The politics of writing: Julia Kavanagh, 1824–77

MANCHESTER
1824

Manchester University Press

The politics of writing:
Julia Kavanagh, 1824–77

EILEEN FAUSET

Manchester University Press

Manchester and New York

distributed exclusively in the USA by Palgrave Macmillan

Published by Manchester University Press
Oxford Road, Manchester M13 9NR, UK
and Room 400, 175 Fifth Avenue, New York, NY 10010, USA
www.manchesteruniversitypress.co.uk

Distributed in the United States exclusively by
Palgrave Macmillan, 175 Fifth Avenue,
New York, NY 10010, USA

Distributed in Canada exclusively by
UBC Press, University of British Columbia, 2029 West Mall,
Vancouver, BC, Canada V6T 1Z2

British Library Cataloguing-in-Publication Data is available

Library of Congress Cataloging-in-Publication Data is available

ISBN 978 0 7190 9013 4 paperback

First published by Manchester University Press in hardback 2009

This paperback edition first published 2013

Printed by Lightning Source

For Peter, Daniel and Paul

Portrait of Julia Kavanagh 1824–77, Henri Chanet. Courtesy of the National Gallery of Ireland, photo © the National Gallery of Ireland.

Contents

Preface and acknowledgements

My interest in Julia Kavanagh came about by chance in the early months of 1995. I was researching material on Irish women writers at Leeds University's Brotherton Library when I came across her name and a list of her major works in an early twentieth-century dictionary of Irish writers. At that time the name Julia Kavanagh meant nothing to me but I was immediately impressed by her literary output. After further enquiry I discovered that, apart from a few entries in nineteenth- and early twentieth-century biographical dictionaries, there appeared to be little else available about her life. However, my curiosity was aroused and I visited the British Library to read her two novels *Nathalie* (1850) and *Adèle* (1858), chosen as a result of their popularity and reviews in *The Athenaeum*. I was not disappointed. While both novels were examples of the domestic fiction of the mid nineteenth century, to my delight they also engaged a strong element of sexual politics that spoke out against the social and sexual imbalance that was characteristic of the time. On the strength of these two novels, and on the little information I had discovered about Kavanagh herself, I wrote a paper on her for a conference organised by the International Association for the Study of Irish Literature (IASIL) held at University College, Cork in 1995. Subsequently the paper was developed into an article for the *Irish Journal of Feminist Studies*, the genesis of which formed the foundations of this book.

During the years of research I encountered a series of elations and disappointments. The joys and discoveries about Kavanagh's works were counterbalanced by the problems emanating from the dearth of information about her life. Genealogical searches in both the UK and Ireland produced little result and there are only a few letters that offer some insight into Kavanagh as an individual. All other available sources of information, including addresses, census reports, family death certificates and testaments, along with documents relating to her father, the writer Morgan Kavanagh, have been thoroughly investigated in my attempts to try to put together some parts, at least, of the jigsaw of her life. The picture is incomplete, but, unless other material comes to light, it may be the best we can hope for.

The dictates of literary production that determined publication during the middle years of the nineteenth century are as much a factor in understanding Kavanagh in the context of women's writing as are the economic, social and psychological variables that are a necessary part of enquiry. While I have drawn on the findings of scholars working in the area of women's literary history, I have not engaged, other than where appropriate, in a wider discourse on the reclamation of nineteenth-century women writers. As it is my intention to introduce Kavanagh to a new audience, I have taken the liberty of quoting extensively from her texts and have combined critical analysis with a more narrative reading of her works. Throughout I have retained Kavanagh's own spellings of various individuals' names, some of which differ from those in other historical sources. This book is divided into five chapters, the first of which is biographical with the other four concentrating on different areas of Kavanagh's literary output and how she impacted her own sexual politics into her writing.

I wish to thank the University of Leeds for awarding me valuable research leave in 2002, and the Research Committee at the Bretton Hall Campus for their generosity in providing grants to enable me to visit libraries in Britain and Ireland. I am indebted to the numerous librarians in many libraries who have searched for rare books on my behalf, particularly the staff at the Bretton Hall Library for their diligence and their enthusiasm for my project. I am grateful to the following institutions for their kind permission to quote from unpublished material in their holdings: the British Library, the National Library of Scotland, the National Library of Ireland, the Board of Trinity College Dublin, Birmingham City Archives. I should also like to thank Cork University Press for permission to use part of my article on Julia Kavanagh from the *Journal of Feminist Studies*; the Harry Ransom Humanities Research Center, at the University of Texas at Austin, for their kind assistance with copies of two letters written by Julia Kavanagh; the Brontë Parsonage Museum, Haworth, for copies of Charlotte Brontë's letters; and the National Gallery of Ireland for providing a copy of the portrait of Julia Kavanagh by Henri Chanet.

Many individuals have helped in a variety of ways towards the completion of this book; too many to name but who have my warmest thanks. I owe a particular debt to several people who gave their help at the beginning of this project and I should like to say thank you to Dolores

Dooley and Mary Eagleton for reading the proposal; to Judith Gantley of the Princess Grace Irish Library, Monaco, for her efforts in seeking out important sources on Kavanagh's final years in Nice, and also to Bruce Stewart for providing valuable related information when he was Literary Adviser at the Library. My thanks also to Professor Michael Kenneally, former Chairman of the IASIL, for his kindness and generous support of my research, and to Sophie Bélot for reading the manuscript and for her good-humoured assistance with the French language. I owe a tremendous debt to Robert Kavanagh for his generosity in sharing his research into his family background and for opening up avenues of information in connection with his great-grandfather and Julia's father, Morgan Kavanagh. Thank you also to Adele Boyte, another member of the Kavanagh family, for allowing me, a stranger, to borrow her own precious copies of three of Kavanagh's novels and for keeping them for much longer than was agreed. I am indebted to the readers and their comments, particularly Danuta Reah and Cristina Andreau for their extremely helpful and positive feedback, to Matthew Frost, literary editor at Manchester University Press, for his understanding and patience in agreeing, several times, to extend the completion date and to John Banks, copy editor at MUP. My greatest thanks, as ever, goes to my husband, Peter, for his enthusiasm and unfailing support during the writing of this book.

1

Julia Kavanagh

Julia Kavanagh was an extraordinarily versatile and significant writer who was held in high esteem by both her contemporaries and her readers. Like many women writers of the nineteenth century she has since been shunted to the sidings of literary history and therefore, it is not surprising that little is known about her or her work today. In writing this book my aim is to introduce this gifted but neglected writer to a new audience and to glean, at least, a small insight into her world.

On 14 June 1861, from an address on the Champs Elysées, Paris, Kavanagh wrote the following letter to Edward Walford, care of Messrs Routledge & Co, London.

> Sir,
> I return the paper you have sent me with a few corrections, of very little importance, as you will perceive. I have also added the titles of the works I have published since *Rachel Gray*. I am happy to say there is nothing else can interest the public in my life, it being of the quiet order.
> With my best wishes for your success in your delicate task.
> I have the honour to subscribe myself yours
> Julia Kavanagh.[1]

It appears that Kavanagh's life was, indeed, 'of the quiet order'. Her letter to Edward Walford, written when she was an established author, is characteristic of this studious and private woman who lived by her pen. To this day very few artefacts concerning Kavanagh's private life have survived and there is little in the way of correspondence. The few letters that have come to light, however, do offer some enlightenment about where she lived and when, whom she knew and with whom she corresponded, and it is through these letters that some of the jigsaw puzzle of Kavanagh's life is pieced together. Each address has its own story and, in spite of the paucity of tangible evidence, connections can be found between the private and the professional person.

Julia Kavanagh was the only child of Bridget and Morgan Kavanagh, born on 7 January 1824 and baptised a Catholic two days later in the 'Big Chapel' in the town of Thurles, Tipperary. However, before she was one year old, she was to leave Ireland, never to return. Some time during the later months of 1824 the family moved to London and then to Paris where they stayed for twenty years,[2] after which they returned in 1844 to London where Julia was to begin her writing career.[3] Around this time Julia and Bridget separated from Morgan, a writer and teacher of languages, and were inseparable until Julia's death in 1877, eleven years before Bridget herself died in 1888.

What is certain, however, is that for Kavanagh writing was an essential part of her life: as she put it, writing '"becomes as necessary to us as food or sleep, and cannot be laid aside"'.[4] In an age when for many middle-class women writing was often the only practicable means of securing an income, Kavanagh was a popular writer who successfully managed to sustain a steady output of both fiction and non-fiction throughout her life.

Like several of her contemporaries whose work was read and enjoyed continuously during their lifetime, Kavanagh has made a significant contribution to literary history. She has been classified as one of the non-canonical 'minor novelists' of the Victorian period who, nevertheless, has shared some recognition alongside more celebrated writers of domestic fiction. Charles Dickens knew her personally and mentioned her along with several other writers, including, 'Ainsworth, Bulwer, Carlyle, D'Israeli, Lady Georgiana Fullerton, Mrs. Gore, Jerrold, Lewes, Macaulay, Thackeray, Warren, Mrs. Marsh, Miss Jewsbury [and] Wilkie Collins'.[5] In a discussion about the lack of discrimination between major and minor novelists in the periodical reviewing of fiction, one modern critic has observed that 'literary surveys which appear in increasing numbers at the end of the century show fascinating preferences and juxtapositions. *Women Novelists of Queen Victoria's Reign* (1897), for example, pays tribute to George Eliot, Mrs. Gaskell and the Brontës, but is not beyond praising Mrs Craik, Mrs Henry Wood or even lesser lights like Julia Kavanagh.'[6] Along with many others, these authors were the mainstay of the circulating libraries. The impact of the latter cannot be underestimated as they provided what was popular – a good family story. Although today this type of entertainment is also provided by film, television, radio and also the internet, during the Victorian period the demand was met by a host of mainly female writers, most of whom have since been characterised as 'writers of their time' and, as such, designated to the annals of forgotten history.[7] Moreover, as John Sutherland has pointed out in his survey of Victorian novelists, the number of women writers who remained anonymous, or published under either sexually neutral or transsexual pseudonyms, suggests that women were more inhibited about 'revealing themselves in the public activity of publication'.[8] This is all the more telling when we learn that not only was writing fiction unique in being a profession 'in which males and females took part in equal numbers', it was also 'unique in Victorian society in being a public and professional activity open both to middle-class men and middle-class women on more or less equal terms'.[9]

As is the case with fiction of any period, much of the output of Victorian women writers of domestic fiction was subject to the demands of popular taste. Novels were concerned with themes that would appeal to the reader's imagination and were required to engage with subject matter that would hold their interest. However, many readers were aware that romance in domestic fiction involved sexual politics and it is ironic that it is this particular genre that became the mainstay of Mudie's Circulating Library.[10] Although there was no written rule of who should read what, these novels were created mainly by women writers for a mainly female readership[11] and, as such, afforded a convenient means of broadening women's political consciousness by drawing attention to social and sexual difference. A recognition of the presence of 'difference' in the historical sense is essential to an understanding of the systematic cultural values of the mid nineteenth century. The gender symbolism in which the woman writer was imbued has helped to construct the historical knowledge of women as second-class writers. In a discussion on the gendering of history Rita Felski has argued: 'If our sense of the past is inevitably shaped by the explanatory logic of narrative, then the stories that we create in turn reveal the inescapable presence and power of gender symbolism.'[12] The discourse of domestic fiction and patterned romance, a genre not generally associated with the political voice and dismissed as mere entertainment and escapism, inadvertently drew on the inconsistencies and contradictions in women's experience.[13] Within the narratives of love and marriage writers were at liberty to explore the sexual difference and gender licence which determined the double standards of the time. Kavanagh's populist appeal bears testimony to these differences and in her novels she often injected an ironic social commentary and at the same time contextualised the political voice in women's writing. Inevitably, in making such claims, I am aware that in arguing for the presence of a political voice in women's writing of the period there are problems associated with the justifiable inherent nature of the subject matter in narrative and the qualitative value of the novels themselves as being worthy of critical acclaim. Nevertheless I would argue that the popularity of domestic novels written by women is itself testimony to women's desire for a political and sexual voice. While I do not wish to overstate the significance of Kavanagh's writing in this context, or in the context of women's cultural history, Kavanagh's relevance lies in the contribution she made to the industry of women's writing at a time when women themselves were increasingly questioning the cultural boundaries and political constraints in their own lives. Kavanagh's stories, which were generally formed around the singular lives of an identified protagonist, were, nevertheless, intertextually inscribed with the exigencies of sexual politics.

Critical enquiry into neglected women writers is a consequence of comparatively recent interest in women's history and the subsequent cultural perspectives which have marginalised many writers into relative obscurity. It is only in relatively recent years, with the reclamation and reappraisal of some neglected women writers, that we are able to see a fuller picture of the significance of women's writing on women's lives.[14] John Sutherland's statistical survey on Victorian novelists has mapped out the field of productivity from the pens of both male and female writers which gives some indication of women's contribution to the fiction 'industry'. And, as Amy Cruse in her 1935 publication of the reading interests of the Victorians,[15] and later Kate Flint's study of women's reading during the nineteenth century,[16] have demonstrated, women's interests were wider and more sociologically placed than was credited by popular belief. These studies are further complemented by Alison Booth's *How to Make It as a Woman: Collective Biographical History from Victoria to the Present*. In this study Booth lists numerous works by and about women and places them in the context of biohistoriography or prosopography. Such an approach, she argues, 'has been instrumental in constructing modern subjectivities and social difference' in our understanding of women's lives.[17] Margaret Kelleher sheds further light on the significance of retrieving forgotten mid-nineteenth-century women writers from obscurity when she suggests that a rereading of writers such as Kavanagh 'from the distance of a century' may offer 'a consciousness of our own historicity and vulnerabilities'.[18]

Progress as a writer

In 1850 Kavanagh was twenty-six years old and was on her way to becoming a commercial success in both Europe and America. She was originally published in London by the established houses of Chapman and Hall, Bentley, Colburn, Hurst and Blackett, and Smith and Elder; and all of her major works went through more than one edition. There are no records of her attempting to publish any work initially in France, although several of her works were translated from English into other European languages, including French, German, Italian and Swedish.[19] In a letter to a Mr Weiderman, written on 10 January 1868, from a Paris address (25 rue des Dames, Aux [Z]ernes), Kavanagh expresses her concerns about translated texts coming on to the market before the original version in English:

> I have much pleasure in forwarding to you the sheets of 'Dora' (complete). The work is to appear next month, but I only received this copy this morning else you should have had it earlier for the convenience of the translator. You will not of course, even should you be ready, publish the German translation before the English edition appears. As the work is to appear in Baron Tauchnitz's series you will know the time of its publication. I shall be much obliged to you if you will kindly acknowledge receipt of the copy I send by this day's post. I shall not fail to let you have two other copies for registering as usual. [20]

Throughout her life Kavanagh wrote numerous stories for different journals including *Chambers Edinburgh Journal, Household Words, All the Year Round, Eliza Cook, The Month, People's Journal, Popular Record, Temple Bar* and *Argosy*. Several of her stories also appeared in America in *Littel's Living Age*, a prominent weekly magazine, published in Boston.[21] In 1846 she published a 32-page pamphlet, *The Montyon Prizes*, describing a series of French prizes for virtue, bequeathed by the Baron Antoine de Montyon (1733–1820). A preliminary version of this pamphlet had previously been published in *Chambers Miscellany*. Between 1848 and 1877 she wrote fourteen known novels including *Madeleine* (1848); *Nathalie* (1850); *Daisy Burns* (1853); *Grace Lee* (1855); *Rachel Gray* (1856); *Adèle* (1858); *Queen Mab* (1863); *Beatrice* (1864); *Sybil's Second Love* (1867); *Dora* (1868); *Sylvia* (1870); *Bessie* (1872); *John Dorrien* (1875); and finally *Two Lilies* (1877). Her fiction also includes a story for children, *The Three Paths* (1848) and a collection of shorter works, several of which had been published initially in *Chambers Journal*, now under the title of *Seven Years and Other Tales* (1859). Her biographical works include: *Woman in France during the Eighteenth Century* (1850); *Women of Christianity* (1852); *French Women of Letters* (1862) and a companion study, *English Women of Letters* (1862); an account of her travels in Southern Italy and Sicily, entitled *A Summer and Winter in the Two Sicilies* (1858). With Bridget she wrote a collection of fairy stories, *The Pearl Fountain* (1877), with another book of tales, *Forget-Me-Nots*, collected by Bridget and published posthumously in 1878.[22] In addition she wrote short pieces on travel and the occasional review for *The Athenaeum*, while her own writing was reviewed consistently in that journal and other periodicals. In 1861 she contributed a short story 'John's Five Pounds', without payment, to a collection, *Victoria Regia*, edited by Adelaide Proctor. Although this collection of poetry and prose was made up of both male and female published authors, it is interesting that it was conspicuously a woman's enterprise, published by Emily Faithful, who headed the first collective women's publishing company, in aid of promoting women in industry.[23] A testimony to her popularity is the fact that Mudie's Library stocked all of Kavanagh's novels until as late as 1900.[24]

Throughout her lifetime Kavanagh was very much respected by her contemporaries. During the 1850s she was celebrated in one biographical source as a 'distinguished writer of the present day' whose style was pleasant and fluent, 'with an *esprit* more French than English'.[25] At the end of her life, however, her fiction was remembered more for its light subject matter, genteel tone and idealised heroines than for its contribution to the politics of women's writing. The writer of her obituary in the *Academy* begins by stating that 'English Literature has been deprived of an accomplished novelist and a skilled writer of biography' and ends with 'Of Julia Kavanagh, if of few other English female novelists, it may be emphatically said that she left "no line which dying she could wish to blot"'.[26] In his obituary of Kavanagh in *The Athenaeum*, which was subsequently reprinted in *The Times*, Charles Wood viewed Kavanagh's writing as 'quiet and simple in style, but pure and chaste, and characterised by the same high toned thought and morality that was part of the author's own nature'.[27] It is this perspective on her writing that characterised biographical entries throughout the late nineteenth until the early twentieth century. A few months after Kavanagh's death Mrs C. Martin in the *Irish Monthly Magazine* recalls that 'The name of Julia Kavanagh is, we think, not so well known in Ireland as it deserves to be, and a few words to remind the readers of this Magazine that a Catholic Irishwoman, who was an accomplished and singularly graceful and pure novelist, as well as a skilled writer of biography'.[28] The entry in The *Dictionary of National Biography* (1892) states that her novels were 'remarkable for graceful style and poetic feeling',[29] while in 1913 the author in *The Catholic Encyclopaedia* offers the view that '[Kavanagh's] studies of French life and character, which are worked into almost all her stories, are excellent and show her at her best'.[30] In his *Memories of Charles Dickens* (1913) Percy Fitzgerald recalls various people who, along with Kavanagh, contributed to *Household Words* and speaks of her as a writer who, though popular in her day, has ceased to be of significance:

Who now thinks of a writer named Julia Kavanagh? I well recall when it was correct to send to the libraries for her last novel, whose merits were discussed at dinner parties. She worked more profitably for the publishers with such things as *English Women of Letters, French Women of Letters,* Women of This and That, *Forget-Me-Nots.* She was considered a very 'respectable' writer.[31]

Kavanagh is also given a mention in Ernest A. Baker's *History of the English Novel* (1937), this time with a little more merit afforded by Fitzgerald and considered alongside Caroline Norton:

The novels of two Irishwomen, Julia Kavanagh (1824–1877) and the Hon. Caroline Norton (1808–1877), were also fondly supposed to be superior, but they have not survived the century in which they were read with admiration. Miss Kavanagh lived part of her life abroad, and was one of the first to put into fiction the observations and experiences which usually go into records of travel. But, unlike so many who have made the Continent the scene of the most incontinent adventures, she tended to idealize both her young girls and their lovers, whether they were French or Italian or English people residing in a foreign land. *Madeleine* (1848) is a pretty love-tale of Auvergne, *Adèle* (1857) presents a charming Norman heroine, the wilful young thing who gives the title to *Sylvia* is a winning and estimable Italian, and so it is with the rest. Miss Kavanagh could paint character and manners, and had a knack for agreeable comedy, or at any rate farce.[32]

Writing in 1988 John Sutherland consolidated the notion of Kavanagh as an accepted and safe novelist when he remarked that Kavanagh's fiction 'was aimed at younger women readers and was fashionably domestic in style while remaining wholly "ladylike" in tone'.[33] Despite this later biographical entry, which focuses on Kavanagh's appeal as a writer of pleasant if somewhat benign novels, from the mid twentieth century onwards critical opinion of Kavanagh as a writer had taken on new perspectives. The few (mainly female) literary scholars who had read Kavanagh were beginning to look beyond the notion that she was just another 'lady novelist' and viewed both her fiction and her biographical writing in more radical terms.[34] In her biographical study of women writers, *The Female Pen* (1946), B. G. MacCarthy considered Kavanagh's *English Women of Letters* to be a perceptive and valuable contribution to women's literary studies and discussed Kavanagh's comments on the writers under discussion.[35] More recently, in *Mothers of the Novel* (1988), Dale Spender has drawn heavily on *English Women of Letters* as a significant source for her own feminist perspective. The entry for Kavanagh in *The Feminist Companion to Literature in English* (1990) also draws attention to the sexual politics in Kavanagh's writing with the comment:

A major concern in all her work is the way in which women can express themselves in the face of restrictive and false conventions: in her *English Women
of Letters*, 1862, and *French Women of Letters*, 1862, she criticises idealised
and sickly depictions of romantic relationships, and in her novels she looks
critically at women's sufferings below the surface ideology of matrimonial
bliss. [. . .] Though never wholly free of sexual stereotypes, her [. . .] fiction
continued to question the sacrifice of womanly freedom in marriage.[36]

In *The Cambridge Guide to Women's Writing in English* (1999), edited
by Lorna Sage, the purpose of which was to 'consolidate and epitomise
the re-reading of women's writing', Kavanagh is introduced as an Irish
novelist who was 'astutely aware of the patriarchal double standards'
and a writer whose 'novels and essays draw on the very core of sexual
politics'.[37] In an earlier article in the *Irish Journal of Feminist Studies* I
argue that Kavanagh's works reflect her consciousness of women's condition in an ideology that worked against them and, in spite of the developments in social and cultural change, she has much in common with
feminists writing today.[38] Interestingly, after over one hundred years
since she was reprinted, Kavanagh's works have now been reissued.[39]

Kavanagh's physical health and appearance

What did Julia Kavanagh look like? A portrait by Henri Chanet in the
National Gallery in Dublin portrays Kavanagh as a handsome woman,
possibly in her late twenties or early thirties, with dark hair and striking
eyes. It may have been commissioned while Kavanagh stayed in Paris in
the early 1860s, but, judging from its style, it is more likely that it was
copied from a photograph and painted later, possibly after her death.[40]
To all accounts, the portrait does not reveal the disability that had
affected Kavanagh all her life. As a child she had suffered severely from
a spinal disorder of which, had money been available for treatment, it
was believed she would have been cured. Her father, Morgan Kavanagh,
earned a living as a teacher of languages, a profession which, evidence
suggests, brought in little remuneration and certainly not enough to
support his daughter's medical requirements.[41] Writing from Paris on 3
September 1839, to the London-based Literary Fund Society, Morgan
expresses his concern over his fifteen-year-old daughter's condition:

My pecuniary embarrassment is consequently very great but what materially tends to heighten my misfortune is the situation of my daughter who
has for several years been suffering from a spinal complaint and may not
yet rise from her bed for at least another year. She has been a patient for
the last fifteen months in Dr. Harrisson's admirable institution, London
where contrary to the predictions of the cleverest of the French faculty she

most wonderfully improved. But notwithstanding the moderate demands of this institution and the benefit my daughter has deserved from it, and the certainty which its medical gentlemen gave me of completing her cure in another year I have been obliged to have her removed back to Paris from my total inadequacy to pay for her any longer.[42]

If, as it was believed at the time, a cure was possible, then the interruption of her treatment had left its mark. In a letter to her friend, Ellen Nussey, dated 12 June 1850, Charlotte Brontë recalls her first meeting with Kavanagh:

Do you remember my speaking of a Miss Kavanagh – a young authoress who supported her mother by her writings? Hearing from Mr Williams that she had a longing to see me I called on her yesterday – I found a little, almost dwarfish figure to which even *I* had to look down – not deformed – that is – not hunchbacked but long-armed and with a large head and (at first sight) a strange face. She met me half-frankly, half tremblingly; we sat down together and when I had talked with her five minutes that face was no longer strange but mournfully familiar – it was Martha Taylor in every lineament – I shall try to find a moment to see her again.[43]

As Brontë herself was only 4 feet 9 inches tall,[44] Kavanagh must have been an extremely tiny woman. However, it appears that Kavanagh's facial features struck a chord in her likeness to Martha Taylor. In Brontë's opinion her friend, Martha Taylor, who had died in 1842, had been a woman who, 'though piquant was not pretty'.[45]

A more empathic observation of Kavanagh's physical appearance is that given by Charles W. Wood, who mentions her briefly in his biographical article on his mother, Mrs Henry Wood, in the April 1877 edition of *Argosy*, published, ironically, a few months before Kavanagh's death in October of that year. He refers to his mother's suffering from a 'curvature of the spine' and recalls his friend, Julia Kavanagh: 'She has told me that in early life she suffered exactly as my mother had suffered; but she was even smaller and shorter, and the mischief in her case was more evident.'[46] This description bears out Brontë's somewhat horror-struck response on meeting Kavanagh and it also suggests further evidence of Kavanagh's physical frailty. There are no existing medical records to indicate the extent of Kavanagh's condition, but Wood's comparative account of his mother's health offers some insight into Kavanagh's own physical state:

At the age of thirteen to seventeen my mother's life may be said to have been spent on her reclining board and couch. [. . .]
   At the age of seventeen the curvature of the spine became confirmed and settled. She was pronounced cured. That is to say, she ceased to suffer.

Nothing more could be done. It was no longer necessary to be always reclining. In earlier life very little amiss was, to be seen with the figure, except that she remained small and short, her height not exceeding five feet two. But, the spine excepted, she was so perfectly formed that her movements were at all times full of grace and dignity. Her constitution was remarkably sound, but the body henceforth was to be frail, delicate, absolutely without muscular power. She could at no time raise an ordinary weight, or ever carry anything heavier than a small book or a parasol.[47]

It is clear from Wood's account that this type of condition imposed limitations on physical endurance. As a woman responsible for her own livelihood, Kavanagh must have found the inevitable restraints disagreeable. However, regardless of her physical shortcomings, Kavanagh's intellectual energy and literary output never ceased throughout her life.

Family and background

Why the Kavanagh family left Ireland for England in 1825 is unknown. One source suggests that it was to find a publisher for Morgan's long poem *The Wanderings of Lucan and Dinah*[48] a work he was later to regret.[49] What is certain, however, is that in London they found themselves without means of any financial support, a predicament that was to emerge with ominous repetition throughout Julia's formative years. It transpires that as a stranger and without friends Morgan was unable to procure work and subsequently found it necessary to apply to the Literary Fund Society for assistance to return to Ireland where he was 'known'.[50] Whether or not the family did return to Ireland is uncertain but evidence suggests that they located to Paris in 1825 where Morgan found employment teaching English. In his letter to the Literary Fund Society dated 3 September 1839 Morgan revealed that with the exception of one year – from the end of 1837 to the end of 1838, when the family was in England – they had lived for the past fourteen years in Paris.[51] During this time Julia remained at Dr Harrisson's clinic for fifteen months from July 1838 to September 1839, after which she returned to Paris to join her parents.[52] After their separation from Morgan some time in the late 1840s,[53] Julia and her mother, Bridget, spent the next sixteen years or so domiciled in London with brief periods spent in France[54] (also taking in a summer and winter in the 'Two Sicilies'[55]), returning to London and then on to Paris some time around 1861. They may also have spent some time in Rouen in 1870, possibly to escape the Siege of Paris at the outbreak of the Franco-Prussian War,[56] before returning to Paris and finally settling in Nice[57] where Julia subsequently died and was buried in the Catholic

Cemetery.[58] Bridget lived on in Nice for another eleven years until her own death at the age of eighty-six.[59]

Nice was certainly a favourite among the British middle-class who were drawn by both the fine weather and the affordable accommodation. Julia and Bridget's last known address in Nice was flat number 93, 24 rue Gioffredo,[60] a district which at that time suited the requirements of their quiet gentility. Whether Bridget had any private income is unknown but it is unlikely as evidence suggests that she was financially dependent on her husband as provider and, later, on Julia's earnings as a writer. All that is known about her is to be found in her Testament and her Death Certificate which gives her birthplace as Montrath (Ireland); her father's name, Guillaume [William] Fitzpatrick, and her mother's name, Catherine Haggarty.[61] Although the 1876 Census form for Nice lists Bridget as a widow, she is, in fact, recorded under her maiden name of Fitzpatrick and not her married name Kavanagh. It may be that she had made this choice as early as the 1840s when she and Morgan separated, or she changed names on his death in 1874.

Morgan and Bridget had been married in Ireland in 1822 when they were aged around twenty-two and twenty years respectively.[62] Why the family split up initially, however, is not known. For the first twenty years or so of their marriage it appears that Morgan made every attempt to care for his wife and daughter and was clearly distraught at his inability to pay for the completion of Julia's hospital treatment. By all accounts he was, at this period in his life, a man who had gained the respect of certain interested parties for his literary endeavours as there exist several letters of recommendation by established persons in London and Paris to the Literary Fund Society, testifying to his moral character and honesty.[63] However, further correspondence from Morgan to this Society suggests that from around 1842 to 1844 he was totally preoccupied with writing his book *The Discovery of the Science of Languages*, a pursuit which, to the detriment of all else, became obsessive. In a letter, written from an address in London on 18 June 1844, Morgan openly admits that his present need for assistance is a consequence of his singular engagement with work, 'My present embarrassment – which is the greatest I have yet experienced is occasioned by the accompanying work on which I have devoted to the exclusion of every other occupation the last two years.'[64] A few years later, about the same time that Julia had published *Women of Christianity* (1852), Morgan was to become engaged in a work that was counterproductive to all that Bridget and Julia, as devout Catholics, wholly believed. In his unpublished manuscript, entitled 'Errors of Religion', and believed to have been written in the early 1850s, Morgan reproves all religious doctrines as the instigators of human chaos. In his enlightening pamphlet on Morgan Kavanagh, Robert Kavanagh notes that:

> In *Errors of Religion* Morgan argues that religions, Christianity in particular, have been the cause of intolerance, prejudice, acts of persecution, mass murder, and many other undesirable acts. He criticizes blind belief in doctrine rather than in reason and rational inquiry. He deplores the role of Christianity in supporting slavery in America. He is clearly supportive of ideas put forward by Thomas Paine. Morgan cites the religious problems in Ireland as another example of the evils brought upon the people by religious intolerance and also refers to the prejudice against the Jews in England at this time. [65]

It may be that Morgan's views on religion were too zealous for Bridget and Julia to tolerate and, over a period of time, difference of opinion may have contributed to the break-up of the marriage.

By all accounts this was a family that lived with ill health, a situation that may well have aggravated their already impecunious lifestyle. Although it appears that Morgan did not suffer from any serious health problems, Bridget was considered an 'invalid' in so far as she had very poor sight. However, this did not deter her from accompanying her daughter on their various travels. She was sufficiently able-bodied to travel around Italy for twelve months or so with Julia in the early 1850s, a time when land journeys in that country were mainly undertaken by coach or horseback, and travel by boat, as Julia records in the *A Summer and Winter in the Two Sicilies* (1858), was, at times, very precarious. In a letter to Charles Wood, concerning a story to be published in *Argosy*, written in September 1877, just a few weeks before she died, Julia gives some indication of her own state of health:

> My dear Mr Wood,
>
> Of course I had previously written to you that I could not let you have another story then woman-like I changed my mind and I sat down and indited the following tale which, to say the truth, had been in my mind *three* years. I think you will like it, perhaps it will do for the Xmas number, but pray do not shorten it!
>
> I write from Piedmont in an old convent, but there is no post office within miles so I should not dispatch my story till we reach Nice at the end of the week I hope for change of air has not done my neuralgia much good, I suppose it escapes general rules.
>
> I cannot tell you what a blessing the Argosy proved here! An English lady who goes wild on a Sunday. This is a very pretty but very dull place, went into transports when I came to the rescue with your precious pages. Mamma & I were especially delighted with Holland. It is as good as travelling without the fatigue of it.

Pray thank Mrs. Wood very kindly for her letter. It cheered and comforted me as a kind sermon [home] always does when one is low as I was so just then.

I have been writing the whole morning and must abridge this epistle as I am far from strong.

Nice
September 30th 1877

I finish my letter here and send it with Clement's Love [short story]. I have taken great pains with it & shall be affronted if you do not like it much. I have no English news of the Fairy Tales, but they are coming out in the Tauchnitz. I mean the edition for children's books.

Saint Dalmas was already very cold when we left and the heat of Nice is very agreeable to such chilly bodies as we are. And now our leaving my dear Mr Wood, many thanks for the Argosy to which I hope to become once more a contributor as though I am still very unwell I think I am a *little* better. Mamma writes in kind regards and I am as ever

Yours Truly,
Julia Kavanagh[66]

In his preface to *Forget-Me-Nots*, published in 1878, after Julia's death, Charles Wood sheds some light on Bridget's state of health when he implies that she was almost totally blind. He records Julia's last moments:

On Sunday, the 28th of October, 1877, at five o'clock in the morning, Mrs. Kavanagh heard, in the adjoining chamber, a noise as of a heavy fall. She immediately rose from her bed, and proceeding to her daughter's room, found her upon the floor. Miss Kavanagh exclaimed in French, the language in which she usually spoke: 'Oh, Mamma, how silly I am to have fallen!' She was assisted back to her couch, doctors were called in, and by eight o'clock that same morning the large, beautiful eyes of Julia Kavanagh had closed in their last sleep. An aged mother, so blind as to be able only to distinguish light from darkness, was left to mourn a daughter whose life had been devoted to her mother, to whom she was all in all: in whom had lived as bright and pure a spirit as ever breathed.

In spite of her physical frailty, Bridget was the co-writer of the collection of fairy tales mentioned in Julia's letter to Charles Wood, entitled *The Pearl Fountain*, which was published in 1876, one year before Julia's death. It appears that Bridget rarely left Julia's side and is herself a contradictory figure. On that same first visit to Julia in the summer of 1850, when the couple were living in London,[67] Charlotte Brontë, in her letter to Ellen Nussey, also commented on the conditions in which Julia was living. She speaks derisively of Bridget and is of the opinion that they had been abandoned by Morgan; she writes:

She lives in a poor but clean and neat little lodging – her mother seems a somewhat weak-minded woman who can be no companion to her – her father has quite deserted his wife and child – and this poor little feeble, intelligent, cordial thing wastes her brain to gain a living. She is twenty five years old.[68]

Brontë's perception of Bridget as 'weak-minded' raises questions concerning the state of Bridget's health and does not fully tally with that of a woman who, later in life, though almost blind, appears to have been of sufficiently sound mind to co-write a book with Julia, present Julia's portrait to the National Gallery in Ireland and arrange for Julia's work to be published posthumously. Notwithstanding these events, circumstantial evidence can distort the real situation which inevitably leaves the question of the extent of Bridget's physical and mental capacities unanswered. However, it is clear that Brontë was undoubtedly affected by what she saw on her visit, which may have further encouraged her professional interest in Julia.

Julia was twenty years of age when she first began to publish after she returned to London from Paris in 1844. Whilst in London, and after they had separated from Morgan, Julia and Bridget stayed in several different lodgings. The correspondence address for 8 August 1846 was 27 Berkeley Street, Lambeth Palace.[69] From 27 February to 9 August 1847 it was 3 Camden Hill Terrace, Kensington,[70] the home of W. S. Williams, Charlotte Brontë's editor and reader for Smith and Elder; although one letter written on 9 July 1847 to W. Chambers is addressed Allason Terrace.[71] It seems that Julia and her mother must have been between addresses during this period as correspondence dated from 26 September 1847 to 23 June 1851 suggests that they resided at 7 Allason Terrace, Church Street, Kensington. Moreover, in her preface to *Women of Christianity* Julia states that on 6 December 1851 she was in Kensington. The 1851 Census, conducted in March, reveals that at that time 7 Allason Terrace, Kensington, was occupied by Mary L. Cursons, widow, aged fifty, milliner and dressmaker, with her mother and daughters. It is likely that Kavanagh had lodged in the same house as these people but as neither Julia or Bridget is recorded on the Census return it is possible that they were in transit.

There could be several reasons why Julia and Bridget chose to live in London at this time and not return to Paris, the more obvious choice, or to Ireland, but all would be conjecture. One good reason for remaining, however, is that Julia had found London publishers who were willing to accept her work and her prospects were better. No evidence has come to light to suggest that Bridget and Julia were in contact with any remaining family or friends in Ireland during this period. Moreover, the mid 1840s was the period of the potato crop failure in Ireland, and the resulting devastation in that country was reason enough not to return. Nevertheless, it must have been an unsettling time for the two women as correspondence suggests that, after living expenses, there would be little money to spare.

The 1840s also saw an increase in the number of Irish seeking work in Britain, mainly as a result of the potato crop failure, and, like several other towns and cities in England, London was host to increasing clusters of Irish migrants.[72] It is not known how long Julia and Bridget stayed in their lodgings in the district of Lambeth Palace, or whether they lived close to an Irish community there.[73] Correspondence suggests that they were not living with Morgan at that time.[74] It is possible that Kavanagh and her mother had lodged with the Williams family for a period of four months before finding more permanent lodgings at Allason Terrace. Several letters written by W. S. Williams to Charlotte Brontë discussing Kavanagh's progress (above) and a letter, dated 13 March 1850, from Kavanagh to Mrs Williams, requesting funds to help Italian refugees,[75] suggests that the two families shared a sense of warmth and trust. It is likely that the 'poor but clean and neat little lodging' to which Charlotte Brontë referred in her letter to Ellen Nussey, in June 1850 was, indeed, 7 Allason Terrace; by all accounts a residence colonised by respectable women who lived by their own industry.

This period is of particular interest as Kavanagh was now on the threshold of success. In 1850 she saw the publication of two separate works: Smith and Elder published the two-volume *Woman in France during the Eighteenth Century* and Colburn published a three-volume version of *Nathalie* which in the same year was also reproduced by Tauchnitz, the German publisher, as a two-volume edition in their Collection of British Authors series. In addition to these longer works she also contributed a short story, 'An Excellent Opportunity', to *Household Words*.[76] Professional progress at this juncture in her life must surely have given Kavanagh a sense of achievement and hope for the future. Whilst living in Kensington, she was also witness to the very different circumstances which befell the increasing number of impoverished Irish migrants who were concentrated in the areas around the back streets of Kensington; a reminder, perhaps, that the current economic and social situation in Ireland, the home to which Kavanagh was never to return, resulted in the enforced migration of its people to make a life elsewhere. Lynn Hollen Lees's study of Irish migrants in Victorian London has shown that Kensington was one district that accommodated different social groups. She notes that 'Irish residents can be separated into two groups: middle or lower-middle-class families who with a few artisans lived in predominantly English areas and families of domestics and laborers who chose to settle near other Irish in the poorer parts of Kensington, Paddington and Hammersmith'.[77] Kensington also had its enclaves of poverty in the form of Irish Roman Catholic migrants, the spectacle of which would have been the cause of much consternation to the established residents of this reputable middle-class area. *Household Words* had reflected the less than picturesque image of these disaffected Irish in terms of a social disease in suggesting that on first entering the High Street of Kensington from the direction of Kensington Palace Gardens, one encounters a '"sore" in the shape of some poor Irish people'. The article continues with the observation:

> They look like people from the old broken-up establishment of Saint Giles's and probably are so; a considerable influx from the 'Rookery' in this; for so it has equally been called. This Rookery has long been a nuisance in Kensington. In the morning you seldom see more of it than this indication at the entrance; but in the evening the inmates mingle with the rest of the inhabitants out of doors, and the naked feet of the children, and the ragged and dissolute looks of men and women, present a painful contrast to the general decency. We understand, however, that some of these poor people are very respectable of their kind, and that the improvements which are taking place in other portions of the kingdom, in late years to the destitute and uneducated, have not been without effect in this quarter. The men for the most part are, or profess to be, labouring bricklayers, and the women market-garden women. They are calculated, at a rough guess, to amount to a thousand; all crammed, perhaps, into a place which ought not to contain above a hundred. [. . .] Most of this unhappy multitude are Roman Catholics.[78]

Kensington High Street is adjacent to Kensington Church Street and Allason Terrace and it must have pained Kavanagh to witness the deprivation and humiliation that is the lot of the Irish Catholic migrant.

Gavan Duffy

It may have been such sights that provoked Kavanagh's innate sense of 'Irishness' and also her interest in Irish affairs which prompted her to initiate a correspondence with Gavan Duffy, editor of the Irish Nationalist newspaper, *The Nation*. She wrote to Duffy in 1849 introducing herself and her interests in writing for *The Nation*, and in his biography, *My Life in two Hemispheres*, Duffy refers to this letter, classifying her among 'gifted women':

> From the beginning gifted women were among the best beloved contributors to the *Nation*, and the revived *Nation* was destined to rally recruits of the same class. Julia Kavanagh, who was earning her income by literary

work for English periodicals, proffered to aid the new experiment, without payment or applause, by her facile pen. Her letter is a touching illustration of the unconquerable sentiment of nationality which lives in the Irish heart:–

'Sir, – I am not, I confess, a constant reader of the *Nation*; I know it chiefly through the extracts and misrepresentations of the English press, but those extracts have sufficed to give me an exalted opinion of your talents as the persecutions you endured formerly gave me your patriotism.

'I should not, however, have troubled you with this letter but for an extract from the *Nation* given in this day's *Times*, by which I find you suggest a very excellent plan of promoting the Irish cause by means of popular tracts, essays, &c. It occurs to me, were this plan to be adopted, I might, perhaps, be of some use.

'I do not suppose my name is known to you, but I have been a writer for five years. I have published a few works and contributed to *Chambers Journal*, to their Miscellany, to the *Popular Record*, to the *People's Journal*. I am now writing for the journal of Eliza Cook. This, if I have not misunderstood you, is the literature you wish to turn into the channel of nationality. I have always felt that of myself I can do nothing, but I might be rendered useful, and nothing could give me greater joy. I make this proposal to you, sir, in the sincere belief that you will not misunderstand me, or think me guilty of indecorous and unwomanly presumption. I live by my labour and have not much time to spare, but in *this cause* I will gladly make time and dispense with payment; nor do I aim in the least at any sort of celebrity which may be connected with this movement. Let my name be known or not, it is a matter of total indifference to me. Let me only be of some use, employed as a common workman, and I am content.

'I speak somewhat earnestly, but I should not like to forfeit your esteem. I am Irish by origin, birth, and feeling, though not by education; but if I have lived far from Ireland she has still been as the faith and religion of my youth. I have ever been taught to love her with my whole soul, to bless her as a sorrowing mother, dear though distant and unknown. I have the honour, sir, to remain yours very sincerely,

Julia Kavanagh'[79]

Duffy first met Kavanagh at a reception in London where there were several people interested in or connected with Irish politics, as Duffy relates:

Later in the evening I met Julia Kavanagh. She is very small, smaller even than Louis Blanc, and, like him, has a good head and fine eyes. She is very much at home in Irish subjects, and tells me she is learning Gaelic. She proposed a volume of sketches from Irish history lately to Colburn and afterwards to Bentley, but neither of them would hear of it. She sent my small proprietors' scheme to Wills of *Household Words*, whom I met last year at Malvern, proposing to make an article about it, but that enlightened

economist told her he had quite another object in view. He meant that
Ireland should be colonised by Englishmen.[80]

Clearly, Kavanagh was interested in Irish history but her attempts to
engage this in print were turned down. She was, of course, only in her
mid-twenties and Colburn, Bentley and the others may have viewed the
subject as too weighty for her. No date is given for this meeting but, as
her publication output indicates, it is likely to be around 1849–50.
Although there is no evidence of Kavanagh actually writing for *The
Nation*, two letters written by Kavanagh to Duffy suggest that he took
her interest in Irish history seriously. The first, dated 19 November 1849,
appears to be a response to his reply to her letter (above):

Dear Sir,
    I sincerely thank you for having answered me so soon and so kindly.
    I regret – since you think it might be of use – that my opportunities of
giving an Irish character to what I write *are* so few. With the exception of
Eliza Cook's journal, I have given up periodical literature, and the two works
on which I have been *sent* am still engaged – one in the press the other in
hand – are both on foreign subjects and cannot admit, therefore, of a national
tendency . . . But this will not I hope always be the case, and I shall endeavour to prepare for a fitting opportunity by reading with much attention the
works you have been so kind as to mention. I could not find them at
B[rookes], T[. . .] Street; I shall perhaps prove more fortunate at Simpkin and
Marshall's. I have in the meantime been looking over them at the reading
room of the British Museum with much interest. When I have finished *those*
works I shall trouble you for the titles of more if our poor country is indeed
so fortunate as to possess many works written in so truly national a spirit.
    With thanks for the interest you express in my behalf.
    Believe me, dear Sir, to remain yours sincerely,
                                                    Julia Kavanagh[81]

Duffy had written a piece for *The Nation*, 16 March 1850, on
Kavanagh's recently published *Woman in France during the Eighteenth
Century*, and, as her letter to him dated 15 April 1850 suggests, she is
grateful for the attention given to her work:

Dear Sir,
    I know not through what mistake the Nation, though one of the earliest
papers that notices 'Woman in France', was not forwarded to me by the
publishers until a month after date. I should not otherwise have delayed so
long in thanking you for taking so much notice of a work possessing few if
any claims on your attention, and for giving to the remarks it suggested so
much space in a paper devoted to the cause – always beaten but never yet
entirely lost – of our poor country.
    You were kind enough a few months back to promise to furnish me with

a list of works on Irish subjects, but declined doing so then, lest you should 'overwhelm me with the avalanche of Irishness.' It was however fear of the 'avalanche' that freed me from applying to you sooner, but a lack of time to read. Now that I have a little more leisure I cannot help reminding you of your promise.

Some of the books I shall probably be able to procure from the local circulating libraries in town, and those that are too difficult [. . .] had or too expensive to purchase will no doubt be found at the British Museum. The volumes you were kind enough to recommend to me were: Davis' poems and essays, The ballad poetry of Ireland, The book of Irish ballads, The writers of the 17th Century, Hugh O'Neill, The plantations of Ulster.

These works I have perused with a degree of interest that makes me wish to read more, even though I am well aware that my own personal instruction and gratification are the chief and probably the only results I can hope to derive from all my reading.

> Believe me, dear Sir,
> Yours very sincerely,
> Julia Kavanagh[82]

This correspondence suggests that, although Kavanagh had a keen interest in Ireland, its culture and history, her years away from her home country had left her with little experiential knowledge about it. For her Ireland remained a distant dream confined to her reading and her imagination.

Morgan Kavanagh

While Julia and Bridget resided in Kensington, Morgan led an itinerant existence. After the separation Morgan appears to have rented rooms in different locations in central London. From mid 1850 to around 1853[83] he was a tenant at 28 Dean Street, Soho, and in turn, sublet two rooms at an annual rent of £22 to Karl Marx and his family.[84] It transpires that Julia was also known to the residents which suggests that during this period she had kept in touch with her estranged father and may have visited him there.[85] The Census returns for 30 March 1851 show that the house was occupied by thirteen people,[86] the Marx family occupying two rooms. They accommodated, at that time, eight people: Marx, his wife Jenny and their four children, their servant Helene Demuth and a midwife. Both Marx and Morgan Kavanagh were exiles from their own countries and, at that time, Soho was a melting pot of assorted European political refugees.[87] Large houses were divided into smaller lodgings and rent was cheap. This is the likely reason why Marx came to be in that part of London. With little money, no security and a family to care for, he lived at 28 Dean Street from December 1850 until some time in 1856.

Soho was a poor area of London with appalling sanitary conditions.[88] Conditions at 28 Dean Street were necessarily cramped,
although this in itself was not unusual at the time. In her biography of
Eleanor Marx, Yvonne Kapp notes, 'That this was not conspicuous
overcrowding for that time and place is made clear by the Report on
the 1851 Census which shows that the 1,354 inhabited buildings in the
Soho parish of St. Anne housed a population of 17,335: an average of
14 persons to each house and 327 to the acre.'[89] Conditions for the
Marx family, certainly, were extremely hard. Kapp leads one to assume
that relations between landlord and tenants were strained, not surprisingly as they were both living on meagre resources. For the Marx family
the domestic situation was particularly sad. They had lost one child to
meningitis when they lodged at number 64 Dean Street, just prior to
moving into number 28, then later another child died of illness while at
that address. Kapp makes a brief but disparaging reference to
Kavanagh and her 'unlasting fame', and in her notes to this section of
the biography she says:

> A quotation from one of her mawkish works [*Madeleine*] has a certain
> relevance:
> " " What has the world done for me that I should love it? . . . Why did I
> see my children die from hunger, when others had more wealth than they
> could spend? I once said . . . that it seemed to my poor judgment the world
> would be better arranged if all human creatures shared in its wealth alike
> . . ." "Well, but what is to be done?" "I know not . . . how should I? But
> there are wise men in the land paid to find out everything. Let them find
> out that . . ."' The authoress might have learnt from the lodger more about
> this subject, including the fact that such men were not exactly paid and that
> their own children also hungered and died.[90]

Kapp's comments suggest that Julia was aware that Morgan had sublet
rooms to the Marx family and knew of their predicament. However, such
deprivation would not have been unusual within the context of the social
surroundings. Kapp continues with the comment:

> But it is to his landlady that Marx refers in his letters, and with no more
> cordial feeling than is usual in that relationship writing to Engels in
> September 1852 to say that the thing most to be desired was that she
> should throw him out, which would at least save the rent, but she was
> unlikely to prove so obliging.

Who was this landlady? Was it Julia, who was only twenty-six years old
at the time? It is possible that, although she lodged separately from her
father, Julia may have paid his rent. Less than one year earlier, Morgan,
then living at 6 Rupert Street, was applying, for the fifth time, to the

Literary Fund Society for financial assistance, this time to return to Paris. In support of his application he states that 'the experience of several years inclines me to suspect that it will be very difficult for me to earn a livelihood in England, the last half year not having brought me in so much as fifteen pounds and the last month – nothing at all'.[91] Whether he was successful in his application is not known; he had had several recommendations from people who thought him a worthy case, including two sisters, Amelia and Elizabeth Pearson, two women who seemed determined to help him find work in England. In their letter of recommendation to the Literary Fund Society, dated 12 June 1850, and signed by Elizabeth Pearson, the sisters relate to the likelihood of change for Morgan, should he stay:

> My sister and myself having signed a testimonial addressed to the Literary Fund Society in favour of Mr. Kavanagh you will allow me to give you the following information which he thinks necessary to lay before the committee. Mr. Kavanagh had resolved upon going to France and called last Saturday to take leave of us.
>
> We regretted much his determination and having formally named him to a friend of ours who has much influence in the management of a large public school now upon the point of choosing a French teacher we repeated the application. Our friend had an interview with Mr. Kavanagh and in the course of conversation perceived that he should be a highly desirable assistant to the Establishment in question and preferred that he should remain in England to await the decision of the council which cannot be had till on or near the 25th of July.
>
> The salary will be about £100 per annum but probably no part receivable in less than three months. Other advantages may be expected to arise with this appointment should Mr K. as we hope be successfull in gaining it.[92]

It would appear that Morgan did not go to Paris on that occasion, and it is not known whether or not he became the French teacher at the said school. On 20 July 1850 he wrote to the French Institute in Paris, as author of *Origin of Language and Myths* (a manuscript in English of 453 pages), offering himself as a candidate for the Prix Volney,[93] giving his address as 28 Dean Street, Soho Square, London.

It seems unlikely that Julia and her mother would have spent time in residence at Dean Street as conditions there would not have been conducive to the two women's sensibilities. Moreover, in the section relating to marital status and family in his application to the Literary Fund Society, Morgan gives Julia and Bridget's address as 7 Allason Terrace, Kensington. However, if Marx was referring to Julia, in his letter to Engels, then his is a particularly poignant comment, considering that, at that time, Julia would have been writing *Women of Christianity*:

Exemplary for Acts of Piety, which was published in 1852. It is significant that the general squalor of domestic poverty which pervaded the
Marx family's everyday routine did not go unnoticed, notwithstanding
the overcrowded household. B. Nicolaievsky and O. Maenchen-Helfen,
in *Karl Marx: Man and Fighter*, give a brief account of conditions for
them at that time, as reported by 'a Prussian spy who contrived to worm
his way into the Dean Street establishment':

> He lives in one of the worst and cheapest neighbourhoods in London. He
> occupies two rooms. There is not one clean or decent piece of furniture
> in either room, everything is broken, tattered and torn, with thick dust
> over everything . . . manuscripts, books and newspapers lie beside the
> children's toys, bits and pieces from his wife's sewing basket, cups with
> broken rims, dirty spoons, knives, forks, lamps, an inkpot, tumblers,
> pipes, tobacco ash – all piled up on the same table. On entering the room
> smoke and tobacco fumes make your eyes water to such an extent that at
> first you seem to be groping about in a cavern – until you get used to it,
> and manage to make out certain objects in the haze. Sitting down is a dan-
> gerous business. Here is a chair with only three legs, there another which
> happens to be whole, on which the children are playing at cooking. That
> is the one that is offered to the visitor, but the children's cooking is not
> removed, and if you sit down you risk a pair of trousers. But all these
> things do not in the least embarrass Marx or his wife. You are received
> in the most friendly way and are cordially offered pipes, tobacco, and
> whatever else there may happen to be. Presently a clever and interesting
> conversation arises which repays for all the domestic deficiencies and this
> makes the discomfort bearable.[94]

By all accounts, the insalubrious circumstance of this household was
partly due to the Marx family lifestyle. There must, surely, have been
constant comings and goings of people strange and exotic, which interrupted Morgan's own domestic routine. Interestingly, at about this time,
Morgan was writing an anti-religious tract, *Errors of Religion*, in which
he argues the merits of reason over religion, a philosophical outlook, one
could argue, that complemented Marx's own views. Could it be that
Morgan was sympathetic to Marx's doctrines? Did they ever converse on
subjects of mutual interest and, if so, was this relationship yet another
contributing factor which kept the Kavanagh family apart? It is a possibility that invites conjecture. Nevertheless, one event which may have
caused friction was the birth of a child to Helene Demuth in June 1851;
and there was little doubt as to the identity of the father. Marx's child
was sent to foster parents, Engels volunteered paternity and the whole
matter was hushed up. If she had known about the pregnancy, Julia's
strict Catholic sensibilities would surely have compelled her to question

Marx's own humanism. By all accounts Marx was extremely unkempt in appearance and I doubt if this would have offered much ardour to Julia's own domestic outlook, which, one imagines, was simple but unpretentiously genteel. It is also difficult to ascertain the degree of her seeming indifference to their poverty. On 8 September 1852 Marx wrote the following to Engels:

> My wife is ill, little Jenny is ill, Leni has a sort of nervous fever. I cannot and could not call the doctor, having no money for medicines. For the last week I have fed my family on bread and potatoes, but I wonder if I shall be able to buy any today[95]

It may have been the case that relations between the two families were so bad that there was no communication. It is also incredible that Julia should knowingly ignore such a devastating and sad situation as evidence suggests that she was assiduously conscious of the suffering of others. On 13 March 1850, just nine months before the Marx family took up residence at 28 Dean Street, in December, Julia, then in residence at Allason Terrace, wrote to the wife of W. S. Williams, requesting funds to help Roman refugees:

> My dear Mrs. Williams,
>
> I know your kind heart and liberal feeling. I know also that you are so happy as to possess liberal and influential friends, and I believe the case I wish to lay before you is fully worthy of their compassion and respect.
>
> I allude to the Roman refugees about fifty of whom are now in London and have been for some time dependent for their daily bread on the funds placed by public liberality at the disposal of a committee chosen for that purpose.
>
> [. . .] funds are now exhausted and next week the unhappy men will be left destitute. Some have been badly wounded; others are in ill health; very few can work or even procure work; banished from Italy, shut out from France, England is their forced place of refuge and here nothing awaits them but starvation.
>
> Is not this a case for an appeal to the generous and liberal feelings now so active and universal? Those who for the sake of principle, a sacred sight, forget selfish wisdom and [. . .] themselves by a resistance to oppression, unavailing resistance perhaps but surely most heroic deserve something beyond mere sympathy.
>
> When a friend of mine as powerless as myself – mentioned these facts to me I immediately thought of Doctor Epps. I thought that his high character and standing; that his well known liberality and love of freedom entitled him to interfere in a matter in which I felt very well that insignificant individuals like myself had no right to meddle; for this I need scarcely say is no case for mere individual charity.

It may be that Doctor Epps already knows of the distress which threatens those unhappy refugees; but if he should not some good and no harm can come from mentioning the matter to him. As you are so happy as to know him you will perhaps do so! I feel at least that I can leave this case to your good judgement and kind heart, and I am too well acquainted with the latter to apologize for troubling you on such a subject.

> Yours truly,
> Julia Kavanagh[96]

There is very little concrete evidence to connect Julia Kavanagh with Morgan's sub-tenants at 28 Dean Street. However, given the fact that Julia was probably still in touch with her father at the time, it is unlikely that she would not have known about the Marx family.

As is the case with many Irish people who had left their home country, little is known about Morgan's origins. In his application in 1844 for financial assistance to the Literary Fund Society, he states that his father was Morgan Kavanagh and his mother was Ellen Read. He is not sure where he was born but believes it was Dublin about the year 1799. He died in London on 10 February 1874.[97] Until 1844 he had given his name as Morgan Peter Kavanagh, but dropped the name Peter in the belief that as it was the name he adopted on his confirmation it was not strictly legal.[98] Morgan Kavanagh is the author of several controversial and much critically maligned books including works on myth, philology and fiction. Throughout his life he had a fascination with language and for much of his adult life he was at odds with the literary establishment, continuously battling to prove his case against those who challenged his theories. All of his works were published in London. His literary output included two lengthy poems, *The Wanderings of Lucan and Dinah, A Poetical Romance, in Ten Cantos* (1824) and *The Reign of Lockrin* (1839); a study of language entitled *The Discovery of the Science of Languages*, in two volumes (1844), also published in French; and two novels, *Aristobulus, The Last of the Maccabees: A Tale of Jerusalem*, in three volumes (1855), and *The Hobbies* (1857). Both novels were published by Newby, with *The Hobbies* becoming the subject of much publicised controversy between Morgan and Julia. As a response to his critics, he produced two lengthy publications, *Myths Traced to their Primary Source through Language*, two volumes (1856), and *An Author His Own Reviewer; or, an analysis of 'Myths traced to their primary source through language' By its author* (1857). This study was followed in 1871 with an investigation into the *Origin of Language and Myths*, two volumes. He applied to the Literary Fund Society for monetary assistance five times in all, the first time in 1825 shortly after his arrival in London, then in 1839,

1844, 1847 and finally in 1850. He was successful on each occasion, with the Literary Fund providing small amounts of £25 and £20 to cover his immediate requirements. However, this assistance offered only temporary relief from financial dificulties. When he was living in London with Bridget and Julia, life for all three must have been very hard as there was little or no financial gain from his books and work as a teacher of languages was insecure.

As a writer Morgan was indefatigable. He had some critical support for his earlier works, but, as Robert Kavanagh has pointed out, his theories on language were much derided by critics and met with severe reviews.[99] The preface to his first published work, *The Wanderings of Lucan and Dinah*, a poetical romance in ten cantos in 'the stanza of Spenser', written by Martin MacDermot, himself the author of articles on Spenser,[100] gives some insight into the circumstances of Morgan's early life:

> Born to no inheritance, though of respectable parents, he seems to have cultivated the Muses from the moment science began to dawn on his infant mind – from the moment perception and observation began to unfold to him the charms of nature, and the consecrated pleasures of sympathy, purity, and refined emotions. Fortune, however, proved less favourable to him than nature, and he had to struggle against evils, which it required physical as well as mental strength to surmount [. . .] In the lottery of fortune, Mr. Kavanagh has been very unsuccessful, and the consequence has been, that he has laboured under all the disadvantages arising from the absence of that glow of feeling which is chilled by adversity; or – if in spirits of the first order there can be no cold, platonic emotion – from the absence of that intensity of feeling and rapidity of perception which cling to genius when suffered to move in its own career, uncontrolled by circumstances. He had also to surmount the disadvantages arising from the want of a classical education. By perseverance and industry, however, he succeeded informing an acquaintance with the poets of other nations, without having recourse to a translation. To his own native and unaided powers of mind he therefore owes whatever portion of acquired knowledge he possesses; and it will be found from the following Poem.[101]

Undeterred by disadvantages and relentless in his pursuit of knowledge, Morgan would surely have had some influence on Julia's education. French biographical sources state that Julia was educated at home,[102] in which case Morgan, who was engaged with his own writing at the time, would have determined the types of books to which Julia was allowed access. He would certainly have encouraged her reading of the classics, which she loved, and he may even have been her tutor. In a letter dated 8 August 1846 Julia wrote to Leitch Ritchie of *Chambers Journal*,

Edinburgh, offering to write several historical pieces, the subject matter of which is sympathetic to Morgan's own interests.

27 Berkeley Street, Lambeth Palace

Dear Sir,

With this letter I have the honour of forwarding to you the tract entitled *The History of the Bastille*. I hope that the manner in which I treated it is suitable to the general spirit of the Miscellany. Should it nevertheless not be found sufficiently interesting I could easily remedy this by adding many particulars which want of space compelled me to omit.

As Mr. W. S. Williams has been kind enough to congratulate me on the English style of *Montyon Prizes*, I trust that the history of the Bastille will not need so many corrections or be found to contain so many gallicisms as *Madame Roland*. With it I send a plan of the Bastille necessary to the intelligence of the whole.

Since I have been engaged in writing this tract several other subjects have occurred to me as being likely to suit the miscellany: namely 1stly, *A History of Abdel Kader*. I need not I believe dwell on the great interest such a subject is likely to offer, nor how opportune its appearance would be at a moment when the attention of Europe is engrossed by this great and memorable struggle of a nation against its invaders. 2ndly *A Tale illustrative of ancient Roman manners and customs*. 3rdly *Annals of Primitive Races* or a comprehensive view of savage life and manners from the inhabitants of Polar regions to the natives of Australia and the Polynesian islands. 4thly A history of Venice and of its government. 5thly Gustavus Wara and Sweden.

If all these subjects are not acceptable some of them may I hope prove so, whichever is the case believe me still.

Dear Sir so remain
Yours very sincerely,
Julia Kavanagh

I have been unable to trace the London address for Julia prior to this date but in late 1844 it is likely to have been 33 Fitzroy Square as this is the address given by Morgan in an application for financial assistance to the Literary Fund Society in November 1844. The family were still together at that time as Morgan declared in his application that he had a wife and a daughter aged twenty who were wholly dependent on him for support.[103] In fact Robert Kavanagh is of the opinion that Morgan was already in London in 1843 as evidence suggests that he visited Longman's the publishers. In the preface to the *Origin of Language and Myths*, Morgan describes an experience which happened soon after the publication in 1844 of his earlier book, *The Discovery of the Science of Languages*, and states that, after leaving a friend, 'I walked to the house in which I lodged. It lay in the neighbourhood of the British Museum'.[104] It may be that he had left Paris before Bridget and Julia, in order to secure employment prior to their joining him later.

By 1849 life had taken on a different turn. Julia had stated to Gavan Duffy that she lived by her labour, which suggests that she was required to write in order to pay the rent, presumably receiving nothing from Morgan. However, as her name became known, she was to encounter an embarrassment which drew on both her professional and her personal circumstances. In 1857 she entered into an extremely unpleasant exchange of correspondence with the publisher Newby concerning the extent of her editorial involvement with Morgan's novel *The Hobbies*. In testimony of Julia's anger with both Newby and her father against the unauthorised use of her name, the letters were subsequently published in the 'Our Weekly Gossip' column of *The Athenaeum*. On 9 June she wrote:

> Mr Newby of Welbeck Street having, during my absence from England, and without my cognizance, published a novel in three volumes called 'The Hobbies', on the title-page and in the advertisements, of which it is stated to be 'Edited by Julia Kavanagh', I am under the painful necessity of stating that my name has been affixed to the book without my knowledge or consent, and that I have, consequently, instructed my solicitors to take such legal measures as will compel Mr. Newby to withdraw my name from the title-page and advertisements for the work.[105]

On 20 June *The Athenaeum* printed Newby's response. It is worth quoting this in full here as the contents offer some insight into relations between Julia and Morgan at that time:

> I am sure I need make no apology in requesting the insertion of the following statement of facts, in reply to a letter which has been printed in your paper from Miss Julia Kavanagh, which absence from town has prevented me from sooner noticing. Nearly twelve months since, Miss Julia Kavanagh's father brought the MS. of 'The Hobbies' to me with a view to its publication, telling me that a considerable portion of it had been written by his daughter who had carefully revised the whole as its editor. The MS. fully bore out this statement inasmuch as I found a large part of it, as well as innumerable emendations, in Miss Kavanagh's handwriting. I was also shown several letters of Miss Kavanagh's in which she wrote in high terms of the merits of the work, and having made such alterations as she thought would make it more acceptable to the public. These circumstances, and the fact of her having previously offered the work to one of the leading publishing firms in London for publication, on the understanding that it was to be announced as *edited by her*, induced me to believe her father's statement, – and in this belief I undertook the publication, upon Mr. Kavanagh's express written authority to publish it 'as edited by his daughter, Miss Julia

Kavanagh, Author of 'Nathalie', 'Daisy Burns', &co., the said work having undergone the editorial revision of the said Julia Kavanagh.' I was unaware when I accepted the MS. that unhappy family differences had arisen between Miss Kavanagh and her father; nor had I reason to suppose that any objections existed to the use of her name as editing her parent's work, until I was called upon by her solicitor to withdraw it. Immediately, however, on being requested to do so, a new title-page was printed and sent to every library to which copies of the work had been sold; and in further compliance with Miss Kavanagh's request, her solicitor was promised that, immediately after my return to town, the fact should be announced to the public in a form that would be most agreeable to her wishes. I was, therefore, much surprised, – and I think I have reason to complain of Miss Kavanagh's publishing her letter of the 9th inst., threatening me with the penalties of the law, when she could not fail to be aware that everything, and even more than any legal proceedings could have effected, had already been done by me to comply with her wishes, and that if any ground of complaint existed, it ought rather to be settled between her father and herself than between herself and me.[106]

Julia's response was printed on 27 June, as follows:

Mr. Newby, with the view of extenuating his conduct in putting my name as Editor on the title page of 'The Hobbies' without my consent, has asserted that I had previously sanctioned such an announcement being made by another publisher. I am therefore compelled to state most distinctly that this is the reverse of the truth, as I positively refused to allow my name to be made use of. I purposely confine my self to this point, because the other circumstances alluded to by Mr. Newby have no direct bearing on his unwarrantable use of my name. I also wish to add, that before writing the letter which I addressed to you on this painful subject, I ascertained from my solicitor that he had not been able to see Mr. Newby, that he had not heard directly from him, and that he was not aware of any steps having been taken to withdraw my name from the title page of 'The Hobbies', copies of which book, with the first title-page, I know to be at the libraries and in circulation at the time.

I remain, &c. Julia Kavanagh[107]

The matter is finally put to rest by *The Athenaeum* on 4 July, in an announcement:

We are tired of the controversy about 'The Hobbies,' and we trust we shall have no need to publish further correspondence on the subject. We must, however, state that Mr. Newby has placed in our hands a copy of a letter from which we gather that Miss Kavanagh formerly offered the novel to Messrs. Chapman & Hall, and proposed to edit for them.[108]

It would appear that Julia was involved initially but had abandoned the project, either because of its poor quality as a novel and the impact it may have had on her own reputation, or for more personal reasons.

Clearly the circumstantial evidence as presented by Newby does not tell the whole story. Moreover, such a course of action on Morgan's part shows how desperate he was to establish himself as a writer. The affair was picked up by *The Spectator*, which viewed the whole event as distasteful to Julia and was of the view that they 'could readily conceive the unwillingness of a writer of established reputation like Miss Kavanagh to be connected as editor with a novel from which no editorial exertions could remove defects that were inherent, not merely in execution but conception'.[109] What this exchange of published correspondence between Julia and Newby suggests is that Julia, on whatever terms, was in contact with Morgan at this time and that the dispute here was professional. The evidence suggests, nevertheless, that she did assist him with this novel, but to what extent remains unclear. Not surprisingly, she wanted nothing to do with the final published version.

Around this time Julia was to endure a much greater form of humiliation than the episode with her father's illicit use of her name, one which, very possibly, was the cause of her desire not to reveal too much of her life to her reading public. It appears that in the late 1850s Morgan Kavanagh had fathered a son, Alfred. No birth certificate has been traced for Alfred but it is believed that he was born in London to Marie Rose, the woman whom Morgan now called his wife. No marriage certificate has been traced for the couple and, of course, as Bridget was still alive, no marriage could have taken place. The couple were to have two more children, Mathilda Rose, born in Paris in 1862, and Alexander (later known as Alexander Morgan), born in Paris in 1866. The birth certificate for Mathilda Rose states that Marie Rose was thirty-two years of age at the time she and Morgan were purportedly married in London in 1859. However, Alexander's birth certificate, four years later, states that Marie Rose was forty years old and that she and Morgan married in London in 1856. Obviously these discrepancies in age can be accounted for by the very nature of untruths pertaining to Marie Rose and Morgan's predicament. It appears that the matter of the mother's age was considered an arbitrary subject and of little consequence. Whether Morgan had known Marie Rose prior to his break-up with Bridget is not known. As Alfred was born some time in the late 1850s, it seems most likely that they began their life together during that period. It is also very likely that Julia was aware of the relationship. She was living in Kensington in October 1858 as she gives this address in her Preface to *A Summer and Winter in the Two Sicilies*. Both Julia and Bridget, and Morgan and his new family were living in Paris in 1862.[110] The address given on the birth certificate for Mathilda Rose is 9 cité du Marché, 18th arrondissement.[111] Morgan's third child, Alexander, was born in 1866 and the address given on his birth certificate is 45 rue Lepic, 18th arrondissement.[112] There are two more known addresses for Morgan. The first is 23 rue Berthe, Montmartre, 18th arrondissement, given in his Will, the beneficiary being Mrs. Kavanagh, presumably Marie Rose, stating that he had left 1,100 francs. Clearly Morgan's fortunes had increased considerably since 1850, when he placed his final application for financial assistance with the Literary Fund Society. In 1868 there is an addition to the Will in which Morgan declares that 'the above sum has considerably increased since above was written' and the second address given here is 95 rue Nollet Batignolles, 17th arrondissement.[113] At this time Julia and Bridget lived at 25 rue des Dames, Aux [Z]ernes.[114] There is no known evidence to suggest that the two families knew each other, but it is unlikely that neither knew about the other's existence. Given Julia's Catholicism and her concern for Bridget especially, Morgan's second family must have been the source of much anguish.

Robert Kavanagh's research into Morgan's life has revealed that in 1874 Morgan was also 'married' to another woman after, one presumes, Marie Rose's death. He states:

> Evidence was given at the Coroner's inquest on Morgan's death in 1874 by Louisa Kavanagh, who was stated to be Morgan's wife. It seems unlikely that she was Morgan's wife in a legal sense, given that his legal wife, Bridget, was still alive. The question arises as to the whereabouts of Marie Rose at this time. The last documented reference to her is in Morgan's Will of 1868. One may conjecture that Marie Rose died during the siege of Paris. [. . .] From the transcript of the Coroner's inquest it is apparent that Morgan must have been living with Louisa for at least several months. No other information is known concerning Louisa.[115]

It is not known whether or not Julia knew of Morgan and Louisa's 'marriage', or of Morgan's whereabouts at this time. He may have returned to London around the time of the Franco-Prussian War in 1870. He wrote in the preface to *Origin of Language and Myths*, 'I have been for years out of England, and without knowing, or much caring to know, what was going on there in the literary world',[116] which suggests that he had an inclination to return for purposes other than publishing his book. Julia never returned to London but remained in Nice with Bridget. It may well be that Morgan's other commitments were as much a reason to avoid London society as the warm weather offered by the South of France was conducive to Julia's and Bridget's health.

The paradigm of father–daughter relations in connection with Julia and Morgan Kavanagh is an important one. Unfortunately, owing to the notable absence of relevant material, and within the context of this study, it has not been possible to enter into a more psychoanalytically based discussion that would significantly draw on what has already been said. This absence is further illuminated when one considers that Kavanagh herself was interested in the social and emotional dynamics of the father–daughter connection and refers to them in *English Women of Letters*. Amongst others she discusses the familial bond between Fanny Burney and her father Dr Charles Burney to the effect that Kavanagh believed that in her writing Fanny strived to secure her father's approval. This observation, though not directly pointed out, is apparent in Kavanagh's discussion, particularly when she alludes to the socially harnessed conformity of Burney's heroines. In the case of Maria Edgeworth, Kavanagh is adamant that, as a novelist, Maria would have benefited considerably without her father, Robert Lovell Edgeworth's, paternal interference. In each case Kavanagh is censorious of the fact that neither of these two women stepped beyond the patriarchal traditions that helped shape their writing.

In her study of women writers and paternal complicity, Elizabeth Kowaleski-Wallace consider both Burney and Edgeworth with reference to the 'myth of the benevolent patriarch'.[117] Both of these women are thus euphemistically identified as 'daddies' girls', the term she uses to suggest that, as writers, Burney and Edgeworth had succumbed to a patriarchal tradition, as she says:

> Literary daughters are special kinds of daughters, women who adapt themselves to both a familial and literary hierarchy. The terms of family romance suggested by modern psychoanalysis might be used metaphorically to describe the daughter's apprenticeship to her father's patriarchal literary tradition. Willingly forsaking her literal mother, the woman writer accepts her place in a literary heritage that is not her own.[118]

She goes on to suggest that in the case of Burney and Edgeworth 'the choice of the patriarchal literary tradition was facilitated, perhaps even necessitated, by the death of the real mother.'[119] Indirectly this suggestion draws attention to the fact that Kavanagh's 'real' mother, Bridget, had played a significant part in encouraging her daughter's literary achievements, further testimony, perhaps, that Kavanagh herself did not adhere to such a tradition. In fact, as Kavanagh's attitude to Burney and Edgeworth suggest, she consciously worked against it. At the same time it is feasible that Kavanagh's unconscious sense of loss brought about by the separation from her father did manifest itself in some of her novels. For example, in her two novels *Rachel Gray* and *Sybil's Second Love*, in each case, the father literally abandons his daughter and the ensuing sense of betrayal is drawn out in the narrative. In *Rachel Gray* the father chooses to turn his back on family life in favour of a more solitary existence, leaving his dependants to fend for themselves. In *Sybil's Second Love*, as a daughter, Sybil is cast aside when her widowed father marries her best friend. It could be argued that, metaphorically, both of these novels harbour elements of Kavanagh's own sense of betrayal and the emotional experience of coping with such feelings. However, in both novels, the sense of abandonment experienced initially by the discarded daughters eventually gives way to that of empowerment as, in each case, the daughter eventually discovers the strength of her own emotional independence.

It is unlikely that the full facts concerning the relationship between Julia and her father will ever come to light. As suggested earlier, one can only conjecture as to why Morgan left his wife and daughter, if he did, in fact, abandon his family, or whether his leaving was decided for him. All available sources suggest that throughout Julia's childhood Morgan did all in his power to educate and care for his daughter, and, although he was himself unsuccessful as an author, he was undoubtedly proud of Julia's achievements. Given the absence of tangible evidence, it would be futile to determine any lasting effect Morgan had on Julia as a writer. Julia's letter to Leitch Ritchie suggests that the choice of material she wished to engage at that time may have been influenced by her father's own interests but as she matured the dynamics of change set a different pattern. As the Newby episode demonstrates, Julia had already consciously set about to distance herself professionally from her father and, in spite of his early paternal guidance, one thing is certain: as a writer she was no 'daddy's girl'.

Julia Kavanagh and Charlotte Brontë

Problematic as it was, Julia's relationship with Morgan did not deter her from her literary ambitions. In 1848, at the beginning of her writing career, she is mentioned several times in the letters of Charlotte Brontë. Writing to W. S. Williams, on 13 January, Brontë speaks of her delight on receiving a letter from Kavanagh sent initially to Williams who appears to have sent it on to her:

> I have just got Miss Kavanagh's letter: her name is Irish – and I seem to hear in that letter a slight, pleasant echo of the Irish accent, as well as to feel the warmth of an Irish heart: there is, I should say, a frankness, a directness in her phrases which is not of Albion. Am I wrong? I will avail myself of your permission to retain the letter, because I like it.[120]

Amongst other reasons, the recognition and respect which Brontë attributes to Kavanagh could well have stemmed from her own desire to hold on to an Irish accent. Brontë could write and speak Irish and had an Irish accent until well into her teens.[121]

A few months earlier, on 6 October 1847, Kavanagh, unaware of the author's real identity, had written to Leitch Ritchie at *Chambers Edinburgh Journal*, offering to write a review of *Jane Eyre*. Although somewhat tentative in tone, she is quietly determined in her intentions: 'I suppose novels are not included amongst the interesting works suitable for reviews? If they were I should propose one now on the eve of publication and which I heard highly recommended by a person of taste; it is entitled Jane Eyre; the author I believe is unknown.'[122] It would seem that from the outset the younger writer's admiration for Brontë (Currer Bell) was to be reciprocated. The two women did not actually meet until June 1850 but Brontë appears to have been informed of Kavanagh's progress via Williams's reports, which, to all accounts, must have been very supportive. Soon after, Brontë expresses her regard for 'Miss Kavanagh' when in a letter to Williams, dated 22 January 1848, she states:

> I was much interested in your account of Miss Kavanagh; the character you sketch belongs to a class I peculiarly esteem: one in which endurance combines with exertion, talent with goodness; where genius is found unmarred by extravagance, self-reliance unalloyed by self-complacency. It is a character which is, I believe, rarely found except where there has been toil to undergo, and adversity to struggle against it; it will only grow to perfection in a poor soil, and in the shade: if the soil be too indigent, the shade too dank and thick, of course it dies where it sprung, but I trust this will not be the case with Miss Kavanagh; I trust she will struggle ere long into the sunshine . . . I should very much like one [copy of *Jane Eyre*] to be given to Miss Kavanagh. If you would have the goodness – you might write on the fly-leaf that the book is presented with the author's best wishes for her welfare here and hereafter. My reason for wishing that she should have a copy is because she said the book had been to her a *suggestive* one, and I know that suggestive books are valuable to authors.[123]

And again, on 29 March, she voices her support for Kavanagh's first novel, *Madeleine*:

> I trust Miss Kavanagh's work will meet with the success that from your account, I am certain she and it [*Madeleine*] deserve. I think I have met with an outline of the facts on which her tale is founded in some periodical, 'Chambers's Journal' I believe. No critic, however rigid, will find fault with 'the tendency' of her work, I should think.[124]

When *Madeleine* was eventually published in October of 1848, Kavanagh sent her novel to Currer Bell with a letter expressing her longing to meet the author of *Jane Eyre*.[125] Brontë appears to have wasted no time in her response: writing to Williams on 2 November, she comments again on *Madeleine*, and on Kavanagh's first publication, *The Three Paths: A Story for Young People*, also published in 1848:

> I am glad, by the by, to hear that 'Madeleine' is come out at last, and was happy to see a favourable notice of that work and of 'The Three Paths' in the 'Morning Herald.' I wish Miss Kavanagh all success.[126]

On 22 November:

> I have just read 'Madeleine.' It is a fine pearl in a simple setting. Julia Kavanagh has my esteem; I would rather know her than many far more brilliant personages. Somehow my heart leans more to her than to Eliza Lynn, for instance.[127]

And on 4 February 1849:

> I have kept 'Madeleine' along with the two other books I mentioned; I shall consider it the gift of Miss Kavanagh and shall value it both for its literary excellence and for the modest merit of the giver.[128]

As Gaye Tuchman has demonstrated, friendship and patronage were instrumental in procuring publishing contracts, particularly for women,[129] and from these letters we can see that Brontë's affection for Kavanagh did not go unheeded. Brontë's interest in Kavanagh continued throughout these early years, and her letters to Williams reveal a growing fondness for this young writer. On 5 September 1850 she wrote:

> I trust your suggestion for Miss Kavanagh's benefit will have all success. It seems to me truly felicitous and excellent, and, I doubt not, she will think so too. The last class of female character will be difficult to manage: there will be nice points in it – yet, well managed, both an attractive and instructive book might result therefrom. One thing may be depended upon in the execution of this plan – Miss Kavanagh will commit no error either of taste, judgement, or principle; and even when she deals with the feeling, I would rather follow the calm course of her quiet pen than the flourishes of a more redundant one, where there is not strength to restrain as well as ardour to impel.[130]

The book in question is likely to have been *Women of Christianity*. In a letter dated 25 March 1852 she refers to this publication with some insightful comments on both Kavanagh's and her own perceptions of Catholic and Protestant difference:

> I ought long since to have acknowledged gratification with which I read Miss Kavanagh's 'Women of Christianity.' Her charity and (on the whole) her impartiality are very beautiful. She touches indeed with too gentle a hand the theme of Elizabeth of Hungary – and in her own mind – she evidently misconstrues the fact of Protestant Charities *seeming* to be fewer than

Catholic. She forgot or does not know that Protestantism is a quieter creed than Romanism – as it does not clothe its priesthood in scarlet, so neither does it set up its good women for Saints, canonize their names and proclaim their good works – In the records of man their almsgiving will not perhaps be found registered – but Heaven has its Account as well as Earth.[131]

Writing to George Smith on 18 September, Brontë proclaimed her displeasure with the publisher, Newby, for his failure to honour an agreement of copyright and unpaid fees to Ellis and Acton Bell. Despite her obvious grief and her frustration in having to deal with Newby's dishonest claims, she shows concern for Kavanagh's economic circumstances:

> If you *should* extract any money from Mr. Newby (of which I am not sanguine), I shall regard it in the light of a providential windfall and dispose of part of it – at least – accordingly; one half of whatever you may realise must be retained in your possession to add to any sum you may decide on giving Miss Kavanagh for her next work. This, however, is a presumptuous enumeration of chickens ere the eggs are hatched.[132]

One year earlier, and in deep mourning after the death of her sister Emily, Brontë had rejected Kavanagh's gesture of condolence when, in a letter to Williams, dated 25 June 1849, she spurns anyone whom she suspects of showing her 'pity' in her grief and claims the right to privacy:

> I by no means ask Miss Kavanagh to write to me – Why should she trouble herself to do it? What claim have I on her? She does not know me – she cannot care for me except vaguely and on hearsay. I have got used to your friendly sympathy and it comforts me – I have tried and trust the fidelity of one or two other friends and I lean upon it – The natural affection of my father and the attachment and solicitude of our two servants are precious and consolatory to me – but I do not look round for general pity – conventional condolence I do not want – either from man or woman.[133]

These sentiments do seem to be the result of Brontë's sadness and depressed state of mind at the time. After she had made Kavanagh's acquaintance, however, she nurtured a watchful and professional benevolence towards the younger woman. On 20 September 1850 her interest in Kavanagh's progress is conveyed to Williams:

> I am truly pleased too to learn that Miss Kavanagh has managed so well with Mr Colburn. Her position seems to me one deserving of all sympathy. I often think of her. Will her novel soon be published? Somehow I expect it to be interesting.[134]

The novel referred to is *Nathalie*, on receipt of a copy, of which Brontë writes to Kavanagh on 21 January 1851, with her response. It is worth citing the whole of this letter as it demonstrates the level of interest and respect that Brontë now had for this young writer:

My Dear Miss Kavanagh,

I fear you will have thought hard things of me ere this – pronounced me ungrateful – uncivil and I know not what, but the fact is I only received 'Nathalie' a few days since; she has been waiting in London to come down in a parcel with some other books. At last however I have made her acquaintance, read her through from title-page to 'Finis.'

Now – do not expect me to criticise; of that ungenial office I wash my hands; it suffices for me to know and to say that I was thoroughly interested and highly pleased. Your reader is made to realize places and persons; he becomes an inmate of the old chateau of Sainville, Normandy spreads green and cultured round him. He numbers amongst his acquaintance the various personage of the tale. Some of the minor characters – the Canoness, Mlle Dantin, the femme de chambre are by no means the least cleverly drawn. Rose Montelieu is excellent; I thought those passages which refer to her illness and death amongst the very best in the book. Nathalie's perverseness as well as her final submission struck me as a little exaggerated – so did some of the traits in M. de Sainville's character – but I said I would not criticise; the contrast in their natures, and the *kind* of contrast is a happy thought; the mutual attraction to which it leads would – I doubt not, be exactly paralleled in nature and real life. In short I have to thank you for a treat; the work merits success, and the favourable notices which have been given by the various literary journals may I trust be taken as evidences that it has secured it.

I earnestly trust your health has been improved by change of air and scene; in England we have thus far had a peculiarly mild open winter; even here, in the North – no snow has yet fallen.

Perhaps ere this you may have left Boulogne; in that case I fear there is small chance of your receiving this note and thus my silence will remain unexplained. I must however trust to fortune and with every good wish for your health and happiness – I beg you to believe me, Yours very sincerely, C. Brontë.[135]

There is no address for Kavanagh on this letter, but, as Brontë's comments imply, she must have been in Boulogne in January 1851.

A few years later, when Kavanagh had become an established writer, Mrs Gaskell also showed an interest in her. In a letter to Edward Coward dated 6 December 1856 she says, '[M]ay I remind you of your kind promise to show me the likenesses of Leigh Hunt and Miss Kavanagh?'[136]

Kavanagh's increasing success ensured that she was able to make her living from writing. Nevertheless her negotiations with Smith and Elder for the publication of *Woman in France during the Eighteenth Century* suggest that, at that time, she was struggling financially. On 11 September 1849 she wrote an apologetic letter to George Smith, which suggests that external pressures compelled her to reconsider the amount of £100 offered for the copyright:

> When I declined your proposal a fortnight ago, I did not in the least intend to reflect upon it as not sufficiently just or liberal. I was actuated – as I explained to Mr. Williams – by purely personal considerations.
>
> It is because my motives were such that I did not feel the reluctance I might otherwise have experienced in offering you my work once more. Had I however been aware that circumstances over which I had no control would render it extremely inconvenient for me to offer it to more than one publisher, I should not have declined your first proposal, and placed myself in the somewhat awkward position of suddenly returning to that which I had refused. [. . .]
>
> To the proposal contained in your letter I fully agree. The provisions made in case of future success are such as to satisfy me, although I begin to fear that my hopes on this head have been too sanguine; but it is a natural and not unjustifiable mistake to value highly that which has cost much labour.[137]

In 1848 she had been paid £25 by Bentley for the copyright of *Madeleine*.[138] In 1853 Bentley had paid £300 for *Daisy Burns* with an agreement of a further £150 for every reprint of five hundred copies.[139] Although these figures suggest that in commercial terms Kavanagh was gaining ground, evidence points to the fact that she needed to continue writing in order to earn a living.[140] It is clear from these payments and also from Charlotte Brontë's letters that during the early 1850s certainly, and probably throughout the remainder of her life, Kavanagh's lifestyle was an undeniably thrifty one.

The politics of writing

Though not considered a political writer of her generation – those whom Elaine Showalter in *A Literature of Their Own* refers to as 'The second generation, born between 1820 and 1840' which 'included Charlotte Brontë, Dinah Mulock Craik, Margaret Oliphant, and Elizabeth Lynn Linton'[141] – Kavanagh was astutely aware of the double standards of her time. Her work bears testimony to the many anomalies concerning women's subjectivity and as such she draws on the very core of sexual politics. It is this aspect of her writing that may well have been the main attraction for Charlotte Brontë. Kavanagh's perspective on French and English women's writing is significant in so far as she is adamant about the importance of the woman's voice and this is demonstrated in the attention to detail and prominence she gives to women writers as writers. She makes this clear in her preface to *French Women of Letters*, when she states:

> I felt that a woman may worthily employ such power as God has given her in rescuing from forgetfulness the labours and the names once honoured and celebrated of other women, [. . .] my object has been to show how far, for the last two centuries and more, women have contributed to the formation of the modern novel in the two great literatures of modern times (I: vi)

Twelve years earlier, she had opened the introductory chapter to *Woman in France during the Eighteenth Century* with the following:

> In times still recent, in a nation celebrated for its power and greatness, and in an age which gave to thought a vast and magnificent, even though perilous, development, a series of most remarkable women exercised a power so extensive, and yet so complete as to be unparalleled in the history of their sex [. . .] This power was not always pure or good; it was often corrupt in its source, evil and fatal in its results; but it was power. Though the historians of the period have never fully or willingly acknowledged its existence, their silence cannot efface that which has been; and without that rule of woman, so reluctantly recognised, many of their pages of statesman's policy, court intrigue, civil strife, or foreign war, need never have been written. To this remarkable feature of modern history, to the analysis of the power of Woman in France during the Eighteenth Century the present work is devoted. (1)

It is evident that Kavanagh felt strongly about the position of women in society and in politics in particular, a conviction she carried into her fiction. It is also clear from these studies that Kavanagh wished to recognise and acknowledge women's potential for power. Her address, however, is not without irony as throughout she draws attention to the secondary positioning of women in the political arena of a male hierarchy. She also brings to light the importance of women's contribution to literary texts. In *French Women of Letters*, for example, Chapter One focuses on Mademoiselle de Gournay, a woman whose literary output was extensive but who as Kavanagh points out, is better known 'for her adopted relationship to Montaigne than for the excellence of her numerous work' (I:1). In the context of her study, Kavanagh is a biographer and a historian who draws attention to the cultural and social positioning of women and how this had affected their lives. She does not offer a specific manifesto for change in the sense of that suggested by Mary Wollstonecraft in *A Vindication of the Rights of Women* (1792) or proposed by Anna Doyle Wheeler, in collaboration with William Thompson, in their *Appeal of One-Half of the Human Race, Women, Against the Pretensions of the Other Half, Men, to Retain Them in*

Political and Thence in Civil and Domestic Slavery (1825). She is, nevertheless, concerned with women's lives and the works they produced in a world, which, for the most part, saw women as adjuncts to male experience. I would argue that, because she is writing about women who previously had been seen primarily in relation to more historically illustrious men, Kavanagh offers a significant contribution to women's history.

Similarly, in her travel writing Kavanagh is equally conscious of women's subordination to patriarchy in her observations of sexual politics. Her two-volume publication *A Summer and Winter in the Two Sicilies* (1858) met with a mixed response in *The Athenaeum*, although the reviewer, Henry Fothergill Chorley, conceded nevertheless that 'the most individual portion of Miss Kavanagh's volume contains her experiences of female life and manners at Sorrento'.[142] Kavanagh records her views, outlining how she was received and how she perceived the people and their customs. Her observations of the everyday lives of people from different social groups are delivered with illuminating clarity. Notwithstanding the historic importance of Italy and its regions and while fully appreciative of its charms as a romantic idyll, Kavanagh is as interested in relating the fortunes, customs and prejudices of the people she engages with as much as she is in describing the scenery. As will be discussed later in a section on Kavanagh's travels in the two Sicilies, her perspective is that of a northern European woman whose outlook is balanced by her observations of the social injustices that she feels many women, especially the poor, are forced to endure.

Kavanagh's views on the injustices of women during the mid nineteenth century are present in all of her works but none so much as in her fiction. As a woman novelist she was all too aware of the fictional representations of women and how the subject is necessarily articulated within the limitations of cultural narrative. In her study *English Women of Letters* she states her distaste for the portrayal of women as mere sex objects in contemporary novels, who, more often than not, are seen as 'silly young creatures made to delight man, to amuse, tease and obey him' (96). In an earlier publication, her novel *Nathalie*, Kavanagh voices a similar observation when Nathalie comments:

> Amongst the 'wrongs of women', few are really more heavy and insupportable than the forced inactivity to which they are condemned in all the life, fire and energy of youth [. . .] They are social prisoners [. . .] a few [. . .] break through their bonds, and throw themselves into social strife; but for one who wins the shore, how many perish miserably. (220)

In the main Kavanagh's novels centre on women's experience as an affirmation of their subjectivity and sense of self in a society that inadvertently works against them. This paradigm is often interwoven into the themes of love and marriage, and in some of her novels she exposes the suffering and frustration born out of the laws of coverture. In those novels which end in marriage it is clear that true marital harmony can be achieved only between equal partners. In the mid nineteenth century the ideological construct of marriage (and motherhood) was promoted as the ultimate fulfilment for women. The Victorian marital home was held to be the pinnacle of domestic happiness, where husband and wife each played out their accepted roles, an idea which was imbued with religious and moral sentiment. While John Ruskin saw the home as a 'place of Peace; the shelter, not only from all injury, but from all terror, doubt, and division',[143] the philanthropic Lord Shaftesbury extolled the virtues of the perfect home where 'the "authority" of the husband and father, and the "genial influence" of the wife and mother, were complementary pillars of both domestic and civil society'.[144] Yet this concept was not without its critics. On his marriage to Harriet Taylor in 1851 John Stuart Mill formally protested against the laws that would govern their marriage, stating that:

> [Marriage] confers upon one of the parties to the contract, legal power & control over the person, property, and freedom of action of the other party, independent of her own wishes and will. [. . .] [H]aving no means of legally divesting myself of these odious powers . . . [I] feel it my duty to put on record a formal protest against the existing law of marriage, in so far as conferring such powers; and a solemn promise never in any case or under any circumstances to use them.[145]

By mid-century the laws pertaining to marriage were no longer acceptable to many women who petitioned for change, the outcome of which was the Matrimonial Causes Act in 1857.

Although the discourse of marriage and happiness was often the mainstay of the romantic novel, paradoxically it is this same genre that also provided a convenient outlet for women writers to expose the inequalities that existed within marriage. In many of her novels Kavanagh both defines and questions the implications and consequences of marriage in an ideology that determines a woman's subjectivity in relation to her husband. It is this recognition of difference in Kavanagh's novels that would certainly have appealed to Charlotte Brontë. Both Robert Colby and Shirley Foster, two modern critics who have looked at Kavanagh's work, have argued that Kavanagh's *Nathalie* had some influence on Brontë's novel *Villette* (1853).[146] It appears that, later, Kavanagh was seen by some women critics as something of an enigma, whose fiction, they claimed, offered an escape from the turmoil of everyday life. Mrs Charles Martin, in her obituary of Kavanagh, suggests that

Miss Kavanagh's stories transport us at once into a delightful region of brightness, romance, gaiety, and fancy dashed, it is true, with graver colours here and there which show the author's capabilities of touching the chords of pathos, and her tender sympathy with sorrow and suffering[147]

This view is complemented by Mrs Macquoid, who, in *Women Novelists of Queen Victoria's Reign, A Book of Appreciations* (1897), observes:

Miss Kavanagh was a keen observer of externals, her types seem to have been created by imaginative faculty rather than by insight into real men and women [. . .] There is something so restful in her books, that it is difficult to believe she was born no longer ago than 1824, and that only twenty years ago she died in middle life; she seems to belong to a farther away age – probably because her secluded life kept her strongly linked to the past, out of touch with the new generation and the new world of thought around her. (251–2)

Shirley Foster expresses a similar opinion in *Victorian Women's Fiction* (1985), when she states, 'The obsessively romantic content of her novels can be seen as a combination of wish-fulfilment – the imaginative enactment of personal fantasies – and pragmatic response to commercial demands.'[148]

These perspectives of Kavanagh depict her as somewhat benign in the area of sexual politics but I would argue that beneath the surface tales of love, courtship and marriage there is a pronounced dissenting voice. In her novels Kavanagh consciously focuses on sexual difference and exposes the illusory world of social decorum through a variety of narrative techniques. She uses the primary and secondary voice in textually dominant positions in order to challenge power structures. In her first novel, *Madeleine – A Tale of the Auvergne* (1848), Kavanagh is intrigued by the woman as hero and the idea of the romanticised liberating male is turned on its head. Here Kavanagh portrays a young woman who, rejected by her fiancé for another, rises above her disappointment and, through her courage and endeavour, manages to raise sufficient money to build a hospital for the poor. This tale is one of Kavanagh's two novels that were 'founded on fact' (the other one is *Rachel Gray*) and the protagonist, Madeleine, is based on Jeanne Jugan, a virtuous and heroic woman whose works of charity Kavanagh had previously recorded in her pamphlet *The Montyon Prizes* (1846). The subtext of *Madeleine* is a strong denial of the nineteenth-century concept of 'manly strength', a staple component of the romantic novel at this time. Indeed, Madeleine's most prolific helpers in her plight are women and the more deviant adversaries and assailants of her plans are men. The significance of the woman who initiates action in this, Kavanagh's first novel for adults, is indicative of her attitude to women and writing and, in one form or another, is present throughout all of her works.

2

The novel

the novel is not merely the great feature of modern literature, it is also the only branch in which women have acquired undisputed eminence. Here they owe nothing to indulgence of courtesy. (*French Women of Letters*, Preface)

So wrote Julia Kavanagh in 1862. Her statement is a testimony against the social and cultural limitations imposed on French and English women novelists during the eighteenth and early nineteenth centuries and, as such, it is as much a comment about women as it is about the novel. As a Catholic Irish woman who had lived most of her life in France before living and writing in England, Kavanagh may have considered herself an outsider in mid-nineteenth-century London. In a discussion of the Brontës, Terry Eagleton made the comment that 'Women and the Irish were sometimes coupled together in the Victorian imagination as equally "childlike" outsiders, affectionate but irrational';[1] a perspective which, perhaps, helps give Kavanagh's own views on the achievements of women novelists a more poignant political edge. By means of placing Kavanagh into perspective I shall begin by looking at cultural attitudes to women novelists in her own lifetime. In this way I aim to demonstrate her significance as a novelist who drew on the cultural contradictions of that time, and to suggest that her insights into class and gender difference were fundamental to her writing. I shall discuss six of Kavanagh's novels, beginning with *Nathalie* and *Adèle*, progressing to more in-depth discussions of *Daisy Burns*, *Sybil's Second Love*, *Grace Lee* and *Rachel Gray*. Although for my purpose I could well engage with any of Kavanagh's fourteen novels, my choice here is simply to demonstrate her diversity as a novelist in her time.

Women novelists and separate spheres

The mid-nineteenth-century hot-house of women's literary productivity in England was a catalyst for debate concerning woman's proper sphere.

The surge of questions pertaining to the aesthetic and moral repercussions brought about by so many women taking up the pen was the inevitable response to an emerging consciousness of women's capabilities, which undoubtedly threatened Victorian perceptions of sexual difference.[2] In this context Kavanagh could be placed alongside those women novelists about whom the late Lorna Sage remarked that, 'while deferring to male knowledge and power, they subtly revise and undermine the world from which they are excluded'.[3] The domestic novel afforded a new voice for women and, along with others who have since been dismissed as simply 'writers of their time', Kavanagh is one writer whose novels, when looked at from the perspective of women's political history, infringe on the sanctity of separate spheres.

The emergence and proliferation of women writers during the mid nineteenth century caused some consternation among both male and female critics. Ideally, woman's mission was that of marriage, as her husband's helpmeet, and motherhood.[4] Moreover, any form of artistic endeavour – other than that which was part of a young lady's education, such as embroidery, drawing and music – was seen as a deviation from this ideal. Although such activities featured regularly in their fiction, by the very act of writing, women novelists were inadvertently engaging in an alternative 'mission' of independence. The domestic novel, the genre that was to become the domain of women writers, was itself the subject of much critical comment and was seen in terms of a sexual divide. Sexual distinction was, in fact, clearly recognised by some women writers as a means of limitation.[5] Ironically, while still maintaining an acceptance of the biological essentialism of separate spheres, Emily Taylor, author of 'The Lady Novelists of Great Britain' in the *Gentleman's Magazine*, was adamant in her appeal for a consciously less separatist approach to reading and reviewing novels written by women when she argued that the 'Mere cessation of authorship, we suspect, will do but little in correcting those tendencies of which authorship is a sign. Let the novel, poem, or essay be written, and let the public criticise it freely.'[6] This writer also mentions several novelists of the day, including Kavanagh, who, in 1853, were considered to be of 'respectable promise'.[7] While the overall perception of the woman novelist remained separatist, it was believed that, at best, she brought to the novel all the 'gifts' attributed to women's experience.

In Britain the 1850s was the decade in which women writers of the domestic novel were the subject of much debate. Although by this time women had been publishing novels for almost two hundred years, the response of the mainly male establishment was still circumspect concerning women's ability to write outside of what was narrowly perceived as 'women's experience'. The general consensus was that this experience was limited by the very nature of being female and, as such, intellectually, women were considered to be the inferior sex. Even amongst those critics who purportedly leaned towards a more balanced view there remained an element of ambiguity. In 'The Lady Novelists' in the *Westminster Review*, 1852, G.H. Lewes acknowledged women's potential for intellectual pursuit when he advocated that

> The man who would deny to woman the cultivation of her intellect, ought, for consistency, to shut her up in a harem. If he recognise in the sex any quality which transcends the qualities demanded in a play-thing or a hand-maid – if he recognise in her the existence of an intellectual life not essentially dissimilar to his own, he must by the plainest logic, admit that life to express itself in all its spontaneous forms of activity.[8]

Lewes celebrates the idea of women's fiction because it is based on a specific 'women's experience' and, as such, brings its own intrinsic value to literary publication. Nevertheless, he goes on to ask, 'What does the literature of women mean?' He responds to his own question by noting the differences to which men and women writers are necessarily subject, suggesting that 'the Masculine mind is characterized by the predominance of the intellect, and the Feminine by the predominance of the emotions'. He argues that in the past women writers had attempted to emulate men and in so doing had stifled their own ability to write as women. Moreover, he sees women's writing as an expression of their emotions, which he pertains to be their proper sphere, and any attempt to do otherwise is doomed, claiming that:

> To write as men write, is the aim and besetting sin of women; to write as women, is the real office they have to perform. [. . .] To imitate is to abdicate. We are in no need of more male writers; we are in need of genuine female experience. [. . .] Fiction is the one to which by nature and by circumstance, women are best adapted [. . .] The domestic experiences which form the bulk of woman's knowledge find an appropriate form in novels; while the very nature of fiction calls for the predominance of Sentiment which we have already attributed to the feminine mind. Love is the staple of fiction, for it 'forms the story of a woman's life.'[9]

Lewes was not alone in his views; five years later, these sentiments were reiterated by Elizabeth Strutt in *The Feminine Soul*, in which she equates the domestic novel to poetry.[10]

Although he was purportedly one of the more enlightened critics of his day, Lewes's opinion still holds an element of condescension. After Jane Austen whom he deems '"the greatest artist that has ever written"', it is to George Sand he gives the honour 'Of greater genius, and incomparably

deeper experience', claiming that 'George Sand represents woman's literature more illustriously and more obviously'.[11] The rest, it appears, though
significant for the particular womanly experience they bring to the novel,
are simply clumped together as a secondary, albeit benign, literary job lot.
Lewes here is surreptitiously dismissing women's writing in that he judges
their experience as insignificant. If women's experience is secondary to
experience outside of the designated sphere, that is, if women write about
their experience, then, Lewes is suggesting, there is nothing really worth
writing about. Moreover, in his review of Currer Bell's *Shirley*, Lewes's
claims for women's intellectual capabilities are, in fact, buffered by the
underlying contention that 'The grand function of woman [. . .] is, and ever
must be *Maternity*'[12] and as such woman is determined by her own biological nature. It is evident, then, that here Lewes is not, in effect, voicing
a recognition of women's intellectual capacities but reinforcing their
'proper sphere'. As Shirley Foster has pointed out, 'Many women novelists themselves recognised that this apparent tribute to female literary skills
was in reality a thinly-disguised weapon of limitation'.[13]

George Eliot's admonitory essay, 'Silly Novels by Lady Novelists', also
for the *Westminster Review* in 1856, written before she herself embarked
on writing fiction, is, as the title suggests, as much a comment on the
acclaim given to women novelists as on the novels themselves. She is concerned by the discrepancy of quantity over quality in women's novels.
Eliot's essay is a stance against the wave of sentiment in women's writing
and, for this reason, she is adamant in her view that the 'seduction of
novel writing to incompetent women'[14] should be curtailed:

> the average intellect of women is unfairly represented by the mass of fem-
> inine literature, and that while the few women who write well are very far
> above the ordinary intellectual level of their sex, the many women who
> write ill are very far below it.[15]

A decade before Eliot's article, the American feminist critic Margaret
Fuller wrote her tributary work *Woman in the Nineteenth Century*
(1845), in which she argues the case for women's independence.[16] This
text may well have influenced Eliot's essay, as is suggested by her
comment in *The Leader* that Fuller exerts

> no exaggeration of women's moral excellence or intellectual capabilities; no
> insistence on her fitness for this or that function hitherto engrossed by men;
> but a calm plea for the removal of unjust laws and artificial restrictions, so
> that the possibilities of her nature may have room for full development.[17]

Eliot's views in 'Silly Novelists' are similarly expressed three years later
by W.R. Gregg in his article 'False Morality of Lady Novelists' for the

National Review. Gregg's concern is that novels influence morality and too many women are writing too many novels that are detrimental to the impressionable women who read them:

> novels constitute a principal part of the reading of women, who are always impressionable, in whom at all times the emotional element is more awake and more powerful than the critical, whose feelings are more easily aroused and whose estimates are more easily influenced than ours, while at the same time the correctness of their feelings and the justice of their estimates are matters of the most special and preeminent concern. [. . .] women [. . .] are the chief readers of novels; they are also, of late at least, the chief writers of them. A great proportion of these authoresses too are *young* ladies.[18]

Regardless of their individual views on women's writing, Lewes, Eliot and Gregg are of the opinion that, in general, women are creatures who, because of the artificial restriction and limitations of their experience, are more prone to allow their emotions to dominate.

In her novel *Cassandra* (1852) Florence Nightingale draws attention to the question of difference and the intellectual impoverishment imposed on middle-class women by the enshrined paucity and induced idleness of their world. Unlike George Eliot, she does not subscribe to the (perceived) 'natural inferiority' of most women. Rather, she focuses on the reality of a socially imposed lack of opportunity for women to develop intellectually within the domestic sphere of feminine decorum:

> Why have women passion, intellect, moral activity – these three – and a place in society where no one of the three can be exercised? [. . .] Women often strive to live by intellect. [. . .] some love its solemn desolation, its silence, its solitude – if they are but *allowed* to live in it; if they are not perpetually baulked or disappointed. But a woman cannot live in the light of intellect. Society forbids it. Those conventional frivolities, which are called her 'duties,' forbid it.[19]

The nurture/nature debate, which was ongoing throughout the nineteenth century, drew much from the concept of sexual difference and was the subject of continuous discussion. In *The Subjection of Women* (1869) John Stuart Mill questioned the nature and history of sexual inequality and in 1860 and 1861, whilst engaged in the first draft of this work, he asked 'that most difficult question, what are the natural differences between the two sexes?' to which he responds with:

> Standing on the ground of common sense and the constitution of the human mind, I deny that any one knows, or can know, the nature of the two sexes, as long as they have only been seen in their present relation to one another . . . What is now called the nature of women is an eminently artificial thing – the result of forced repression in some directions, unnatural stimulation in others.[20]

The Darwinian perception of women – that they are biologically and intellectually less developed than men – sanctioned the notion that women were driven by the emotions, and the emotions were the means by which they engaged with the writing and reading of fiction. The novel, being the preferred form of reading for most women and that which was judged to be the most suited form for women writers, was the vehicle through which the emotions and morality were both subjected and exploited. Obviously, the conflicts and arguments surrounding the phenomenon of women novelists covers a much wider area than this discussion allows but the examples given here give some indication of the general opinion and character of thought concerning women writers and their readership which was dominant during the mid nineteenth century and as such have a direct bearing on Kavanagh's choice of subject matter.

Much discussion has been concerned with the notion of women writers adopting male or gender-free pseudonyms during this period. The mid nineteenth century, otherwise referred to as the 'feminine phase' of women's writing, was very much characterised by this practice. It began in the mid-1840s and lasted until the death of George Eliot in 1880.[21] One reason for this usage seems to have been the need to detract from prejudice against women writers and the desire to be received simply as a writer, the norm being the male writer.[22] Charlotte Brontë expressed anxieties concerning the response to *Jane Eyre* when in a letter to W. S. Williams she wrote, 'A mere domestic novel will, I fear, seem trivial to men of large views, and solid attainments.'[23] Women's experience was itself demeaned by the establishment because it was perceived as domestic. However, although socially and culturally women were, by necessity, engaged in and contained by this world, their subjectivity was not necessarily confined to it. The real issue here was not so much that some women chose a male pseudonym but that more women were writing and publishing than ever before. The consequence of such activity was a form of Bakhtinian carnivalesque disruption in the cultural status-quo, threatening the boundaries of difference as more and more women became independent, paradoxically, by writing both from within and about the world which patriarchy had placed them.

Voicing sexual politics

Kavanagh's career proper began at the very beginning of the 1850s after the success of *Madeleine* in 1848 and then in 1850 *Nathalie*, the novel which was to launch her as a writer of domestic fiction. However, the reviewer in *The Athenaeum*[24] noted that 'we cannot but think that

"Nathalie" would hardly have been born had not Currer Bell's daughter been her ancestress. The first fancy of Miss Kavanagh's story, however, thus ascribed to its origin, – the rest seems to us all her own.' He placed the novel 'high among books of its class, and which will be recognized by most select readers of novels as distinguished from romances'.[25]

The domestic novel was a means through which many women writers voiced a criticism of patriarchy and, of course, Kavanagh was not unique in this sense. Many writers, including Charlotte Yonge and Dinah Mulock Craik, two writers who were looked upon as conservative in their affirmation of Victorian values, were also critical of women's position in that society, particularly with reference to marriage. During the period in which Kavanagh was writing, 1846–77, reforms for women's rights were slow to materialise and consequently women were economically and politically restrained with little legislative protection.[26] Until the 1857 Matrimonial Causes Act[27] in England, which extended the possibilities of grounds for divorce, a married woman was completely at the mercy of her husband, having no rights to property or, if her husband saw fit, the care of her own children. By mid-century the novel was the genre in which the concept of the 'angel in the house' was increasingly contested as the institution of marriage and the relational expectations within marriage were scrutinised. Interestingly, although Mary Wollstonecraft in *A Vindication of the Rights of Women* (1792) had attacked the 'divine right of husbands', she fully supported the institution of marriage, calling it 'the cement of society'. Marriage was, after all, a very convenient institution, which, in spite of the economic and social inequalities it imposed, suited most people.[28] Marriage was the 'norm' for the Victorian middle class, but, as Valerie Saunders, one of several modern critics writing on this area, has noted, 'it was a highly uneasy norm, constantly under attack from lawyers, reformers, moralists, and feminists'.[29] As a subject, marriage was fundamental to the domestic novel as it reflected the mores and attitudes not just towards marriage as an institution but to love, romance and obligations within both marriage and events leading up to marriage. These events, of course, were the very currency of romance, the narrative entity through which many issues within domestic fiction were delivered. As mentioned above, the portrayal of 'women's role' in the domestic novel was, paradoxically, a catalyst for the exposure of double standards as these were identified via the different trajectories of judicial, social and sexual mores for men and women. Accordingly, the novelist was able to engage directly in subverting women's proposed role by playing on a number of alternative truths, which the 'role' subsequently harboured. The real-life marriages of some women writing at this time became the subject of their novels. Lady Caroline Norton and Rosina Bulwer Lytton both wrote novels which alluded directly to their experience of disastrous marriages. Caroline Norton's *Lost and Saved* (1863) is based on her own life, with the heroine becoming embroiled within the entanglements of illicit love.[30] Two of Rosina Bulwer Lytton's novels, *Cheveley, or the Man of Honour* (1839) and *Very Successful* (1856), allude to her estranged husband, Edward Bulwer Lytton, while her *Miriam Sedley* (1851) is largely autobiographical. The legislative 'non-existence' status of the married woman – whose signature was void without the agreement of her husband – ensured that in matrimony a woman was wholly the property of her husband.[31] The parliamentary debates on property and divorce prior to the passing of the Divorce Act of 1857 revealed a patriarchal fear of women's independence, which threatened to upset the status quo not just of a husband's authority but of society in general.[32] Although it was Caroline Norton's experience of the divorce laws that led her to campaign for change, she believed entirely in the superiority of men. At the same time, women were in need of legal protection and in her pamphlet entitled *English Laws for Women in the Nineteenth Century*, printed for private circulation in 1854, she states that:

> when a woman was failing her natural protector, the law should be able to protect; that some direct court of appeal should exist, in which [. . .] the circumstances of each case should guide its result, and the LAW exercise remedial control. [. . .] What I write is written in no spirit of rebellion; it puts forward no absurd claim of equality; it is simply an appeal for protection [. . .] I, for one (I, with millions more), believe in the natural superiority of men, as I do in the existence of God. [. . .] Masculine Superiority is incontestable; and with superiority should come protection.[33]

Norton's pamphlet has since been the cause of much debate amongst modern scholars who have argued that it merely serves to denigrate woman's position in that she simply exchanges dependence on a husband for dependence on the state.[34] Nevertheless, given the obstacles in her path for equality, her courage in writing her pamphlet is a radical statement in favour of change. In challenging the laws pertaining to women and divorce, Caroline Norton drew attention to the sexual inequalities that depended on an adherence to the laws of coverture. She found some outlet for voicing these injustices in writing her novels, which, inadvertently, also drew attention to the need for change.

Paradoxically, although many of Kavanagh's novels end in marriage, they engage wholly with the sexual politics of marriage. She may have read William Thompson and Anna Doyle Wheeler's philosophical treatise on rights for women, as many of the objectives and sympathies towards women's position in her novels are similar to those offered by Thompson and Wheeler in the *Appeal*, particularly their views on women's sexuality when they state that:

> An adult human being, though a woman, and though a wife, is possessed of all the senses, the appetites, the faculties and capabilities of enjoyment of any other human being. To hold the gratification of these and of all power over her voluntary actions at the bidding of another, deprives her of more than half of the happiness which she might enjoy, though such debasing and unnecessary power were ever so kindly exercised.[35]

Nathalie *(1850) and* Adèle *(1858)*

In her two novels *Nathalie* and *Adèle* Kavanagh questions the concept of marriage as an ideal in that she undercuts the illusion of a 'naturalised' symbolic order in her heroines' recriminations against convention. As with so many novels of this period, the interest today now lies in the contradictions they raise. Set in Normandy, *Nathalie* is the story of a young woman, Nathalie Montolieu, who, in spite of misadventure and adversity, finally marries a much older man with whom she has fallen in love. Through marriage Nathalie becomes mistress of the chateau where she had previously been offered refuge following her unfair dismissal as a schoolteacher from a nearby boarding school. As with most of Kavanagh's novels, it is a story of self-discovery and survival in which the protagonist is determined to maintain her integrity in a world riddled not only with hypocrisy and self-interest but also with illusion and false idealism. Similarly, in *Adèle*, published eight years later, and also set in northern France, Kavanagh repeats the idea of an independent-minded young woman who, though almost penniless, likewise marries an older man whom she admires but is yet to love. In this story Adèle eventually learns to love her husband, who, like Rochester with Jane Eyre, in turn accepts her as his equal. While the two novels contain elements of patterned romance in which Kavanagh adheres to commercial demands, she consciously exposes the double standards required to maintain patriarchal hegemony. This aspect of women's experience has been well documented in feminist criticism but I refer to Jenni Calder's study of Victorian fiction, which for the purpose of this discussion articulates the position succinctly:

> Novelists were writing romances, yet love, even sexual attraction, has little to do with marriage, not only in Thackeray's novels, which are concerned to expose this, but also in general attitudes. Young women were told that they would 'grow to love' their husbands after marriage, and conventions of courtship were such that there was little opportunity to know one's future spouse well before marriage. [. . .] men chose their wives for their value, whether it was economic, moral or decorative, or, if very lucky, all three.[36]

In her study of *Jane Eyre* and marriage Patsy Stoneman identifies a similar awareness of the consciousness of the loss of liberty in Kavanagh's novel *Adèle*:

> Even with a civilized husband, marriage can appear like a prison.
>
> Contemplating marriage with St. John Rivers, Jane Eyre fears the self-repression which would make her life 'a rayless dungeon' and 'an iron shroud' (*JE* 425) [. . .] Julia Kavanagh's [. . .] novel, *Adèle* (1858), also examines the situation which ensues when the sixteen-year-old heroine accepts marriage from an older man whom she hero-worships; the couple spend the final two volumes of the novel in a kind of soap-opera of emotional shifts, painfully negotiating the imbalances of power, incompatible needs and misunderstandings which arise even between two well-disposed, unneurotic and articulate people. At one point Adèle wishes she were dead: 'it makes me mad to be married – because I feel like one that is bound hand and foot – stifled like one that has not air to breath' (II 107). She records her dread of her husband's 'tenderness' in a context which makes it seem possible that this is a euphemism for sexual attentions (II 322). At the opening of the final volume, the stages of her wifedom – oppression, resignation, jealousy – are recapitulated in a way that makes it clear that this is the major theme of the novel (III 9), though their difficulties are compounded by scheming and unsympathetic relatives. Several other unhappy marriages provide an ominous prophecy of what may be to come, and this novel also has recourse to the devices of fire and major illness to 'prove' the marriage, before the wicked are confounded and the good hasten together to perfect felicity.[37]

Within Kavanagh's narrative there is a prominent authorial voice, which harnesses the sense of outrage that Kavanagh herself feels on behalf of women's subjugation to patriarchy. Shirley Foster views this aspect of Kavanagh's work with some reservation however, when she argues that 'the "anti-romantic" elements of Kavanagh's novels are often clumsily and unconvincingly interpolated into the narrative'. Nevertheless, she goes on to suggest that

> Her depiction of conflicting feelings in the heroines themselves, as well as her own tentative affirmation of the importance of female individuality, do however, indicate her reluctance to accept unquestioningly the sexual ideologies of her age.[38]

Without necessarily disagreeing with this view, I would argue that Julia Kavanagh's 'interpolations' are interesting in that they are often a significant expression of political comment in her work. In the novels *Nathalie* and *Adèle*, Kavanagh plays to her reader on several levels. She subverts normative codes of conduct by *seemingly* conforming to established expectations of femininity – both Nathalie and Adèle are referred to throughout as either 'birdlike' or 'childlike' – while subtextually exposing the construct of femininity as an illusory concept. The underside of the bird imagery in this context, of course, is that of the caged bird, the loss of liberty as demonstrated throughout Charlotte Brontë's *Jane Eyre*.[39] Inherent in the subtexts of *Nathalie* and *Adèle* is the challenge to social order in so far as Kavanagh actually defies a received 'accepted knowledge' of that order. This is apparent in both texts in the injustices imposed on women who are caught up in the dominant constructs of economics and class. Both Nathalie and Adèle are manifestations of this consciousness when they respectively fear the dissolution of self through marriage. We are given some indication of Kavanagh's views on sexual difference when, during a lengthy discussion on marriage between Nathalie and her suitor, Monsieur de Sainville, he extols the virtue of '"authority on the side of the husband, and submission on that of the wife"', to which Nathalie exclaims:

> 'Surely I have misunderstood you, [. . .] you do not mean to say a woman must obey her husband!' 'A woman's husband ought to have all the authority of a father,' gravely replied monsieur de Sainville. 'And of a Master, it would seem,' bitterly exclaimed Nathalie, who on this subject had all the rebellious feelings of her sex. (397)

Similarly, the newly married Adèle reflects on her situation as a wife and we are told:

> It pained her, they were married: but what availed marriage if they were not one? She had revolted against that union because it made her suffer; but the pain had died of its own excess. Duty, inexorable necessity, sincere admiration, attention deep and true, had conquered rebellion. It was over, and it had left behind a great truth – Adèle was Mr Osborne's wife; she had felt it too keenly, too bitterly not to feel it both strongly and deeply now. 'He must not dream so,' she thought, impatiently, 'I will not be his little girl to be kissed, caressed, then set aside. He is fond of me but he must be more than fond of me.' (II: 183)

While there is resistance in Adèle to give herself in marriage to a man who, as yet, does not see her as a grown woman, the message is clear – a woman has a right to sexual fulfilment and consummation is acceptable only when desire is mutual. At the same time, Kavanagh deconstructs the construction of identities as she destabilises the popular notion of 'woman as child', an idea which developed through Darwin in the mid nineteenth century to become the subject of scientific enquiry. In her study on Victorian 'Womanhood', Cynthia Eagle Russett notes the 'findings' of several studies, undertaken by men, aiming to prove the 'natural childlike characteristics of women'. Among others she refers to a study by the psychologist George John Romanes, who proclaimed:

> 'We find in women, as contrasted with men, (the emotions) are almost always less under control of the will – more apt to break away, as it were, from restraint of reason, and to overwhelm the mental chariot in disaster.' In extremis, the result was hysteriam but even the normal emotional state of women was one of 'comparative childishness'.[40]

To perceive a woman as a child is to disclaim her experience as a woman. Notwithstanding the social and historical considerations around which the construct of 'woman' is determined, I would argue that Kavanagh's intentions are overtly political. Viewed as a child, a woman will remain an inferior adult and as such poses no threat to patriarchy.

In all of her novels Kavanagh raises questions concerning woman's subjectivity through the experience of the women subjects themselves. In *Nathalie* and *Adèle* there is a strong sense of indignation against the 'powerlessness' a woman feels in a world predominantly biased towards male authority. It is interesting that Kavanagh felt the need to preface *Nathalie* with an explanation of her choice of heroine and hero:

> I had no other definite object in view than to draw two very opposite characters, and show as truthfully as I could how those characters attracted, repelled, and influenced each other. I by no means intend to imply that these pages contain no other moral; I hope they do: but I cannot claim the merit of having made any peculiar moral my aim.

Clearly, Kavanagh is conscious that, in spite of her disclaimer, her novel is an exposé of patriarchal injustices to women. In *Nathalie* the two women of the de Sainville family, a personable aged spinster, Aunt Radegone, known affectionately as 'the Canoness', and Monsieur de Sainville's widowed sister, Madame Marceau, along with Nathalie herself, are each a vehicle through which the unacknowledged voice of outrage can be heard. In a voice scarcely disguising a sense of disappointment and resignation, the 'Canoness' exhorts the virtues of celibacy to the young Nathalie as the only means through which a woman can find lasting peace. Madame Marceau likewise attempts to compensate her own disappointment in society through the political aspirations of her brother and the economic ambitions of her son. Nathalie, on the other hand, though eventually submitting herself to a marriage in which she adheres to the authority of her now tempered and accepting husband, is able to hold on to her own sense of self, and, by implication, her subjectivity. However, there is a shadow in Nathalie's life in the form of her sister, Rose, who lives in the nearby village as a companion to their cantankerous, half-blind old aunt. Rose, an obedient, put-upon and physically frail person, is the epitome of the woman who is forced to accept her destiny of 'death in life'. As such, she finds solace in her own spirituality and, to her, death is seen as a welcomed escape. Rose struck a chord with Charlotte Brontë who thought her character 'excellent',[41] and Mrs Charles Martin found Rose's character 'almost ideal in its saintly resignation to a sorrowful and crushing fate'.[42] Kavanagh's voice, however, tells its own story when, after Rose's death, and in a state of deep sorrow, Nathalie's thoughts and feelings are relayed in the narrative.

> One sorrow seems to wed us to all the sorrows of humanity. There is a secret link between even the disappointments of the heart, and the disappointments of the social strife called life. To women and their altered position is owing this vague and almost querulous sorrow. They are the living embodiment of the most heavy social wrongs, and their secret discontent swells the voice of general murmur. (430)

Rose is an easily identifiable subject in the social hegemony of mid-nineteenth-century sexual politics. In one sense she is Nathalie turned inside out. In the bourgeois world of patriarchy she is superfluous. She is without status, in seriously poor health, without money and, to all accounts, without physical beauty. In Rose, Kavanagh seems to be suggesting that woman's identity, her subjectivity, is culturally void. Moreover, if subjectivity is itself subject to cultural determination, then Kavanagh is outlining the social and psychological criminality of patriarchy. Rose has no acceptable identity. As Foucault has demonstrated, in the nineteenth century in particular, woman was defined as 'body'[43] and femininity was contrived around a strictly controlled set of rules. In her novels Kavanagh actively dislodges the notion of a singularly constructed femininity. The concept of 'woman' as such was an illusion masking the reality of the person beneath the façade of bourgeois respectability, and here Kavanagh's narrative disrupts the notion of the revered 'angel in the house'. Paradoxically, Rose, who, in reality, is the embodiment of the 'angel', is a single woman, dispossessed of her subjectivity. As Shirley Foster has argued, she is 'Kavanagh's vision of spinsterhood as a state of mournful resignation'.[44] Rose is the unacceptable image of woman, unproductive, without culturally saleable attributes, the unwanted child.

In *Adèle* the women openly state their awareness of social and sexual injustice. One of the more prolific accounts of dissent is through Alice Lascours, a young woman in her twenties who, for the sake of material security, was forced by her mother to marry a rich but much older man. In a bitter account of her marriage Alice confides in Adèle when she remonstrates, 'God help me! I am like the reed, made to bend. I tell you

I was born to yield and obey – to be conquered and even broken' (I: 42).
Compare Alice's outburst with another young woman, Adèle's sister-in-
law, Isabella, whose resignation and sense of bitterness in a woman's lot
is illustrated in her conviction that love in the romantic sense is an illusion. Her distaste for marriage as an institution is encompassed in her
ambition to marry, not for love but for money and status. In this way she
feels she will, at least, have some control over her destiny. Isabella's anger
at her own social impotence as a woman is expressed openly as she
declares her feelings to her brother:

> 'you are a man, and you can command life! I am a woman and it will take
> me years to be where you were at twenty. Ah! to be a man!' she exclaimed
> . . . 'to be a man, young, well born, well educated, handsome, not poor, and
> to have a world before me – how I would laugh at women, at marriage, at
> all bonds.' (II: 178)

Here Isabella's rage at her own condition is a direct metaphor for
woman's consciousness; moreover, it demonstrates the extent of
Kavanagh's own consciousness of women's condition in an ideology that
works against them. Kavanagh's distaste for unsuitable marriages was
voiced in most of her novels. She was not alone of course in her observations, and the discontent as much as the contentment which is created
by a bad or a good marriage is the discourse of romance in fiction of any
period. Writing in her time, Kavanagh was also very much aware that
the entities of romance, courtship and marriage also allowed for a
narrative of deconstruction of those entities.

Kavanagh was constantly juxtaposing the concepts of the socially
'ideal' with the socially subversive to the extent that sexual and social
dissent was manifested in the narratives. This dissent takes form through
the experience of different characters: sometimes it is related directly to
the central protagonist, often the female subject, but it is just as likely to
be associated with minor characters, such as Alice and Isabella in *Adèle*.
Moreover, in this way, Kavanagh's novels, while contained within the
patterns of romance, surreptitiously explore the nature of knowledge
and women's place through the interior of domestic space, that which is
representative of the 'feminine' ideal. Here, literally within the designated walls of houses and gardens, gender boundaries undergo a form of
deconstruction as notions of social and sexual power are constantly
questioned. Feminist criticism has argued that the social constructions of
knowledge can be interpreted as part of a larger construct of culture and
ideology.[45] In the light of this perspective, one can see how the discourse
of romance in Kavanagh's novels is a means through which knowledge
as a construct is both re-evaluated and reinterpreted in her fiction.

In her study of the development of the novel Nancy Armstrong maintains that the history of sexuality is important to the history of the novel as it was the novel that helped to turn 'political information into the discourse of sexuality', suggesting that 'These novels made the novel respectable, and it is significant that they so often were entitled with female names such as Pamela, Evelina, Jane Eyre'.[46] It is no coincidence then that so many novels written by women in the mid nineteenth century were entitled with female names, and thirteen of Kavanagh's fourteen novels follow this pattern. Instigated by the domestic novel in the eighteenth century, in the mid nineteenth century this practice becomes a conscious recognition of woman's presence as more than just the subject of social empowerment.

In the main Kavanagh's novels engage directly with the complexities of social standing and the reclamation of self in so far as the protagonist's subjectivity is both explored and questioned within the framework of a questionable ideology. Her narratives adopt several recurring patterns, which draw on themes well known within the genre of domestic fiction, yet also question the very notions of acceptance within these themes. These include the concept of the marriage of convenience, which often works against any form of genuine happiness and becomes itself a form of prison. This paradigm is tied in with the illusion that happiness can be bought and sold, a consumable commodity, which, in the end, leaves the protagonist bereft of a sense of self.

The dual self

In several of her novels Kavanagh engages a form of psychological dualism when one character serves as a mirror image, or *doppelgänger* to the main protagonist, usually the heroine. These two characters who, on the surface, appear to be opposites may each subconsciously harbour aspects of the other's psychological make-up. She adopts this technique for both male and female protagonists. Issues of masculinity and strength in the hero are often set against another weaker and more 'feminine' male character with whom the hero is socially connected. It is as though this secondary figure acts as the shadow or the darker side of the hero's higher self – a constant reminder of his own vulnerability and weakness. Kavanagh adopts a similar pattern in several of her novels including *Grace Lee, Two Lilies* and *John Dorrien*. However, there is an element of ambivalence in her portrayal of women as stereotypical opposites, which, although clearly represented, are never wholly defined as such. Structurally, the narrative device of dual representation is a means of demonstrating the existence of other, latent aspects of the heroine's character which might otherwise be unexplored within the parameter of romantic domestic fiction. As such, Kavanagh is able to engage with the dynamics of human psychology within the framework of 'populist' themes.

As is the case with other women writers of the Victorian period, Kavanagh's novels draw on the contradictions of that time. In her discussion of the impact of medical science and subjectivity in Charlotte Brontë's novels, Sally Shuttleworth has argued that

> one must look beyond the surface texture of the novels to the conflicting ideologies of self-control and female sexuality which permeated Victorian economic and psychological discourse, and inevitably affected not only Brontë's representation of her heroines, but also her attitudes to her own authorial role.[47]

This is a claim, which, undoubtedly, also applied to many of Brontë's female contemporaries, including Kavanagh. As discussed above, in *Nathalie,* Rose represents another aspect of Nathalie in so far as, symbolically, she is a living spectre of Nathalie's deeper, non-material self. The sisters are portrayed as physical opposites. Nathalie is dark and strong while Rose is fair and frail. While Nathalie is independent, resourceful and able to engage in a loving and equal relationship with the man she loves, Rose succumbs to a secondary, subservient role, devoid of love and fulfilment in this world but which, inadvertently, enables her to develop spiritually and to engage in the notion of an afterlife. Kavanagh also makes it clear, nevertheless, that Rose's illness is symptomatic of her sense of non-life in this world. Other examples of female dualism occur, more predominantly, in *Sybil's Second Love, Bessie, Two Lilies* and, to a lesser extent, in an earlier novel, *Daisy Burns,* which suggests that, from early on in her writing career, Kavanagh was conscious of the singular perception and misrepresentation of women in society.

Daisy Burns *(1853)*

Daisy Burns, Kavanagh's third novel, was overwhelmingly dismissed by the critics, and, although at this time women novelists were still generally reviewed more harshly than male writers,[48] Charlotte Brontë herself found the novel deeply disappointing. Writing to Williams, she compares it unfavourably to *Madeleine*:

> I have tried to read 'Daisy Burns'; at the close of the 1st Vol. I stopped. I must not give an opinion of it for I should seem severe. Miss Kavanagh's intentions are thoroughly good – her execution in this case seems to me disastrous. 'Madeleine' her first quiet, unpretending book – is worth a hundred such tawdry deformities as 'Daisy Burns' – I find in it no real blood or life; it is painted and cold.[49]

Fothergill Chorley in *The Athenaeum*, was no less sparing in his response, stating that

> The tale, in brief, is a sickly one, – and no qualification of the truth will mend the matter. Many passages are written with Miss Kavanagh's usual sentiment and delicacy; but we can wish her no better wish than the earliest, possible deliverance from that desire to exhibit feminine originalities in fiction which, as we have elsewhere said, bids fair, just now, to spoil so much that is brightest and bravest in the richly-cultivated and peculiar domain of our female authorship.[50]

The reviewer in the *Westminster Review* was of a similar opinion that 'Miss Kavanagh has richer stores than she has drawn from in "Daisy Burns;" and she would do well to work upon a larger canvass [sic], and study nature with closer attention'.[51] In spite of the poor critical response, *Daisy Burns* proved to be a popular novel. One reason for its success could have been the accepted appeal of the young orphaned child, which was widely recognised by readers at the time. Written in the first person narrative, *Daisy Burns* is directly influenced by *Jane Eyre*. The story is narrated by the adult Daisy who is looking back over her life and, as with Jane Eyre, events are seen from the heroine's perspective. In this scenario Kavanagh picks up on the names of characters in Brontë's novel and adapts them accordingly in her own narrative. It is the repetition here, more than in any other of Kavanagh's novels, that justifies Mrs Oliphant's concern that Kavanagh is simply rewriting *Jane Eyre*.[52]

The opening chapters centre on the protagonist, ten-year-old Margaret (who later becomes Daisy),[53] a plain, motherless girl whose circumstances place her in the care of her late father's *protégé*, Cornelius O'Reilly, a young artist of twenty years of age, and his older sister, Kate, in their cottage in a leafy part of London. It is out of loyalty and respect for Daisy's late father, an Irish gentleman and a physician, that these two take her in and become surrogate guardians. However, their guardianship becomes possible only after Cornelius has gained permission from Daisy's estranged and embittered maternal grandfather, George Thornton, to whose dilapidated ancestral home she is delivered soon after her father's death. Because she had married a man of whom he disapproved, George Thornton had disinherited his daughter, Daisy's mother, and, in his wrath, had irretrievably cut all emotional ties. Consequently, he shows only a grudging acceptance of his granddaughter whose entire care he leaves to his indifferent housekeeper. From the beginning Daisy had formed a very strong attachment to Cornelius in her perception of him as her handsome saviour, rescuing her from a dull, loveless existence at Thornton House. At first

Cornelius's interest in Daisy is that of an older brother, but as she matures his affections openly turn to that of a lover and the novel ends, predictably, with their marriage.

While domiciled with her grandfather, who has expressed his intention that Daisy will receive a commonplace education, thus denying her right to be a lady, the unhappy child implores Cornelius to take her away from Thornton House. Cornelius's outrage at the unfairness of her grandfather's decision spurs him on to put things right. Daisy recalls the scene:

> 'Your father, who was an Irish gentleman born and bred, gave me the education of a gentleman: and I will give you the education of a lady, – so help me God!'
>
> He drew and pressed me to him. I looked up at him, and said, 'I should not take up much room.' [. . .]
>
> 'Will you take me with you?' I asked earnestly. Cornelius drew in a long breath.
>
> 'You are an odd child!' he said.
>
> I passed my arms around his neck, and asked again, 'Will you take me with you?'
>
> 'Why do you want me to take you?'
>
> I hung down my head, and did not answer. The strange unconquerable shyness of childhood was on me, and rendered me tongue-tied. Cornelius gently raised my face, so that it met his look, and smiled at seeing it grow hot and flushed beneath his gaze.
>
> 'Do you really want me to take you?' he asked, after a pause.
>
> I looked up quickly; I said nothing; but if childhood has no words to render its feeling, it has eloquent looks easily read. Cornelius was at no loss to understand the meaning of mine. (I: 53)

It is interesting that here, particularly, the associations of the protective mentor and, possibly, substitute father figure are closely connected and the passage lends itself openly to a Freudian perspective, which, it has been noted, still dominates our understanding of subjectivity.[54] This passage is the second reference to a pre-pubescent sexual awakening in Daisy. Prior to her father's death. Daisy had led an idyllic life in their appropriately named Rock Cottage, a name that symbolised the solid security of Daisy's childlike happiness under her father's paternal care. It is here that Daisy first encounters Cornelius. He comes to collect her and finds her weeping, literally on the threshold of the cottage, and in an encounter that symbolises the transitional nature of change Kavanagh lays down the foundations of their relationship:

> 'Poor little thing!' he said, 'poor little thing!'
>
> He took my cold hands in his, and drew me closer to him. Subdued by grief, I yielded. I had refused his presents, shunned his caress, been jealous,

proud and insolent, hated the very thought of his presence in my father's house, and now he came to seek me on the threshold of that house, to take me – a miserable outcast child – in his embrace.

The thrill of a strange and rapid emotion ran through me. I disengaged my hands from those of Cornelius, and, with a sudden impulse, threw my arms around his neck. My cheek lay near his; his lips touched mine; I mutely returned the caress. I was conquered.

I was a child, how could I but feel with a child's feelings, entirely? I kept back nothing; I knew not how or why, but I gave him my whole heart from that hour. (I: 22–3)

Although these passages may strike the modern reader as oddly disturbing in their suggestions of child sexuality, it has to be remembered that, at the time Kavanagh was writing, in England the age of sexual consent for girls was twelve. As a writer, Kavanagh is drawing on the Victorian ambiguity of childhood innocence while at the same time acknowledging a sense of unconscious change in Daisy's subjectivity. Although two of her later novels, *Adèle* and *Two Lilies*, also engage similar themes, Kavanagh's narrative here is couched in a sense of ambivalence concerning childhood and sexuality. It is tempting to suggest that Kavanagh was herself unaware of the disconcerting eroticism encoded in the delivery. However, as it is the adult Daisy who is giving a retrospective account of the incident, and in the light of Shuttleworth's argument, it is feasible that Kavanagh was aware of the unconscious sexuality in Daisy's 'spontaneous' response. As there are no disembodied emotions laid down separately from the young girl's immediate reaction, I would suggest that her feelings here are intended to signify her future adult relationship with Cornelius.

During the nineteenth century new theories of subjectivity were beginning to shape the way that women writers approached the novel and, as Sally Shuttleworth suggests, 'Selfhood no longer resided in the open texture of social act and exchange, but within a new interior space, hidden from view, inaccessible even to the subject's own consciousness.'[55] She goes on to suggest that 'with reference to the interpretative gaze: condition of femininity was dependent on the woman retaining her impenetrability'.[56] Similarly, in this early novel Kavanagh engages directly with the notion of interior space when she focuses on the otherwise inaccessible unconscious sexuality of the young female. Moreover, it is significant that these 'textually open' feelings in Daisy are connected (in the text) with her desire to be educated as a 'lady', the Victorian ideal of accepted femininity. Contextually, this section of Kavanagh's narrative is an attempt to engage with the contradictions that are a direct result of the interpretative male gaze, the imposition of which served to control women's sexuality.

Throughout this novel Kavanagh explores the relational dynamics of power and vulnerability as these two entities direct the outcome of emotional control in the lives of the two main protagonists, Daisy and Cornelius. Interestingly, it is within this same context that Kavanagh introduces the element of dualism in the narrative. Roughly two years after Daisy had joined the O'Reilly household there is a significant interlude that affects the otherwise conventional romantic developments associated with this type of fiction. Cornelius falls in love and subsequently becomes engaged to the twenty-six-year-old Miriam Russell, a beautiful, independent-minded older woman. The relationship between Daisy and Miriam is one of distance and Kavanagh here plays on the sense of ambivalence associated with notions of childhood innocence and adult experience as these are apportioned to the two women who appear to see each other solely in terms of their relationship with Cornelius. Throughout this episode the young Daisy's dislike of Miriam is rooted in jealousy as she sees her heart's desire snatched from her by a woman who has all the physical attributes and self-composure that she herself lacks. At this stage in the narrative Cornelius perceives Daisy as his adopted child and adoring pupil. He is both her trusted protector and her intellectual mentor and over time had developed a sense of deep friendship and love for her. Miriam, however, is the woman of his dreams. While Daisy is spontaneous and open in her affections towards him, Miriam is calm and controlled, a trait he considers an attribute of the classical beauty he so admires.

Domestic life is interrupted by a series of small, testing incidents which imply that Miriam is attempting either to discredit or compromise Daisy's character, or to draw attention to her lack of physical beauty. All comes to a head with the defacement of a painting of Medora, the beautiful heroine in Byron's *The Corsair*, which Cornelius had been working on and for which Miriam was the sitter. However, circumstantial evidence points to Daisy as the guilty party and, although she professes her innocence, a trust is broken to the extent that it is enough to cause a temporary rift between her and Cornelius. It soon transpires that the perpetrator of this act is, in fact, Miriam herself who, in her frustration and anger at what she sees as ignominious sensibility on Cornelius's part, attempts to expose the delusions he has about both herself and Daisy.

This revelation, though unpredictable, is not surprising as there have been several pointers in the narrative to indicate that Miriam is not all she seems. The air of mystery that, from the beginning, has surrounded her character and, indeed, manifested her as the more interesting of the two women, has enabled Kavanagh to politicise her subject material. Miriam is portrayed as a woman who neither accepts nor endorses the pedestal upon which the patriarchal ideal of the feminine woman is placed. It is her observation that Cornelius, in his attempts to mould both herself and Daisy into projections of his own ideal woman, is incapable of seeing either of them as possessing a sense of self independent of his perceptions of them. Kavanagh was by no means unique in this respect. It was for a similar reason that Christina Rossetti wrote her poem, 'In an artist's studio',[57] in which she protested against her brother Dante Gabriel Rossetti's attempts to objectify women for his own aesthetic reasons. The poem has the lines, 'He feeds upon her face by day and night / And she with true kind eyes looks back on him / [. . .] / Not as she is, but as she fills his dream.' These lines are testimony to the sense of self-alienation Christina felt in her recognition of the power of patriarchal discourse, which, by implication, diminishes any sense of 'reality' she may have. Both within the framework of the painting and outside of it she exists as part of another's ideology, which has little to do with her own sense of existence. As these lines suggest, she is imprisoned by another's illusory consciousness. Similarly, Kavanagh draws attention to the misconceptions Cornelius has concerning women but there is a particularly revealing moment when, commenting on the beauty he has created in his painting of Medora, Miriam retorts:

> 'Medora is not my portrait, but an ideal woman for whom you have borrowed my form and face.'
> 'What will not an artist attempt to idealize?' asked Cornelius with a touch of embarrassment.
> 'Oh!' she observed very sweetly, 'I do not mean to imply it was not required. Only if this were a portrait, I should object to having Daisy's eyes and brow given to me.' (I: 195)

Moreover, and more importantly, she observes in him an incapacity to experience passion. For Miriam, passion is the emotion that conquers all boundaries and without it there is no understanding of life. It is for this reason, above all, that she is determined to break the enchantment he has over the younger Daisy. Miriam believes that the devotion Daisy has for Cornelius will prevent her from developing her own sense of self and, subsequently, her own sense of womanhood. In defacing the painting she thus gives vent to her pent-up frustrations and feelings at being perceived as merely the object of Cornelius's own creation, manifested in the painting itself. Shocked by this revelation, Cornelius questions his love for Miriam and she answers him by exposing his lack of understanding of both her and Daisy and, by implication, all women.

> 'Are you the woman whom I have loved?'
> 'You never understood me,' she said impatiently. 'You might have

guessed that I had, from my youth upwards, lived in the fever of passion inspired or felt; you might have known that I should master or be mastered. I warned you that though I could promise nothing, I should exact much, and you defied me to exact too much. Yet when it came to the test – what did you give me? a feeling weak as water, cold as ice! Why, you would not so much as have given up what you call Art for my sake!'

'Nor for that of mortal woman,' indignantly replied Cornelius. 'Give up painting! Do you forget I told you I would love you as a man should love?'

'That is, I suppose, a little more than Daisy, and something less than your pictures. I have been accustomed to other love.'

Cornelius reddened.

'An unworthy passion,' he said, 'stops at nothing to secure its gratification; a noble one is bound by honour.'

'I leave you to such passions,' calmly answered Miriam: 'to painting, which you love so much; to the domestic affections in which you weakly thought to include me, I have tried to make you feel what I call passion, I have failed; it is well that we should part; let us do so quietly, and without recriminations.'

Cornelius looked at her like one confounded. She spoke composedly, as if she neither cared for nor felt that, on her own confession, she was guilty. Of excuse or justification she evidently thought not.

'You think of Daisy,' she continued; 'think of my conduct to her what you choose. I will only say this, though she, poor child, has hated me, as she loved you, with her whole heart, you may have been, are still, and will remain, her greatest enemy.'

'I!' indignantly exclaimed Cornelius.

'Yes: and you must be blind not to see that, by seeking to sever from you a child whom a few years will make a woman, I was her best friend; and so she will know some day, when you break her heart, and tell her you never meant it.' (I: 355–6)

Cornelius's duty to his own art is also a reflection of the Victorian concept of male honour. The dialogue continues with Miriam indignant at Cornelius's inability to feel genuine passion, the emotion that can both enslave and bind two people together. Although it is Cornelius's energy that spurs him on, it is an energy given predominantly to Art. At first Miriam mistakes this energy for passion, but soon concludes that he is a man who could neither truly understand nor love any woman. It is at this point that she sets about her attempts to end their relationship and also attempts to undo the emotional ties that hold Daisy to him. In time, however, like Rochester in *Jane Eyre*, Cornelius is to be humbled by circumstances before he proves a worthy suitor for the heroine.

From the beginning Kavanagh makes it clear that Cornelius has an unconscious fear of adult women. He changes Margaret's name to Daisy,

this being the botanical diminutive of Margaret, perhaps in an attempt
to harness her childhood and keep her locked within his safety net of
dependency. She also exposes Cornelius's need for power over Daisy with
the use of bird imagery, a pattern she deploys in several of her novels to
demonstrate male desire for dominance. As in *Nathalie* and *Adèle*, her
narrative here is not without irony. When Cornelius rejects Daisy's constant pleas of innocence and is still convinced that she is the guilty party
concerning the spoiled painting, Daisy becomes extremely despondent
and takes to her bed. In his attempt to draw her back into the household,
Cornelius brings her food and relates to her an experience of his boyhood
when, after he caught and caged a wild bird, it died:

> 'I caught a wild bird, and caged it, thinking it would sing; but it would not
> eat; it hung its head and pined away. I was half afraid this evening you were
> going to do like my poor bird.'
>   'I hope I know better than a bird,' I replied, rather piqued at the com-
> parison, 'and that was a very foolish bird not to take the cage where you
> had put it – so kind of you,' (I: 346–7)

Daisy's retort is ambivalent and Kavanagh here sports with irony in her
allusion to Jane Eyre's response to Rochester who, when comparing her
to a 'wild frantic bird', replies, 'I am no bird and no net ensnares me, I
am a free human being with an independent will.'[58] Kavanagh alludes
further to the folly of male delusion and vanity when, later that evening,
after Cornelius and Daisy are reconciled and have resumed their usual
familiarity, Daisy playfully attempts to cut off a lock of Cornelius's hair.
Kavanagh parodies the penetrative (cutting) action of the male gaze – a
symbolic castration – in a comic allusion to the story of Samson who,
when Delilah cut off his hair, lost his strength:

> [W]ith the secure familiarity of an indulged child, I untwined one of his
> dark locks to its full extent, observing –
>   'It is too long; let me cut it off with Kate's scissors.'
>   'No, faith,' he replied hastily, and shaking back his head with an alarmed
> air, as if he already felt the cold steel, 'do not dream of such a thing. Cut it off
> indeed!' and he slowly passed his fingers through his raven hair, in the glossy
> and luxuriant beauty of which he took a certain complacency. (I: 347–8)

At length, as Cornelius gains more experience of the challenges and disappointments he must learn to endure, his feelings for Daisy mature and
several years later, after a period of separation, the two eventually marry
and live harmoniously with Kate in the cottage. However, it is Miriam
who is the catalyst for change and also Kavanagh's voice of protest against
the imbalance of power which determined gender difference.

Although contemporary critical response was damning of this novel and the *Westminster Review* placed *Daisy Burns* in a category of 'novel without a purpose',[59] modern critical perspectives have engaged a wider sphere and it could be argued that Kavanagh did have a 'purpose', or at least a sense of the Victorian notion of sexual difference that influenced her narrative.

Sybil's Second Love (1867)

In *Sybil's Second Love* Kavanagh tentatively dipped a toe into the murky waters of the sensation novel, a departure that enabled her to explore the nature of dual representation in theatrical detail. In her later novels particularly there are elements of the 'sensation' genre which prolong the sense of melodrama in the story but never divert from the sexual politics in the narrative. In *Sybil's Second Love*, Kavanagh's delivery and aptitude for suspense and intrigue are evident in her gift for storytelling. The complex love story around which she weaves her narrative is also a template upon which to attach an intriguing satire on the connection between money and social aspirations during the industrial mid nineteenth century.

The book is set within the broader spectrum of romance, mystery and commercial enterprise, and bourgeois values are systematically unwrapped and decoded against the backdrop of a decadent and diminishing aristocracy. It is within this maelstrom of cultural change that Kavanagh lays bare an ideology based on the predominance of male honour in an increasingly commercial world and one in which the interconnected destiny of two women is perilously balanced. Within this world women are seen as objects to be owned and, metaphorically, bought and sold in an open market. Moreover, Kavanagh leaves little doubt that it is the expediently male-orientated world of capitalism and the associative effects of an ownership-dominated culture that leave women culturally disadvantaged. In this novel she actively dislodges the convenient concept of a polarised femininity, exposing the specious misconceptions of the angel/demon dichotomy, which served to nurture the cultural and scientific discourse of women's lives.

In a fictitious small, socially censorious town, Saint Vincent, in northern France, seventeen-year-old Sybil Kennedy lives with her industrialist father, a handsome fifty-year-old, in their beloved home, a converted ex-convent, the Abbey Saint Vincent. Mr James Kennedy had come over from Ireland to advance his commercial interests and, contrary to advice from the local residents who were opposed to any change that might disrupt their little community, saw an opportunity to develop the area by growing rape seed. Subsequently, he bought land, built his own water mill on the river that passed through the abbey grounds to extract the oil from the seed, and made a fortune.[60] However, it is significant that

Kavanagh's choice of crop is linguistically associated with the physical act of rape. Capital enterprise here is tainted by the suggestion of exploitation, the theme of which is encoded throughout the narrative.

The novel's thematic dualism is set in motion when, against her father's wishes, Sybil invites her old music teacher, Blanche Cains, to stay. In fact Sybil is completely infatuated with this beautiful young woman but when she extols the virtues of her friend to others (especially her father) she is met with an unpalatable fact – that a woman's value is judged largely in commercial terms. On hearing that Miss Cains is of a very good, but impoverished family, Mr Kennedy draws attention to the reality of her situation and considers her social prospects bleak when measured against those of his plain but much wealthier daughter. However, Blanche is by far the most compelling character in the novel; she is beautiful, charming, clever and manipulative – as the reviewer in *The Athenaeum* put it, 'that adorable creature Miss Blanche Cains'.[61] Moreover, Blanche is Kavanagh's ultimate *femme fatale* in that she manages to enchant all of the men who, in one way or another, are associated with Sybil. Reminiscent of Lucy Graham, the self-seeking anti-heroine of Mary Elizabeth Braddon's novel *Lady Audley's Secret* (1862), Blanche is driven not by love or vanity but by a desire for material security: she will stop at nothing in her pursuit of riches. As a woman who had to make her own living, Kavanagh was clearly aware of the relative, if unpalatable, material security that money brings; a truism that, no doubt, informed the sense of prosaic realism of Blanche's predicament. Whilst conversing with Sybil on the subject of marriage, the twenty-five-year-old Blanche confesses that she could neither love nor marry a poor man. She contrasts her own situation with that of Sybil's and in response to Sybil's questions she retorts:

> 'Remember, you have the theory of poverty, and I have the bitter practice. It is cruel, it is selfish in a poor girl to marry a poor man. It is dragging him down to life-long sorrow. But, oh! you lucky little girl, what a place is this Saint Vincent!' (I: 152)

Unlike Blanche, Sybil has been protected from life's social injuries; typical of Kavanagh's heroines, she is trusting, loving and generous in nature and, although she is not beautiful, she is pretty and kind and, moreover, she is loved. At this stage she believes fully that Blanche is one of the deserving good and 'wished ardently' that she and Blanche 'could live and die together in Saint Vincent' (I: 152). Inevitably, she loses all to her more beautiful friend who, through a series of carefully planned manoeuvres, manages to supplant Sybil as the centre of her father's affections and marries him, thereby gaining the wealth, position and power she desperately craves. Consequently the protected idyllic world, the only one Sybil had ever known, is shattered and she is sent off to live with her aunt in the country.

As with other women in her novels who, faced with a sense of economic powerlessness, succumb to dubious actions, Kavanagh also offers an alternative perspective. Throughout there is an element of ambivalence towards Blanche and, without condoning her actions, Kavanagh gives some insight into her background, thereby shedding light on her insecurity and fear of poverty. Born into a wealthy family, her status and social position are curtailed after her father had gambled everything they had, leaving her without any means of support other than by her own labour, which she bitterly resents. Moreover, his activities leave her with a deep distrust of all men. Her relationship with Sybil is also ambiguous. Although she is clearly very fond of Sybil, she is also proud and her genteel but impecunious presence is a constant reminder that she is a penniless guest in her friend's house. Sybil's relative indifference to her own material surroundings is contrasted throughout with Blanche's love of consumerism, and that which Sybil takes for granted is coveted by her more ambitious friend. Paradoxically this is one way in which Kavanagh's narrative draws the two women together.

The title of the novel, *Sybil's Second Love*, refers to Sybil's only true love, Edward Dermot, her father's thirty-year-old business partner whom she finally marries. Sybil's first encounter with romantic love turns out to be infatuation and is founded on an arranged courtship and proposed marriage with an eligible but impoverished young aristocrat, Count André de Renneville. The alliance is orchestrated by two of Saint Vincent's society ladies, Mrs Ronald and Madame de Lonville, who, together, see it as their duty to take a professional interest in such matters. These two, engaging in the French custom of matchmaking, agree that Sybil's fortune and the Count's elevated position in society are destined for the mutual benefit of the two young people. The de Rennevilles had been one of the leading aristocratic families in the area and the Kennedy home, the Abbey Saint Vincent, had once been part of their estate. However, similarly to Blanche's family misfortune, their wealth had also been squandered as a result of the old Count, André's father's, gambling debts. André courts and charms Sybil and declares his love for her and, although she is aware that she is not 'in love' with him – an emotion she feels she is never likely to experience with anyone – she is enchanted by the 'romance' of the situation and she believes she will be content as his wife. Nevertheless, with Sybil's best interests in mind, Blanche advises her against the marriage. A few days before the wedding is to take place, it is disclosed that the Count is in love with Blanche, and his motive for marrying Sybil is her wealth, and consequently she refuses him.

In his proposal to marry a rich but socially inferior woman, the Count is merely following convention in a society that condones such practice, and all are shocked by Sybil's refusal. However, Kavanagh's interpolative voice suggests a turning point in Sybil's experience when, in proffering an insight into the young woman's romantic imagination, there is a suggestion that Sybil had also been attracted to rank and social position:

> There is always imagination in a young girl's first love. It was not merely André de Renneville who had won Sybil's affections, it was the gentleman of noble birth, of refined feelings, of stainless honour, and of many heavy troubles. Had he been a gay and rich young man she might not have cared for him; or if she had liked him, it would assuredly have been on different grounds, and in a different way. He had conquered her by his sorrows, and the supposed greatness and goodness of his nature. But his griefs now wore a sordid look and his very virtues were unread – the mere creatures of her brain. Sybil had sense enough to see this, and as pity and esteem had helped the birth of love, so contempt now helped to kill it, surely and very swiftly. She would not go on lamenting a man who had deceived her so basely, and sold himself more basely still. Sybil had learned that men do betray, that girls can be deceived, but she could not connect these sad truths with herself, or think them woven in her destiny. Her lover was to be great, and good, and true, and the very soul of honour; her love was to be faithful and eternal. There might be trouble in store for her, partings bitter as death, calamities, too, but not treachery – not falsehood! (I: 286)

In her naivety Sybil has mistakenly equated social rank with a nobility of character, and her disappointment on learning of the Count's real intentions for marrying her is the first of a series of awakenings into a wider experience of life. Moreover Blanche is of the belief that the Count's love for herself is not true and she feels that, because she is beautiful and poor, he is using her merely to satisfy his own sexual desires:

> 'I suppose that, being poor and handsome, I am made for that sort of thing – to be insolently liked, I mean [. . .]' [Sybil's response is that she] '[. . .] must ever more hate the man: he was not true [. . .]' [Whereupon Blanche retorts] 'He was a contemptible wretch!' [. . .] 'You do well to discard him; but for all that, you had his better liking. I have seen it a hundred times. The baser part he gave to me, and, I will be honest, I saw that too and I hated him for it' [. . .] 'If I had him under my foot, so, I would crush him! How dare he betray you, and insult me!' (I: 288–9)

Angry and defiant, Sybil now believes that love in the romantic sense is an illusion and vows that she will never fall in love. In time, she does, of course, and with Edward Dermot. Throughout this section of the narrative Sybil's affection for Blanche is as strong as ever. She even suggests that Blanche should marry Edward (I: 107) but, as yet, she is unaware that Blanche and Edward had already been lovers. It transpires that their relationship had ended when Blanche believed that Edward was no longer rich and, as she was set on marrying into riches, she refused his love, leaving him bitter and angry towards her.

Prior to her marrying Mr Kennedy, Blanche continually reminds Sybil of their different economic circumstances, for which Sybil, in her own way, attempts to make amends. Until Blanche's arrival Sybil's world had never been challenged; all her material comforts were catered for and taken for granted. Nevertheless her world has become sterile and, unconsciously, Sybil is ripe to break free from her cloistered existence in her abbey home and experience the awakening of a deeper sense of self, for which Blanche is the catalyst. Psychologically the two women are, in fact, an example of latent doubling.[62] It is significant that it is Sybil who invites Blanche, the older, worldly woman, into her life. When Blanche says to Sybil, 'at times I am like the Sybil, child – a voice which is not mine own speaks from within me' (I: 262), not only is she echoing the Sibyl[63] of Greek mythology who could see into the future, she is demonstrating an aspect of her own finer self, which she unconsciously attributes to her friend, Sybil. Following the exposé of the Count's true intentions for wishing to marry Sybil, Blanche professes that, because Sybil has a 'finer, larger, greater nature' than herself, it is Edward who Sybil should marry. There are numerous examples of this psychological dualism throughout the novel; not only do Sybil and Blanche inadvertently share the same men, there are times when they literally share the same bed and, at one point, Blanche suggests that they wear the same colour of dress for a local ball. Thus, via a narrative suggestion of metonymic transference, any sexual ambivalence associated with the heroine, Sybil, is safely imbued in her opposite figure, Blanche. Conversely, Sybil is a manifestation of Blanche's lost innocence.

The sense of 'otherness' or doubling in nineteenth-century literature has been well documented with Mary Shelley's *Frankenstein* (1818) and R. L. Stevenson's *Jeckyll and Hyde* (1886) as obvious examples. In a discussion on literary doubling Marina Warner makes the comment that 'the metamorphic beings who issue from you, or whom you project or somehow generate, may be unruly, unbidden, disobedient selves inside you whom you do not know, do not own, and cannot keep in check'. As a means of demonstrating this point she refers to an Emily Dickinson poem from around 1863 which includes the line 'Ourself behind ourself, concealed'.[64] I would add that Dickinson's line also appropriates the sensibilities of psychological dualism that Kavanagh attempted to portray in Sybil and Blanche.

The baser sense of self – that which cannot be openly acknowledged in the heroine in Romance – is conveniently manifested in the form of relational other, usually one who is also closely connected to the heroine by a third party, in this case Sybil's lovers and, ultimately, her father.[65] It is also significant that Kavanagh makes a conscious reference to the concept of 'Romance' in her allusion to Spenser's *The Faerie Queene*, reminding her reader that Romance is itself an artificial device through which it is possible to make social and political comment. Duessa and Una are echoed in Blanche and Sybil and the Red Knight in Edward Dermot, whose noted 'red hair' is, no doubt, of emblematic significance. In a discussion with Sybil on the nature of truth and deception, Edward refers to Spenser's epic, '"You have never read Spenser, Sybil? Well I have; and I remember Una, my second love; and like all second loves, the purest and the best"' (I: 169). Edward is equating Sybil with Una here and in so doing he is, like Cornelius in *Daisy Burns*, inadvertently using art to project his own values on to women. He equates Blanche, his first love, with Duessa, telling the unsuspecting Sybil that his first love was a Cinderella whom he loved out of pity. There follows a series of episodes wherein Sybil is forced to make choices involving Edward, thus enabling her to mature intellectually and emotionally. In time the small animal-related *noms d'amitié* of 'Pussy' and 'Birdie', which both Mr Kennedy and Edward had attached to the childlike Sybil are eventually dropped, thereby signalling an acceptance of her blossoming adult self.

There are many examples in nineteenth-century fiction where the duplicitous nature of femininity is unveiled as a means of dissipating any singular concept of self. One of the more sensational examples, of course, is that of Jane Eyre and Bertha Mason who, it has been argued, represent two sides of the same psyche made manifest by their connection with a closely related third person, Edward Rochester. The passing influence of Brontë's *Jane Eyre* is also registered here and it is interesting that Kavanagh chose to give the two characters, Edward and Blanche, similar names to Edward (Rochester) and Blanche (Ingram) in Brontë's novel. Unlike Rochester, however, Edward Dermot is not an aristocrat, but, in keeping with the idea of the new 'industrious' manufacturing aristocracy of the mid nineteenth century, he embodies all that is progressive, thus supplanting an older diminishing aristocratic presence with that of the respectable self-made man. In this sense he projects a different image from his business partner, Mr Kennedy, who, to all accounts, reflects a more mercantile profile of capitalist enterprise. Blanche Cains, like Blanche Ingram, is conscious of her notable handsome looks. She is described as being 'tall and rather large' with a 'grand look' (I: 130) and Blanche Ingram, being less slender than her sister Mary, is 'moulded like a Diana'.[66] Both are hunters, or, it could be argued, within the context of their social ambitions, predators. It is also conceivable that Blanche Cains is so named as a reference to the biblical Cain who killed his brother Abel, suggesting that, like Cain, Blanche would like to 'kill off' her oppositional other, Sybil. She could then take Sybil's place, literally within the comfort of her home as well as in her father's affections. In Kavanagh's novel Blanche is given a much more significant role to play than her Brontë namesake. In associating Blanche Cains with Brontë's Blanche Ingram, Kavanagh is drawing a comparison with Blanche's external exploitative material self. Another aspect of Blanche, and more significant, is the allusion to Bertha Mason. As Bertha Mason, it has been suggested, is a personification of the unacknowledged sexuality of Jane Eyre's unconscious self, so Blanche Cains portrays an external aspect of Sybil's interior consciousness, ostensibly her unacknowledged sexual self. Again, the texture of Kavanagh's prose owes much to Brontë. On first meeting Blanche, Mr Kennedy comments on her physical characteristics and, much to Sybil's consternation, his comments concerning Blanche's large size cause her distress. In her discomfort Sybil also wishes that her father would not accuse Blanche of 'showing her teeth' (I: 149). Similarly, when Jane first encounters Bertha, she describes her as being 'tall and large [. . .] reminding her 'Of the foul German spectre – the vampire'.[67] Concerning the latter, both Kavanagh and Brontë are alluding to the idea of biting through the outer skin that houses the interior self.

Significantly, it has been argued that, in the mid nineteenth century, for a woman to be 'big' was considered to be unladylike. Brontë portrays 'bigness' in a woman as monstrous: while the cold, aristocratic Blanche Ingram is the object of her own narcissistic gaze, depleted of passion, Bertha was locked away because of her passionate excess. The associations of size and sexual attraction are displayed throughout nineteenth-century fiction. While heroines were usually depicted as small and slender, bordering on the anorexic – a reassuring physical evidence of sensual sparcity and moral surety – female plumpness suggested a fallen nature.[68] Paradoxically it is significant that, for reproductive reasons, the medical professions advocated the more developed female as the desired choice for marriage: a logical assumption made easy for Mr Kennedy. Shortly after her arrival at the abbey, Mr Kennedy observes that Blanche is 'a big, fair, fat girl' (I: 147), signifying his perception of her as a sexual entity.[69]

Kavanagh makes it clear, however, that Blanche Cains's 'bigness' and physical beauty accounted for more than her sexual attraction. We are told that during a conversation with Sybil imploring her not to marry Count de Renneville, 'She held a light in one hand, and laid her other hand – and though not a small hand, it was a handsome one, with white fingers, slender and firm – on the supple shoulder of her friend' (I: 262). In this manner Blanche is reminiscent of Holman Hunt's painting *The Light of the World*. The painting depicts the figure of Christ holding a light in his left hand while his right hand is raised and about to knock on a cottage door. It illustrates a passage from Revelation: 'Behold, I stand at the door, and knock; if any man hear my voice, and open the door, I will come in to him, and will sup with him, and he with me.' It is surely no coincidence that Kavanagh chose to portray Blanche in a similar pose to that of Hunt's Christ at this point in the narrative. On the surface, Kavanagh's portrayal of Blanche is encoded with traits of the woman who is morally suspect but she is also a vehicle through which static concepts of femininity could be broken. It is Blanche, the woman of sensuous appetite, who refuses to endorse the politics of self-denial and imposed artificial femininity. Paradoxically, Blanche is a symbol of strength. Positioned in the pose of an administering angel, Kavanagh's subtle allusion to Hunt's feminine Christ figure would not have been overlooked.[70] Blanche literally sheds light on Sybil's future when she advises her against this unsuitable marriage. Significantly, gender and size are encoded into the narrative here as metaphors for breaking down a cultural prejudice that works against human understanding. Kavanagh encoded her narrative with the rhetoric of the female body but she makes it clear that, while Sybil, the more culturally acceptable of the two women, is the official 'angelic' heroine, Blanche is the representative of the woman who is able to subvert the concept of the 'angel in the house' by empowering her and all she represents. Towards the end of the novel Sybil is given opportunities to prove her mettle and comes through as one of Kavanagh's strong heroines.

The lack of economic power and freedom apportioned to women during the mid nineteenth century was at the core of *Sybil's Second Love*. And while this novel ends on the expected note of hope, the dominant echo of the novel is one that disrupts the notion of female subjugation to patriarchy. Kavanagh's satirical comments on the bargaining power of money and the idea that happiness can be bought and sold are as significant as the tale of romance and regeneration in which it is encased.

Fiction, romance and fantasy: *Grace Lee* (1855)

Published in 1855, *Grace Lee* is Kavanagh's fourth novel and also her most experimental in that it attempts to widen the perimeters of romance in domestic fiction. *Grace Lee* is a novel that celebrates the power of fiction and its capacity to engage the imaginative concept of worlds within worlds. There are constant references to ancient books and the act of reading itself is a prominent *leitmotif* in the narrative. As her name suggests, the heroine, Grace Lee, is both a symbol of hope and regeneration – indicated by the 'golden light' that surrounds her – and a woman of earthly substance. *Grace Lee* was received well in America,[71] but less so in England. Geraldine Jewsbury[72] disliked it intensely and criticised it for what she considered its lack of realism and somewhat fanciful abstract notions of self, as exemplified in the main protagonist, Grace. She saw *Grace Lee* as a novel that failed in its execution of ideas – mainly that they contradict a sense of social realism from which the domestic novel derives its narrative. Jewsbury's contemporary Mrs Oliphant was more straightforward in her view of this novel, saying that it was simply another version of *Jane Eyre*. Nevertheless, it is possible to embark on a rereading of *Grace Lee* from a modern perspective and focus on the independence and liberty which the young heroine makes her own. Such a reading not only sheds light on the critical boundaries suggested by Jewsbury's response but introduces the idea that in this novel Kavanagh was attempting to break through these boundaries. It also draws attention to the appeal of the novel for its readers. US sales of six thousand copies within the first few months of publication are an indication of the novel's popularity in that country certainly, while (as was the case with Kavanagh's other novels) many readers in England would have had access mainly through the circulating libraries, of which Mudie's alone held four hundred copies. Monica Correa Fryckstedt has noted that an indication of Kavanagh's growing popularity is suggested by the action of Mudie himself when on 3 March 1856 he placed the title 'GRACE LEE' at the head of his advertisement, then listed all the other books in small print below this eye-catching heading.[73]

Grace Lee is one of Kavanagh's more independent and resilient heroines who, like most of her main protagonists, is not conventionally beautiful, but has qualities of strength, endurance and kindness in her nature. The genesis of the resilient and independent heroine lies in earlier writers and, of course, is not unique to Kavanagh (or Brontë). Arguably the qualities invested in Grace Lee and Jane Eyre are characteristic of mid-century domestic fiction. Dinah Craik's *Olive*, in her novel of the same name (1850), and Charlotte Yonge's Rachel Curtis, in *The Clever Woman of the Family* (1865), are just two examples of heroines who, each in her own way, break through the mould of the patterned, decorous 'feminine' woman and sustain the virtues of resilience and independence. And though *Grace Lee* and *Jane Eyre* are thematically similar in many respects, there are also differences; while both heroines are realists in the material sense, *Grace Lee* is a novel that ventures further into the realms of fantasy and surrealism. Both Jane and Grace are orphans; they are also 'plain' women who enjoy study and have a sense of wonder about the world. However, unlike Jane, Grace is not sent away to a boarding school but educated at home; her childhood, though restricted, is a happy one and she experiences none of the humiliations and persecutions suffered by Jane as a child. Money is a prominent entity in both novels and is the means towards liberation for both Jane and Grace. Although they both come into an inheritance, this occurs at different times in their lives, which undoubtedly determines the outcome of their response to their respective change of fortune. Jane receives her inheritance only after she has been through much hardship and has experienced many disappointments in life, while Grace comes into hers at the age of sixteen, content and happy under the congenial protection of her kindly guardian. While Jane's inheritance of £5000 is fundamental to her sense of liberation – money frees her from the toil of teaching and allows her to find Rochester – Grace has a different philosophical outlook. Money enables Grace to seek out worlds that lie beyond those partitioned by the propriety of domestic decorum. Moreover, while it is Jane's destiny to remain in Yorkshire, Kavanagh informs us that Grace, 'now one of the wealthiest women in all England' (9), is able to live out a fantasy to travel to exotic places and money is the source through which she can realise her dreams. After her adventures she has no need of wealth and neither does she seek it, choosing to live off a small legacy left to her by her father, along with the earnings of her own labour.

In both novels the narrative consciously engages with the human delusions and social inequalities that are a direct result of an imbalanced distribution of wealth. At the same time money and love are closely connected, woven into the fabric of each story. Both Jane and Grace marry men who have undergone change through experience and, notably, both novels end with the respective couples living in domestic harmony. Rochester loses much of his fortune as Jane gains hers; Grace relinquishes her wealth and finds love with a man who lives by his profession as a lawyer. However, as Jane retreats into the protection of Ferndean, overgrown and 'deep buried in a wood',[74] separated from the ills of the world, Grace divides her time between her peaceful rose garden and her house, which is appropriately named Eden and built in the open country, and an active life in London. In both novels the dynamics of gender, wealth and power are finally balanced by the accepted consensus of love and marriage.

Throughout *Grace Lee* the juxtaposition of social realism, gothic landscape and dream fantasy are all pertinent to the telling of the story while remaining within the prescribed perimeters of domestic fiction.

Kavanagh integrates her heroine's experiences within a series of related themes of social and political consciousness, all of which engage the narrative in an interplay of dissenting voices which are interwoven into the main structure of the story. The basis of the narrative is outlined in the opening chapter when Grace, aged fourteen, and her stepsister, Lily Blount, aged eleven, have each lost a parent and a step-parent. In their youth Grace's father and Lily's mother were lovers but circumstances led them to marry other people and, after sixteen years when they each find themselves widowed with a child, they meet again. Their old love is revived and they marry and live happily for a year before they both die within days of each other, 'each ignorant of the other's fate; each bequeathing to the other's care his or her child' (5). Grace, who, we are told, will always be plain, and Lily, who will grow into a beauty, are to have separate guardians. Grace is placed in the hands of an old scholarly cleric, Dr Crankey (a distant relative of her mother) and his cousin Amy Crankey. She will live in 'one of the wildest nooks of northern England' (3), where her mind will be charmed 'with classic lore, Hebrew, and romantic dreams' (7). Conversely, Lily is to live in the south of England with her cousin, the elderly Miss Blount, presumably a relative on her father's side, whose eccentricity is such that, after they had settled, Lily 'daily wished herself dead' (7). It was assumed that Grace would have been placed with her wealthy aunt, Old Miss Lee, but was rejected by this lady on the grounds that her mother was a 'Papist'. Moreover, at this stage, Miss Lee had favoured Grace's cousin, the London banker Mr Gerald Lee as the heir to her fortune. He soon fell out of favour, however, by marrying against Miss Lee's wishes and, subsequently, her vast fortune was bequeathed to Grace; the only proviso being that she divide it with her cousin at a time appropriate to her circumstances. During this opening chapter we are also introduced to John Owen, the young man whom Grace will eventually marry and around whom many of the events are placed. At this juncture, Mr Owen is the young assistant to a Dr Marsh, physician to Grace and Lily's parents, in whose hands lies the responsibility of placing the two girls with appropriate guardians. Although he qualifies as a surgeon he forsakes medicine to study law, a profession that determines his fluctuating fortunes and later leads him into politics.

In the first chapter Kavanagh introduces several themes, which, in turn, determine the issues behind events in the narrative. The concept of equality of the sexes in the professions is touched on lightly when John Owen suggests that Grace and Lily might follow in their respective father's footsteps and take up law as a profession. His idea is immediately dismissed on the grounds that their gender renders them unsuitable for such an undertaking, an attitude with which Kavanagh clearly disagrees and which becomes apparent as her novel unfolds. Not the least of her themes concerns the nature of love and she determines the difference between the entities of romance and passion. Romantic love is presented as a commodity, which may or may not develop into a deeper and more lasting form of love based on human understanding and compassion. As with her other heroines who eventually marry, Grace and John Owen's relationship culminates in an acceptance of each other as independent and autonomous beings. Their friendship is one that is built on a process of discovery and Kavanagh suggests that, above all else, it is their mutual ability to feel and express passion that finally liberates the spirit and determines the truth of the love they share. The notion of enduring love is manifested in the first chapter with the marriage of Grace's father and Lily's mother, but Kavanagh also draws attention to the fact that love of this kind is not necessarily open to everyone. The rekindling of love between Grace's father and Lily's mother and their subsequently happy but short-lived life together is counterbalanced by a brief reference to Dr Crankey and his cousin, Amy, who, in the past, had been on the verge of love but allowed other factors to determine their future otherwise. Because these two lacked the potential for passion, their early relationship could not develop on these lines, Kavanagh writes:

> [Miss Amy] had once been young, and the gray Doctor too; and then they had been on the very verge of love: but Miss Amy was capricious, and John Crankey was exacting; they parted coldly, he to take priest's orders, she to settle down into a calm old maid. When they met again, years had passed, and he could ask Miss Amy to keep house for him, and she could accept the office. Of the passage of their youth he remembered nothing, she but a little and that not often. (8)

Kavanagh also distinguishes the difference between the pursuit of material pleasure, which can be enjoyed for its own sake but is temporary, and that of lasting joy, which is brought about by love.

The novel begins with the seventeen-year-old Grace living in the Crankeys' cottage. Dr Crankey, now an elderly priest and accomplished scholar, spends much of his time on his lifelong work, *A History of the Church*, while Miss Amy, an accomplished needlewoman, engages herself in her own little world. Significantly we learn that these two 'both zealously taught the young girl all they knew'. Grace is introduced in the semblance of a romantic motif. She is 'a slender, dark-haired and dark-eyed girl', engaged in scholarly activities. Her eyes are 'fixed' on the 'strange eastern characters' of a Hebrew Bible over which her 'long drooping curls half veiled the page'. We are told that:

She was not, and never could be, pretty; yet her dark face had warmth and character, her eyes great beauty, and her young form much grace. [. . .] She was born far away, amongst Welsh hills, but she was an orphan, and for two years she had lived with her guardian [. . .] in a bleak and lonely home. (3)

From the outset there is ambiguity in the narrative as Kavanagh fixes the oppositional positioned worlds of tangible reality and dream fantasy within the space of the opening paragraphs. Within the protective shelter of the simple cottage Grace, the contented young scholar, is capable of imagining a completely different world, one that would enable her to achieve great things. The romantic delivery, abound with recognisable fairy-tale motifs, serves as a backdrop for her own fervent imagination:

The snow fell fast; soft, white, and noiseless it was borne past the parlour window. A gray sky, a white, hilly horizon bounded the outward prospect. Within all was touched with the red firelight: tables, chairs, cabinet, and mirror gave back the same warm and burning glow [. . .]

A gust of wind swept by the house; it died far away with a faint murmur on wild moors. The young girl bent her ear and listened. 'How far that wind has come,' she thought; 'how far it must be going – how wide the world must be.' She put her book away; she left the room; she went up to the highest part of the house, a terrace on the roof. The snow fell on her bare head; the keen north wind blew back her hair from her face, but her blood was ardent and young; her cheek only freshened to feel the blast, she only shook her head and smiled at the falling snow. She looked around her; a wide, white plain spread to the foot of white hills; a pale sky met a paler horizon; she clasped her hands on her bosom; she raised herself on tiptoe; she stretched her slender neck, and bent a keen, eagle look that seemed as if it would pierce every barrier. 'Ah! she thought again, "how wide the world must be!"' and seized with a wanderer's longing, she thought of burning Africa, of the luxuriant New World, of fair southern Europe with the sun shining on her brown ruins, and the blue Mediterranean washing her antique shores.

'I wish I were a queen,' she thought, her head pensively inclined towards her right shoulder, 'but a queen without her state, without her kingdom; what place, beautiful or famous, would I not see! what delight should not be mine! I would do great things; I would build cathedrals; I would found hospitals; I would erect palaces; I would make a cardinal of Dr. Crankey, a duchess of Miss Amy, a princess of Lily. I would have more jewels than a sultana, more robes than there are days in the year, and withal I would be so generous and so good, that everyone should love and praise Queen Grace'. (3–4)

Kavanagh's romantic pastiche here may help to put Geraldine Jewsbury's dislike of this novel into perspective as it does not fit neatly into the usual paradigm of domestic fiction. There is no clear demarcation between the events that take place in Grace's imagination, which, as Kavanagh's interpolations in the narrative suggest, are as real, nevertheless, as any event the reader absorbs in the act of reading itself. In the textual transference between the imaginary world and the events that seemingly materialise from this world, we are never quite sure what is and what is not actualised outside of Grace's imagination. Grace's daydream appears to turn into reality when she inherits money and Kavanagh takes her heroine into the realm of fairy-tale romance, consciously parodying the world of the privileged princess who is coveted, courted and esteemed; in Grace's case, not for beauty which, traditionally, is often expected in fairy tale but for her wealth. In this way Kavanagh simultaneously utilises and caricatures the ideals perpetuated by romance. Furthermore, as the reader is drawn into the story, Kavanagh exploits the possibilities of fictional representation by drawing a parallel with the reader's own experience of textual engagement and Grace's daydreams, which are a by-product of her own reading. Thus, the consciousness of reading a story within a story is romantic in the sense that the text itself is a celebration of storytelling. Moreover, it becomes progressively unclear which *story* we are reading. The story set within the narrative ceases to be part of that story as it merges into the narrative itself. After hearing that she is one of the wealthiest women in England, Grace vows that she too will be like Alexander who visited the oracle at Delphi and chose the 'short and glorious life'(10), a prophecy made possible for her by the acquisition of money. Subsequently, Kavanagh engages Grace in the ultimate romantic experience:

> Who would not travel? Who would not feel strange suns; behold new skies; hear the greeting of foreign speech, and pass a wanderer among scenes beautiful and still; amongst nations living and moving, yet left behind with their passions, their contests, their hopes and sorrows, like the images of a dream.
>
> Six years were past and gone. In a strange place – in a strange land the dreaming girl, who on a snowy day had wished herself a queen, read, as in a book, the vivid story of years of wandering. She saw broad seas and circling horizons; a boat cutting through the green billows, and leaving its brilliant track behind; long blue liens of coast glittering through white mists; open ports with shipping, with bronzed sailors and fishermen, with all the life and all the noise of commerce. Then came sunny plains with their harvests, and brown peasant men and women looking up by the dusty road, as the carriage passed and vanished through scenes of soft rural beauty, by green hills with hamlet, church, and church-yards, by calm valleys with hidden streams softly flowing in cool evening shadows. Then gay cities, all mirth and splendour, followed; then wild scenes, deep lakes sleeping midst stern mountains, with fir tree forests and snowy brows, and sounding

cataracts, above which on broad wing the royal eagle flew screaming. Then, past the mountain ranges, past the wildness and grandeur of nature, spread lands all light, all warmth and softness; lands of poetry, art, and beauty, with ruined temples and heroic battle-fields, now trodden by enslaved races; still farther and farther in the spreading desert, within the shadow of the pyramids, by the ancient Nile, by forsaken kingdoms, she followed her own track until she came to an Eastern city, rising on an Eastern sky, to the gloom church where lamps burned before a sacred shrine, and like one wakening from a dream, she found herself kneeling by the Holy Sepulchre of Jerusalem. For two years and more she had been a wanderer, and now her pilgrimage over, she had come to pray a last time where she knew she never could pray again.

Long before sunrise Grace had left Jerusalem. We will not follow her through the whole of her homeward track; it gave to her story a few bright pages more; it left images that enchanted her whole life, but it had no influence on her destiny. At Rome she paused and rested.

Miss Lee travelled alone; she was twenty-three, wealthy and fearless. Until her twenty-first birthday, she had remained in the North with Doctor Crankey and Miss Amy, exactly as if no change in her life had occurred. Not until the very day she was of age had Grace entered on the full and double enjoyment of fortune and liberty. Then, indeed, spreading her wings like a long captive bird, she had taken her flight towards the burning East. Gold smoothed a path else too rough, and charmed away peril. She travelled in the style, with the suite, and with all the privileges of a princess. The world might have reproved this adventurous spirit in a poorer woman, but it admired and extolled it in the wealthy lady. Wherever she went, she left behind her a golden shower that won her still more golden opinions. In France she was Lady Lee, la grande dame Anglaise; in Italy, an English Principessa; in the East, she was the Sultana from the West, and she all but eclipsed the fame of Lady Esther Stanhope. In England she was plain Miss Lee, an eccentric, independent girl, who had travelled over half the globe, who was prodigiously rich, and every one knows what *that* is in England, whom no one knew personally, and whom everybody was dying to know. (11–12)

Kavanagh is suggesting that money is the pivot around which public opinion is formed. Her comment, 'The world might have reproved this adventurous spirit in a poorer woman, but it admired and extolled it in the wealthy lady', bears witness to the element of difference afforded to both gender and class in Victorian England. Although there are echoes of Madame de Staël's enigmatic heroine, Corinne, in Grace's desire for liberty, Kavanagh may well have found the inspiration for her heroine's adventures in the Catholic scholar Lamartine's account of Lady Esther Stanhope, whom he met on his travels in the Orient. Lady Esther Stanhope was the beautiful and eccentric wealthy daughter of the Earl of Stanhope and grand-daughter of the Earl of Chatham.[75] Until his death in 1806 Lady Esther was hostess to her uncle, William Pitt the Younger, after which she travelled in style throughout Europe before venturing east on a voyage of discovery and finally settling in Lebanon. It was in this country that she spent her vast fortune, living in luxury in the village of Djoun where she built several houses and created her own estate. Unfortunately, almost three decades of eastern opulence and the neglect of her business interests in Europe left her destitute and she died forgotten and forsaken by those she had befriended. From 1810 to her death in 1839 she became known in Europe as the 'Mystery lady of the Orient'. Like Lamartine, Kavanagh would have been attracted to Lady Stanhope because of her intelligence, her sense of adventure and her religious leanings, which, to all accounts, were compounded in variations of eastern and western belief.

Throughout this section in Kavanagh's novel, parody is merged with the hedonistic experience of travel and, in the manner of Lady Stanhope, Grace embraces the delights of fortune and liberty that only money can bring. While 'spreading her wings like a long captive bird', she takes flight, a pilgrim of adventure, 'towards the burning East', paradoxically, the direction of spiritual enlightenment. It is clear, however, that in the novel the hedonism is tempered by a sense of transience and its worth is only the sum of its experience. Not surprisingly, she encounters the impact of her wealth on others by the very nature of money as an entity of social currency. Grace's world is showered in a golden glow and it is the allure of gold and money that attracts others to her – 'gold smoothed a path else too rough, and charmed away peril' and 'Wherever she went, she left behind her a golden shower that won her still more golden opinions'. These 'opinions' stem from those representatives of the collective *mélange* of European society, including assorted aristocrats, politicians, military *émigrés* and revolutionaries who, to one extent or another, have been the recipients of Grace's generosity. At one point in her journey, dressed in eastern silks, the preferred costume of Lady Stanhope, and reminiscent of a heroine from the *Arabian Nights*, Grace is symbolically emblematic of her own dream. Whilst in Rome, she is sought by the beautiful aristocratic widow, Mrs Chesterfield, 'whose praise or censure gave life or death in the fashionable world' (53), albeit a woman whose circumstances have reduced her to genteel poverty and who is now forced to trade on her beauty as a means of securing a rich husband. In this novel the issue of human delusion and worldly ambition reverberates throughout the text. In the following passage, lured by her own opportunism, Mrs Chesterfield slowly makes her way through a garden that is reminiscent of a forsaken Eden in pursuit of Grace, the woman she believes is in possession of the holy grail of wealth.

Mrs Chesterfield walked slowly through that beautiful old Italian garden; the summer flowers of other lands there bloomed and grew in the winter air, redolent with the sweet scent of violets. The red orange glowed through its sombre leaves; the yellow lemon hung from its bending boughs, or Hesperides like, the golden fruit was strewn on the dark earth. A clear fountain poured down from a stone niche full of green ferns, and flowed away with a broken sound. The whole place had a forsaken look; the mutilated ancient statues grouped around seemed to gaze with a melancholy air down the silent and neglected path.

Mrs. Chesterfield took that to her right. It brought her to the last terrace. Gray sculptured masses of what was once a Temple of the Sun lay half buried in the earth. The God of Light looked down carelessly on his ruined shrine. On a fragment sat, or rather half reclined, Grace Lee. She wore a striped Tunis silk, of light texture; it had the hues of a land of the sun, gorgeous, not gaudy. It was made in Eastern fashion, and suited both her figure and dark complexion. The vest and sleeves were fastened by carbuncle buttons, set with brilliants; a narrow striped scarf carelessly tied around her ebon hair completed her attire. The sun that shone on her whole figure gave warmth and brilliancy. She basked in its heat like one to whom it was life. (13–14)

In this garden the juxtaposing images of life and death are bathed in a redeeming sunshine, the 'The God of Light', which guides Mrs Chesterfield, herself a relic of a delusive material world, out of the world of darkness towards Grace. However, it is immediately made clear that Mrs Chesterfield is not seeking spiritual enlightenment when, on finding Grace, she remarks, "How can you bear that sun?".[76] Kavanagh may be indebted to Lamartine for the origin of this garden as it is not dissimilar to his account of Lady Stanhope's garden at Djoun, which evokes the same heady attraction:

she created a charming garden of flowers and fruits, cradles of vines, kiosks, nouveau riches of sculptures and paintings arabesques; running waters in marble drains; water jets in the medium of the paving stones of the kiosks; arch orange trees, fig trees and lemon trees. There Lady Stanhope lived several years in a completely Eastern luxury.[77]

Symbolically, Grace has undergone a form of spiritual enlightenment and has ventured to the edge of the world and back, travelling to the limits of material experience. The narrative draws attention to the two sides of experience that money can impose. The golden fruit guarded by the Hesperides[78] is 'strewn upon the dark earth' and the 'clear fountain' of life is shadowed by a sense of darkness and spiritual neglect, as symbolised in Mrs Chesterfield. Kavanagh also engages with the visual impact of costume and masquerade as text and, again, she may have been inspired by Lamartine. On one occasion during his stay in Djoun, Lady Stanhope greeted Lamartine and his companions, dressed in oriental costume:

> She wore a white turban, on her face a strip of wool the colour of crimson which covered the side of her head until it lay on her shoulders. A yellow length shawl of cashmere, and immense Turkish white silk dress with loose sleeves, wrapped around her in simple and majestic folds, and one only saw, in the opening that this first tunic left on her chest, one second fabric dress of perse with thousands of flowers which went up to the collar and tied itself there by staples of pearl. Turkish boots of yellow morocco embroidered out of silk supplemented this beautiful Eastern costume.[79]

While Grace is aware, literally, of the impact of her emblematic attire, she is conscious of the illusion it represents as the fantastic and the prosaic worlds are literally materialised (*textualised*) in costume. Kavanagh is suggesting that, in her imagination, Grace is weaving her own text here. The obvious reference to the linguistic associations of text and texture lies in the fact that the scholar, Dr Crankey and Aunt Amy, the accomplished needlewoman, had 'both zealously taught the young girl all they knew'. Costume becomes text and the story unfolds in Grace's masquerade of the exotic. In contrast Mrs Chesterfield's self-delusion is projected in her own fading beauty. Her beauty is the sum of her reality but its worth is based on illusion,[80] i.e. that it will bring her happiness by attracting a rich husband, and as such she is empowered by her own materialistic delusions of grandeur. Mrs Chesterfield's subjectivity is based on the values of the material world and, although beauty in this sense is a marketable commodity, it is, by its very nature, transient and loses its value with time.

Grace is placed on a pedestal by those who covet her wealth and, much to the chagrin of Mrs Chesterfield, she is pursued by the rich and the titled. However, while she indulges their compliments she remains detached from the embrace of their flattery. Throughout this section of the novel the whole sycophantic world of money is presented like a dream. Grace enters into it and enjoys the ephemeral pleasures of material comforts and excess only to return to the 'real' world to begin her life proper. Kavanagh exposes the transience of the material world and politicises the concept of power and money by disempowering its importance for the heroine. Grace is indifferent to the wealth of others and she freely gives to those who are themselves convinced that money will help their cause.

Grace returns to London and for a short while sets up home in a grand house in Park Lane where she becomes a 'patroness of the arts', enjoying all the spoils of a celebrated hostess. After two years of lavish entertaining she embarks on a final party as a means of farewell to one kind of world and entry into another, one she perceives as the world of liberty. Having now enjoyed the 'short and sweet life' to the full she has come to the end of her fortune whereupon, honouring Old Miss Lee's request, she calmly relinquishes the remaining half to her cousin, Gerald Lee. Throughout the novel there is the notion that money can swallow a person's integrity. Grace is not a hypocrite, she had set out to enjoy without guilt the money she had inherited by living life to the full; as she said, she 'spent more on others' than on herself. Nevertheless, she is also conscious that wealth can corrupt and she decides to leave the world of privilege 'before disgust has replaced delight' and, having achieved what she set out to do, she looks forward to a new liberty and sense of freedom.

Whilst in London, Grace is host to the cream of fashionable society and on one occasion her former acquaintance, Mrs Chesterfield, turns up. She informs Grace that Mr Gerald Lee, now widowed, has 'given himself up to philanthropy' (43) and is on the board of a charitable establishment for destitute girls, The Female Asylum, set up by one Abigail Smith, herself a poor girl, in Clapham. It transpires that Grace, who was sympathetic to this particular cause, had anonymously donated £1000 to this same charity under the pseudonym of one Princess Amelia. In another attempt to ingratiate herself with the person whom she believes to be the very wealthy Miss Lee, Mrs Chesterfield suggests that they might visit the Asylum to survey the progress and also to meet the now wealthy Gerald Lee. Here Kavanagh's satire is significant in its comic rendition of the two separate worlds of rich and poor. Mrs Chesterfield's condescension and indifference to social inequality is the vehicle through which Kavanagh is able to voice a protest against such attitudes:

> Through the windows the sunlight streamed in rays of gold. It lit up every group of girls in their plain but neat attire, with their young and cheerful faces. Grace was charmed, and turning to Gerald Lee, warmly expressed her approbation.
>
> 'Yes,' said Mr Lee, 'it is not amiss. The person,' (poor Abigail you were a 'person,' not a lady), 'who first established the Female Asylum, was certainly most praiseworthy; but she was ignorant and had narrow views; we have certainly improved on her plan.'
>
> 'Oh! it is beautiful!' enthusiastically exclaimed Mrs. Chesterfield, 'and you have no idea how cheap they work: French cambric handkerchiefs, beautifully embroidered, seven-and-sixpence a-piece. Everything was much dearer in the time of that Abby Smith. But as Mr. Lee says, it is all now on an improved plan. Thanks to an excellent committee, and admirable chairman,' she added, laughing. (45)

In this passage money is presented as the means through which progress can be made in charitable circumstances. However, Kavanagh is always conscious that money as an entity in itself is also a contentious subject and its value depends on the context in which it is utilised.

As Grace lives the privileged existence made possible by her inheritance, John Owen, who is yet to make his way in the legal world, ekes out a living writing articles for 'third class magazines' (49). We are told that 'Hatred of obscurity had induced John Owen to forsake his original profession for the bar' (48) and at this juncture his bitterness at the disappointment of his progress is projected in his outlook on the world. Kavanagh's introduction to his current predicament contrasts sharply with the image evoked by the sunlight shining through the windows of The Female Asylum which 'streamed in rays of gold'. Where Kavanagh chooses hyperbole as a stylistic device to emphasise hope for the destitute girls, she inverts this image and reverts to journalistic prose to introduce John Owen's circumstances, 'The dull light of a London day stole in through the dim glazed window of a miserable London attic' (48). Owen's lodgings are a reflection of his impoverished state, 'It was low, narrow, meanly furnished, with an indifferent bed, a rickety chest of drawers, a ragged carpet, plenty of heavy books, and no dearth of dust' (48). Oblivious to hunger or thirst but fed by ambition, John Owen reflects on the wild natural beauty of his native Wales, recalling his own boyhood 'in whose heart already burned the pride and ambition of man' (50) when he hears the voices of children outside:

> They sang a monotonous chaunt, yet it had a strange charm for them; day after day, hour after hour, Mr. Owen had heard them sing that endless song. It had but one word, ever repeated – 'Money, money, money.'
>
> Money was the song, and money was the burden.
>
> 'The very children know it,' thought Mr. Owen, as after listening he closed the window. ''Tis not genius, though splendid; tis not character, though strong; tis not virtue, though immaculate, rule this world. Money is her God, her lord, and her master. Patience, truly, patience!'

On reading a newspaper report on 'Miss Lee's visit to the Female Asylum', he conjectures:

> 'Oh, money! money! thou dost indeed rule the world,' thought John Owen, laying down the paper with involuntary bitterness. '"Lovely and munificent!" I remember her a plain, sallow girl, who never could be handsome; and what is a thousand pounds to her wealth, if report speaks true? A drop of water from the deep sea; a grain of sand from the wide shore. Well, may the very children catch up the cry, well may they too, sing, "Money, money!"'. (50–1)

Throughout money and the artificial is pitched against nature; town and country each have their negative and positive attributes but it is in the countryside that Kavanagh's sympathies lie. In his garret Owen compares his miserable existence with that of his youth and Kavanagh emphasises the fact that he is, indeed, a man of nature:

> He sat reading, as we said, vainly studying a profession that had never yet given him his daily bread. At length daylight failed; he rose and paced up and down his narrow room that imprisoned a spirit as restless as that of any wild creature of the woods; then suddenly pausing near the window, he threw it open. Before him rose brick walls, red with the flush of dying day: above roofs and tall chimneys spread a blue sky, dimmed with London smoke. A sudden vision passed athwart his mind or his heart, – for is it not with the heart that we remember a loved spot? He saw a wild Welsh dell, the warm sunlight gliding down the green mountain side; above, a breezy blue sky, below a rushing torrent white with foam; and by the torrent, vainly dreaming, a boy, in whose heart already burned the pride and ambition of a man. (50)

At this juncture Owen is suffering the humiliations of thwarted ambition. Like Rochester he is a romantic hero who is destined to undertake a journey into self-realisation before he can be reconciled with the woman he loves. Kavanagh's description of him has its own narrative here. As a young man and assistant to Dr Marsh he is described as 'dark and saturnine' (5), locked within his own thoughts. It is not until we meet him a few years later, however, that a fuller insight of his character is offered. Whilst he is brooding in his London garret, we are told:

> He was a man of thirty or so, tall, thin, and stern in aspect. His dark, deep-set eyes, and swarthy face, were both ardent and resolute; every line was deep and passionate; every feature had its meaning, but that meaning, though not mean or evil, was not pleasant. There was too much indifference, and too little of true content in the seeming repose of the brow; something too unquiet and gloomy in the bent look; too reckless a smile played around the scornful lips; the face, though evidently that of a man of intellect and education, bore too much the wild and lawless cast which may become a life of liberty, but which jars with the restraints of civilisation. It betokened, and truly, one to whom inward or external subjection was unknown; a proud, stiff-necked, self-willed man, whose temper had no more of the beautiful or loveable than his outward appearance, and yet, like that too, was not without certain careless and unconscious greatness, as plainly pervading his whole nature as it was stamped on his brow, and impressed in every dark lineament of his mien and motion of his bearing. (48)

Owen's sexuality is suggested in his dark brooding demeanour and is itself characteristic of the romantic hero. In line with Victorian ideology, his 'self-will' is synonymous with his animal nature and, as such, needs to be tamed. He must develop his higher, spiritual nature if he is to be worthy of Grace's acceptance. As is the case with most of Kavanagh's heroines, Grace's own (unconscious) animal nature is, by association, reflected in the man she loves.

Owen's progress is documented in the various professional and sexual encounters he experiences throughout the novel, all of which, inadvertently, help to bring him closer to Grace. At the end of the novel Kavanagh engages once more in the game of illusion and reality as, once again, she adopts the language of dream realism. The reader is not told whether events are, in fact, part of the tangible, material world or part of the dream world. After seven years of separation, a time in the wilderness of bitter experience, John Owen finally finds his Grace, literally *receives grace*. In an episode in which it is not clear whether it is 'Dream or truth' (387), the narrative engages with the reader's suspension of disbelief as John Owen's reverie on life fulfilment challenges the boundaries of fictionality and we are not sure if events in the narrative are the culmination of his own wish-fulfilment or are actually taking place. The most significant debt this novel has to *Jane Eyre* is when, like Rochester, John Owen is transformed by love which comes to him only after he is able to accept his own humility. Towards the end of *Jane Eyre*, Jane, in a state of much anticipation, follows the dictates of her imagination and she appears to converse directly with nature when she hears Rochester calling her:

I saw nothing, but I heard a voice somewhere cry –
'Jane! Jane! Jane! – nothing more.
'O God! what is it?' I gasped.
I might have said, 'Where is it?' for it did not seem in the room, nor in the house, nor in the garden; it did not come out of the air, nor from under the earth, nor from overhead. I had heard it – where, or whence, for ever impossible to know! And it was the voice of a human being – a known, loved, well-remembered voice – that of Edward Fairfax Rochester; and it spoke in pain and woe, wildly, eerily, urgently.
'I am coming!' I cried. 'Wait for me! Oh, I will come!' I flew to the door and looked into the passage: it was dark. I ran out into the garden: it was void.
'Where are you?' I exclaimed.
The hills beyond March Glen sent the answer faintly back, 'Where are you!' I listened. The wind sighed low in the firs: all was moorland loneliness and midnight hush.
'Down superstition!' I commented, as that spectre rose up black by the black yew at the gate. 'This is not thy deception, nor thy witchcraft: it is the work of nature. She was roused, and did – no miracle – but her best.'[81]

In *Grace Lee* it is Owen, who, after momentarily thinking that Grace is dead, experiences a surge of feeling, in an 'unuttered voice' that calls out to Grace. At the same time Owen undergoes a new sense of liberation from his former ambitious self, as we are told, 'ambition, that master-passion of his life folded her wings, and wearied of her long flight, pined for repose' (386). In the same tone of eerie romanticism that charac-terises much of Brontë's novel, Kavanagh continues in prose that recalls Rochester's plea:

> But brief was the rest of that ardent heart. Strong in his will, he recalled Grace; he bade her return, not pale but vivid as the light of day, not dead but overflowing with the fullness of life. He looked at the setting sun; the broad round orb slowly sank down to a yellow horizon, encircling the dark earth like a golden zone, then melting in the hollow air into vast depths of palest blue. But below all was splendour, all was light and flame; a wooded slope was a still forest of bronze and gold, a tame field a purple sea: the dust-worn way a path of light leading to a burning world. In that fervid glow he sought the loved and lost image he had ever known, all warmth and all light, and again with passionate longing, there rose an inward cry from the depths of his heart, an unuttered voice that said: 'Come back, Grace, come back!' (386–7)

Towards the end of the narrative Kavanagh reverts to a dream realism wherein the language of romance is interspersed with a reference to the classics: Homer, Agamemnon and Achilles. The novel returns to its beginning, a cottage in which Grace, suitably enveloped in a light of heavenly gold, sits with her old guardian, the now blind Dr Crankey, reading an ancient language, not Hebrew but Greek, suggestive, perhaps of a progression of events. Owen, relieved in his belief that he has found Grace, continues his reverie:

> Suddenly he breathed deep. Dream or truth, he saw and heard her. He saw an isolated dwelling, a poor home, rising bare and lone by the road side, an open door, a narrow room with boarded floor, with white-washed walls, with gilt-edged books on a low shelf, with bright crimson and yellow flowers in the window, with the rich sunlight streaming in; and half lost in the evening gloom, an old man who sat gray and blind in a deep arch-chair, whilst in the bright red light a woman leaning back on a low seat with a heavy book on her knees, read in a clear, musical voice, in a foreign tongue, a tongue long dead and unspoken, a strain of full and ancient verse.
>
> 'How fine that Homer is!' said the slow admiring voice of Doctor Crankey.
>
> The blood rushed to John Owen's heart with a force that might have proved fatal to a man less strong. Like a vision come to him at his bidding from the depths of the west, he saw her through the flood of living gold that

flowed behind and around her. She sat turned towards him; she looked her years, but unaltered, save in time, was her aspect. Her hair was as dark and as abundant as in youth, her eyes were as brilliant, her figure was as full and as graceful, her voice was as sweet, her tongue, too, was as ready.

'Oh! Homer, old Homer!' she said suddenly pausing; 'I like you certainly, but why do Agamemnon and Achilles make such long speeches? Surely –'

A shadow fell on the floor. She looked, saw him, and sprang to her feet with a joyful cry.

What passed in that first moment, neither could have told, for neither knew. She had sunk back on her chair, and he was at her feet. His arms clasped her trembling, hers thrown around his neck drew and pressed to her bosom his throbbing brow. He looked up flushed and burning. She bent down red as fire. One feeling like a chain wrapped and bound them both in that ardent embrace. Alas! some might have smiled to see so impassioned a meeting between a man whose hair was gray and a woman who was not young, but none were by, none save a blind old man who with his two hands resting on his chair vainly turned towards them his troubled face and sightless eyes.

'I knew you would come,' she said at length, looking and laughing down at him with proud yet fond triumph. 'I knew you would.' (386–7)

The novel turns full circle when the couple, married and with children, live in their intended home, Eden, a living domestic paradise. After several years as John Owen's wife Grace muses on her life and here Kavanagh's narrative is drawn to the power of passion which is born out of love:

If Grace wished for quiet, domestic happiness, her wish was not granted. Her husband loved her as passionately after as before marriage. She yielded to this stormy bliss, but looked for the day that should calm it down to silence and repose. She knew that there are pauses of rest in the sweetest music; that when the human heart overflows its bed long remains barren and dry. She watched for the ebbing of the tide. It never ebbed for her. Years have passed over her head, children have grown up around her; and her lover, unsated by possession, unwearied by habit, has never sunk down into the mere husband.

Grace is silent, but she often marvels in her heart at this great love of John Owen for her. She knows not that poverty and ambition had saved him from much sin; but that with prosperity he might, like many a better man, have grown cynical and profligate; that Providence has sent him this heavenly guest to guard him from temptation, to absorb in a generous passion other passions less noble, to atone for many a dark sin of anger and pride, and lead him to the judgment seat a man not unblemished, but redeemed and forgiven. (392)

Kavanagh is conscious here that the accepted utopian 'happy ending' of romance is a paradox. It is the awareness of the conflicts of true love that produces a more acceptable finale and one that she herself can more readily accept and which is the basis of romance in this novel. Catherine Belsey has argued that there are no perfectly happy endings in romance, noting that 'Desire is not a property, [. . .] of mind or body, still less of mind *and* body. On the contrary, it exceeds the duality of their relationship, and in this excess lies the impossibility of the healing unity the romances promise.'[82] Both Grace and John Owen are the recipients of a passion which, as Kavanagh suggests in this novel, is greater than the culmination of desire and is sent by Providence. Happiness in the romantic sense is of less consequence than the reality of their acceptance of each other, which, in accordance with the dictates of Victorian ideology, was tantamount to happiness in marriage. Nevertheless, the final voice is given entirely to Kavanagh. Although it is the narrator who informs the reader that it is through Providence that Grace is able 'to guard him from temptation, to absorb in a generous passion other passions less noble' – a sentiment that would certainly have met with a sense of Victorian approval – Kavanagh does more than tell the reader that, Grace 'married him'. Paradoxically, it is through Grace's very *silence* that she is able to sustain her voice and, by implication, her subjectivity while fully engaging in married life. In this way Kavanagh disrupts the notion of closure; the happy ending is present but the prevailing voice transcends the domestic harmony to suggest that the text itself houses other considerations. Grace is portrayed here as the *Angel in the house*, a guardian angel to John Owen – 'Providence has sent him this heavenly guest' – but, unlike Patmore's creation[83] whose happiness is to be found solely through administering to her husband, Kavanagh is adamant that Grace's marital contentment emanates from a partnership built on equal terms. As his wife, Grace has become one with Owen but she has not been absorbed by him. At no time does Grace become her husband's possession. In this novel Kavanagh engages the politics of writing in her deconstruction of the symbolic order of romance. In Grace's wish to remain silent, Kavanagh is, in fact, defying the rules of conventional romance and endorsing woman's control over her autonomous self.

The social novel: *Rachel Gray* (1856)

Geraldine Jewsbury may not have approved of *Grace Lee*, but she totally endorsed Kavanagh's next novel, *Rachel Gray*:

> 'Rachel Gray' is a charming and touching story [. . .] No one can read the story and not feel a good influence from it. The characters are vigorously sketched, and have a life-like reality about them which makes a favourable contrast to the dreamy, morbid phantasms of bad dreams which usurped

the place of human beings in Miss Kavanagh's last novel, 'Grace Lee.' She
has in the present work well retrieved her credit.[84]

It may have been Jewsbury's adverse critical response to *Grace Lee* that
prompted Kavanagh to focus her energies consciously on producing a
novel with a more prosaic subject, the reasons for which she outlines in
her preface:

> This tale, as the title-page implies, is founded on fact. Its truth is its chief
> merit, and the Author claims no other share in it, than that of telling it to
> the best of her power.
>
> I do not mean to aver that every word is a positive and literal truth, that
> every incident occurred exactly as I have related it, and in no other fashion,
> but this I mean to say: that I have invented nothing in the character
> of Rachel Gray, and that the sorrows of Richard Jones are not imaginary
> sorrows.
>
> My purpose in giving this story to the world is twofold. I have found
> that my first, and in many respects, most imperfect work 'Madeleine,' is
> nevertheless that which has won the greatest share of interest and sym-
> pathy; a result which I may, I think, safely attribute to its truth, and which
> has induced me to believe that on similar grounds, a similar distinction
> might be awarded to a heroine very different indeed from 'Madeleine,'
> but whose silent virtues have perhaps as strong a claim to admiration
> and respect.
>
> I had also another purpose, and though I mention it last, it was that
> which mainly contributed to make me intrude on public attention; I wished
> to show the intellectual, the educated, the fortunate, that minds which they
> are apt to slight as narrow, that lives which they pity as moving in the
> straight and gloomy paths of mediocrity, are often blessed and graced
> beyond the usual lot, with those lovely aspirations towards better deeds
> and immortal things, without which life is indeed a thing of little worth;
> cold and dull as a sunless day.

The story opens with an account of the drab day-to-day existence of
twenty-six-year-old Rachel Gray, a seamstress who lives in a small house
in one of London's more neglected suburbs with her ill-tempered but
loving stepmother and her two young apprentices, Jane Smith and Mary
Jones. Rachel makes a meagre living but is uncomplaining and, characteristically of Kavanagh's heroines, she is not beautiful but has 'fine eyes'
and is of a strong and naturally independent character. Her existence is
clouded not simply by the bleakness of her profession but by the fact that
she is unloved and ignored by her estranged father, Tom Gray. Before the
heartbreaking death of her mother and, later, her thirteen-year-old half-
sister, the child of her father's second marriage, Tom Gray had abandoned his family for a life in America, only to return to England three

years later to live a separate life. Tom Gray, a carpenter by profession, is a totally self-absorbed man who shows no feelings for his daughter and is indifferent to her attempts to engage with him. We are told that he was a 'thorough Republican' and it is interesting to learn that, like Kavanagh's own father, Morgan, Tom Gray had read Thomas Paine.[85] In spite of his detachment, Rachel loves her father and pays him several visits to his home in another part of London where he lives above his workshop. On one occasion she makes him a gift of six fine linen shirts that she has made especially for him, a gesture he treats with cold indifference. It is not until several years later, when a stroke leaves him paralysed and totally helpless, that Rachel, resolute on looking after him in her own home – the alternative is the workhouse – is able to care for him. After several years of constant nursing she is finally rewarded by his feeble recognition of her when he utters her name.

The narrative also relates to the story of the unfortunate Mr Richard Jones, a widower and adoring father of Rachel's young apprentice, Mary. In his attempts to better himself, Mr Jones opens a small grocery shop in the area only to lose his custom to a more commercially viable grocery, which opens on the opposite corner to his shop and forces him into bankruptcy. At this time his much loved child, Mary, now aged sixteen, dies of consumption. Consequently, he is left bereft and destitute and falls ill from grief and a sense of failure. In her kindness Rachel takes him in and cares for him until he is well. However, she is able to act on her charity only because of the natural death of her aged stepmother and a series of domestic encounters she had endured over the years. Under Rachel's care Mr Jones grows stronger and accepts a position as a grocery assistant in the very shop which, by the nature of competition, contributed to the ruin of his own business. Now resigned to his fate, his thoughts are constantly of his dead child and his only comfort is visiting Rachel to whom he can express his endless sadness.

George Eliot considered the novel a failure but she also found it commendable in many ways:

> Rachel Gray is not a story of a fine lady's sorrows wept into embroidered pocket-handkerchiefs, or of a genius thrust into the background by toad-eating stupidity. It does not harrow us with the sufferings and temptations of a destitute needlewoman, or abash us by the refined sentiments and heroic deeds of navvies and ratcatchers. It tells the trials of a dressmaker who *could* get work, and of a small grocer, very vulgar, and not at all heroic, whose business was gradually swallowed up by the large shop over the way. Thus far 'Rachel Gray' is commendable: it occupies ground which is very far from being exhausted, and it undertakes to impress us with the everyday sorrows of our commonplace fellow men [. . .] 'Rachel Gray' further professes to

show how Christianity exhibits itself as a refining and consoling influence in that most prosaic stratum of society, the small shopkeeping class; and here is really a new sphere for a great artist who can paint from close observation, and who is neither a caricaturist nor a rose-colour sentimentalist.[86]

In spite of these commendations, while she accepts that the story is 'founded on fact' Eliot suggests that Kavanagh's 'portrait' of Rachel is less than believable. Amongst her reasons for considering the novel a failure was Kavanagh's lack of realism in her depiction of Rachel as a representative of her class or profession and whose sense of piety she judged as unreal, as she says:

We do not feel that the story of 'Rachel Gray' brings any nearer to us the real life of the class it attempts to depict; still less that 'Rachel Gray's' piety gives the reader any true idea of piety as it exists in any possible dressmaker.[87]

The authenticity of any literary work that purported to be 'founded on fact' during this time must be balanced by other non-fictional sources, of which, as Eliot recognised, Kavanagh was fully aware. Although in her preface Kavanagh omits any direct reference to her original source, she was obviously conscious of the divisions amongst the lower middle classes, which included small shopkeepers as well as the plight of the poor. Moreover, it is probable that she had some first-hand knowledge of the toil of the seamstress. As mentioned in Chapter 1, correspondence shows that from September 1847 to June 1851 Kavanagh had lodged at 7 Allason Terrace, which, according to the Census conducted in March 1851, had been occupied by a milliner and dressmaker, her mother and two daughters.[88] Generally speaking there were three main divisions in the needlework industry, the top level belonging to those who made clothes for the aristocracy, the next those who serviced the middle classes and who appointed residential apprentices, and, at the bottom of the ladder, outworkers who were employed in the 'slop' or 'dishonourable trades'. For all its sweated labour and low pay, needlework undertaken in the privacy of the home was considered a 'genteel' occupation and, though it paid less than factory work, it was often the preferred socially accepted option.[89] Rachel Gray belonged to this group of workers, as, it is likely, did the needlewoman who occupied 7 Allason Terrace.

Written against a background of political and cultural change – Kavanagh makes a brief reference to the Chartists' petition presented to Parliament on 10 April 1848 – the narrative reflects the reasoning behind a system of laissez-faire economics and the effects this has on the lives of those who are either unable or unwilling to keep up with the dictates of its demands. Mr Jones, a man who is brimming with love for his daughter and full of good intentions, unfortunately lacks the ability and the acumen to be a success in business. Kavanagh draws attention to the fact that, like many others, he is the product of his own mediocrity and as such falls prey to those who are better placed to succeed in this mid-century period of economic transition. In a discussion on women novel-ists and the social narrative of the 1850s, Joseph Kestner has drawn attention to the fact that, in *Rachel Gray*, Kavanagh was, in fact, writing against the myth of self-help that was summarised in such novels as Dinah Craik's *John Halifax, Gentleman*, published just after Kavanagh's novel in 1856. Kestner argues that, 'Despite the fact that many were able to subscribe to this myth of assimilation, self-help, and upward mobil-ity, and perhaps to realize it, there were thousands who could not or would not'.[90] Kavanagh's Mr Jones was one of those who did subscribe to the myth but, as George Eliot noted, he was not 'heroic'; he was, as Kavanagh intended him, vulgar as well as psychologically and intellec-tually too ill equipped to realise his dream. Kavanagh was extremely conscious of the selectivity inscribed in the 'self-help' myth; as she inti-mated in her preface, commercial success is no measure of human worth. And while George Eliot found Rachel to be unrepresentative of needle-workers,[91] Kavanagh's portrayal of her heroine was, in fact, twofold. As stated in her preface, she wanted to 'intrude on public attention' the fact that such people had their own share of finer sensibilities;[92] she also intended that *Rachel Gray* would help to deflect the different forms of social prejudice that were directed at women who lived by their labour.[93] In this way she wished to repudiate the notion that such people are seen as mere commodities, valued only in terms of their commercial useful-ness. Moreover Kavanagh suggests that human sensibilities were not necessarily determined by education or social class, as is clear in her ref-erence to her stepmother old Mrs Gray's comparative choice of reading matter. Her delivery is poignant in its scathing association of privilege and indifference:

> Mrs. Gray was an ignorant woman, and she spoke bad English; but her lit-erary tastes were superior to her education and to her language. Her few books were good – they were priceless; they included the poetical works of one John Milton. Whether Mrs. Gray understood him in all his beauty and sublimity, we know not, but at least she read him, seriously conscientiously – and many a fine lady cannot say as much. (88)

Although Rachel herself is not particularly clever and can even be 'slow witted', as Kavanagh points out, she is blessed with a 'fine mind' and is sensitive to her environment and to the needs of people around her.

Her favourite private occupation is to sit and meditate in the quiet of her tiny, poorly furnished upstairs room. Rachel also finds much solace in her stepmother's books, particularly Milton's sonnets. Here again, Kavanagh takes the opportunity to engage her scepticism of the assumed literary knowledge of the more privileged reader:

> Rachel, too read Milton, and loved him as a fine mind must ever love that noble poet. That very morning, she had been reading one of his sonnets, too little read, and too little known. We will give it here, for though, of course, all our readers are already acquainted with it, it might not be present to their memory. (88–9)

Rachel reads Milton's Sonnet XVI, and reflects on the final line, 'They also serve who only stand and wait',[94]

> 'They also serve who only stand and wait.' thought Rachel, brooding over the words, as was her wont, 'and thus is my case. Oh, God! I stand and wait, and alas! I do nothing, for I am blind, and ignorant, and helpless, and what am I that the Lord should make use of me; yet, in His goodness, my simple readiness to do his will, he takes as good service. Oh, Rachel! happy Rachel! to serve so kind a master.' (89–90)

Cloaked in this Christian message of humility and acceptance is the infinite sadness Rachel feels in the absence of her father's love, a sadness that is further compounded by the demonstrable love expressed daily by Mr Jones for his daughter. Tom Gray's total indifference to love is manifested in his self-absorption and his disregard for others. Later on in the novel Rachel lives with her invalid and insensible father in quiet acceptance of what life has bestowed upon her. In her thoughts she is conscious of her need for a fuller, richer love that had been denied her, as is apparent in Kavanagh's final paragraph:

> And Rachel Gray, too, has her thoughts. As she looks at her father, and whilst thankful for what she has obtained, as she yet longs, perhaps, for the full gift she never can possess; if her heart feels a pang, if repining it questions and says: 'Oh! why have I not too a father to love and know me, not imperfectly, but fully – completely,' a sweet and secret voice replies: 'You had set your heart on human love, and because you had set your heart upon it, it was not granted to you. Complain not, murmur not, Rachel, if thou hast not thy father upon earth, remember that thou has thy Father in Heaven!'

It is ironic that Tom Gray's paralysis, a living metaphor of dependency and, in a sense, the antithesis of 'self-help', is the agency through which he is forced to accept his daughter's love. Given Kavanagh's estranged relations with her own father, which began a few years prior to the publication of this novel, it is tempting to suggest that, in relating to Rachel's paternal estrangement, she was also accommodating her own sense of sadness and loss.

Rachel Gray is a novel that looks towards love as a reconciliation of the human spirit over adversity, and Kavanagh's Christian message is present in the unflinching selflessness and charity that Rachel shows to others. Rachel's selflessness is mirrored in a minor character, a tiny, eccentric Frenchwoman, 'mad Madame Rose', a member of the London underclass who lives near Rachel in a low damp cellar in 'a narrow court, inhabited by the poorest of the poor' (53). One of Kavanagh's strengths as a writer is her power of description, and her portrayal of Madame Rose is significant in the dignity and tenderness she bestows on this tiny outcast:

> Madame Rose, as she called herself, was a very diminutive old woman – unusually so, but small and neat in all her limbs, and brisk in all her movements. She was dry, too, and brown as a nut, with a restless black eye, and a voluble tongue, which she exercised mostly in her native language – not that Madame Rose could not speak English; she had resided some fifteen years in London, and could say 'yes' and 'no,' &c., quite fluently. Her attire looked peculiar, in this country, but it suited her person excellently well; it was simply that of a French peasant woman, with high peaked cap, and kerchief, both snow-white, short petticoats, and full, a wide apron, clattering wooden shoes, and blue stockings. (53–4)

Although much of Kavanagh's tale is 'founded on fact', it may be that Madame Rose is Kavanagh's invention or that, in creating her, she drew her inspiration from someone she had encountered whilst living in France. While Madame Rose lives off the charity of others, she is herself the very epitome of charity and also a reminder that kindness exists in an otherwise indifferent society. Madame Rose spends her weekdays knitting and generally keeping busy, but on Sundays she is to be found sitting on a little wooden stool which she has placed on the steps of a nearby French chapel, giving 'unasked for information' to passers-by. However, she asks for nothing but receives enough to maintain her meagre subsistence of mainly onion soup and bread and cheese, food she shares willingly with the many outcasts who seek shelter in her cellar. In contrast to the grey existence, also suggested in Rachel's surname, Kavanagh introduces an element of colour, not the sunlit gold that in its different percolations permeated the narrative of *Grace Lee* but the subtle colour of Dutch paintings. One evening Rachel looks out from the window of her upstairs room and takes great pleasure in the scene presented in Madame Rose's cellar:

> As she saw it this evening, with the tallow light that burned on the table, rendering every object minutely distinct, Rachel looked with another

feeling than that of mere curiosity. She looked with the artistic pleasure we feel, when we gaze at some clearly-painted Dutch picture, with its background of soft gloom, and its homely details of domestic life, relieved by touches of brilliant light. Poor as this cellar was, a painter would have liked it well. (56)

The authorial effect of Dutch paintings was utilised by several writers during the 1850s. In a review of Elizabeth Gaskell's *Ruth*, J. M. Ludlow referred to women novelists who evoke the 'Dutch painter's accuracy in describing the surfaces and outer aspects of social or domestic life'.[95] However, while it is Kavanagh's voice that draws on the comparative associations of this scene and the paintings of the Dutch masters, her intention is to demonstrate Rachel's aesthetic sensibility in the pleasure it gives her.

It is significant that the romantic love that sustains most of Kavanagh's other novels is totally absent in *Rachel Gray*. Marriage is cut short either through death or abandonment, or it is linked with the success of commercial enterprise. In the early days of running his grocery business, Mr Jones had taken in a lodger, an energetic young man in whom he saw a suitable husband for his daughter and, eventually, his successor in business. And while the idea had furnished Mary's mind with romantic visions of the future and set her dreams in motion, she was soon disappointed when she learned that it was this same man who was managing the rival grocery shop and had married her co-apprentice needlewoman, Jane Smith.

In *Rachel Gray*, Kavanagh has attempted to illuminate the grim realities of existence endured by many in mid-nineteenth-century London. Rachel is one of the many thousands of women who were a source of immovable labour and whose work ensured a livelihood that was bound by the conditions and demands of enterprise. She is not rescued by Providence, there is no romantic escape route, no lasting source of joy, only her acceptance and her Christian faith. Compassion is measured by the sensibilities and actions of the individual, the paradox of which belies the mid-nineteenth-century concept of self-help, a philosophy that, in practice, as Kavanagh implies, has little room for charity.

While *Rachel Gray* ends on a note of resignation, all of Kavanagh's other novels end in regeneration, mainly through marriage. Many of the themes related to in the novels discussed here appear in their various incarnations in Kavanagh's other novels. Kavanagh's insistence on passion over contentment is to be found repeatedly, whether in connection with the main protagonists or in minor characters. For example, in *Two Lilies*, published in 1877 and Kavanagh's last novel, the protagonist Edward Graham, after a former engagement to the gentle and dutiful

Lily Scott, finds himself attracted to the more volatile and, by implication, more exciting Lily Bertram, the woman he will eventually marry. In this novel Kavanagh also draws on the visual narratives expressed in architecture and painting. Edward Graham is an architect and many of his struggles relate to the rules and regulations that accompany this occupation. In her novel *Bessie* the paintings of Watteau provide a significant backdrop for the story of the two young protagonists, the plain, introspective Bessie and her beautiful, extroverted opposite number, Elizabeth, two women who, like the two Lilies, and as their names suggest, are portrayed in terms of dual representation. Some of Kavanagh's heroines have artistic talents, which are utilised to eke out a living. At one stage in her life Grace Lee chooses to paint decorative patterns on ladies' fans as a means of earning money. Similarly, in her novel *Dora* the heroine attempts to sell her drawings in order to make ends meet. Whether artistic, studious or otherwise, Kavanagh's heroines have one thing in common; they are all women who challenge the imposition of the nineteenth-century concept of the feminine woman. By adopting the convenience of patterned romance and engaging with popular themes, Kavanagh was able to question the many misconceptions concerning women's subjectivity in the mid nineteenth century and as such her novels have played a significant role in women's literary history.

3

Woman in France during the Eighteenth Century

To judge of the intellect and influence of the women of those times, we must therefore consider them in their social relations, and often in their private affections. (*Woman in France during the Eighteenth Century* (I: 164))

Introduction

Kavanagh was born within three decades of the onset of the French Revolution, so it is not surprising that, with her French education and her interest in women's lives, she chose to write a history of women in France during the eighteenth century. It is clear from her novels that she was deeply interested in women's place in society and it follows that eighteenth-century France would have been the source of much interest and fascination. Her two-volume study covers the period from the end of Louis XIV's reign to Napoleon Bonaparte and engages not only with the celebrated and famous but also with the unsung heroines of the Revolution.

The aim of this chapter is not to look at Kavanagh's study of French women as a work of unparalleled scholarship, as there are too many gaps and discrepancies in her research. Neither is it my purpose to disengage Kavanagh's views by conducting further research into the original French sources of her material.[1] I intend to look at her perspectives on some of the women she discusses and consider her views in the light of her own objectives. Her purpose was, indeed, a celebration of women and of women's presence in history. She concentrates mainly, but not exclusively, on women of privilege whose position, she claims, afforded them tremendous social power and influence over those men who were prominent in the changing course of eighteenth-century France. Kavanagh argues that the power held by women in France during that protracted period had been largely ignored by historians, their negligence being the reason for her own endeavours to redress the balance in favour of those women who, she believed, played a significant part. To this end her purpose is clearly outlined in her introduction:

Though the historians of the period have never fully or willingly acknowledged its existence, their silence cannot efface that which has been; and
without that rule of woman so reluctantly recognised, many of their pages
of statesman's policy, court intrigue, civil strife, or foreign war, need never
have been written. To this remarkable feature of modern history, to the
analysis of power of Woman in France during the Eighteenth Century, the
present work is devoted.' (I: 4)

Women's power, she declares, was not always 'pure or good: it was often
corrupt in its source, evil and fatal in its results; but it was power' (I: 3–4).
She was amongst the few English-speaking writers of her day to offer
such a lengthy study of French women of this period and her aim was to
draw them out of the closet and into the mainstream of history.[2]

Both Charlotte Brontë and Mrs Gaskell were eager to read Kavanagh's
study, although, given the subject matter, she may well have anticipated a
mixed response from the reviewers. Fothergill Chorley in *The Athenaeum*
was of the opinion that, as a historian, Kavanagh's own 'purity of mind'
threw obstacles in her way. Writing in the mid-Victorian period,
Kavanagh's cautious approach to the sexual mores of the aristocracy in
eighteenth-century France would have been determined by her sense of
propriety on such matters. Nevertheless, Fothergill Chorley attributed her
with her own 'pathetic power which gives depth and repose to a book that
in other hands might have become wearying from its unmitigated
sparkle'.[3] The conservative *Quarterly Review*, while acknowledging the
fact that she had undertaken a delicate task, went on to suggest that 'her
biographical partialities mislead her, and her desire to establish the
supremacy of her sex has induced her to invest her heroines, their age, and
their country, with a brilliancy for which facts afford no warrant, and by
which the cause of morality suffers'.[4] In contrast, the more sympathetic
Gavan Duffy writing in *The Nation*, claimed that Kavanagh had produced 'A work which would trace the progress and even attempt to define
the bounds of this immense yet vague influence often so fatally abused'.
Moreover, he declared that it 'was loudly called for, and it has been con-
scientiously and faithfully executed'.[5] Interestingly, Kavanagh's study
embodies elements of both the praise and the objections raised by all three
reviewers here and, as such, offers a revealing insight into her attitude and
representation of her subject matter.

Although Kavanagh focuses more frequently on privileged women,
her interest extends to those others who were knowingly active during
the revolution along with the numerous women whose courage and
silent heroism had been largely unacknowledged by historians. In this
chapter I will look in greater or lesser depth at some of the women in
Kavanagh's study whom she considered significant either for their

prominence or simply for their virtue. These include: Madame de Maintenon (1635–1719), Elisabeth Charlotte, Duchesse d'Orléans (1652–1722), Madame de Berri (1695–1719), Madame du Maine (1676–1753), Mademoiselle de Launay (later Madame de Staal) (1684–1750), Mademoiselle Aïssé (1694–1733), Mademoiselle de Lespinasse (1732–76), Madame du Châtelet (1706–49), Madame d'Epinay (1726–83), Madame du Deffand (1697–1780), Madame de Pompadour (1721–64), Madame du Barry (1743–93), Madame de Genlis (1746–1830), Marie Antoinette (1755–93) and Madame Roland (1754–93). In Kavanagh's view each of these women, in her way, epitomised women's presence in either the aristocratic or revolutionary France of the eighteenth century. She opens her discussion with the aged Madame de Maintenon, the enduring mistress of Louis XIV, and concludes with her recognition of the forgotten heroines of the Reign of Terror. It is ironic, therefore, that she gave her final word to a woman whom she declined to discuss in any significant detail, Madame de Staël, about whom she states: 'With this woman, the greatest and most gifted in intellect her sex has yet produced, closed the social and political power of women in France during the eighteenth century' (II: 257). The paucity of space afforded to such an illustrious figure in this work is rectified by her prominence in Kavanagh's later study *French Women of Letters*.

Kavanagh's biographical perspectives are directed by the fact that, up to the last quarter of the eighteenth century, women's power emanated from a sense of their own political insignificance. As she says in the opening pages, women 'were denied all political rights but society gave them the power denied by the law' (I: 4). By way of placing Kavanagh's views into a historical context, this observation is given a slightly different perspective by one modern critic, who, in a discussion of the novels of French women writers of the period, suggests that their contents indicate

> limits which are imposed on the representation of women as active participants in history. History remains above all the privilege of the male; female participation is passive, influencing the course of history only in so far as it provokes male activity. Where the catalytic function is translated into a more active response, it immediately becomes suspect and liable to censure.[6]

The extent that women had power, as Kavanagh recognised, was confined to the social contradictions imposed on women at the time. As a consequence it has more recently been argued that any power held by women was illusory, one of 'form rather than substance'.[7] Women were subject to various forms of oppression, as Maïté Albistur and Daniel Armogathe in their study of French feminism have noted:

An astonishing contradiction in the eighteenth century juxtaposed a freedom of social behavior with the total dependency that was women's lot. On the one hand, there was a greater participation for women in social activities – according to class, obviously – and on the other hand, a very clear oppression of women by men in order to preserve their power.[8]

This contradiction is manifested in the fact that marriages in the upper classes were still arranged, with many women betrothed at a very young age and often to much older men. Their lives were invariably subject to their husband's whim and they were often left alone. Given the licence of the age, it is not surprising that many women took the liberty of seeking solace outside of marriage. Kavanagh actually says little about power and marriage as an institution, preferring to engage her reservations within a more contained argument on social mores. She maintains that both gender and rank dictated the boundaries of influence which were instrumental in restraining woman's potential to do 'more good' when she states, 'If she did not do more good, let it be remembered that her power was conditional: it was confined within the fixed limits, and submissive to that spirit of the times which both men and women obeyed' (II: 259). However, Kavanagh disabuses any accepted notion that women were vested with an inherent goodness in her frank discussion of the various women's lives included in her study.

In her concluding section Kavanagh acknowledges that in the aftermath of the Revolution, under the auspices of Napoleon Bonaparte, women's political voice had little influence. The closure in 1793 of the politically minded female clubs initiated by the revolutionary Olympe de Gouges, and later headed by the actress Rose Lacombe, had halted a progress which was itself propelled by social inequality. 'The power of such women', Kavanagh suggests, 'could not endure beyond the excesses from which it had arisen. It disappeared when the Reign of Terror vanished, and society resumed its rights' (II: 252). In spite of their intent on change, Kavanagh argues, women were hindered by their own lack of restraint and impatience for reform; 'The passionate impulse which precipitated France in her career was partly owing to women: had they tempered instead of accelerated the fever of the day, so many dark and mournful pages need not have been found in the history of their country' (II: 259). Nevertheless, recalling her comment on her opening page that, 'when their failing power seemed at its last ebb, it was still a woman who overthrew Robespierre, a woman who raised a solitary voice against the despotism of Napoleon' (I: 3),[9] she closes her discussion on a celebratory note, adamant in her endeavour to bring women into the foreground of history. Notwithstanding the post-revolutionary halt to women's political activities, she writes of the significance of their accomplishments and the legacy of reform which, she argues, deserves recognition:

> For those who know how to look beyond the mere surface of history, the action of woman in France during the eighteenth century will not soon be forgotten. She appears in that age – the most remarkable since that of the Reformation – connected with every important question. We behold her giving a stronger impulse to literature, aiding the development of philosophy and thought; and, like man, earnestly seeking, through all the mists and errors of human knowledge, to solve the great social and political problems which still agitate us in our day: the legacy of the past to the future. (II: 259)

Kavanagh is passionate in her attempts to override the restrictive perspectives that predominated against women during the mid nineteenth century. The resounding emphasis she gives to women's intervention in literary, social and political developments in eighteenth-century France is clearly felt throughout her discussion.

During the fifteenth and sixteenth centuries French women had become more active in the country's political and religious struggles, a phenomenon Kavanagh attributes to the progress of civilisation which, she suggests, 'raised the moral and intellectual standard of woman, naturally extending her power'. 'This influence', she contends, 'was increased in France by the three Queens-Regent, Catherine of Medici, Mary, her niece, and Anne of Austria' (I: 4–5). After the political upheaval of the wars of the Fronde,[10] a period in which, Kavanagh states, 'Women now took the lead in every intrigue' (I: 5), the influence of women was becoming more visibly significant. Madame de Maintenon, she asserts, cannot be ignored, and as the companion of Louis XIV she 'can almost be said to have governed France under the name of the *Grande Monarque*' (I: 5).[11] The influence of Madame de Maintenon was all the more pertinent when, at the height of his reign, Louis's claim, '*L'état c'est moi*', Kavanagh argues, was said in the spirit of one for whom mistresses were influential to his changing moods, and she attributes the rise of women's power to the vanity of Louis's despotic need for personal honour and glory. So much so, Kavanagh declares, 'It was, therefore, only through Louis himself that women could rule' (I: 5). However, encouraged by Madame de Maintenon in his attempt to restore France to its ancient faith, the court had become a place of oppression, and ennui amongst Louis's children and friends was rife.

The nation, now drained of its resources as a result of wars and Louis's extravagance, was open to what Kavanagh interprets as an 'irrepressible longing for a new and younger reign', the outcome of which was a new religious scepticism and an added 'force and freedom to woman's power' (I: 6). Times were changing and the privileged indulgence of the aristocracy was threatened by a more enterprising and intelligent group of financiers. The increasing ambitions of the wealthy bourgeoisie infiltrated the families of the aristocracy, which was to set a new precedence in French society. Kavanagh records that 'The nobles, while they hated the plebeian intruders into their order, married their richly-dowered daughters; protesting, however, like one Madame de Grignan, "that they were only manuring their barren ancestral lands, in order to render them once more fertile"' (I: 10). By the middle of the eighteenth century the financiers, though lacking the polish and elegance of their aristocratic contemporaries, were gaining ground. Kavanagh argues that, consequently, women 'eagerly seized on influence', quickly checking her comment with the provisionary parenthetic, 'whatever the means of influence might be' (I: 11). Her moral perspective on the women in question is paramount to her study as she argues that social corruption determined the conditions, which, in turn, determined the means of women's influence. She contends that women

> had received from their male relatives a shameless example of profligacy, which they were not slow to follow. [. . .] The corrupting tendency of a despotic government had reached the women who lived beneath its sway. The men, deprived of political rights, used their female friends as the means of their ambition. Indirect power is necessarily immoral: when exercised by women, it is still more so. (I: 11).

By means of qualification Kavanagh adds levity to her argument by citing Montesquieu, who, in his observation of the shifting patterns of establishment, declared that, '"the individual who would attempt to judge of the government by the men at the head of affairs, and not by the women who swayed those men, would fall into the same errors as he who judges of a machine by its outward action, and not by its secret springs"' (I: 11). Kavanagh's argument rests on the contention that the immorality of courtly life itself fed on the overall moral weakness, which, in turn, pervaded women's ambitions:

> There was nothing likely to purify or exalt the female character in influence so exercised; we accordingly find few of the women who possessed any power, remarkable for moral excellence. Their intellect, from not being allowed a free scope, was perverted to evil ends. (I: 13)

In her moral censuring of the 'few' women who gained access to power, she is expressing her indignation, not simply at the means through which power was gained but at the lack of political opportunity otherwise available to women who, she feels, might have used it for more positive ends. Although Kavanagh's concern with morality and power is central to her objections here, she was not alone, of course, in drawing attention to the morality of eighteenth-century France. The subject of French morals had been well covered by writers during Kavanagh's lifetime; Lady Morgan had already noted that the French were 'a people so vehemently accused of having no morals',[12] and later George Eliot interrupted a discussion on the intellectual effectiveness of French women with her pointedly ironic exclamation, 'Heaven forbid that we should enter on a defence of French morals, most of all in relation to marriage!'[13] In this context Kavanagh's study seems all the more significant in her attempt to engage with her subject, 'warts and all'.

Whilst acknowledging the fact that the salons and the celebrated *soirées* of the famed Hôtel de Rambouillet had already established a breeding ground for women's voice, Kavanagh's proclamation that a new impetus was given to the literature of the day by such writers as Mademoiselle de Scudéry, Madame de Sévigné and Madame de La Fayette. Four years after the publication of *Woman in France*, George Eliot echoed Kavanagh's sentiments with an even more appreciative appraisal of the literary contribution of French women writers. Writing in *The Westminster Review*, she argued:

> in France alone woman has had a vital influence on the development of literature; in France alone the mind of woman has passed like an electric current through the language, making crisp and definite what is elsewhere heavy and blurred; in France alone, if the writings of women were swept away, a serious gap would be made in the national history.[14]

Louis XIV had virtually shackled literary freedom and, subsequently, prejudice against high-ranking female authorship was rife. Kavanagh records that women authors, peppered with the ridicule of Molière and Boileau,[15] ceased to write; so much so, she informs us, that the accomplished Marchioness of Lambert would never allow her productions to be published, although her manuscripts were subsequently obtained from friends and eventually did find their way into print.

Kavanagh claims that a great cultural and social debt is owed to women by France itself. She notes that 'The action of literary men on society was chiefly exercised through women, in whose select assemblies they were admitted, and who naturally influenced their views, and their mode of expressing them' (I: 15). As mentioned above, this desire to engage and influence was due to women's 'want of political liberty' and the salons offered a refuge where discussions on politics, literature and philosophy were openly met. This is why, Kavanagh argues, the influence of women can be traced 'through all the philosophy and literature of the eighteenth century' (I: 16). It is complimentary to Kavanagh that one modern scholar, Susan R. Kinsey, in her essay on the Memorialists, argues that in a society where women were confined to passive roles, the act of writing 'could only be called revolutionary', maintaining that in their memoirs 'Mme de Staal-Delaunay, Mme Roland, and Mme Campan rewrote history to include women'. Kinsey goes on to suggest that, 'While these women felt that their lives were worthy of consideration because of their proximity to certain events, they did not want to disappear against that backdrop. A balance was needed between the personal story to be told and the broader historical drama'[16]. In her argument to attain a 'balance' Kinsey addresses those issues that Kavanagh had found relevant in her own study. Kavanagh's emphasis on the social relations and private affections of the women she discusses is, for her, the key to a wider understanding of their influence and place in society.

It was not until the death of Louis XIV and, later, with the accession of Louis XV in 1715, Kavanagh asserts, that the eighteenth century began. The increasing animosity by the French people towards the old King had effectually consolidated the power of the regent, Louis's nephew, Philippe II, Duc d'Orléans.[17] Kavanagh's brief outline of the Duc d'Orléans's contradictory character is interesting in her perception of his temperament and disposition. The overwhelming sense of ennui, which dominated this 'atheistic' man for whom the material world could not assuage, is sympathetic if somewhat selectively drawn, as she notes:

> This unhappy scepticism neutralised the effects of the regent's best qualities: his kindness of heart was only shewn in good-humoured forbearance towards his enemies; the activity of his intellect, wasted on trifles, could not save him from ennui; and he fully verified his mother's ingenious apologue: 'That though good fairies had gifted her son, at his birth, with numerous qualities, one envious member of the sisterhood had spitefully decreed that he should never know how to use any of these gifts'. (I: 26–7)[18]

Thus, Kavanagh conjectures, the court was resumed into an age of profligacy and into the most 'shameless and corrupt' period in French history – opening opportunities for numerous 'clever and unprincipled women' to ingratiate themselves with the regent, only to discover that he offered no confidences to any of his mistresses, or even female members of his family. Moreover, she argues that this man only had contempt for women, as he 'only held intercourse with the most profligate of their sex' (I: 28). In terms of her argument, he avoided surrounding himself with women who were considered too clever, favouring the less intellectually inclined Madame de Parabère whose main interests, Kavanagh contends, were concerned only with her own pleasure. The insouciant Madame de Parabère may have possessed those attributes required of the Regent's mistress, but, as Kavanagh's source, Saint-Simon, confirms, generally women could exercise no influence through him.[19]

Elisabeth Charlotte ('Madame') and Madame de Berri

In her biographical sketches Kavanagh gives momentary attention to women who, she claims, were of no political importance but who were significant within the context of family relations. Elisabeth Charlotte (1652–1722), mother of the Duc d'Orléans and known generally as 'Madame', is one such woman. Kavanagh offers a scant portrait of Madame, a morally rigid and haughty Palatine princess who was overtly proud of her German ancestry and for whom Paris was a second Babylon. She had been married to the only brother of Louis XIV (Philippe I, Duc d'Orléans), who, Kavanagh notes, was an 'indolent, narrow-minded man, whose highest pleasure lay in wearing rouge, patches and female apparel' while 'Madame, on the contrary, had all the breadth and masculine vigour which her husband lacked' (I: 29). Kavanagh's description of Madame's physical demeanour is characteristic of her more general interest in the aesthetic aspect of women's appearance. In this instance she focuses on the physical disadvantages attributed to Madame, describing her almost in terms of caricature:

> Her manners were, like her person, eccentric, and somewhat coarse. Her short, square figure, heavy German countenance, and hands of unrivalled ugliness, contrasted unfavourably with the beauty of the Duke of Orleans's first wife, the lovely and accomplished Henrietta of England. Courtly amusements had no charms for her; her masculine tastes and robust constitution made her delight in dogs, horses, hunting and every species of violent exercise; she disliked dress, as only calculated to draw attention to the plainness of her person: her general costume of a round, close wig like that of a man, and a tight-fitting riding-habit, somewhat increased, however, the grotesque appearance of her square and thick figure. (I: 29)

It is not without a sense of irony, Kavanagh notes, that Madame's greatest boast was to have introduced 'sauer kraut into France, and caused Louis XIV to relish her favourite omelet of salt herrings' (I: 29). Moreover, she was a woman who was of the opinion that she had highly honoured her husband by marrying him and, indifferent to the overall allure of courtly life, preferred engaging in her personal interests and writing to her numerous relatives rather than in matters of state. Kavanagh also notes that 'Madame did not possess more power under the regency: she was of the opinion that France had already been too much governed by women' (I: 31). Her opinion of women and politics is likely to have been influenced by her immediate relations with other women. Her hatred of Madame de

Maintenon was renowned;[20] an understandable enmity, Kavanagh suggests, in view of the rivalry between the Duc d'Orléans and the Duc du
Maine, Madame de Maintenon's favourite. Madame was furious when her
son married Madame de Blois, daughter of Louis XIV and his former mistress Madame de Montespan and sister of the Duc du Maine. Moreover,
her sense of injury was compounded when she was not consulted about the
match, which she considered a 'degrading alliance'. Her anger over the
union was such that 'on meeting her son in the gallery of Versailles, she
gave him a slap on the face, in the presence of a host of witnesses'.
Kavanagh relates further that 'The poor prince, who had only yielded a
reluctant consent to the match, needed not this new mortification' (I: 31).
However, later on, although she could not forgive her daughter-in-law for
being the daughter of one of the late King's mistresses, she did take over
the superintendence of her three eldest daughters who became the Duchesse
de Berri, Mademoiselle de Valois[21] and Mademoiselle de Chartres.

Madame's relations with her grand-daughters were complex. While dis-
liking the two elder sisters, she doted on the youngest, Mademoiselle de
Chartres, whose interests in 'masculine amusements', including dogs,
horses and the firing of pistols all day long, reflected her grandmother's
tastes. Madame's dislike of the spirited and 'profligate' Madame de Berri
was quite a different matter and was a response to her grand-daughter's
overall intemperance and notorious licentious behaviour. Taking much of
her information on Madame de Berri from Saint-Simon, Kavanagh herself
likens the Duchesse to 'those dissolute princesses, who filled Rome with
the scandal of their excesses, towards the decline of the empire' (I: 33).
Four years after her marriage at the age of fourteen to her cousin, the Duc
de Berri, youngest grandson of Louis XIV, she was to find herself a childless, if very rich, widow. From here on, her newly acquired independence
was to grant her an existence in which she could fully indulge her sense of
personal liberty.[22] Amongst the many scandals connected with Madame
de Berri during this time were potent rumours of an incestuous relationship with her father. Kavanagh would undoubtedly have considered inves-
tigative comment here to be indecorous and, subsequently, her
commentary on Madame de Berri's relationship with the Duc d'Orléans is
guarded. Christian propriety, always a determining factor for Kavanagh,
takes precedence and she merely states that 'Her husband who was at first
passionately attached to her, soon grew disgusted with her conduct. This
feeling was increased by the impiety she affected in her conversations with
her father, who had brought her up in his atheistical principles' (I: 33).
Although there was no genuine proof of incest, Madame was incensed by
notices that were stuck on the Palais Royal stating: 'Here be Lotteries and
most subtle poisonings'; by Lotteries, Madame wrote, 'they imply that my

son lives with his daughter after the manner of Lot'.[23] Kavanagh omits this particular reference but does mention that Madame du Maine, whose hatred of the regent was well known, took advantage of this particular scandal by promoting Voltaire's drama *Oedipe*. Although Voltaire had the patronage of the regent, his publication was actually an attack against the Duc d'Orléans's alleged relationship with Madame de Berri. The allusion was such that she became known as Berri-Jocaste, an intimation she chose to ignore, as Kavanagh informs us; 'she assisted five times at the popular tragedy for which Voltaire was pensioned by her father' (I: 50). Madame de Berri died at the age of twenty-four and throughout her short life her conduct was such as to cause great embarrassment to her relatives. Her death, after an agonising illness, at first caused Madame grief but on learning of her grand-daughter's secret marriage to her lover, the much despised Comte de Rions,[24] Kavanagh records, 'she indignantly dried her tears. The pride of birth superseded every other feeling' (I: 35). Madame disliked her eldest grand-daughter, not least because her conduct reflected badly on her own high principles but she was also incensed by the relationship between Mademoiselle de Valois, her second grand-daughter, and her lover, the Duc de Richelieu, which she considered unfitting and immoral. Her anger was such that she was instrumental in preventing a match suggested by the regent between Mademoiselle de Valois and the Prince of Piedmont by informing the prince's mother, the Queen of Sicily, of the young princess's previous relationship with Richelieu.[25] Madame's death at the age of seventy-one[26] effected no great loss although she was universally acknowledged for her virtue. Kavanagh may well have been attracted to Madame primarily because of her strong individuality and consistent eccentricity, which, in her view, signalled a refreshing departure from the general 'profligacy' of the court.

Madame du Maine

Kavanagh's account of courtly life at this time also gives an insight into the private unhappiness of the many aristocratic women in her study. She notes that it was the celebrated *salonière* Madame du Deffand who, in later life, wrote in a letter to her beloved friend, D'Alembert, 'Give me a secret to ward off ennui [. . .] and you will lay me under a greater obligation than if you had bestowed on me the philosopher's stone' (I: 169). As was the case with many members of the French court, ennui was the enemy that threatened their existence. She introduces Louise-Bénédicte de Bourbon-Conde, Duchesse du Maine, as the tiny, formidable woman who opposed the Duc d'Orléans's regency in favour of her husband, the Duc du Maine. Kavanagh's sketch on Madame du Maine is, nevertheless, both circumscribed and exposing. Again she gives a description of her subject's personage but suggests that Madame du Maine's undoubted allure owed less to her physical attributes and more to the 'universal seduction she exercised, – a seduction the more remarkable that she was neither beautiful nor striking in her personal appearance' (I: 39). Although she was the recipient of an excellent classical education, was bold, active and gifted with a felicitous wit, Kavanagh records also that she was superficial, capricious and deficient in moral courage and had a violent, fickle and selfish temper, a character not suited to 'the high political part she was anxious to act' (I: 40). Such was the nature of her temperament that the regent referred to her as 'the little wasp at Sceaux'[27] and his mother, Madame, more vehemently called her 'the little dwarf'. A more revealing aspect of this woman's character, however, was her 'great horror of solitude and ennui' and subsequently she 'was seldom to be found alone' (I: 40). When an old admirer enquired as to why she kept company with 'persons so little suited to her', she replied: '"I am so unhappy as not to be able to do without that which I do not need in the least"' (I: 40). It appears that Madame du Maine suffered from the same malady as her long-standing friend, Madame du Deffand, who, in Kavanagh's judgement, although she 'imparted amusement to others, she could not always receive it herself' (I: 170). Madame du Maine's desire for company at her magnificent chateau at Sceaux was known to all. Another close friend, Madame de Staal, and also a regular visitor at Sceaux, intimates in her correspondence to Madame du Deffand, that the Duchesse's 'desire of being surrounded increases daily' (I: 167).[28] Her unhappiness was, no doubt, compounded by the fact that it was the Duc d'Orléans and not her husband who had been appointed regent to the young Louis XV; a predicament that, perhaps, reflected more on her own ambitions for her husband than his personal desire for that office.

Kavanagh writes at length on the differences of personality between the energetic Madame du Maine and her more introspective husband. They both excelled in the art of talking and engaged their talents accordingly with society at their chateau, a residence rivalled only by Versailles for its splendour and brilliance. Her irrepressible attempts to secure the regency for her husband were matched only by his timidity; whilst he spent much of his time translating the classics, she surrounded herself with the company he shunned. While she was a woman whose sharp tongue and restlessness were the cause of derision, Kavanagh notes that 'she never learned to bear, with even common equanimity, the misfortunes occasioned by her imprudence'. She was, nevertheless, emphatically capable of charming others: 'there was about this clever and volatile princess an irresistible charm, that never failed to fascinate those who lived in her intimacy' (I: 40). However, it was her political imprudence that proved the greater consequence. The princes of the blood, those born within the dictates of legitimacy and who had historically opposed the legitimisation of Louis XIV's illegitimate children, were successful in their attempts to deprive them of this status. As a consequence the Duc du Maine no longer held any successive rights to the crown. Subsequently he was stripped of his privileges after a disagreement incurred with the Duc d'Orléans, who held the presidency of the regency council concerning the Quadruple Alliance among England, France, Austria and Holland. With this change of status the Duc du Maine was required to forfeit his parliamentary position. His humiliation was complete when, as a direct consequence of his wife's threats of revenge, Kavanagh informs us, 'the regent, moreover, took from her husband the superintendence of the young King's education, in presence of the parliament' (I: 48). Madame du Maine's vehemence was such that on being forced to quit the apartment in the Tuilleries, attached to her husband's former office, she vandalised its contents, breaking all the mirrors, porcelains and fragile objects she could lay her hands on. Her contempt for her now crestfallen husband and his brothers and her hatred for the regent was such that she exclaimed: '"My husband and his brothers are cowards: I – though only a woman – feel myself capable of asking an audience from the regent, and plunging a dagger in his heart"' (I: 49). Though her threats were not taken literally, she caused sufficient concern in the Orléans camp that for a while after she was put under strict surveillance by their sympathisers.

Kavanagh discusses the political consequences of the regent's policies, which had led to a general discontent throughout Paris and the provinces.[29] Intent on revenge, Madame du Maine siezed on the regent's loss of popularity to plot against him. Accordingly, plans were set in place to usurp him in favour of Philip V of Spain and the subsequent aggrandisement of the Duc du Maine. This episode in French history, otherwise known as the Cellamare Conspiracy, named after Antoine-Guidice, prince de Cellamare, ambassador to Philip V, failed owing to the imprudence of one of Cellamare's secretaries. The plot was discovered in December of 1718 and the ambassador and those involved were subsequently arrested and dealt with accordingly, some more leniently than others. From a historical perspective Kavanagh is of the opinion that all was doomed from the start: 'Even if it had not been discovered by accident, the Cellamare conspiracy must have proved a failure: it had none of the elements of success or popularity' (I: 57–8). While some of those involved were sent to the Bastille and others were executed, by virtue of their rank the Duc and Duchesse du Maine were dealt with lightly. Kavanagh informs us: 'It has been asserted that Dubois[30] and the regent suppressed the strongest proofs against the Duke and Duchess of Main, and only produced those necessary to justify their apprehension' (I: 52). Under the surveillance of her nephew, the Duc de Bourbon, the Duchesse was confined to the castle of Dijon of which he was governor. The regent, fully aware of the enmity between aunt and nephew, considered this action appropriate as he wished to 'impress on the public mind the reality of her guilt, without the necessity of a trial: which her sex and high rank would have rendered embarrassing' (I: 52–3). Madame du Maine met this decision with passionate rage as she had been under the impression that she would be delivered to Fontainebleau or some other royal palace. The boredom of her confinement soon tempered her spirit, however, and after several months of card-playing activity she wrote to the regent confessing her guilt. By using her gender as her trump card, she sought to procure her freedom, as Kavanagh states: 'as she felt protected by her sex, laid the whole blame on herself, and completely exonerated her husband'. Subsequently she gained freedom for herself and her husband but in so doing she incriminated others and, as Kavanagh notes, her letter 'which was read in the regent's assembled council, has remained as an indelible stain on the character of the weak and selfish princess'. Moreover, she goes on, 'Madame du Maine was highly indignant to see herself exposed: even while reaping the benefit of her treachery, she wished to be spared the shame it so fully deserved' (I: 55). Kavanagh reports that the political part of Madame du Maine's life ended with her captivity and, despite her ambitious spirit, the regent's political strategies prevented any future intrigues.

Kavanagh's source material for life at Sceaux comes predominantly from the memoirs of Madame de Staal,[31] from which she conjectures that, with all its wit, politeness and refinement, Sceaux remained a cold and heartless place where its members were acquaintances rather than friends and ennui was rife. She maintains that, although the court may have been a centre of '*style*' characterised by the 'purity, clearness and elegance' of Madame du Maine's own language, the appreciation of genius was lacking, so much so that on her death literary society at Sceaux merely dissolved. As Kavanagh says, 'The authors received amongst them belonged, with few exceptions, to that class of writers whose ephemeral compositions seldom outlive the epoch of their birth' (I: 59). Of Madame de Staal herself Kavanagh is somewhat circumspect. While acknowledging that her 'delightful memoirs' offer an authentic account of life at Sceaux, she confesses that it is difficult to imagine a more cold and unpoetic personage than Madame de Staal and suggests that 'Any feeling like tenderness, enthusiasm, or fervour, was evidently foreign to her nature' (I: 58). Kavanagh's reproof here throws light on her own perceptions of Madame de Staal's written style which was clearly too austere to fit within the aesthetic parameters of Kavanagh's stylistic preferences. Her opinion differs from at least one modern scholar who attributes Madame de Staal's written style to her sense of discipline and emotional containment. In direct contrast to Kavanagh, Judith Curtis has argued that 'Not coldness but discipline and elegance of expression, a piquant counterpoint to the underlying emotion, are marks of everything she wrote'.[32] Before she was married, Madame de Staal was one Mademoiselle de Launay, a woman who enchanted many celebrated dignitaries with her intelligence and charm. It comes as something of a surprise then to discover that, in Madame de Staal's earlier existence as Mademoiselle de Launay, Kavanagh was wholly sympathetic with her circumstances.

Mademoiselle de Launay

Kavanagh writes affectionately of the young Mademoiselle de Launay, whom she introduces as a highly educated and refined young woman of obscure birth.[33] Later, Madame de Staal herself was under no illusion about her birth as the pragmatic opening to her memoirs suggests:

> What happened to me was just the reverse of what one sees in romantic novels, where the heroine, raised as a simple shepherdess, discovers that she is a princess. I was treated in my childhood as a person of distinction; and subsequently, I discovered that I was nothing, and that nothing in the world belonged to me.[34]

At the age of seventeen and following the death of her 'benefactress', she was taken into the household of Madame du Maine's close friend, the Duchesse de la Ferté. Delighted with the young woman's intelligence, we are told that this 'kind, though capricious' lady was apt to parade her in company as her adopted *protégée*, a role that was to cause Mademoiselle de Launay much embarrassment. Kavanagh gives some sense of the general situation by relating one such occasion when the Duchesse de la Ferté directed events: '"Come mademoiselle," she once exclaimed, in the presence of a friend, "speak." To the visitor: "You will hear how she talks. Speak a little about religion, – you can say something else afterwards." Though thus put to the test, Mademoiselle de Launay's conversational powers did not desert her' (I: 45). Mademoiselle de Launay's reputation was such that Madame du Maine took an interest in her to the extent that she considered the young woman a suitable tutor for her own daughter. However, there followed a period when the Duchesse de la Ferté lost interest in the talents of her young ward and, after a series of mishaps, broken promises and disappointments, Mademoiselle de Launay was obliged to take up the more lowly position of *femme de chambre* to Madame du Maine. Kavanagh informs her reader that 'Those persons who had admired her most during her temporary éclat, now affected to shun her; and Madame du Maine, on whom she waited daily, scarcely deigned to seem conscious of her existence' (I: 46). As the first lines of her *Memoires* testify, this proved to be an extremely unhappy period in Mademoiselle de Launay's life. Judith Curtis sheds light on her sensibilities at this time when she argues that Mademoiselle Delaunay invites the reader to see in her life the disadvantages of being '"educated above one's station"'.[35] She was rescued from this obscurity by a chance occurrence. In a careless aside Madame du Maine advised her to write to Fontenelle, the 'celebrated author of the *"Histoire des Oracles"*', whose authority had been challenged by a young woman who presumed herself an inspired sibyl. Already being acquainted with Fontenelle, Mademoiselle de Launay wrote to him immediately. The author was delighted with her letter and so it was read, admired and circulated throughout Paris. The comic irony here is not lost on Kavanagh, as she points out: 'In those times, when a well-turned madrigal could open the doors of the French Academy to Saint-Aulaire, it was only natural that Mademoiselle de Launay's letter should enjoy great success' (I: 46). With the success of this celebrated letter, Mademoiselle now found herself, once more, in the spotlight, and the haughty Madame du Maine, learning of her attendant's celebrity, found her worthy of her notice.

Notwithstanding this change in fortune, it was, as Kavanagh reports, 'Mademoiselle de Launay; around whom now secretly gathered many of the remarkable men who came to Sceaux, and who often deserted the saloons of their princely hostess, for the gloomy and comfortless room of her witty femme de chambre' (I: 46). As a result of her newly found acceptance, Mademoiselle de Launay was soon the recipient of much attention and, for her, life took on a more pleasurable turn. However, this phase was short-lived as, still in the service of Madame du Maine, she became implicated in the Cellamare Conspiracy for which she was imprisoned in the Bastille for a period of a year and a half. During this time she remained loyal to Madame du Maine and refused to be tricked into disclosing any information that might further incriminate her mistress and her friends. Her allegiance did not go unnoticed by Madame du Maine who then interceded with the Duc d'Orléans to effect Mademoiselle de Launay's release. Impressed by her loyalty and steadfastness, Madame du Maine took her back into her household whereupon she developed a deeper affection for her young attendant and they soon became true friends. However, concerned over Mademoiselle de

Launay's lack of rank, Madame du Maine wished to secure her friend's future and, before long, found a suitable husband for her in the Baron de Staal, a Swiss officer in the French service. Kavanagh's account of the marriage is economic in detail, relating only that, though this was strictly a marriage of convenience, the couple were 'tolerably happy and gave Madame de Staal a rank in the household of the Duchess' (I: 57). This particular marriage of convenience says much about the differences of social class at the time. Mademoiselle de Launay was undoubtedly bitter about its necessity and, in her own words, referred to her marriage as a form of sacrifice, contesting that 'The victim, bound and decorated, was sadly led to the altar'.[36] Dependent on others for her security, she was subsequently obliged to place herself into what she perceived as institutionalised bondage as a means of survival. It is clear from Kavanagh's lack of detail here that, in this case, she was less concerned with the consequences of Mademoiselle de Launay's psychological response than with noting the social acceptance that an appropriate marriage effectively guaranteed.

The intrigue of romance: Mademoiselle de Launay, Mademoiselle Aïssé and Mademoiselle de Lespinasse

Kavanagh was drawn as much to stories of romantic liaisons as she was to the political intrigues in which the women of the period became embroiled. Whilst focusing on the status of birthright, she inadvertently exposes the importance of class and rank within the aristocratic world of eighteenth-century France. She took a particular interest in women who, in one way or another, were dependent on those more economically and socially established. Mademoiselle de Launay was one of a trio who attracted Kavanagh's attention, the other two being Mademoiselle Aïssé and Mademoiselle de Lespinasse; interestingly, three women who, like Kavanagh herself, were without pedigree or wealth. They each wrote copiously of their experiences in their letters and revealed themselves to be deeply unhappy in their respective lives. In this section of her discussion Kavanagh's construction of events is contextualised within the framework of relational sentiment in that her narrative invites the reader into a sense of solidarity with each respective 'heroine'. As Kavanagh sees it, their suffering and implied moral superiority is positioned against an otherwise inferior immoral society.

Kavanagh was intrigued by the events and circumstances of unfulfilled love, which, in the case of Mademoiselle Aïssé and Mademoiselle de Lespinasse, had tragic consequences. Mademoiselle de Launay was to experience disappointment at an early age by the infidelities of her lover.

Kavanagh relates that, while in the Bastille, Mademoiselle de Launay entered into a flirtatious correspondence with another prisoner, the Chevalier de Ménil, a young man who had been indirectly implicated in the Cellamare Conspiracy. However, the liaison proved to be short-lived for Mademoiselle when, on his release, the Chevalier married another. In this instance Kavanagh concludes that the relationship was based more on fantasy than fact:

> Though Mademoiselle de Launay's love for the chevalier appears to have been very sincere, the letters in which it is expressed do not convey the impression of a deep or fervent affection. The style is invariably cold, precise, and elegant, and, notwithstanding the occasional tenderness of the sentiments, it is difficult not to think with the Chevalier de Ménil, that the feelings of the writer resided chiefly in her brain. (I: 54)

Given the fact that Mademoiselle de Launay's written style had no appeal for Kavanagh, it is her opinion that it was the very nature of 'romance' itself that sustained Mademoiselle de Launay to endure the long months in the Bastille.

By contrast, Kavanagh's reading of the history of Mademoiselle Aïssé may have appealed more to her sense of moral values. This particular story reads like a French romantic novel in which, she reports, two lovers are at odds with the 'heartlessness of the world around them' (I: 75). Kavanagh introduces Aïssé as the young woman who, in time, was to become an alternative attraction at the residence of her protector, Madame de Ferriol, a woman who, though handsome like her more celebrated sister, Madame de Tencin, unfortunately lacked her subtlety and wit. Married at an early age to an indifferent husband, Madame de Ferriol embarked on a long and open liaison with the socially influential Maréchal d'Uxilles. This connection suited her ambitious nature and gave her a social power with which, as long as the Maréchal remained constant, she was able to play host to all those who required some favour or other. Visitors came from 'every class and party' including the young Madame du Deffand, Madame de Parabère and even the Englishman Bolingbroke when he visited Paris. However, Kavanagh notes that, as she grew older, Madame de Ferriol's faded charms held less attraction for the Maréchal and, without his patronage, her social world would have taken on a different character had it not been for the attractions of her young ward, the exquisitely beautiful young woman, Aïssé.

To the modern reader the history of Aïssé reads more like fiction than fact but sufficient written evidence exists to verify its truth. Said to be the daughter of a Circassian prince, Aïssé was about four years of age when in 1698 she was bought from a Turkish slave market for 1500 livres by

Madame de Ferriol's brother-in-law, a diplomat travelling in that country. Kavanagh informs us that the practice of purchasing beautiful female slaves was not a new venture for M. de Ferriol. On a previous occasion he had returned to France with two of them, one for himself and one who so enchanted his friend the Comte de Nogent that he made her his wife.[37] Leaving Aïssé in the care of Madame de Ferriol, M. de Ferriol then returned to Constantinople to resume his ambassadorial duties. Aïssé was accepted in the household where, to all accounts she was treated kindly, brought up on an equal footing with Madame de Ferriol's two sons, D'Argental and Pent-de Veyle, and introduced into French society, where she attracted much attention. In 1711 when Aïssé was seventeen, M. de Ferriol, then aged seventy, returned to France to claim his purchase as his own. It was only through the intervention of her adopted brother, D'Argental, who persuaded his uncle of the inappropriateness of the match, that Aïssé escaped the old man's carnal intentions; after which, it appears, he treated her as an affectionate daughter.

Aïssé's beauty was such, however, that amongst her many admirers she attracted the uninvited attentions of the Prince Regent himself, thereafter shocking society by her refusal to become his mistress. Madame de Ferriol, whom Kavanagh deems as profligate as any of the guests she entertained, was deeply concerned by this refusal as she saw the union as a means of progressing her own social ambitions. However, Kavanagh's applause of the young woman's decision is loudly heard in her comment: 'Unlike the noble and freeborn ladies of France, the Circassian slave, bought in the market of Constantinople, inexorably refused to sell herself for gold or power' (I: 78). As ever, Kavanagh here also seizes the opportunity to contrast unprecedented virtue with the mercenary and self-seeking opportunism that proliferated in the ranks of French aristocratic society.

Defiant in her resolve not to compromise her virtue, Aïssé was, nevertheless, conquered by love and it is this part of the story that fully engages Kavanagh's imagination. Whilst on a visit to Madame du Deffand, with whom she was acquainted through Madame de Ferriol, Aïssé met and fell in love with a young Knight of Malta, the Chevalier d'Aydie. Unfortunately there were obstacles to their union; it mattered little that he was poor, but several years before their meeting, and in accordance with the dictates of his military order, the Knights of St John, he had taken a vow of celibacy. Aïssé found herself caught in an internal struggle between virtue and passion, the outcome of which, according to Kavanagh, was determined by the society into which she was placed. It was inevitable that, in time, Aïssé's love for her chevalier was such that passion proved stronger than virtue and she secretly gave birth to a daughter.[38] Such was the strength of his love that the Chevalier offered to procure a dispensation from the Pope so that they could marry. However, Aïssé refused as she believed that the origins of her birth and the prejudices of the age would only degrade such a union.[39] Although the ensuing years only strengthened their affection, her sense of sin was such that her health suffered and she became very weak. Finally, overcome with a sense of shame and repentance, against the wishes of Madame de Ferriol, who wished to maintain the secrecy of the affair, she sought the services of a priest and in her final days found solace in confession. After her death in 1733, Kavanagh writes that the Chevalier took care of their child but was to spend the rest of his life grieving for Aïssé, who remained his only true love.

Much of Kavanagh's information is taken from letters written by Mademoiselle Aïssé and one Madame Calandrini, who was both Aïssé's friend and her spiritual mentor. Kavanagh introduces Madame Calandrini as 'a lady of much piety and virtue, residing at Geneva, and who had endeavoured to awaken Aïssé to a sense of her error' (I: 80). However, sources reveal that there is some discrepancy as to the authenticity of these letters. Thirty-three letters were written over a period of seven years and were first published in 1787 along with notes by Voltaire and a highly sentimental biography which, Judith Curtis suggests, 'contributed at least as much as the letters to the enduring legend'.[40] The publication of faked correspondence during the late eighteenth and early nineteenth centuries has been a cause for concern for historians and, although the authenticity of Madame Calandrini's letters was challenged when they were first published in 1787, Kavanagh does not allude to this fact. It appears that she has cited extracts only from letters that supported her own perspective on Aïssé insofar as Aïssé very much reflected the type of heroine found in French Romance, a genre with which, Kavanagh, of course, was familiar.[41] Moreover, she has focused on those letters that appropriate her own reading of Aïssé's battle between passion and duty: a dilemma, it has been suggested, that enabled Madame Calandrini to manipulate the young woman's sense of guilt.[42] It seems that Kavanagh had picked up on the dynamics of the relationship between Aïssé and her religious mentor and noted that this was also the cause of much anguish for Aïssé's young lover. She states, 'The Chevalier d'Aydie had been well aware of Madame Calandrini's efforts to reclaim his mistress. He never sought to oppose that lady's influence, but in the most touching terms he besought Aïssé not to deprive him of her love' (I: 82). In foregrounding the plight of the lovers, Kavanagh attributes Aïssé's dilemma of conscience to the profligacy of the age, which, she contends, distorted the boundaries of love and innocence. She rounds off the correspondence by citing a section from Aïssé's final letter to Madame Calandrini, which outlines her unhappiness and leaves her longing for death:

> The life I have led has been very wretched. Have I ever had an instant's joy? I could never be with myself. I dreaded to think. Remorse never abandoned me from the time that I opened my eyes to the extent of my errors. Why, then, should I dread the separation of my soul, since I feel convinced that God is all goodness, and that my real happiness shall date from the moment when I leave this miserable body? (I: 84)

Above all, for Kavanagh, it was the sense of spiritual 'purity' which exemplified this young woman's character against a background of 'shameless licence' that she wished to convey in her sketch. She saw Aïssé as one who had the potential for power, if the social mores of the time had allowed: 'Her power was limited; but within its sphere it was a severe, and – strange as it may seem – a moral power' (I: 84). Given the nature of Kavanagh's love of Romance and her interest in exemplary women, it is not difficult to see why she was attracted to this story; she saw in Aïssé a woman of independent mind and a moral template for the perfect heroine.

Of all the women in her study, Mademoiselle de Lespinasse was probably the one who Kavanagh most admired. She saw Julie de Lespinasse as the culmination of all that was noble in humanity and one of the many who were trapped in a society at odds with their natural selves. As she states, Mademoiselle de Lespinasse was, 'one of the vast multitude who, though surrounded and contaminated by the sceptical and corrupting influences of the eighteenth century, had yet in them the germ of a nobler nature, and yearned for a purer and freer air than the heated and artificial atmosphere they breathed' (I: 192). Kavanagh's perspective on Julie de Lespinasse suggests that she perceived her as one who, notwithstanding the corrupting influences of the period, was more in touch with her own sense of reality. In this particular instance Kavanagh is somewhat protective of her subject, which explains her own fascination for this woman who, to all accounts, spent her life in a constant state of emotional turmoil.

Born in Lyon, the illegitimate child of the Comtesse d'Albon, Julie was brought up as the daughter of one Claude de Lespinasse and spent her early years in a convent near to her mother's home. On coming of age she was later obliged to live as a poor dependant in her mother's household and act as a governess to her legitimate half-sister's children. Without the same privilege of recognition, Julie's situation was one of precarious social imbalance; having been made aware of her real origins her predicament was doubly humiliating. As Kavanagh notes, since she was illegiti-mate, her mother could show her due affection only in private.[43] Moreover, Julie's half-sister was married to Gaspard de Vichy, Comte de Champrond, who, evidence suggests, was Julie's real father. Kavanagh makes no reference to this possibility but, as the Marquis de Ségur,[44] one of Kavanagh's sources, had presented evidence for this conclusion, it is unlikely that she was not aware of the situation. Julie was, in fact, the child of her half-sister's husband. To complicate matters further, with this marriage, Julie's mother also became Julie's father's mother-in-law. It has been suggested that the Vichys wanted to keep Julie under their roof in order to contain her movements. It appears that their intentions were twofold: they wished to prevent the possibility of a public scandal con-cerning Julie's origins and also to stop her from making a claim to an inheritance to which she may have been entitled. However, Julie received no money in this respect. To all accounts, apart from the annual income of 300 livres she received as governess, she was penniless.[45] On her mother's death, Kavanagh notes that the proofs of Julie's birth, along with a large sum of money set aside for her, had been 'basely wrested' away by her relatives. Without the singular affection of her mother, her only real source of comfort, Julie's unhappiness in the Vichy household increased daily.

Gaspard de Vichy, Julie's biological father, was also the brother of the celebrated *femme d'esprit*, Madame du Deffand (which, technically, would make her Julie's aunt). Impressed by the younger woman's intel-ligent and affectionate personality and touched by her unhappy situa-tion, Madame du Deffand eventually procured Julie away from the Vichys to reside with her in Paris as her *demoiselle de compagnie*. It is interesting that letters between Madame du Deffand and Julie reveal that, owing to the perfidious nature of Julie's position in the Vichy house-hold, Madame du Deffand, along with the assistance of a number of friends, took two years to manipulate the circumstances suitable for Julie's release.[46] Finally, in April 1754 when Julie was twenty-four years of age, she moved to Paris.[47]

As Madame du Deffand's companion, Julie's life was, at first, a mixed blessing. She resided in the Convent of St Joseph, in a small apartment next to Madame's, an arrangement that suited both women and lasted for approximately ten years. During this period the elderly, and now almost totally blind, Madame du Deffand received some of the most celebrated men and women in France who, in turn, were intrigued by her younger companion. Julie became acquainted with many distinguished people, including the illegitimate son of Madame de Tencin, Jean Le Rond d'Alembert. Sensitive to Julie's own burden of illegitimacy, D'Alembert found in her a kindred spirit and became her closest friend. However, towards the end of the ten-year period, Julie's relationship with Madame du Deffand had deteriorated and in 1764 they went their separate ways. The relationship between the two women has been much alluded to in relevant studies[48] and, although Kavanagh's account is relatively brief, again she concentrates only on those areas that suit her purpose. Relating to the daily pattern of life at St Joseph, Kavanagh states:

> The cold and selfish Madame du Deffand treated her young dependant with little kindness. She made her sleep, like her, during the day-time, and sit up all night, in order to read aloud to her. This unnatural mode of life completely destroyed the health of Mademoiselle de Lespinasse. [. . .] The loneliness and suffering which embittered her early youth seemed to have added only new intensity to the natural fervour of her feelings. (I: 178)

Notwithstanding the nature of her discomfort, however, Julie, who had neither beauty nor rank, was compensated by the friendship and admiration she received from those guests who frequented Madame du Deffand's salon. Such was Julie's charm that before long certain members of this select group, wishing to engage in Mademoiselle's company without the restraining presence of Madame du Deffand, took to visiting Julie for an hour in her own room prior to calling on her mistress. When Madame du Deffand discovered the arrangement, she was furious, accusing Julie of the 'blackest treachery' and threatening her with immediate dismissal. As a result, Kavanagh reports, Julie took laudanum but 'Timely remedies saved her from the consequences of this rash act' (I: 179). With the help of influential friends, who were able to provide her with her own apartment and procure her a modest pension, Julie acquired a new independence. She was now able to receive visitors without recrimination including some who, forced by Madame du Deffand to choose between the two, abandoned this great lady in favour of her former companion. The uninhibited intellectual stimulation that Julie derived from her guests prompted her to engage fully in the political and economic discourse of the day, as Kavanagh records:

> Ideas of reform and the doctrines of political economy were then beginning to agitate and divide French society; Mademoiselle de Lespinasse sided with the economists and philosophic reformers. Turgot, the future minister of state; the bitter Morellet who expounded his theories, and whom Voltaire aptly called Mord-les (bite-them), Diderot, D'Alembert, Marmontel, Chastellux, and Saint-Lambert, were her constant guests; they made her house the central point whence they disseminated their doctrines in financial, political and literary matters. (I: 181–2)

However, it is interesting that Kavanagh makes no reference to the fact that, owing to Mademoiselle de Lespinasse's own engagement with intellectual discussion, her salon became known as the 'laboratory of the Encyclopédie' out of which stemmed her reputation as the 'Muse of the Encyclopédie'.[49]

The loss of D'Alembert in particular embittered Madame du Deffand against Julie even more, as Kavanagh states:

> D'Alembert was one of the few individuals who had the power of banishing Madame du Deffand's ennui: his unaffected manners, the calm and dispassionate turn of his mind, and the engaging mirth and frankness which distinguished him, were all extremely agreeable to her: the loss of his society accordingly embittered her still more against her former companion, of whom she always spoke with the strongest animosity. (I: 180)

Kavanagh's account suggests that Madame du Deffand had few feelings of genuine regard for her young companion and treated her merely to suit her own convenience. While this may be the case in the long term, it is not the whole story.[50] As already mentioned, Kavanagh has chosen her sources to suit her own purpose which, it seems, was to present Julie as the fascinating, if overtly sensitive, heroine who was rescued from the selfish machinations of a cold-hearted woman. It appears that Kavanagh's main source for this part of her sketch is Marmontel, who had described Madame du Deffand as 'an intelligent woman full of caprice and malice',[51] and who, according to one modern critic, Benedetta Craveri, gives a 'partisan and oversimplified' account of Julie's life with Madame du Deffand. Craveri suggests that 'The conflict between the two women developed gradually and the outcome of it was complex. Above all, it could not be reduced to a simple tale of oppression'.[52] Kavanagh may have chosen not to question Marmontel's account of the relationship because of her own bias towards Julie and, arguably, because Madame du Deffand, who featured high as one of Kavanagh's 'profligates', gave Kavanagh licence to place Julie on a higher moral plateau. In her account of the split between the two women Kavanagh reports only that Madame du Deffand was enraged. She focuses more on the now homeless Julie, who, she states, 'seeing herself thrown upon the world without a home or the means of procuring one, was driven to despair [. . .] she swallowed a dose of laudanum' (I: 179). However, evidence suggests that rather than it being the direct result of Madame du Deffand's dismissal of Julie, as Kavanagh implies, the laudanum episode may have occurred earlier. During her first months with Madame du Deffand, Julie had formed a relationship with an Irishman, John Taaffe, an aristocratic adventurer who had moved from Ireland to

Paris.[53] On 19 June 1756 Madame du Deffand wrote to Taaffe asking him to declare his intentions towards Julie. The letter, which had been shown to Julie and written with her consent, also suggests that at this time Madame du Deffand's feelings towards her were maternal and her motive for writing was to safeguard Julie's reputation. She writes:

> The friendship I have for her is so tender and so sincere, the fear of losing her is so great that there is nothing that I would not do to keep her. Here then, monsieur, is what I propose; it is that you profit from your absence to examine your feelings carefully and to decide what you will do in consequence. If your passion for her is stronger than . . . [sic] you make haste to reassure both her and me that your intentions are both honest and legitimate. If they are not so, do all you can to detach her from you. You owe it to her happiness and to the consideration which I have a right to demand of you.
>   [. . .] I bear her the love of a mother; you should not be surprised if I also have the language, the behaviour and the firmness of a mother.[54]

Taaffe's response was to disengage himself from Julie while still hoping to retain the friendship of Madame du Deffand. In her disappointment Julie is reported to have become hysterical. La Harpe (who is not listed as one of Kavanagh's sources) gives a description of Julie's state of mind at the time, which, he reports, led to her taking an overdose of opium. Whether her action was the consequence of Taaffe's decision is open to question.[55] Warren Hunting Smith seems to suggest that Julie had already taken the opium before Taaffe's letter (dated 1 July 1756)[56] had arrived.[57] As Craveri points out, although La Harpe does not significantly relate Julie's crisis specifically to the episode with Taaffe, he reports:

> Her already lively mind became so excited that she wished to poison herself. She took sixty grains of opium, which did not bring about the death she desired, but gave her appalling convulsions which left a permanent mark on her nerves. Madame du Deffand dissolved into bitter tears at her bedside: 'It is too late now, Madame,' said Mademoiselle de Lespinasse who thought she would not recover.[58]

Kavanagh gives no mention of either Taaffe or Madame du Deffand's tears. She attributes Julie's overdose and her reply, 'Madame, it is too late', solely to Madame's 'cold and insincere expressions of regret' (I:179). It seems then that Kavanagh is either genuinely confused about this episode or she has misinterpreted her sources. In any event it appears that she is skipping over certain details that might otherwise reveal her heroine in a different light from that which she wished to convey.

Kavanagh chose to ignore the more emotionally volatile aspects of Mademoiselle de Lespinasse's character in favour of those positive traits. Throughout her sketch Kavanagh has a tendency to romanticize her heroine's suffering.[59] It could be argued that, historically, her aim was to protect Mademoiselle de Lespinasse from negative exposure and present her as a woman whose search for genuine love and acceptance was at odds with the world around her. As a biographer, it is evident that the then twenty-six-year-old Kavanagh was drawn by the magnet of Mademoiselle de Lespinasse's legendary charm and was herself enchanted by this woman's vivacity and ability to enchant others, as she says:

> Mademoiselle de Lespinasse was perhaps one of the most fascinating women of her day. [. . .] Her power was not merely intellectual: it sprang less from the activity of her mind than from the depth and fervour of her feelings. This very fervour seemed to say that she was not formed for happiness: she was too ardent and excitable for this calm state of mind. Secluded from affection during her unhappy youth, her whole soul, on regaining its freedom, gave itself up, not to ordinary love, but to a bewildering and intoxicating passion never meant for earth. It was this inward fire which, whilst it consumed her frail being, gave her so deep a charm, and imparted to her language a passion and eloquence rarely surpassed. (I: 182–3)

The romantic pedestal upon which Kavanagh places Mademoiselle de Lespinasse suggests that her sense of empathy with her subject is also drawn from her novelist's imagination. Like several of the heroines in Kavanagh's own novels, Julie de Lespinasse possessed that inexplicable essence of inner beauty that Kavanagh found so alluring.

There are echoes of Mademoiselle de Launay's earlier experience in Mademoiselle de Lespinasse's life: their illegitimate status and their relations with high-born women; their intelligence and ability to engage others and their disappointments in love. However, Kavanagh shows the greater sympathy for Mademoiselle de Lespinasse. To her contemporaries Mademoiselle de Lespinasse was volatile and unstable but Kavanagh is infatuated by the complexity of her emotions and turns them into a virtue:

> Indifference was a feeling unknown to her: she either revelled in enthusiastic bliss, or she was overwhelmed with despair. A calm and even state of mind was insupportable to her; and, fatal as it proved to her peace of mind, it was perhaps this perpetual mobility of feeling and impressions which rendered her presence so deeply attractive. (I: 184)

Above all Kavanagh saw Mademoiselle de Lespinasse as a romantic, one for whom life without passion was non-life. The psychological affect of her circumstances was such that her life was characterised by her unstable emotions, a predicament for which she found solace in opiates. Her life was also dominated by tragic love affairs. After the earlier debacle of

her affair with Taaffe, she became embroiled in two separate love relationships, which were to culminate in grief and unhappiness. The first
was with the Marquis of Mora, a young Spanish noble of delicate health,
whose family disapproved of his choice of love because of her lack of
wealth and rank. Subsequently, the Marquis was called back to Spain
where, by way of convalescence, he languished for three years before a
means was put in place to enable him to return to Paris to be with Julie.
Unfortunately, the journey proved too much for the physically frail
Marquis and he died at Bordeaux before the union was realised. Julie's
grief was such that she soon became extremely ill. Although it was regret
for her lover that was thought to be the cause of her decline, Kavanagh
reports that this was not the reason. During the Marquis's absence, Julie
had secretly fallen irretrievably in love with another man, the charming
and socially successful Count of Guibert, who, after the initial novelty of
their relationship had wavered, treated Julie with a callous indifference.
According to Kavanagh, his success lay mainly in his ability to charm
through his gift of conversation and for Mademoiselle de Lespinasse, 'the
universal fascination which he exercised became, in her ardent soul, a
deeper feeling' (I: 186). However, it soon became clear to Julie that all he
wanted from her was friendship, a situation unbearable to her. Their
altercations of feelings were to last for several years until Guibert's marriage to another was too much for Julie to bear, upon which she soon
wasted away and died. Although Kavanagh does not give the cause of
death, which was tuberculosis, she focuses on Julie's heart-broken grief
as a result of Guibert's rejection. Her reading of Julie's correspondence
to Guibert emphasises the contrition and sense of remorse Julie felt for
her betrayal of the young Marquis, the man who had returned her love,
and the contradictions of passion she felt for Guibert, the man who
rejected her. It was this love that Mademoiselle de Lespinasse wished to
take with her to her grave, but, as Kavanagh points out, had she been
happy and beloved, her name would now be scarcely known.

The biographical histories of Mademoiselle de Launay, Mademoiselle
Aïssé and Mademoiselle de Lespinasse appealed to both Kavanagh's
romantic imagination and her sense of social propriety. The tragic circumstances of the heroine without a pedigree caught in a world which
sets wealth and rank above all else reflects her own sensibilities of social
injustice, a theme which is consistently explored in her own novels.

Madame du Châtelet

Kavanagh's sketch of the Marquise du Châtelet is devoid of the romantic connotations she associates with the above three women. She depicts

Madame du Châtelet as a woman of independent mind who cared little for the opinion of others and followed her own inclination for scientific interest.

> The good qualities of Madame du Châtelet consisted more in a certain haughty independence of mind, in an untiring affection for those whom she loved, than in any very amiable traits. She was deficient in gentleness and in many of the most winning qualities of woman, but there was neverthe- less in her so little affectation and intrigue, and so much of what was good and true, as to command respect at an epoch when other women, possess- ing her position in life and her great mental acquirements, would not have rested satisfied until they had made France and all Europe echo with their praises. (I: 128)

Born in December 1706 into an aristocratic family, Emilie Gabrielle de Breteuil was fortunate in that she received a classical education superior to most women of her rank. She had a knowledge of several languages including Latin, Italian and English, as well as an interest in mathemat- ics. She soon developed an interest in metaphysics and the natural sci- ences, which led her to publish several short pieces on these subjects.[60] However, her ambitions for scientific advancement were restricted. Like those of others in her position, Madame du Châtelet's life was circum- scribed by gender. Women were not admitted to the academic institutions where most of the scientific debates took place and so were obliged to seek out scientific contact via a more personal route, relying on individ- uals, usually men, with similar interests. Kavanagh's respect for Madame du Châtelet's interests in science and her scholarly achievements is evident in her account of this woman's life. While she could not condone Madame du Châtelet's extra-marital relations – she mentions both Richelieu and Saint-Lambert[61] in this context – she does acknowledge that Madame du Châtelet was merely acting in accordance with the con- vention of the day. On Madame du Châtelet's long-acclaimed relation- ship with Voltaire, Kavanagh limits her discussion to the effect that their friendship was the result of a mutual interest in Newton.

Married in 1725 at the age of nineteen to the much older Marquis du Châtelet, Emilie was to see little of her husband who, being a military man, spent most of his time with his regiment. During this time and with the consent of the Marquis himself, who had no objection to accommo- dating his distinguished guest, Voltaire took up residence at Cirey, the Marquis's estate in Lorraine.[62] It was here that he and Emilie spent fifteen very happy years engaging their mutual philosophical and scientific inter- ests and generally enjoying each other's company. Kavanagh notes that, in order to preserve appearances, the pretence of a platonic friendship was, indeed, a cover for a more intimate relationship. Such was Voltaire's part in this cover-up that his protestations were loudly expressed in his confession that his Emilie '"is tyrannical: one must talk about metaphysics when the temptation is to talk of love. Ovid was formerly my master, it is now the turn of Locke"' (I: 126). Madame du Châtelet's love of science was also the cause of much envy, particularly from Madame du Deffand and Madame de Staal. Madame du Châtelet was herself conscious of her high rank and status and Kavanagh reports that 'She treated her inferiors with a cold superciliousness, that shewed she fully felt their vast distance from herself' (I: 128). Madame de Staal's response to Madame du Châtelet's scientific pursuits was one of ridicule and Madame du Deffand accused her of seeking out a superiority over her sex.[63]

Along with her subject's interest in scientific knowledge, Kavanagh turns her attentions to Madame du Châtelet's love of pleasure and her 'excessive love of dress' which, she reports, 'often led her into serious expenses'. However, it was her equally serious love of gambling and the large sums of money lost at play – losing on one night no less than 80,000 livres at Versailles – that dented her finances. On hearing about the debt, Voltaire, attributing her loss to cheats, was immediately pursued by those he had insulted and was forced to take refuge at Sceaux. For six weeks his whereabouts were known only to Madame du Maine with whom he met, secretly, each night for supper. It was not long before Voltaire was accepted into society but only after Madame du Châtelet had managed to appease the insulted players by paying her debt and pacifying their indignation against the accuser. Kavanagh also gives some indication of the couple's impact on society and how they were received. While she proffers some doubt on the trustworthiness of Madame de Staal, Kavanagh refers to her account of the couple's cool reception at Sceaux in 1747: 'If we may trust the petulant effusions of the ennuyée Madame de Staal to her friend Madame du Deffand, the learned pair were little appreciated by the society of Sceaux, on this visit, as well as on the subsequent ones they paid to Madame du Maine' (I: 133). The couple's relationship was also the subject of much speculation and, as Kavanagh contends, it was Madame de Staal who had 'pithily observed, "She is the mistress; and he is the slave"' (I: 134). However, in time, his passions tempered into friendship, as Kavanagh says, 'Long as the love of Voltaire and Madame du Châtelet had lasted, it was not destined to resist time and habit' (I: 135).[64] This change from love and passion to deep friendship, though initiated by Voltaire, did not prevent him from feelings of jealousy towards Madame du Châtelet's admirers, particularly Saint-Lambert, whose friendship was, as Kavanagh records, 'destined to prove so fatal to her' (I: 136). Kavanagh's obvious distaste for this period in Madame du Châtelet's life is expressed in the brevity of detail she offers in relation to her death. After a stay at the 'polished and elegant little court' at Lunéville (in Lorraine), where Madame du Châtelet was introduced to Saint-Lambert, she returned to Cirey, pregnant with his child, to finish her translation of Newton's *Principia*. Now in the throes of an unshakable despondency, she went back to Lunéville where, Kavanagh reports, 'her health, which had been failing for some time, became worse, and on the 10 August 1749, she died in childbed, after a few days of brief illness' (I: 136). Voltaire's grief was such that, in a letter to D'Argental, he declared, '"It is not a mistress that I have lost: I have lost half of my being – a soul for which mine was made"' (I: 137). The friendship between Madame du Châtelet and Voltaire was unique in that they openly shared their intellectual interests at a time when it was considered unfeminine for women to openly engage in the sciences. Nevertheless, Madame du Châtelet was the epiphany of a new, more unselfconsciously active woman who cared little about gender prejudice. To this effect Voltaire attributed to her the status of 'honorary male' when he referred to her as '"that lady whom I look upon as a great man. [. . .] She understands Newton, she despises superstition and in short, she makes me happy."'[65] Madame du Châtelet's relationship with Voltaire was built on mutual respect and it is now considered that, without Madame du Châtelet's involvement, Voltaire would not have been able to complete his *Eléments de la philosophie de Newton*.[66]

Kavanagh argues that the relationship between Madame du Châtelet and Voltaire caused Madame de Staal and Madame du Deffand to rally against her, later exposing their resentment in bitter outpourings against the dead woman. She states, 'There is something literally revolting in the brutality with which the errors of Madame du Châtelet were attacked' (I: 137). Madame du Deffand circulated a portrait she had written of Madame du Châtelet in which 'her person and life were equally villified' (I: 137). Kavanagh's indignation at this distasteful gesture is expressed in her comparison of the two women. Without condoning Madame du Châtelet's conduct, she argues that, because of the extent of their practised profligacy, her attackers are the greater sinners:

> She was frail, when they were profligate: she yielded to passion, when they gave themselves up to licentiousness. The real cause why Madame du Châtelet's memory was treated with so much bitterness was her great superiority to most of the women with whom she associated. [. . .] It was this, and to have fascinated such a man as Voltaire, that could not be, and was not, forgiven. (I: 137–8)

Kavanagh rationalises her inclusion of Madame du Châtelet on the grounds that, notwithstanding her critics, she was a 'favourable and appropriate illustration of her class' (I: 139). She also considers her important for the part she played in introducing all things English to the French, in her view, an influence 'not to be slighted' (I: 140). In concluding her section on Madame du Châtelet, it is Kavanagh's judgement that it was her diligence and interest in science, rather than the lasting value of her works themselves, that will be 'long and gratefully' remembered.

Madame d'Epinay

In her sketches of women it is clear that Kavanagh engaged her interests with some more than others. It is against the background of philosophical and religious debate and the *bureaux d'esprits* that she introduces Madame d'Epinay. While she was of the opinion that Madame d'Epinay was neither very clever nor handsome, Kavanagh sees her as an attractive woman who was accepted less for her originality of wit than for her free and natural nature. It was, she suggests, this very characteristic that encouraged Madame d'Epinay's distinguished guests to shake off their 'philosophical armour', thus creating a more relaxed and comforting atmosphere while in her company. Nevertheless, other than a brief mention of her early relationship with her patron, M. de Francoeil, and her acquaintance with Grimm and, later, Rousseau, Kavanagh gives very little space to Madame d'Epinay. She attributes any historical recognition she may have acquired to her association with Rousseau and her relevance as a writer on education only significant when unfavourably compared to Madame de Genlis. In fact, it was much to the chagrin of Madame de Genlis that the Academy sought fit to bestow the Montyon prize not on one of her own works but on Madame d'Epinay's *Conversations d'Emilie*.[67] Married to a profligate but very wealthy man, Madame d'Epinay was one whose social position rendered her independent of the opinion of others and gave her a freedom not normally afforded to ladies of a higher rank. The impression Kavanagh offers of this 'less important' woman in her study is that of one who seemed to engage readily in the intellectual circles of her day, without necessarily proffering much other than her easy charm.

The bureaux d'esprits

Throughout this section of her text Kavanagh discusses the importance of the salons in the context of women's influence and male ambition, identifying the three most celebrated as those hosted by Madame du Deffand, Mademoiselle de Lespinasse and Madame Geoffrin. She had already referred to the fact that the 'clever and unprincipled' Madame de Tencin, otherwise known as 'that *queen of beaux-esprits*', had hosted 'one of the earliest and most celebrated bureaux of the eighteenth century' and it was 'Under the superintendence of a cold, worldly woman, the germ of the future encyclopaedists was being slowly but surely developed' (I: 97). Political change rendered women's 'interference unavoidable' and, as Kavanagh notes, 'Madame de Tencin was well aware of the power of her sex. Her advice to Marmontel on his conduct in the world, was, above all things, to secure the friendship of women. It is, indeed, certain that without their aid nothing could have been done in France for freedom' (I: 99). However, concerned by the increasing distance between religion and philosophical ideas, Kavanagh was instinctively sceptical of the Encyclopaedists. In a short chapter on the developments of change in the eighteenth century she states, 'Philosophy, which had previously been linked with religion now became its irreconcilable foe. Ideas replaced creeds and doctrines' (I: 142). She saw the *bureaux d'esprits* as artificial, superficial gatherings only, claiming that solitary contemplation was the way to genuine philosophical thought. To this end she engages much of her commentary in two separate chapters given to two of the more celebrated *salonières*, Madame du Deffand and Madame Geoffrin, who, she reports, were rivals locked in enmity.

While she appreciates the significance of Madame du Deffand as 'a brilliant and Epicurean woman of the world' (I: 195), Kavanagh's sympathies lie more with the equally wealthy, but considerably less brilliant, Madame Geoffrin, 'the quiet and prudent bourgeoise, who wished to reconcile her religious feelings with the patronage of professed sceptics' (I: 164). She speaks extensively of Madame Geoffrin's benevolence and the friends and acquaintances she gathered around her. Her generosity to the Encyclopaedists gained her the reputation of foster-mother of the philosophers,[68] whilst the endearment of 'mother' was conferred upon her by another recipient of her salutary altruism, her great friend Stanislaus Poniatowski (Stanislaus I of Poland).[69] Kavanagh informs us that, on being crowned, one of his first acts was to write to Madame Geoffrin, simply stating, '"Mamma, your son is king"' (I: 201). His allegiance to Madame Geoffrin stems from his gratitude for the kindness shown to him when he required it most. Kavanagh does not give any dates but tells us that, owing to his extravagance while in France, Stanislaus was imprisoned in Fort l'Evêque for debt and released only after Madame Geoffrin had paid his creditors. Subsequently he invited Madame Geoffrin, now a well-travelled woman in her seventies, to visit him in Poland where she was received with distinguished honours.

In 1780, the year of Madame du Deffand's death, Kavanagh states that 'The times were altered, [. . .] the philosophic power had progressed, and no longer sought the patronage of narrow circles; it had become the spirit of the whole nation' (I: 174).[70] However, she declares that it was with the death of Madame Geoffrin in 1777 that France was to see the closure of that particular class of *bureaux d'esprits* and she asks what influence did these assemblies have during the eighteenth century? Each salon was determined by the style and *gravitas* of the company assembled and such influence depended greatly on the individual characters of the women who hosted them. She attributes the success of the salons to the polish and elegance of these women while also recognising their limitations. Whilst acknowledging that the salons allowed for open discussion, she is unconvinced about their genuine significance as centres of philosophical debate and it is with a hint of satire that she notes:

> Every subject was treated with heartless levity: enthusiasm, serious thought, or generous impulses, were alike proscribed and withered by the cold, worldly spirit which then prevailed. [. . .] At the same time, and with all their defects, these assemblies had a singular power in arousing the intellects, and that vivacity of thought, in itself a very indifferent accomplishment, but which is so often mistaken for a higher faculty. It was to this their awakening power on the mind that Rousseau alluded, when he exclaimed – 'Are you in doubt whether you have or not any genius? go to Paris, and if you have got any you will soon feel it fermenting in your breast.' (I: 204–5)

The demise of the salons as places of productive enquiry and profitable discussion was also equally, if somewhat less passionately, expressed by George Eliot who was of the opinion that, 'although many salons of that period were worthy successors of the Hôtel de Rambouillet, they were simply a recreation, not an influence. [. . .] The *salon* retained its attractions, but its power was gone: the stream of life had become too broad and deep for such small rills to affect it.'[71] For Kavanagh, the salons had become merely fashionable drawing rooms of entertainment, places where people gathered as a means of staving off the enemy – ennui.

Madame de Genlis

The decline of the *bureaux d'esprits* measured a change in the direction of women's influence, as Kavanagh argues:

> The golden days when woman ruled arbitrarily over the French social world, were now nearly over [. . .] many women could still, when sufficiently attractive, obtain a considerable share of the dominion which had

at one time been so liberally granted to their sex; but the difference between their former and their actual power was that the latter proved to be essentially personal, and could no longer be exercised through the medium of a coterie. (II: 34)

Charming, multi-talented and enviably musical, the attractive, witty woman of fashion Madame de Genlis slotted easily into this new era. However, as Kavanagh argues, despite the highly moral and useful aim of her most important works, she was not without her critics.[72] Kavanagh introduces her as one who is remembered for her works on education, but she is more intrigued by her clever use of personal influence during the early reign of Louis XVI. However, as with Madame de Staël, it is not until the publication of *French Women of Letters* that she gives a fuller account of Madame de Genlis's life and works.

Like Mademoiselle de Launay and Mademoiselle de Lespinasse, Madame de Genlis was also one of those higher-ranking women who fell hostage to fortune. Born into a noble but impoverished family, she made her first appearance in Parisian society as Mademoiselle Stephanie de Saint-Aubin. While her father was compelled to leave France due to 'pecuniary distress,' she, still a young child, remained in Paris with her handsome and charismatic mother. Mother and daughter soon won the favour of the rich financier M. de la Popelinière who, at the age of sixty-six, lamented the fact that marriage to the then thirteen-year-old Stephanie was out of the question. However, Mademoiselle, as Kavanagh puts it, 'soon wormed herself into the favour of her ancient admirer, by an easy, caressing manner, of which her dependent position early taught her the value' (II: 36). M. de la Popelinière was quick to appreciate the potential of his *protégée* and financed her extensive and progressive education, engaging the best of tutors. Amongst her many accomplishments she excelled in music, a talent which brought her both celebrity and reproach. On the death of her benefactor Kavanagh notes that Madame de Saint-Aubin found it necessary to turn her daughter's talents into 'pecuniary advantage'. They were accepted into 'the most fashionable societies' where Stephanie's musical performances proved to be highly remunerative. However, despite her high-ranking origins, recognised by many, a far greater number saw her only as a 'musicale artiste' and patronised her as such. Deliverance from this subordinate position came, as it often did, in the form of marriage. The 'witty and profligate' Comte de Genlis, charmed by the grace and style of letters written to her father and shown to him in confidence by M. de Saint-Aubin, on his return to France met with the young Stephanie who, surpassing all his expectations, married him.

Kavanagh's account of how Madame de Genlis procured the engagement of her aunt, Madame de Montesson, to the old Duc d'Orléans as a means of securing her own status is an intriguing insight into how domestic politics were used for social progression. The marriage finally took place in 1773, after which Madame de Genlis became, by association, connected to the Orléans family via one of the first princes of the royal blood. This advantage served her well as she was able to exploit her position to gain access into the household of the Duc et la Duchesse de Chartres, who, after entrusting the education of their daughters to her care, later appointed her '*gouverneur*' to their sons.[73] Such were her gifts as a teacher and author of educational works that Buffon attributed to her the title 'angel of light' (II: 42). However, while fully endorsing the moral intentions of Madame de Genlis's educational pursuits, Kavanagh is deliberately vague about other aspects of her life. She skims over any references to an illicit relationship with the Duc de Chartres, noting only that 'The very pointed attentions he paid her gave rise to some rumours unheeded by the guileless Duchess of Chartres' (II: 42). Later when the Duc became known as Philippe Egalité, the name given to him by the Commune, Kavanagh remains reticent and she refers only to Madame de Genlis's 'intrigues for his party during the revolution' (II: 35).[74] It is apparent that even within the context of her sketch Kavanagh here has left a significant gap in her account of this woman's life. At the same time, Kavanagh notes that for all her charm and her talents, Madame de Genlis was not the most popular of women. There existed a professional rivalry between her and Madame Necker, who, in Kavanagh's opinion, was a much more 'rigid and pedantic' woman whose mind, she judged, 'was too calm and too well-disciplined for passion' (II: 31). More significantly, there existed a very bitter animosity between her and the young Queen, Marie Antoinette. For example, Kavanagh notes that, on being given an apology by the Duchesse de Chartres on behalf of Madame de Genlis, who was unable to pay the customary visit after the birth of the Queen's first child, 'Marie Antoinette haughtily replied that, although the celebrity of Madame de Genlis might cause her absence from court to be noticed, her rank did not authorise her to send in excuses' (II: 59). Her connection with the Duc de Chartres, who was vehemently disliked by Marie Antoinette, no doubt contributed to the young Queen's acrimony. Kavanagh is of the opinion that, although Madame de Genlis was not generally liked, her position and talents gave her great influence and that Marie Antoinette, who, she says, 'disliked most of the women of her time', would have gained more from cultivating her friendship than from allowing her animosity to dictate her response.[75]

Louis XV's mistresses: Madame de Châteauroux, Madame de Pompadour and Madame du Barry

Given the fact that the pious but plain Marie Lecsinska, wife of Louis XV, was held in such high esteem by Kavanagh – she devotes a chapter to her in *Women of Christianity* (1852)[76] – it is predictable that her general distaste and reluctant acknowledgement of the power held by Louis's mistresses is given short shrift. It is here that Kavanagh engages wholly in her narrative of censure. Her reluctance to endorse these women with any singularly redeeming feature is expressed in her statement:

> However degrading for society it may be to confess it, it is nevertheless true, that, besides the democratic influence of the bureaux d'esprit, there existed another power in French society during the eighteenth century – the power of royal mistresses; exercised, not because they were clever or intelligent women, but because they were the acknowledged favourites of a profligate monarch. (I: 207)

Apart from Madame de Châteauroux, for whom, Kavanagh relates, Louis had genuine affection, it is her belief that the earlier mistresses were nothing more than ambitious opportunists who, in their turn, served only to satisfy the King's desire for novelty. She speaks briefly of Madame de Châteauroux, and her four sisters, 'all fascinating in various respects, and who were destined to act a conspicuous part in the life of Louis XV – four by their profligacy and one by her virtue' (I: 108). The eldest, namely the plain but 'good tempered' Madame de Mailly, was soon ousted by her younger 'ugly' sister, Mademoiselle de Nesle, whose 'brilliant and audacious wit' and 'inexhaustible power of yielding amusement' to an indolent monarch proved a more attractive option. However, Louis's liaison with Mademoiselle de Nesle was short-lived[77] and she, in turn, was succeeded by the more handsome and still younger Madame de la Tournelle, who later became Madame de Châteauroux (1717–44)[78] and was to gain notoriety as the 'Royal Mistress'. Though she was unpopular and frowned upon by the people of France, she was energetic and ambitious and made it her mission to rouse the indolent King from his noticeable indifference to his government – a lethargy judged by Madame de Tencin sufficiently apathetic to prove fatal to France. The Royal Mistress's endeavours were not without their rewards, however, and, though the extent of her political influence has since been questioned, Kavanagh writes that Madame de Châteauroux used her position to yield a significant political influence which did not go unnoticed. At the same time she records that Madame de Lauragais, the fourth sister, was also believed to be romantically involved with the King. It was after the death of Madame de Châteauroux, who had been Louis's mistress for four years, that Richelieu approached Madame de Flavacour, the youngest of the five sisters, in an unsuccessful attempt to procure her as Madame de Châteauroux's successor. However, as Kavanagh notes, although there were many women who coveted such a role, Madame de Flavacour's preference was for a different kind of honour, as her reply to Richelieu suggests, "'I prefer to what you offer me, the esteem of my contemporaries'" (I: 206). Kavanagh mentions Madame de Flavacour specifically to make a point of contrast. As she advances through the line of mistresses, she emphasises that the mere respect of contemporaries was not a foremost consideration of the infamous Madame de Pompadour, whose ambition it was to progress from Louis's mistress to becoming Louis's wife.

Kavanagh was also intrigued by the gains and losses of being a King's mistress. In her view such a contemptible position promised only drudgery and depravation. She saw Madame de Pompadour's relationship with Louis XV as nothing more than a wearisome attachment and a high price to pay for this dubious privilege. Moreover, she makes it clear that she had only the most profound contempt for Madame de Pompadour and refers to her as a 'cold, selfish and ambitious' woman whose sole intention was to govern both Louis and the state. While acknowledging her grace and beauty and her carefully orchestrated education,[79] Kavanagh pays little heed to Madame de Pompadour's patronage of the arts. She briefly endorses her active involvement with the theatre but only as a means of demonstrating her relentless pursuit of finding ways to entertain the King. As she says, 'From the time she became the king's mistress to the epoch of her death, to please and amuse her royal lover was the sole study of her life [. . .] What was such a life but one of endless, degrading slavery' (I: 208–9). In the same breath Kavanagh relates to the fact that, in time, Madame de Pompadour had even made contingency plans for when the King tired of her. As a means of maintaining her position by his side and thus assuring a sense of political power, Kavanagh attributes Madame de Pompadour with the proposition that Louis might gratify his sexual appetite from a source outside of court. To this end Louis rented a little house in the Parc-aux-Cerfs in the town of Versailles for the sole purpose of procuring young virgins with whom he could take his pleasure. In Kavanagh's words:

> [Madame de Pompadour] [. . .] had no sooner secured a firm hold on the king's heart than she resolved to govern the state. Her penetration shewed her that Louis XV might not love her long, but that, if she could render herself necessary to him, her position would nevertheless remain safe. It was for this that she did not scruple to encourage and assist his obscure

intrigues, from which she felt that she had little to fear. The foundation of that infamous establishment where Louis XV kept young girls, whom he had in many instances caused to be forcibly taken from their parents, is even attributed to Madame de Pompadour. From the first she resolved to be not only the king's mistress, but also his prime minister. (I: 209)

In her biography of Madame de Pompadour, Christine Pevitt Algrant raises questions as to who actually instigated such a plan, Madame de Pompadour or Louis himself. In the main she concurs with Kavanagh's reading but her perspective on the situation differs in that she sees Madame de Pompadour as a woman who acts not simply out of political contingency but also out of a desire to hold on to his heart: 'She would tolerate Louis's escapades on the understanding that these girls would be no threat to her. "It is his heart I want! All these little girls with no education will not take it from me. I would not be so calm, if I saw some pretty woman of the court or the capital trying to conquer it."'[80] Kavanagh, of course, saw little romance in their relationship; throughout she presents Madame de Pompadour as an obsessive whose need for power takes precedence over her need for Louis's love.

In Kavanagh's view Madame de Pompadour hastened the ruin of the monarchy while it increased the evils of France. However, although Kavanagh had little sympathy for Louis's mistress, she was even less inclined to recognise the woman who took her place. On the death of Madame de Pompadour, Kavanagh reports that 'a common courtesan was destined to succeed the bourgeoise, and to rule over the court of France' (I: 225). Compared to this unmitigated mistress, she states, Madame de Pompadour was nothing less than 'an immaculate woman'. It is, of course, Madame du Barry, the mistress *en titre* of Louis XV, who was given credit for such a perilous honour. Fascinated by the contrast of her 'Madonna-like beauty' and the 'coarseness of her language', Louis found her irresistible. From Madame de Maintenon, mistress to Louis XIV, to Madame du Barry, Kavanagh considers the succession from high-born ladies to low-born commoner a metaphor for the decline of the French court. As she says, 'Even in the choice of royal mistresses may be traced the descending tendency so characteristic of the times. From the daughters of nobles to the wife of a bourgeoise, and from her again to a woman of the people, the differences were sufficiently striking' (I: 226). As if wishing to distance herself from her subject, she deals briefly with Madame du Barry, focusing on her unpopularity at court, her enmity of Choiseul, Louis's chief minister, and her influence in the suppression of parliament. Such is Kavanagh's distaste for this woman during this period that her scant discussion is drawn to an abrupt end when she relates that, upon the King taking the last rites, a sacrament that dictated that he should renounce his mistress and that she should be removed from court, Madame du Barry was thus forced into retirement in May 1774. However, later on in her discussion, Kavanagh considers it pertinent to draw attention to Madame du Barry's generous conduct towards her old enemy, Marie Antoinette. As a result of the enforced constitutional monarchy in 1791, the difficulties of Louis XVI's position 'had materially increased'; consequently many court privileges were withdrawn and several nobles held Marie Antoinette responsible for her part in events. Kavanagh notes that their conduct towards the Queen was contrasted by that of Madame du Barry who, she records:

> From the commencement of the revolution the ex-mistress of Louis XV. distinguished herself by her zeal in favour of the queen; at whose court she knew, however, that she could never hope to appear. At one period, hearing that the queen was in want of money, she offered her the costly and magnificent diamonds she had received from the late king. The queen thanked her and declined. After the events of the 6th of October,[81] Madame du Barry, at risk of her life, received the wounded gardes du corps who had defended the apartment of Marie Antoinette, and attended them with the utmost devotedness. More affected by this trait than if she had received a personal favour from her former antagonist, Marie Antoinette commissioned one of her friends to go and thank Madame du Barry in her name. (II: 101).

However, Kavanagh balances these heroics with her account of Madame du Barry's lack of courage when Madame du Barry, in turn, faced her own death:

> Of all the women who perished during the Reign of Terror, one only, Madame du Barry, knew not how to die courageously. She was safe in England, assisting the emigrated nobles, when she resolved to return to France to possess herself of the treasures she had hidden at Luciennes; without which she could not continue her generous task. [On finding herself betrayed] she was taken before the tribunal, and condemned. Horror-struck at her fate, she wept bitterly on going to the guillotine, and passionately entreated the people to save her. Heedless of the example and remonstrances of those who were going to die with her, she continued to wring her hands and to bewail her fate; she struggled with the executioner on reaching the scaffold, and filled the whole Place de la Revolution with agonising shrieks (II: 216).

Although Kavanagh protests that while Madame du Barry's tears and lamentations did not save her, it was her shrieks and cries for mercy, rather than the stoic silence of the other victims, that epitomised the butchery of the scaffold.

Marie Antoinette

It is ironic that on first meeting Madame du Barry, the fifteen-year-old Marie Antoinette innocently claimed that she would be her rival for the affection of Louis XV. On the evening of her arrival at the French court, a supper was arranged at the Château de Compiègne where Louis and several court ladies were present, including the 'profligate' Madame du Barry. Kavanagh reports that the youthful Marie Antoinette deeply resented the indignity of supping with a courtesan[82] and merely asked, 'what was the beautiful Madame du Barry's office at court. "To please and amuse the king," was the courtier-like and ambiguous reply. "Then I shall become her rival," answered the dauphiness, with a smile' (II: 6).[83] Kavanagh introduces Marie Antoinette as a gauche young Austrian whose errors in etiquette drew many enemies at the French court. While Louis was still alive, she engaged in an 'unacknowledged struggle' with Madame du Barry, or, as one modern critic suggests, the two women shared a sense of 'barbed neutrality'.[84] Madame du Barry's influence during this time was considerable and the younger Marie Antoinette, already mistrusted by many members of the nobility, must have felt the impact of this strongly, as Kavanagh states:

> Madame du Barry was all powerful during the latter years of Louis XV's reign. Whilst *she* was surrounded by assiduous courtiers, the proud young dauphiness was scarcely allowed to share that general influence of which women are often more jealous than of the substantial realities of power. An unacknowledged struggle was incessantly carried on between the dauphin's wife and the king's mistress. Madame du Barry protected the retrograde party, and Marie Antoinette gave what little power she possessed to the Duke of Choiseul and the philosophers; the very men whose imprudence was preparing the Revolution. (II: 9)

In the aftermath of Louis XV's reign France was in a state of political uncertainty and the young Dauphin and his new wife faced a precarious future. Kavanagh's portrayal of Marie Antoinette as Queen is that of an independent-minded woman who was generally indifferent to the rigours of courtly existence. However, it was her relatively free approach to the rules of etiquette that jarred against the strict formalities of the French court, and her innocent improprieties often resulted in the many calumnies that were to blight her life. As Kavanagh says:

> Her generous nature deceived her with respect to the real worth of popularity. Heedless of the future, she welcomed royalty as a glorious vision, fraught with happiness and joy. Time alone shewed her that even the bright diadem she wore might in the end become a sharp and heavy crown of thorns. (II: 11)

Of course Kavanagh's portrayal embraces the unignorable fact that Marie Antoinette was treated with suspicion because she was an Austrian. It was with an ironic sense of hindsight that during her final days of imprisonment, on observing an attendant superintending her food lest it should contain poison, she is reported to have said: "'Remember [. . .] it is not by poison, but by calumny, that I shall die'" (II: 06). She was disliked immensely by 'Mesdames', Louis's aunts, not simply on the grounds of her nationality but because she came to favour Choiseul, who had been a close friend of Madame de Pompadour and whom they detested. To them, Marie Antoinette was an outsider who had attempted to usurp their influence over her husband. Kavanagh also notes the paradoxical situation of Marie Antoinette's impotence in political matters before the birth of her children. After her children were born she gained confidence and though she presumed to engage with her husband's ministry, it was to her detriment as it was then that the populace began to truly hate her.

With the odds stacked against her in all directions, Marie Antoinette was to find herself the victim of a major fraud known historically as the Diamond Necklace Affair. The 'affair' involved the duping of Cardinal Rohan who, as a means of gaining favour with the Queen, consented in January 1785 to purchase on her behalf a necklace originally commissioned by Louis XV for Madame du Barry and purported to have been worth around 1,800,000 livres. Throughout, Marie Antoinette was kept in complete ignorance of the venture, which came to light only after the necklace had been stolen and taken to England by the other parties involved and Cardinal Rohan was put on trial for his part in the transaction. However, as Kavanagh notes:

> The trial did not only give rise to the most injurious surmises against Marie Antoinette, it inflicted on [the] monarchy a deep irremediable stain. The queen might be pure as snow; but the prestige of royalty had been broken. [. . .] The Parliament acquitted the cardinal; less, it is said, from a belief in his innocence, than from a feeling of animosity against the queen. (II: 68)[85]

The whole business, which, as Kavanagh says, 'brought in contact the names of a profligate cardinal, a noted intriguer, a courtesan, two common sharpers, and the queen of France!' (II: 63), merely exacerbated Marie Antoinette's unpopularity.[86] The scandal of the affair was itself fodder to those who hated her. Malicious and prurient speculations – including the distribution of pornographic caricatures and fantasies – to the detriment of the Queen's reputation were widespread. Kavanagh undoubtedly sympathises with the anguish and suffering that Marie Antoinette was forced to endure as a direct result of these speculations while decorously avoiding any direct reference to them.

Another area in which Kavanagh shows a reluctance to engage is Marie Antoinette's relations with the Swedish-born nobleman Count Axel Fersen, who, along with several others, Kavanagh argues, was himself the subject of calumnies involving the Queen. She claims that, because Marie Antoinette carried friendships to the height of a passion, her affections went beyond her 'sincere and devoted' love for the King which gave courtiers a reason to engage in 'uncharitable thoughts'. 'Calumny', she exhorts:

> successively attributed to the Count of Artois, the Duke of Lauzun, and the Count of Fersen, a share in the favour of the queen. No proofs of her alleged errors have ever been produced. Her favourite attendant, Madame Campan, when pressed on this subject, many years after the death of her royal mistress, confessed that Marie Antoinette had indeed once experienced a deep and unhappy attachment, but averred with solemn energy that this involuntary feeling had ever remained pure and unsullied. (II: 53)

In her biography of Marie Antoinette, Antonia Fraser has gathered a wealth of evidence which suggests that since the summer of 1783 the Queen and Count Fersen had engaged in a lifelong relationship which, over the years, changed from carnal to romantic.[87] Given Kavanagh's own feelings towards the open licentiousness of the period, it is not surprising that she ignored all evidence that might have proved the Queen an adulterer. Moreover, for her to engage in a discussion around Marie Antoinette yielding to feelings of sexual love with a man who was not her husband would not have found a place in her argument. In Kavanagh's view free licence of such a nature was not for queens but for courtesans.

Kavanagh is more interested in the contradictory character of Marie Antoinette as a woman and as a queen who was capable of both great bravery and foolish actions. She gives numerous examples of her politically myopic and ill-timed decisions as well as her personal heroism:

> Whenever she was personally exposed to danger, Marie Antoinette shewed herself the heroic and fearless daughter of Maria Theresa; but in her political conduct there was neither heroism nor greatness. She opposed the revolution vehemently and blindly, and without seeking to work the salvation of royalty through any settled plan of conduct . . . She considered the revolution as the ambitious struggle of a few headlong men, when it was the awakening of a long-oppressed people; she sought to check, not to guide its course. (II: 81)

However, as Kavanagh points out, during the three years which had elapsed between 6 October 1789, when Marie Antoinette held out against an attempt on her life, and the fall of the monarchy in 1792, '[She] had acted in direct opposition to the principle of passive submission' (II: 94) and, as a means of maintaining safety, found herself in the company of men–Mirabeau, Barnave and Danton–who were otherwise her enemies. Kavanagh notes the memorable interview with Mirabeau, who, impressed by the Queen's 'grace, dignity and energy', concluded with his confident, if somewhat ill-fated claim, "Madam, the monarchy is saved". Moreover, after this meeting, he is reported to have observed, "She is the only man of the family!" (II: 95), an expression, Kavanagh notes, that Napoleon later borrowed, and applied to Marie Antoinette's daughter, the Duchess of Angoulème (II: 96). Much as she was hated by the people of France, it was as a mother that Marie Antoinette was to find momentary sympathy with other women and, in this respect, Kavanagh engages all her sympathies. At her trial, held at the Palais de Justice on 14 October 1793, Marie Antoinette was confronted with her crimes against the state, read out by the infamous prosecutor, Fouquier Tinville. Knowing that it would be futile to say anything in her defence, she followed the example of her husband who had offered no protest during his own trial, and spoke only as required. It was the maleficent accusation, made by another member of the tribunal, Jacques Hébert, that she had depraved her young son, the Dauphin, that gave the greatest sense of grief and outrage. When pressed by a member of the jury to answer, Kavanagh writes:

> she turned towards the crowd, her countenance lit up by scorn and indignant majesty, merely saying, "I appeal to all the mothers present." The mothers who heard her then were the furious Tricotteuses, who daily accompanied victims to the scaffold; but even they had not so far given up all the feelings of womanhood as to remain insensible to such an appeal, and a murmur of horror and indignation against Hébert ran throughout the court. (II: 167)

Kavanagh's sympathies for Marie Antoinette are for the woman who, she feels, showed a sense of true heroism throughout the ordeal of her imprisonment and her trial. Her silent composure and sense of self-possession shown in the face of death were the outward manifestations of a woman who felt she was punished for her "faults, not crimes", a verdict Kavanagh seems to have agreed with, as she said, 'Her errors were those of her judgment, never of her heart' (II: 170). Had Marie Antoinette survived the Revolution, however, Kavanagh is of the opinion that as 'the whole nation did not disdain to avenge itself on a woman' (II: 170), she would have been judged even more severely.

Madame Roland

It is interesting that Kavanagh sees a connection between Marie Antoinette and one of the women who was active in her downfall, the revolutionary Madame Roland, who, like Marie Antoinette, went to the scaffold in 1793:

> There was a strange link between the destinies of those two women. Born within a few months of each other – one in the sheltering obscurity of the French bougeoisie, the other on the steps of an imperial throne – they met in antagonism on the stormy path of the French revolution. Both were beautiful, ardent, and heroic, and helped to ruin, by their imprudence, the opposite causes to which they clung. In her republican ardour, Madame Roland hastened the fall of Marie Antoinette; but it was, after enjoying a brief triumph, to end by following the fallen queen in her dungeon, and to perish on the same scaffold. Opposed in life, the two rivals met in death: the revolutionary axe knew no distinction of victims. (II:1 78)

These were two very different women who, for different reasons, were tried and condemned to death for crimes against the state. It is interesting that both women were also the victims of calumnies, which were directly expressed in terms derogatory to their gender. In the case of Madame Roland, Danton had called her the 'Circe of the Republic' (II: 138) and Marat saw her as a sexually promiscuous siren, comparing her not just to historical women of disrepute but to the hated Marie Antoinette herself.[88]

Kavanagh's account of Madame Roland, however, is, in the main, expressively idealistic and sympathetic. She portrays her as a stoic and studious young romantic whose greatest pleasure was absorbing the writings of the ancients, particularly Plutarch's *Lives*, which fed the young woman's imagination with its tales of heroism and courage. Later, Kavanagh sees her as a woman of vision and pious resolution in her dreams of a republic. Her famous utterance, 'Ah, Liberty! how many crimes are committed in thy name!' spoken immediately before she died is, for Kavanagh, a fitting testament to the values for which she gave her life.

Manon Philipon was born in 1756 the daughter of respectable parents; her father, an engraver of some talent, and an adoring and gentle mother. One of the likely reasons for Kavanagh's sympathetic view is that, as a child, Manon was content and curious about her faith and even later, when, influenced by the writings of Rousseau, scepticism and doubt took over, she found solace in basic Christian principles. Her marriage in 1781, at the age of twenty-four, to Roland de la Plâtière, a man on the verge of fifty, was one based on respect and a mutual interest for the republican cause, rather than love. Dutiful and compliant, she assisted her husband in his literary enterprises, finding relaxation in country walks and domestic tasks. However, Kavanagh speaks of Roland with an element of disdain and, one feels, regret that such a marriage took place; as she says, 'The love of Roland was a love selfish and domineering, to which he expected every feeling of his wife to yield. So jealous was he of her exclusive affection, that he exacted from her the sacrifice of every female friendship of her youth' (II: 122). The marriage was based on principles outside of those favoured by romantic love and Kavanagh's disapproval is clearly heard in her account of their daily routine.

Having spent several years in Paris and Amiens, where Roland was 'the inspector of several important manufactories', the couple moved to Lyons where, because of his political leanings, he was elected one of the first members of the municipality of Lyons. It was this body that sent him, accompanied by his wife, to Paris in the early part of 1791. It was also at this time, Kavanagh conjoins, that Madame Roland, while casting doubt on the lasting effectiveness of the newly formed constitutional monarchy, exercised a powerful fascination over her husband's friends who were charmed by her beauty and intelligence. As events took their course, the couple became more involved in political debate. The Girondist ministry was formed in 1792 and, subsequently, Roland was made the Minister of the Interior, a position which gave Madame Roland a platform from which she could voice her own opinions and engage her own influence. As Kavanagh sees it, 'Her political power during this her husband's first ministry was, like that she had previously exercised, great though occult. She influenced not only the acts of her husband, who reposed unbounded confidence in her, but likewise those of the entire Girondist party' (II: 127). Kavanagh goes on to relate the mood and changes that developed as a result of the revolutionary fervour and the residual bloodshed that epitomised the reign of terror. Although Madame Roland was to look back with shame at the human carnage in the name of republican idealism, Kavanagh argues that she and the Girondist party had brought this devastation on themselves.[89] As she says, 'Madame Roland instinctively imparted to the Girondists that feeling of mistrust against the King, which was strengthened in her by the earnestness of her republican tendencies'. Moreover, she maintains that it was this mistrust, 'caused by a jealous love of freedom' (II: 128), that was the only stain on her political career.

Kavanagh's intense dislike of Roland himself drew her to make 'a vague conjecture' that Madame Roland held a secret passion for one of their party, the handsome Girondist, Charles Barbaroux, whose family hailed from Marseilles. As with a story in a romantic novel, she contrasts the aged, prosaic husband from the temperate North with the youthful, poetic lover from the passionate, sultry South with the heroine caught between her duty to one and her love for the other. Conscious that her reasoning is based on flimsy evidence, it is as if she has willed their union because of the romantic connotations suggested by this young and beautiful couple. Her 'vague conjecture' asserts that Barbaroux appears 'to have been the object of that secret passion to which Madame Roland remotely alludes in a passage of her Memoirs' (II: 130). This passage, along with her reading of a short section from Barbaroux's memoirs, is sufficient to feed Kavanagh's imagination, as she notes: 'Once, when Roland had been expressing his mournful apprehensions, "his wife," observes Barbaroux in his memoirs, "wept as she listened to him; I wept myself, as I looked upon her"' (II: 130). In fact Madame Roland did have a love affair; however, it was not with the exuberant Barbaroux, as Kavanagh conjectured, but with the more serious and pensive young deputy François-Léonard Buzot. Along with other political figures, including Robespierre, Buzot was a frequent guest of the Rolands in Paris in 1792. In her biography of Madame Roland, Gita May gives an account of the relationship between the two. Recognising that the love Madame Roland had for her husband was nothing more than an *amour de tête,* she records that at the age of thirty-eight Madame Roland 'encountered true passion for the first time'. However (not unlike Kavanagh), May also sees this relationship in terms of a French novel, namely, Madame de La Fayette's *Princesse de Clèves,* and Rousseau's *La Nouvelle Héloise.* The true situation, in fact, emulates Kavanagh's conjecture that Madame Roland, caught between duty and love, is faced with an impossible dilemma. May notes that, 'Caught up between a respected elderly husband and an adored young lover, both the Princesse de Clèves in the novel of that name and Julie de Wolmar in *La Nouvelle Héloise* had determined to confess to their own husbands. With her usual directness, Manon did the same thing.'[90] Kavanagh makes no reference to this affair, yet her 'vague conjecture' with reference to Barbaroux appears to follow a similar pattern. One can only guess as to the reasons why Kavanagh omitted to comment on Madame Roland's affair with Buzot. It is unlikely that she was not aware of their relationship as she had access to Madame Roland's *Mémoires.* It may be that because Buzot was already married to a woman who was sixteen years his senior that Kavanagh chose to ignore the fact that there was anything other than friendship between the two. Moreover, given the strictures that determined her own moral outlook – as was the case with Marie Antoinette and Count Fersen – she would not have been able to condone an adulterous relationship, even if she were sympathetic. Her deliberate vagueness concerning the possibility of a liaison with Barbaroux could well have been her way of expressing an awareness of Madame Roland's capacity for genuine passionate love, an entity all the more real because of its notable absence in her marriage to Roland. In the light of her conjectures one can only wonder why Kavanagh makes a specific reference to Buzot who, on hearing of Madame Roland's death, she reports, 'remained for several days delirious: the depth of his grief revealed the fervour of the attachment he is asserted to have felt for Madame Roland' (II: 182). Madame Roland intrigued Kavanagh who saw her as a woman who, in spite of the purity of her intentions, was misled in her understanding of events. She believed that, like Marie Antoinette, the woman she sought to bring to justice, Madame Roland was herself persecuted as much for her sex as for her actions.

Kavanagh concludes her study of women in the eighteenth century by drawing attention to some lesser known and many unknown women who were active in fighting the injustices and terrors of the Revolution. Of these women she singles out Theresa Cabarrus, who later became Madame Tallien, for her part in bringing down Robespierre. She tells us that Charlotte Corday, for her assassination of Marat, was called by Madame Roland 'a heroine worthy of a better age' (II: 156). The historical precedence accorded by Kavanagh to these revolutionary women is testament to her understanding of their courage and determination in their fight against injustice.

Throughout her study Kavanagh takes licence with her subjects which only serves to expose her bias and her prejudices, the result of which, one could argue, detracts from the purpose of her intentions. Nevertheless, in spite of these impediments, *Woman in France during the Eighteenth Century* is a significant contribution to women's history as it succeeds in drawing attention to women's lives and experience during that long and turbulent period: 'For those who know how to look beyond the mere surface of history, the action of woman in France during the eighteenth century will not soon be forgotten' (II: 259).

4

French Women of Letters and *English Women of Letters*

French Women of Letters and its companion volume, *English Women of Letters*, are Kavanagh's testimony to the progress and achievements in women's writing during the previous two hundred years. Both volumes were published in 1862, twelve years after *Woman in France during the Eighteenth Century*, and, as she states in her preface to *English Women of Letters*:

> Both are parts of one whole, conceived and written at the same time, and with the same object – namely, 'to show how far, for the last two centuries and more, women have contributed to the formation of the modern novel in the two great literatures of modern times – the French and the English.'

Women's lives, and women writers particularly, never ceased to fascinate Kavanagh. She believed wholeheartedly that the novel was an important means of expression for women; as she states in the final paragraph of *English Women of Letters*, 'It is the only branch of literature in which women have acquired a genuine distinction and exercised undoubted influence'. She maintains that during the past two hundred years the French novel has held precedence in Europe as the most popular, adding that it may have been abused, even hated, but it has always been read.[1] The English novel, she claims, is less universally fascinating but more durable. She attributes a change in the novel over the previous seventy years or so to the influence of women who, she implies, extended a sense of 'truth' in the telling of a plain tale. To this end she applies the term 'delicacy'. In the context of the mid-nineteenth-century concept of sexual difference, Kavanagh makes it clear that in her regular usage of this term she is, in fact, addressing the literary developments that took place during the period about which she was writing. In *Writing Women's Literary History* (1996) Margaret Ezell notes that 'Between 1675 and 1875, there were at least twenty-five biographical encyclopedias and anthologies specifically devoted to chronicling the lives and labours of literary Englishwomen', all of which establish an ideology of the 'feminine'.[2] She reminds us that in Kavanagh's literary history the term 'delicacy' had evolved from earlier eighteenth-century usage to represent 'the primary standard of literary merit for women writers'. However, she contends that in *English Women of Letters*, Kavanagh 'faces the charge that nineteenth-century novels suffer from overrefinement because of the domination of female authors'. And, as such, she maintains that Kavanagh 'turns to the history of the novel seeking solutions'.[3] I would suggest that Ezell's argument is too reductive in that it fails to accommodate a wider understanding of Kavanagh's purpose. Though Kavanagh's perspective is one of gender difference, she does not singularly reflect a historically received allegiance to the ideal of 'feminine', as Ezell suggests, but also determines a political position. By the end of the eighteenth century, delicacy of tone in women's writing had become the accepted norm.[4] Kavanagh utilises the word in terms of understanding women's contribution to the novel and sees it as a positive attribute of women writers:

> Delicacy, both natural and acquired, has especially been their gift. The laws of society have given women a marvellous faculty for implying that which cannot be told; this refinement is a part of delicacy and good-breeding, and is excellent until it prevents truth. It must not give us a world too sweet, too fair, too good. (*EWL*: 3)

Later on she picks up on this argument:

> The writings of women are betrayed by their merits as well as their faults. If weaknesses and vagueness often characterize them, they also possess when excellent, or singularly good, three great redeeming qualities, which have frequently betrayed anonymous female writers. These qualities are: Delicacy, Tenderness, and Sympathy. We do not know if there exists, for instance, a novel of any merit written by a woman, which fails in one of these three attributes. (*EWL*: 251)

The attribute of 'Delicacy' she notes is the 'most common – delicacy in its broadest sense, not in its conventional meaning' (*EWL*: 251).

However, much of Kavanagh's argument rests on the associations of women's ability to compound a sense of delicacy with the telling of a plain tale. Such tales, she claims, are now 'rarely written by men' as their interests have taken them elsewhere. Later on in her section on Jane Austen she states that:

> Delicacy was the great attribute of the writer under our notice. Mademoiselle de Scudéry alone equalled Miss Austen in delicacy, with this difference, however, that one applied hers to thought, feeling, and intellectual speculation, and that the other turned hers to the broader and more living field of character and human nature. (*EWL*: 251)

Nineteenth-century perceptions of the seventeenth and eighteenth centuries were dictated by the mores of the time and Kavanagh, understandably, abhorred that which she perceived as 'coarse'. At the same time she was not so censorious as to ignore the significant observations of society that women writers incorporated into their narratives. Her approbation of 'delicacy' in fiction was not to be achieved at the expense of what she saw as truth and it is in this light that she discusses the first writer in her study of English women, Aphra Behn. Kavanagh believed that the purpose of fiction is to inadvertently teach noble lessons, to avoid coarseness, to show human greatness and virtue but, above all, not to 'belie truth' if it is to survive. 'These strictures', she suggests, 'whether just or not, will not, at least, apply to the woman who opens this line of English novelists. Too much delicacy or refinement was not the sin of poor Aphra Benn, or of the times when she wrote' (*EWL*: 3). Her disapprobation of the cultural attitude that works against female creativity is voiced later on in her discussion: '[men] are trained to act a part in life, [. . .] whilst girls are either taught to look on life, or, worse still, told how to practise its light and unworthy arts' (*EWL*: 202–3). For Kavanagh, Aphra Behn was one who, regardless of her 'faults', was 'at least, free and open' (*EWL*: 10). Whilst she admired Aphra Behn's sense of freedom, she also noted the ability of French women writers to circumnavigate the difficulties of social restraint. By engaging their literary energies, she argues, they were able to make a stand against sexual difference. Moreover, she suggests that, whether for good or bad, it is this quality of purpose that gives French women their great superiority over women of other nations. Above all, she contends, they have been able to maintain their feminine charm while being equal to action. For French women writers, much of this action was captured in their writing, not the least of which was expressed through the medium of romance, the genre that helped to accommodate women's consciousness and imagination. In Kavanagh's view this action signalled the beginning of a change in literary culture.

Kavanagh was fascinated by what she termed the 'generic and easily-understood name of Romance' (*FWL*: I: 2), the entity which she translated as the imaginary with the reality of human existence. In her introduction to *French Women of Letters*, she declares that the purpose of romance is to invent, to offer tales that are larger and more colourful than the reality of everyday life. Moreover, romance, she proclaims, has nurtured the minds of writers from the ancient Greeks to her own contemporaries. It is her view that the imagination, the mainstay of romance, builds on the prosaic and allows for a greater understanding of human nature: 'we read once more the great struggle between the spirit and the flesh, which every man carries on from his birth to his grave, which is the real story of humanity'. At the same time she impresses on her reader that 'The share of woman in transmitting this ideal history from generation to generation has ever been great' (*FWL*: I: 5). It is interesting that, while Kavanagh gives a brief mention of Clara Reeve later on in *English Women of Letters*, she makes no reference here to Reeve's *The Progress of Romance* (1785), a publication that attempted to outline the progress of romance and its influence over time.[5] One reason may be that Kavanagh considered Reeve too narrow in her understanding of romance. In *English Women of Letters*, she momentarily refers to Reeve in relation to her novel *The Old English Baron* (1778), which she dismisses outright as 'a very cold and commonplace production' (*EWL*: 116). Kavanagh's comments on this novel also go some way to explaining her dismissal of Reeve's work on romance. She believed that Reeve did not convey the necessary element of 'truth' that she considered was the purpose of romance:

> It was, indeed, inevitable that, in dealing with ages where birth was every-thing, authors should unconsciously forsake the humble, the poor, and the oppressed classes, to tell us of the fortunes of the strong and mighty. But they did so, without reaching the truth they aimed at. Clara Reeve designed her 'Old English Baron' as 'a picture of Gothic times and manners.' She failed; but probably died unconscious of her failure, a misfortune which she shared with the greatest who have made the attempt. In reality, it is impossible to succeed in painting the Middle ages with anything like truth. Clara Reeve, like Walpole, who preceded, like Sir Walter Scott himself who followed her, could only give us a onesided picture. The method she followed, which Walpole had opened which every one has adopted since then, is the only one that is feasible, but it is bad. She gave us the romantic customs of that wonderful period, customs in which ferocity was so strongly blended with romance – the lists, the judgment of God, the law of the sword – things remote from our own manners; but neither she nor her successors ever dared to give us the rudeness, and with it the breadth and geniality of those wonderful times. It could not be. Modern delicacy and refinement would have shrunk aghast from some of the pictures in the romances that were sung and told in feudal homes, in the ear of noble ladies, and with the sanction of grave men. (*EWL*: 116–17)

She argues the case that the romances of the past, with their chivalrous extravagance, were a reflex of the times and no longer hold sway in the modern world. In France developments in prose fiction from romance to the pastoral and eventually the novel in its various incarnations dictated the need for a new form of realism, a sense of 'probability' in so far as 'the characters and incidents must be such as we can believe in' (*FWL*: I:

8). Kavanagh's perspective here is, in fact, an earlier variant of the findings of more recent scholars of the French novel. English Showalter, for
example, argues that 'The novel's believability depends on the imagination quite as much as the romance's appeal to fantasy or idealism'.[6]
Whilst drawing his references from the conventions and inevitable over-
laps pertaining to the different genres in prose fiction, Showalter goes on
to suggest that 'the theory of the *roman* pointed fiction in the direction
of greater realism in our modern sense, and both authors and readers of
the seventeenth century appreciated the superiority of the realistic elements for achieving the kind of verisimilitude they sought from fiction'.[7]
Debates concerning both the matter and the form of the novel were
ongoing throughout the seventeenth and into the eighteenth century and
were mainly centred on ways in which this new form accommodated the
transition of older, more historical genres, such as the epic and the
romance. French women writers were often at the centre of discussion,
and Kavanagh occasionally alludes to the arguments put forward by
critics such as Nicolas Boileau, who saw romance as nothing more than
a frivolous exercise, and to Pierre-Daniel Huet, whose views were more
conciliatory.[8] Kavanagh's aim is to show how romance was a genre that
proved particularly accommodating for women, and her discussion
centres on the recognition, achievements and failures of those who chose
to make this genre the mainstay of their literary contribution.

French Women of Letters

By means of an introduction to the influx of women's writing in France
during the period loosely covering the early seventeenth and up to the
late eighteenth century, Kavanagh draws on her own perceptions of
romance as the genre which was to infiltrate much of the writing of the
period. In line with those sentiments voiced by George Eliot, who, in
1854, attributed a particular historical significance to earlier French
women writers,[9] it was Kavanagh's objective to manifest this significance
in her own contribution to women's literary history. She discusses ten
writers overall and, in each case, offers a biographical sketch of her
subject followed by a brief outline and a short critical response to a selection of their novels. In her preface she notes that the women she will
discuss 'are strictly novelists' because it is with the novel that women
have 'acquired undisputed eminence'. She goes on to say that her selection will be found 'impartial and is based on great celebrity, original or
suggestive power, and individual attraction', adding that 'none but dead
authors, or such as have already stood the test of time, are included'. Her
compilation of women writers is interesting in so far as she observes their

differences as well as the generic element of romance in each writer's work. They are presented in more or less chronological order, and she also considers each one from the perspective of their historical and literary significance. In order of presentation they are: Mademoiselle de Gournay (1565–1645), Mademoiselle de Scudéry (1627–1711), Madame de La Fayette (1634–93),[10] Madame de Tencin (1685–1749), Madame Riccoboni (1714–92), Madame de Genlis (1746–1830), Madame de Charrière (1740–1805), Madame de Krüdener (1764–1824), Madame Cottin (1770–1807) and, finally, Madame de Staël (1766–1817). By necessity of selection, my intention is to look at how Kavanagh's perspectives contributed to her own understanding of women's writing during the period. I will concentrate mainly, but not exclusively, on Mademoiselle de Scudéry, Madame de La Fayette and Madame de Staël, the three novelists who, for Kavanagh, signified a notable change in women's literary accomplishments.

Breaking through boundaries: French women novelists and cultural change

In seventeenth-century France women who took up the pen were, by definition, beginning to break down the barriers of cultural restraint by transgressing traditional boundaries. As Faith Beasley has pointed out, during the period 1640–1715 alone, there were over 220 women who actively participated in the literary scene.[11] Much of the literature produced by women during the seventeenth and into the eighteenth century came within the parameters of romantic fiction. Thus romance was considered a predominantly feminine entity and, as such, was believed by its detractors to lack reason, the claimed natural reserve of the male gender. In Louis XIV's reign particularly, it was considered undesirable and improper for women to practise intellectual pursuits and there had been a genuine fear that women's engagement with writing would upset the natural order of the state and thus lead to the feminisation of France. Novels written by women were suspect in so far as it was believed their content could influence women away from their natural 'subservient' roles as wives, mothers and/or aesthetic ornament. Not surprisingly, in such a culture women feared social ostracism and as a result anonymity of authorship became the norm.[12] The fear of feminisation continued well into the eighteenth century. It was the view of the Abbé Jacquin, one of the more prominent critics of the novel, that the 'feminisation of literature had seduced writers from their true calling'.[13] In his *Entretiens sur les romans* (1755) he objected strongly to the progression of literary women, pronouncing them a danger to morality, the state and women's proper function in society. Novels were thought to confuse fiction and historical fact, and the debates around the dangers of the novel's influence argued strongly against women novelists.[14] However, by the mid eighteenth century the manacles of cultural boundaries had loosened, and more and more women took to writing as a means of creative expression. Historically, the cultural developments that led to the influx of women's writing were gradual and often subversive. Most notably it was the aftermath of civil wars in France, the Fronde uprisings, in which several aristocratic women had been involved,[15] that signified a change in women's intellectual activities. Later on, Germaine de Staël was to write in *De la littérature* (1800) that women's writing was the natural outcome of their sense of difference and as such had posed a genuine threat to absolute monarchies that objected to such an open display of intellectual ability in women. Amongst other forms of writing, including memoirs and letters, novels were also vehicles via which women could write themselves into history, a trend that went against Louis's absolutism.[16] Kavanagh's comments on this aspect of the development of the novel are located mainly in relation to her section on Mademoiselle de Scudéry, whose novel *Artamène, ou le Grand Cyrus* (1649–53) is based on a thinly disguised chronicle of court life. As Kavanagh points out, 'Every one knew that the past was but a convenient cloak for the present; [. . .] beneath that veil of fiction every one also knew that there lay truths and realities' (I: 45). As with other critics who came after her, Kavanagh's understanding of Mademoiselle de Scudéry's novels determines the foundations upon which she bases her critical appraisal of those novelists who followed.

The first writer in Kavanagh's study is Marie le Jars de Gournay (1565–1645), the adopted daughter of Montaigne, who, she states, produced the first genuine prose story written by a woman, *Le Promenoir de Montaigne* (1589), which preceded Honoré d'Urfé's *Astrée* (1607–10) – the work acclaimed to have paved the way for the novel in France – by several years. Though Mademoiselle de Gournay's story went through several editions, Kavanagh suggests that it is more significant for its historic value than for its content, which, she contends, is not remarkable. Her comments on Mademoiselle de Gournay's enthusiasm and zeal for literary pursuits are astute but sympathetic. She refers to Mademoiselle de Gournay's idiosyncratic use of language manifested in the 'antiquated French' of Montaigne, which, as she grew older, was deemed oddly old-fashioned by her contemporaries. However, as Kavanagh notes, Mademoiselle de Gournay was not averse to the introduction of new and 'often necessary' words.[17] Although Kavanagh states that it is not known whether Mademoiselle de Gournay had ever visited the Hôtel Rambouillet, the Paris establishment responsible for the fashionable new trends of expression and, later, made famous for its nurturing of the Précieuses,[18] she sees her as a woman who spoke out against the all-pervasive prejudice of a male establishment to women writers:

> She wrote much, and almost on every subject; philosophic and moral matters were her favourite themes. She did not fail either to do her best in favour of her sex, and with much warmth and some sharpness she censured those men 'who despise absolutely the works of women, without deigning to read them, in order to know of what stuff they were made, and without first inquiring if they could themselves write such books as would deserve being read by all sorts of women'. (I: 15)

Mademoiselle de Gournay's disdain for those men who blindly ignored women's writing is a starting point for Kavanagh's own investigations into the emergence and developments of French women writers. Her education and her fluency and understanding of the French language would certainly have prepared her for such a venture and it is likely that she undertook her own translations of the passages she cites in her discussion. However, in her biographical sketches she only occasionally refers to her original French sources, which can be frustrating for the modern reader who is accustomed to informed bibliographical references.

Kavanagh quite rightly traces the germ of women's writing, particularly the novel, to the established salons[19] of the seventeenth century where she acknowledges that 'the authority of women took the shape of legislation, a fact the more singular, with few exceptions, women of rank and good-breeding scarcely knew how to spell' (I: 16). Notwithstanding the fact that, in the main, the education of aristocratic women at that time was deficient in many ways, the desire to explore language took precedence in the cultivated art of conversation, as Kavanagh argues: 'it is not always book knowledge that educates society – conversation and discussion form and refine minds as books never can' (I: 16). She goes on to suggest that the seventeenth century produced some of France's 'finest and noblest works' (I: 16). However, the eloquence and purity of language so revered by society was, in Kavanagh's view, 'a somewhat cold idiom', which, she argues, 'has remained to this day the language of pure and perfect prose, the speech in which conversation can most agreeably be carried on, and ingenious ideas best expressed' (I: 16). Although aristocratic women in general were not taught to spell correctly, there were, of course, the exceptions and Kavanagh points to Madame de Rambouillet as a pioneer of genuine accomplishment. Catherine de Vivonne de Pisani married the Marquis de Rambouillet, and the Hôtel Pisani, which she inherited from her father (situated between the Tuileries and the Louvre) became the famous Hôtel Rambouillet. It was from here that Madame de Rambouillet soon gained the 'deserved' love and respect of those she entertained, keeping up the famous establishment for over half a century from 1600 to 1650 when, as Kavanagh puts it, 'the storm of the Fronde dispersed the guests' (I: 19) and, subsequently, it became extinct.[20]

It is to the legacy of the Hôtel Rambouillet that Kavanagh attributes the purity of the French language. The celebrated Précieuses, whom she identifies as 'ladies, whom their admirers considered of so exalted a nature that no adjective meaner than "precious" could qualify them' (I: 24) numbered more than eight hundred and were savagely ridiculed by Molière in his play *Précieuses Ridicules* (1659). While she acknowledges what she perceives as the many faults of 'bad taste' that, no doubt, were committed by the Précieuses, she also considers their notable attempts at linguistic refinement. In spite of their failure to spell correctly, she acknowledges these women as pioneers and moral guardians of the French language, claiming that 'To them we owe it that the French literature of their age can, with few exceptions, be read without shame in ours' (I: 25). The converse side of the Précieuses' influence on language was, however, one with which Kavanagh could not comply. For all its refinement she found their approach lacked both spontaneity and the flow of poetic expression. However, the legacy of the Précieuses, Kavanagh claims, was to last longer than the Hôtel Rambouillet, the evidence of which she was to experience in her own lifetime.

Mademoiselle de Scudéry

By far the longest singular discussion in Kavanagh's study is devoted to Mademoiselle Madeleine de Scudéry, a prolonged visitor to the Hôtel de Rambouillet and a woman whom Kavanagh clearly admired for her energy and enterprise: 'women will ever acknowledge with gratitude the efforts Mademoiselle de Scudéry made to waken the women of her time from intellectual sloth and ignorance' (I: 163). Kavanagh sees Mademoiselle de Scudéry, the 'acknowledged foundress of the psychological novel' (*EWL*: 219), in particular as a woman whose contribution helped to open the floodgates of women's writing. It is also with a sense of regret, Kavanagh notes, that Paris in the mid nineteenth century had little recollection of this once celebrated writer of the grand heroic novel, reflecting that 'it would take years, a lifetime perhaps, to collect a complete edition of Mademoiselle de Scudéry's works in that city where her fame reached its fullness; saddest of all, her name has remained as a byword with a posterity that has never cared to read her' (I: 39). Given the fact that by the mid nineteenth century Mademoiselle de Scudéry was virtually a forgotten writer, Kavanagh raises questions pertaining to the influence and meaning of her works during her age. As she says, 'Her meaning is obvious – more than one she had; but one was eminent and apparent above the rest; the wish to improve the moral, social and intellectual condition of women' (I: 157). Kavanagh sets Mademoiselle de Scudéry, the acclaimed writer of several novels, in which seventeenth-century society was set against the backdrop of ancient Greece or Rome, apart from other less influential writers. Mademoiselle de Gournay's *Promenoir de Montaigne*, she notes, 'had neither universal interest nor success' and, she tells us, the subject matter of the Princess of Conté's *Amours du Grand Alcandre* was chiefly confined to the scandals of the court. In contrast Mademoiselle de Scudéry had produced 'real romances' that not only attracted a 'large and genuine public' but 'pleased and interested thousands' (I: 72). However, it seems that Kavanagh was less impressed by the quality of Mademoiselle de Scudéry's writing than by its moral impact on her readers. She notes with irony, 'Her books were read and admired by the whole world, and the most distinguished amongst her contemporaries praised both them and the author in language which shows but too forcibly how unstable is the tenure of literary reputation' (I: 60). She follows this comment with a reminder that, 'if Mademoiselle de Scudéry was admired and read with transport, she was also criticised with some severity. Tallemant des Réaux said she had done more to spoil the French language than any other writer living'; but she is careful to add that 'he liked her stories, however' (I: 63). Kavanagh's own critical stance is that not only were Mademoiselle de Scudéry's tales too long, she also pandered to popular taste, as she candidly points out: 'where honour was not at stake, Mademoiselle de Scudéry was too prudent to quarrel with the world and its opinions. It gives us a key to her literary weakness and success. She wrote badly, because the taste of the majority was bad – and she succeeded, because she pleased that taste' (I: 54). At the same time Kavanagh sees this practice as Mademoiselle de Scudéry's own form of rebellion against a society invoked by the projections of the Précieuses: 'whilst she always argued in favour of female education, she never ceased to talk and write against female pedantry, to plead for modesty and moderation' (I: 54).[21] Evidently Kavanagh considered Mademoiselle de Scudéry less significant as a stylist and more as a legislator of morals.

Accordingly, Kavanagh introduces Madeleine de Scudéry as one remarkable more for her fame than for her influence. She tells us that Scudéry's 'fifty volumes of poetry and prose were the delight of the most exquisitely polished society France has yet known [. . .] They were translated into every European language, and found their way, it is asserted, into Eastern tongues' (I: 37). Moreover, as Kavanagh readily notes,

'None of the women who have written during the last two centuries received more honours, more flattering distinctions, and more substantial rewards' (I: 39). Amongst Mademoiselle de Scudéry's many honours, she won the French Academy's first prize of eloquence for her discourse on Glory and she replaced Helen Cornaro amongst the Ricovrati of Padua.[22] It is, therefore, with some qualification that Kavanagh declares that, although Mademoiselle de Scudéry's influence does not extend to that of Madame de Staël, she surpassed that writer in fame. Mademoiselle de Scudéry's ten-volumed work *Clélie, histoire romaine* (1654–60), or "Clelia" in which she introduced the map of the Kingdom of Tenderness, the *carte de tendre*, a system that outlined the different pathways of love, was a work that in his youth even Boileau, the man who would later become one of her most adverse critics, found endearing. As Kavanagh informs us, 'Boileau himself, then a young man – lingered with delight over those seven thousand pages of lively or tender controversy' (I: 39). However, she argues that the bitter criticism Mademoiselle de Scudéry would later receive from both Boileau and Molière was partly justified:

> If her tales had been short, and not in ten volumes a piece – if she had dropped historical narratives, which she only disfigured, and had professed to give us the men and women of her own day, neither Molière nor Boileau, with all the genius of the one and the bitterness of the other, could have inflicted upon her an enduring stigma. (I: 39–40)

This infliction of ridicule, as much as any stylistic failings attributed to Mademoiselle de Scudéry, Kavanagh sees as a product of the age. At the same time she is also aware that Mademoiselle de Scudéry had the capacity to charm and delight the most cultivated minds of the time and is of the opinion that she could still be read with entertainment and profit in her own time. Reason enough, she claims, to attempt a better understanding of this writer.

Kavanagh offers a brief biographical sketch of this physically plain[23] but notably sensible Neapolitan woman who, regardless of family setbacks, was the recipient of an excellent all-round education, which went beyond languages and literary knowledge.[24] However, on the death of her uncle and benefactor, she found herself destitute and, 'somewhere between her thirtieth and fortieth year', was obliged to take up her abode in Paris with her older brother George, under whose name she first published her work. Kavanagh acknowledges George's contribution to Mademoiselle de Scudéry's two romances, *Ibrahim, ou l'illustre Bassa*, or "Ibrahim" (1641) in four volumes, and *Artamène, ou le Grand Cyrus*, or "Grand Cyrus" (1649–53) in ten volumes, both written in the 'grand historical style', but notes that it was generally known that these works were those of his sister, Madeleine.[25] In *Grand Cyrus*, Mademoiselle de Scudéry incorporated a *mise en abyme* of the Hôtel de Rambouillet and her own *Samedis*, her Saturday salons. Response to this novel was generally one of glee and fully appreciated by those who identified themselves on the page, as Kavanagh records:

> Her readers were delighted to recognize themselves, their friends, and their enemies, painted to the very life in her pages. [. . .] The long description of Cléomire's palace had a charm for every reader; for everyone knew that it was the Hôtel Rambouillet – that the rooms, pictures, and very couches were those of the celebrated and accomplished Marquise. Many a provincial girl sighed as she read of those splendors she must never hope to see; many a faded beauty or exiled courtier lingered with regret over the page that recorded the scene of past triumphs. (I:45–6)

However, as much as Kavanagh acknowledged Mademoiselle de Scudéry's appeal as a writer, as is the case with the Précieuses, she is adamant in her opinion that it is the moral and not the literary content of her writing that deserves merit:

> if [Mademoiselle de Scudéry] unfortunately helped to pervert the literary taste of her age – or rather if she had not power, genius, and originality enough to reform it – she conferred incalculable benefits on the moral tone of literature. She put into books what Madame de Rambouillet and the 'Précieuses' had introduced into society – modesty, and with modesty she helped to develop a purer moral feeling than she had found before her. (I: 70)

While Kavanagh appreciated the impact of Mademoiselle de Scudéry's popularity in her time, she expresses her disappointment that this writer of 'real romances' had little appeal, even for the less discriminating reader of her own lifetime, as she asks: 'by what melancholy magic have they [Scudéry's novels] lost all power to amuse the least exacting class of all readers' (I: 72). She reasons the fact that Mademoiselle de Scudéry's works, notably her three celebrated novels, *Ibrahim*, *Grand Cyrus* and *Clelia*, were not read in the nineteenth century because her tales of heroes and heroines are too unbelievable, too lofty and noble. It was Kavanagh's view that Mademoiselle de Scudéry's characters lacked the true magnitude of humanity as they were beyond belief and as such were brought down by their own imposed perfection. Moreover, although Kavanagh contends that, in their day, these romances were intended and taken as a code of morals, taste and good breeding, she is of the opinion that Mademoiselle de Scudéry herself was not wholly convinced of the credibility of the stories: 'Her lofty histories she wrote to please the age; but, alas! she did not believe in them much more than we do' (I: 77). She argues:

'Ibrahim' bears abundantly the stamp of its age, but can still afford amusement – the ignorant, the young, would read it with pleasure; whereas the
'Grand Cyrus' and the 'Clélia,' precisely because they are of a higher cast,
and appeal to feelings and tastes that have passed away, have now nothing
left save for the intellectual and the educated. (I: 84)

Kavanagh is also of the opinion that Mademoiselle de Scudéry mistook
her vocation in attempting prose epics. In so doing she compromised her
talents and thus yielded too readily to the tastes of the day. She argues
that it is the 'conversations' rather than the romance and episodes that
run throughout these three novels that reveal the real talent of this writer.
The conversations, she contends, are 'Ingenious, subtle, full of delicate
perception and excellent matter, they delighted the most refined minds in
her own times, and have much that must always please persons of taste'.
However, she goes on to say that 'Both episodes and conversations prove
her to have been an ingenious tale writer and an agreeable moralist' (I:
78–9). In this context it is interesting to note that these conversations
were modelled on those already conducted in the salons before they were
incorporated into her novels.[26]

Notwithstanding Kavanagh's critical stance on the believability of
their content, she takes note of the significance afforded to women in
Mademoiselle de Scudéry's novels. By drawing attention to the ways in
which women featured in the numerous digressions and interlocking
tales that permeated all three of the novels under discussion, Kavanagh
also focuses on the area of sexual politics. She puts into perspective
Mademoiselle de Scudéry's own attitude to women and knowledge in an
age which deemed learning in women undesirable and unfeminine.
Mademoiselle de Scudéry's arguments pertaining to knowledge were
more often linked with both the nature and the conventions of love and,
in this context, Kavanagh acknowledges the relevance and significance
of this writer in her age. In her discussion of Mademoiselle de Scudéry's
attitude to matters of love Kavanagh argues that, 'Mademoiselle de
Scudéry maintained the superior attractions of mind over person,
though she prudently avoided severing them' (I: 160). She contends that,
though Mademoiselle de Scudéry's reasons may themselves be open to
question, they do not detract from her purpose, which was the improvement of women. Going back to Kavanagh's questioning of the meaning
of Mademoiselle de Scudéry's work in relation to women's moral, social
and intellectual condition, she impacts her reasoning with an understanding of Mademoiselle de Scudéry's own attitude to love. Kavanagh
argues that it was with the intention of improving women's understanding of their position that, in her novels, Mademoiselle de Scudéry
made the subject of love so 'potent' because she believed that love

was the 'source of woman's power' (I: 157). Nevertheless, Kavanagh presents her readers with a psychological conundrum concerning Mademoiselle de Scudéry's own literary renderings on the subject of love. She was not convinced that Mademoiselle de Scudéry was successful in her attempts to convey the sentiments and real meaning of love. She argues that, for all her moral intentions, Mademoiselle de Scudéry's concept of love lacks passion and, for all its delicacy, finesse and 'general perception of truth', it has 'none of the grand marks of love in every time'. For Mademoiselle de Scudéry, it is, she says, 'a moral agent, meant to refine man and raise woman' (I: 158–9). Kavanagh's reservations stem from the fact that, like other women writers, namely Madame de Genlis, Madame de Staël and even Maria Edgeworth, Mademoiselle de Scudéry was primarily a teacher (I: 78). Later on she adds, 'It is always hard to be true when there is an intention of teaching' (I: 158). Kavanagh notes the passage in *Grand Cyrus* where Cydmon asks Sappho, the 'Lesbian poetess', how she wishes to be loved. Sappho's reply is one that denotes a happiness that comes from her lover's total compliance and faithfulness. When Sappho is required to tell how she, in turn, would wish to love, Sappho replies, '"When I told you one I told you the other"' (I: 159). Kavanagh notes that 'This love, indeed, is not to end in marriage, which Sappho proclaims a long slavery; but Sappho is here for Mademoiselle de Scudéry, and this is but an allusion to her private life, not a broad theory' (I: 159).[27] In fact Kavanagh says little about Mademoiselle de Scudéry's private life. Mademoiselle de Scudéry never married and was said to have remained a celibate. Her long friendship with Paul Pélisson, who acted as secretary at her Saturday meetings, her *Samedis*, was understood, to have been of a spiritual nature only, based on intellectual interest and mutual trust. He appears under the name of Herminius in her novel *Clelia* in which she speaks of him as all that is noble, kind and admirable. Kavanagh puts this reference into context when, later on, she is sceptical about the quality of their relationship when she asks, 'How pure and true was the long affection of Mademoiselle de Scudéry and Pélisson! – scarcely love, though the fashion of the age made them call it such' (I: 194). Several reasons have been suggested as to why the two did not marry. In her biography of Mademoiselle de Scudéry, Nicole Aronson notes that in 1654 'Sapho' (the name by which Mademoiselle de Scudéry was known by her friends) was in her forties, and Pélisson was seventeen years her junior.[28] Evidence suggests that it is likely that Mademoiselle de Scudéry, above all else, did not marry because she wished to safeguard her freedom as a single woman. Kavanagh refers to Pélisson only briefly when she notes that the two friends agreed to a form of platonic love in preference to marriage. By means of qualification she cites the French philosopher Victor Cousin[29] who, she says:

> in his interesting analysis of the "Grand Cyrus," considers the following passage relating to Sappho and Phaon, as an allusion to this agreement between Pélisson and his mistress: 'They even agreed on the conditions of their love; for Phaon solemnly promised Sappho, who wished it to be so, never to require more than the possession of her heart from her, and she also promised never to receive any one else in hers'. (I: 65)

It is precisely these sentiments that Kavanagh takes exception to when she suggests that Mademoiselle de Scudéry exploited the idea of love for political ends. However, as Joan DeJean has argued, novels about love and marriage were overtly political in that they were vehicles through which women could stress the social implications of affective choice.[30] DeJean's twentieth-century perspective may explain why Kavanagh believed that Mademoiselle de Scudéry was unsuccessful when writing about love. For Kavanagh true love needed no such instruction. While she appreciated the political and cultural differences between her own time and that of Mademoiselle de Scudéry, she could not accept that in fiction the explication of true love could be delivered, as she perceived it, with such didactic intention.

In spite of her reservations on the subject of love, however, Kavanagh recognised the importance of Mademoiselle de Scudéry's contribution to sexual politics in her writing. Whereas she declared that the story in *Clelia* is 'painfully absurd' (I: 141), she was more forgiving of the accompanying 'conversations' in the novel. One such conversation on freedom and gender between a young woman, Tullia, and her sister, a princess, is, as Kavanagh acknowledged, a protest against the imbalance of gender politics and an example of Mademoiselle de Scudéry's message to women. As Kavanagh says, it is 'a whole declaration of the rights of woman, suited to the age in which it was written; and instructive, as showing against what obstacles Mademoiselle de Scudéry had to contend' (I: 142). The young princess says that she is happy and enjoys perpetual peace because of the '"thousand advantages"' she derives from being a woman and would not wish to change her sex. She argues:

> 'Honour compels men to go to war, and forbids us. Beauty [. . .] is ours; we share the honours of our parents, and all the advantages of those to whom we are united. We need not even take the trouble of studying arts and sciences; ignorance is not a fault in us; we are not asked to be brave; in short, a small share of personal attractions, a mediocre intellect, and a great deal of modesty, are enough for a woman; whereas a man, to be distinguished, requires a thousand great qualities, natural or acquired.' (I: 114)

Tullia's response is one of defiance and indignation at such reasoning and she dismisses the princess's claims as those that merely diminish her sex. She offers a catalogue of women's wrongs including the lack of social liberty, the suppression of their intellect, the restraints that virtue imposes and the condemnation of perpetual obedience, all of which are women's lot. She continues:

> "When I see a man walking alone, I envy his freedom; when another goes off travelling, I envy him again; and I envy the anger and the vengeance of some – for it is not thought strange that a man should resent a wrong and avenge it, and it can scarcely be tolerated that a woman should complain of anything, or, if she does complain, it must be so meekly that her colour does not change, and that her eyes lose none of their softness. Indeed, one might imagine that nature has given us no feelings, such are the laws custom enjoins on us; and I can assure you that I murmur strangely against all who made them." (I: 144–5)

It is interesting that while Kavanagh notes the frequency of such uncompromisingly political sections throughout Mademoiselle de Scudéry's work, it is her opinion that Mademoiselle de Scudéry's own sexual politics lay somewhere between those proffered by the two women in her story (I: 145). It appears that while she openly endorses the sexual politics in this writer's work, above all else, she sees her as a moralist whose literary accomplishments voiced the importance of women's liberty and helped to refine an age.

Madame de La Fayette

While Kavanagh argued that, with all her talents, Mademoiselle de Scudéry was lost to 'bad taste', she contends that it was 'good taste' that gave Madame de La Fayette 'a fixed and exalted place in French Literature' (I: 205). Unlike Mademoiselle de Scudéry, however, who, she argues, was a leader in her field, she makes the somewhat puzzlingly contradictory comment that Madame de La Fayette, in obeying the tastes and feelings of her age, was neither remarkable nor original. However, Kavanagh's judgement of Madame de La Fayette engages different perspectives, particularly as, later on in her discussion, she acknowledges her as one who 'founded a new school of fiction' (I: 201–2). Kavanagh justifies her claim by the fact that, in her ability to convey a sense of 'truth', Madame de La Fayette injected a new form of realism into her stories. This element of realism may have been the reason why Kavanagh had previously referred to 'that pitiless derider of Mademoiselle de Scudéry', Boileau, who, she notes, 'declared that Madame de la Fayette wrote the best, and had most *esprit* of any woman in France' (I: 182).

She argues that though Madame de La Fayette's novels were devoid of that element of monumental power associated with Mademoiselle de Scudéry, she brought to fiction the freshness and simplicity of more 'delicate', 'womanlike' and 'refined' qualities that have enabled her to survive the test of time, ones which, no doubt, Kavanagh would deem the very essence of good taste.

Madame de La Fayette was significant for her intervention, or, as Kavanagh puts it, 'her romantic adventures', in the wars of the Fronde and her intimacy with Madame de Sévigné, Mademoiselle de La Fayette and the Duc de la Rochefoucauld, the man to whom she was devoted.[31] Paradoxically, although Kavanagh notes the influence of her novel *La Princesse de Clèves* since it was first published in 1678, her historical assessment of Madame de La Fayette is that of merely an acceptable and pleasant writer: 'To posterity she is known as the writer of a few agreeable letters addressed to Madame de Sévigné, and as the author of some charming memoirs, and more charming tales' (I: 183). Born in the year 1633 and as the recipient of a superior education, even by the standards of the day, the aristocratic and extremely pretty Marie Madeleine Pioche de la Vergne attracted much attention. In this connection Kavanagh tells us that one of her tutors, the learned Ménage, fell in love with his precocious young pupil and wrote verses in her honour. It was one of these verses that was to cause her displeasure however, when he called her by the 'euphonious, but not pleasing, name of Laverna' (I: 184), the classical goddess of dishonesty, an appendage that, she notes, 'availed him nought with the prudent Marie' (I: 184). Marie's indifferent marriage in 1655, at the age of twenty-two, to the Marquis de La Fayette, brought her into contact with a wider aristocratic audience, including her sister-in-law, Mademoiselle de La Fayette, the platonic favourite of Louis XIII, through whom she later became known to Henrietta, the first wife of Louis XIV's brother, the Duc d'Orléans. Friendship between Henrietta and Madame de La Fayette soon blossomed to the extent that Henrietta encouraged her friend's writing. Kavanagh attributes much significance to women's friendship during this period, a phenomenon she associates with the political and social constraints imposed on women at the time. As she says:

> It has been the happy lot of Frenchwomen to experience and receive in its fullness that gentlest feeling of the human heart. No friends have been so universally faithful and true, and none have been more beloved. If we read the social and literary history of France during the last two hundred years, we shall find more instances of the tender and enduring affection of women than can be the boast of any other nation during the same space of time. (I: 193)

She goes on to remind her reader that friendship was also the great passion of Madame de Rambouillet, whose circle included Madame de La Fayette, and from whose salon the art of portraiture was encouraged. Madame de La Fayette was famous in her day for her written portraits, particularly of Madame de Sévigné and Madame Scarron, with whom she later parted company when this lady became Madame de Maintenon, friend, then wife, of Louis XIV. The reason why their friendship ended, Kavanagh claims, was Madame de La Fayette's candour and propensity for truth, traits that were rarely welcome at court. Madame de La Fayette's enduring friendship with Madame de Sévigné was particularly significant. As was the custom at the Hôtel de Rambouillet, the establishment where the two women socialised, Madame de La Fayette was so taken with her delightful friend that she celebrated her beauty and her talents in a portrait. Kavanagh adds that Madame de Sévigné's brilliance, coupled with her lively disposition, was the perfect complement to Madame de La Fayette's more subdued and quieter nature.

Unlike Madame de Sévigné, who is celebrated for her correspondence, Madame de La Fayette spurned letter writing, finding the practice distasteful, as Kavanagh notes: 'She praised and admired Madame de Sévigné's epistolatory facility, but neither could nor would imitate it' (I:190). Sustained by the friendship of women and assisted primarily by Rochefoucauld and her *protégé*, Ségrais,[32] under whose name her work appeared, her energies were reserved for her novels which, Kavanagh suggests, relate directly to her own disappointments in love. She argues:

> Her three tales, 'Madame de Montpensier', 'The Princesse de Clèves', and 'Madame de Tende', tell but one story, which in its main features is her own; the struggle between duty and passion in the heart of a virtuous woman, united to a man whom she cannot love. We do not think that Madame de la Fayette went so far as passion; but she had to strive against indifference and *ennui*, a weary load to bear in married life. (I. 193)

Madame de La Fayette's novel *Madame de Montpensier* (1662) is dismissed by Kavanagh as neither interesting nor remarkable, although it has since been noted as the novel that ushered in a new era in French women's writing.[33] This novel's questioning of the politics both of marriage and of the state reaches a culmination in *La Princesse de Clèves* (1679). Both novels deal with a form of symbolic adultery but, while Kavanagh is reluctant to engage with the former, in her discussion of *La Princesse de Clèves* she readily outlines the sad consequences of a woman's adherence to marital duty over unfulfilled passion and desire for another man. However, Kavanagh is less concerned with the sexual politics projected in Madame de La Fayette's stories as, more often than not, her readings of them lack political analysis. Her discussion focuses more on the impact of their invention which she puts down to Madame de La Fayette's 'perfect judgement, "her divine reason"'. She goes on to suggest:

> Her power of excellence was limited; but had she only written the 'Princess of Clèves,' we should say that she could not do wrong. Her first tale, 'Madame de Montpensier,' a slight sketch, and her second, 'Zayde,' a novel of some length, prove with all their merit, that her third and most perfect work [*Princesse de Clèves*] was the fruit of thought and experience, even more than of inspiration. (I: 204–5)

Kavanagh attributes much of Madame de La Fayette's success to what she perceived as her impeccable style. Whereas she considered the writing of Mademoiselle de Scudéry to be careless and loose, Madame de La Fayette, she proclaimed, 'wrote as she spoke, with clearness, elegance and precision' (I: 206). Madame de La Fayette was for Kavanagh more successful than her predecessors because she was more 'graceful' when writing about love; for this reason, her stories, though not without their failings, she claims, can still be read with pleasure: 'The experience of two centuries has given her successors more passion and more power; it has not given them more delicacy and more grace' (I: 223). Kavanagh viewed Madame de La Fayette as one who was true to her age, her depiction of court life was, she believed, somewhat idealised but truthful. Kavanagh argues that in her stories Madame de La Fayette captured the 'spirit' of the women of the seventeenth century. Her perspective is essentially romantic when she concludes that in the most accomplished of her novels, La *Princesse de Clèves*, Madame de La Fayette had 'reached the centre of all interest – the heart and conscience of a human being' (I: 253). This sentiment says much about Kavanagh's perspective in that she viewed Madame de La Fayette as a writer who had the ability to convey a sense of realism concerning the human condition in a world in which women, in particular, were subjected to the politics of duty, family and state.

Madame de Staël

Kavanagh's appreciation of Madame de Staël is determined by a different set of criteria. She argues that 'There are few persons living in recent times, and having left so great a name, who are in reality less known to us than is Madame de Staël' (II: 269). While she acknowledges her gifts as an intellectual, she writes that owing to the complexity of Madame de Staël's character, she is reticent about disclosing her full opinion of her as a woman. Restricted by the lack of more 'private resources' available to her at that time, Kavanagh reveals her frustration and awareness of the necessarily reductive stance of her own views on Madame de Staël.

She attributes much of Madame de Staël's character to her 'unchild-like' upbringing, which ensured that she was precocious beyond her years. To this end she gives a brief outline of the young Germaine Necker's childhood; her classical education at the hands of her 'learned, religious, and austere' (II: 192) Protestant mother, Madame Suzanne Necker; her early leanings towards metaphysics which were augmented by her acquaintance and conversations with the many learned men who frequented Madame Necker's salon;[34] and her lifelong devotion to her father, M. Jacques Necker, the prodigious banker and adviser to Louis XVI.

The discipline of Madame de Staël's early years, Kavanagh writes, was gratefully tempered by her generous nature and friendship with her lifelong friend and companion, Mademoiselle (Catherine Rilliet) Huber.[35] The two girls engaged in more creative talents such as acting out the dramas they had written together, a detour which delighted Germaine but met with disapproval from her mother. She was of the opinion that Madame de Genlis, who is reported to have regretted not having the young Germaine as either a daughter or a pupil, would have been a better literary instructor than Madame Necker.[36] Kavanagh concludes, nevertheless, that Germaine grew into an 'eloquent, impassioned, and brilliant girl, whom some beauty would have made queen of all hearts' (II: 202). Like so many of the women she writes about, Kavanagh accords much significance to physical appearance and its subsequent effect on a woman's life. Of the young Germaine she reports that 'Neither her face nor her person gave promise of beauty; her complexion was swarthy, her features were irregular, though mobile and full of expression, and her large dark eyes were what they ever remained – magnificent' (II: 193). However, Germaine's lack of beauty did not deter her admirers (including Guibert)[37] or her lovers, and herein, Kavanagh suggests, lay her charm: 'The fascination she exercised was unrivalled: it was that of a genius and a woman' (II: 205). She relates briefly to Germaine's (indifferent) marriage in 1786, at the age of twenty, to the Swedish nobleman Baron Erik de Staël, (Erik Staël von Holstein) who, although seventeen years her senior, was chosen by her parents as a suitable husband, an arrangement that was based on respect rather than love and so met with Germaine's compliance.[38] While Kavanagh speculates on the reasons for Germaine's agreeing to this marriage, she notes the irony of such a match, seeing it as nothing more than a 'cold destiny for one who never ceased to feel a woman's longing for what she considered woman's only perfect happiness – love in marriage' (II: 207). She judges that the decision was a fatal one: 'for, by binding her to duties she had not always the heroism and self denial to fulfil, this unhappy union marred the best and fairest portion of her life' (II: 207). It is clear in

Kavanagh's discussion that, as a biographer, she was uneasy about many issues in Madame de Staël's life. While accepting that Madame de Staël was not happy in her marriage, she was clearly uncomfortable with the ease with which Madame de Staël openly conducted intimate relationships with men other than her husband, even after they were officially separated and later after his death in 1802. For example, there is no mention of Madame de Staël's first lover, Tallyrand, and she gives only the briefest of details about Louis de Narbonne, the lover by whom she had two sons and whom she helped escape to England at the height of the Reign of Terror in 1792. She is equally cautious in her references to Benjamin Constant, the father of Madame de Staël's daughter, Albertine, with whom she had a relationship for over twenty years. She speaks warmly of her as a mother, but only acknowledges her three children as those from her first marriage (II: 247). It is possible that Kavanagh was unaware of the true paternity of the children but, given her sense of moral propriety, it is more likely that she thought it better to avoid comment: 'Her errors are authentic enough to leave a stain on her name as a woman, but not to mollify the severity of our judgment' (II: 269). True to her belief in the redeeming qualities of love, Kavanagh is more accepting of Madame de Staël's conduct in later life:

> Her late marriage with M. de Rocca [in 1816] is the truest clue we have to this portion of her life; it was a folly, but an honourable one, and it does more to absolve her than all that her friends have said in her favour. The woman who at forty-five could still hope and believe in love in marriage, and endeavour to secure it to herself, may have been an erring, but surely she was not a vicious woman. (II: 269)

Nevertheless, she makes no mention of the fact that, four years before their marriage, Madame de Staël had given birth to Rocca's son.[39] A few pages later she considers that, if the weak point of Madame de Staël's life was want of principle with regard to her own conduct, her generous magnanimity and concern for others was paramount.

Madame de Staël's political interests are only briefly touched upon, mainly in connection with her father's fluctuating career and the reasons for her exile, initially from her beloved Paris and then France itself.[40] Her passionate belief in constitutional liberty later brought her into conflict with Napoleon who opposed all she stood for. As she was a powerful force in her political opinions, she had posed too much of a threat to his egotistical nature, the result of which was a sense of lifelong enmity between the two. Already disturbed by the political inferences of her two novels, *Delphine* (1802) and *Corinne* (1807), in 1910 Napoleon demonstrated his wrath with this troublesome woman when he took umbrage over her publication of *D'Allemagne*. He saw this publication as anti-French in content as it questioned French political structures and subsequently ordered the destruction of all the ten thousand copies published in France.[41] After several years in exile, and in spite of poor health, Madame de Staël returned to Paris in 1814 and lived for three years before dying of a stroke in July 1817. Kavanagh writes that Madame de Staël's death was met with a sense of indifference and 'save for the social few Madame de Staël was not lamented' (II: 268). Such was, in her view, a fitting epilogue to the life Madame de Staël had chosen to lead. It was also Kavanagh's opinion that, although Madame de Staël had attracted and delighted in the company of others, she was full of deficiencies, the results of which had a detrimental affect on how people perceived her. She refers to the words of Madame Necker Saussure, Madame de Staël's adopted sister, as testimony to Madame de Staël's single-minded disregard for anything other than the execution of her own intentions: '"Her scruples, which had always had the consequences of her actions for their object, became more and more fixed on their motives"' (II: 271). Kavanagh concludes that the consequences of Madame de Staël's actions outweighed the motives, whether for good or evil. She argues that Madame de Staël's 'great error, and her great sorrow' was due to her preference of impulse to cold duty. Her conclusion is that history has thrown a 'lenient veil' over Madame de Staël's errors to the effect that the more 'dearly prized' and 'honourable' features of this woman's life have been justly recorded.

Kavanagh addresses the beginning of Madame de Staël's literary career with a brief reference to the publication of her letters on the writings of Rousseau (*Lettres sur les ouvrages et le caractère de J. J. Rousseau* (*Letters on the Works and Character of J. J. Rousseau*) (1788)):

> The delicacy of analysis and power of reasoning displayed in this essay were very remarkable in an author who had scarcely passed her twentieth year. Power, indeed, is always Madame de Staël's attribute. She is often wrong, but she is never weak; and she rarely fails to be original. (II: 208)

Clearly Kavanagh attributes Madame de Staël's attractions here to her force of opinion rather than the content of her argument. However, regardless of her own reservations, she gives Madame de Staël credit for originality. As it was often the (acceptable) practice of many writers who profited from salon interactions, she refutes certain accusations that the ideas Madame de Staël presented were not necessarily her own, that she gathered these in conversation from her friends, including Marmontel, Thomas, Grimm and Raynal. In 1795 Madame de Staël published *De l'Influence des passions sur le bonheur des individus et des nations* (*The*

Influence of Passions on the Happiness of Individuals and Nations), a work which, Kavanagh states, not only includes the 'admirable analysis of the passions' but in which, in the wake of a post-revolutionary Reign of Terror, the sceptical young writer condemns passionate feelings as fatal to human happiness. While Kavanagh notes Madame de Staël's sensibilities concerning her detached approach to faith and the study of philosophies pertaining to human 'goodness', she also denotes a sense of irony in the relationship between writer and reader: 'The cold and the wise she did not write for; yet we think that the cold and the wise alone could apply lessons so stern' (II: 232). It is interesting that modern perspectives of Madame de Staël's work contest that she was, in fact, unable to reconcile her theories with her actual belief. In this context Angelica Goodden, for example, draws attention to the conflict between the neo-Stoic philosophy of the sixteenth and early seventeenth centuries which emphasised the destructive nature of the passions and the later eighteenth-century opinion that human passions were a source for creativity and potential good. The philosophers of Madame de Staël's youth had contended that 'the purging of intense feeling was tantamount to a loss, not a gain',[42] and the tragic outcome of both *Delphine* and *Corinne* suggests that, notwithstanding her theoretical beliefs, Madame de Staël was sympathetic to this view. Given Kavanagh's leanings towards romanticism, it is not surprising that she would react unsympathetically to an argument that proffered the neutralising of passion.

In the main Kavanagh was dismissive of Madame de Staël as a novelist. On the opening page of her chapter on *Delphine* she declares that 'Madame de Staël was not a good novelist. Her mind was too metaphysical for romance. Incidents were nothing with her unless they had a meaning. Her characters were controversial; her subjects were long arguments' (II: 275). Madame de Staël's love of conversation has been blamed for the 'verbosity that mars some of her writing',[43] indeed, the novelist Madame de Charrière referred to her as a talking machine[44] and, as Kavanagh noted, 'Châteaubriand said of her that had she not spoken so well, she would have written better' (II: 275). While fully agreeing with Châteaubriand, Kavanagh adds, 'had she not thought so much, her novels would have been more natural and pleasing' (II: 275). Kavanagh's opinion, no doubt, stems from the fact that her own penchant for romantic vision was in direct opposition to Madame de Staël's literary view of the world. In some ways Kavanagh's perspective is not unlike that put forward by Schiller when, in a letter to Goethe, he writes of his experience of Madame de Staël, whom he had met in Weimer in 1803–4:

> She insists on explaining everything, on seeing into it, measuring it; she allows nothing dark, inaccessible; withersoever her torch cannot throw its light, there nothing exists for her. Hence follows an aversion, a horror, for the transcendental philosophy, which in her view leads to mysticism and superstition. This is the carbonic gas in which she dies. For what we call poetry there is no sense in her: for in such works it is only the passionate, the oratorical, and the intellectual, that she can appreciate: yet she will endure no falsehood there, only does not always recognise the true.[45]

Madame de Staël's failing, as Kavanagh saw it, was her inability to free her mind of metaphysical thought long enough to allow her imagination to conduct a good story. As a result she was not suited to write romance. Of Madame de Staël's two novels, *Delphine* and *Corinne*, she argues that, as novels, neither is satisfactory: '"Corinne" is a splendid guide-book – "Delphine" is a history of passion, from which all that does not bear upon passion has been excluded' (II: 276). Amongst other things *Delphine* is a novel that draws on the inequality of the sexes. In a letter dated 10 August 1800, Madame de Staël had written that *Delphine* was becoming 'l'histoire de la destinée des femmes présentée sous différents rapports' (the history of women's destiny), dedicating it to 'la France silencieuse' (silent France), which, Angelica Goodden has suggested, 'may or may not have been the silent body of *women*: Maria Edgeworth, who disparaged the book remarked that it might have been subtitled "Le malheur d'être femme" (the misfortune of being a woman).[46] Notwithstanding the social commentary in the novel, the sexual imbalance in the story may have contributed to Kavanagh's general disapprobation and dislike of *Delphine* as a romance. She gives her approval to its epistolary form which she suggests gave Madame de Staël 'many opportunities of developing principles she wished to advocate' (II: 278), but her main objection to *Delphine* as a novel is that it adheres to the principles of deism and as such it bears no relation to the realities of life. Her argument stems from her reservations with Madame de Staël's own philosophy that religious dogma is an impediment to thought and the imagination. While Kavanagh declared that, by its very nature, the absence of 'tame realities' was systematic of fiction, she believed that religious dogma was a fundamental part of French life and, whether for good or bad, she could not accept a novel that ignored the consequential reality of its influence. As she says:

> to banish dogmatic religion from fiction means that it should be left out from life – for what is fiction but a life more noble, more imaginative than the real? The dogmas of religion must be blended with our whole existence, or they are nothing – nay, we are better without them – and if a tale soar on sublime wing beyond the belief which guides daily life, it is weak, it has no hold on reality. (II: 276–7)

Kavanagh takes issue with Madame de Stael's representation of deism or natural religion over the laws of revealed religion. She argues:

> Besides the general moral of the story, that implied in the epigraph – that man must brave opinion, and woman submit to it – was used by Madame de Staël to unfold three arguments, which she elaborated with some care: the superiority of natural over revealed religion as a rule of life – the necessity of divorce for general happiness in marriage – the ennobling nature of love. (II: 288–9)

All of these issues, Kavanagh argues, conflict with the realities of social behaviour, which is not addressed in the novel. Unconvinced by the credibility of the tale, Kavanagh goes on to unfold the narrative that connects Mathilda, a 'rigid Catholic', to the fated love between the two main protagonists in the novel, Léonce, an atheist, and Delphine, a deist. Kavanagh argues that it is a love story that defies all probability of time or place: 'It is said to happen at the time of the French Revolution. It might happen in Fairyland, for all we know of that gloomy crisis, until it is brought in to produce the catastrophe' (II: 276). Based on the conflicting principles of honour, passion and duty, the moral of the tale is built around the principle endorsed in the epigraph. The misfortunes of the two lovers arise from their disobedience of that axiom, the consequence of which becomes clear as the narrative unfolds. Delphine is a woman who contributes to her own wretched fate by giving in to her impulse, her passion for Léonce after he has married another woman, Mathilde. It is not the impulse that is wrong – Delphine was the 'true wife of her husband's heart' (II: 291) – but the acting upon it, Kavanagh argues, that determines her downfall. The two lovers are marked out by society and, subsequently, Delphine suffers all the perils inflicted upon women who violate those rules dictated by social and religious convention. Kavanagh focuses her argument on what she sees as a contradiction in Madame de Staël's intentions here. She states that Madame de Staël had declared that she had made Delphine 'wretched, "because she could not forgive her for loving a married man"' (II: 288). The fact that Delphine suffers for her action, Kavanagh contends, 'does not efface the immoral because untrue fact that [as a deist] she has every virtue and practises none. [. . .] she can resist no temptation' and goes on to ask: 'what is the meaning of such teaching?' (II: 288). She argues that Madame de Staël's application of natural religion in the narrative does not support that which she wished to convey. Because of the nature of deism, Kavanagh suggests, Delphine does not know what is lawful and what is forbidden and as such it is her 'absolute want of principle' that undoes her. (II: 290). She goes on to question Madame de Staël's understanding of love, marriage and divorce and the implications of such entities in the novel. Léonce is wretched in his marriage with Mathilde, she says, not because marriage is binding but because he had no respect for marriage; nor does she believe that the love between Léonce and Delphine is ennobling, 'The love which, like that of Léonce, has no faith in the loved one – the love which, like that of Delphine, is weak and debasing – never was a great love' (II: 292). It is society, she notes, that is made the scapegoat for their downfall, a convenience, she concludes, that is the consequence of six volumes of metaphysics and speculation on 'some of the saddest and most perplexing problems of society and life' (II: 293). The saving grace of this novel for Kavanagh is the heroine's faith. It is this aspect of Delphine's character, which, she contends, leaves the reader not convinced but conquered.

Like those of the heroine in her novel of the same name, *Corinne*, Kavanagh suggests that: 'In its indifference to detail, and to the sad suffering aspect of northern nature' (II: 298), Madame de Staël's leanings were towards what she termed a 'Southern mind'. The warmth of Italy, so welcome to her on a visit she made after the death of her father in 1804, drew from her a friendliness to nature that was otherwise absent in northern climates. In literary terms Kavanagh often attributed characters with either a southern or a northern countenance, which she engaged in her own novels. In contrast to her Normandy surroundings, her heroine Nathalie longs for the landscape of Provence, and in her novel *Sylvia* the young protagonist brings the sunshine of Sorrento with her to the cold damp environment of the north of England. The sense of poetic freedom that Grace Lee experiences while travelling southwards and the love of nature and simplicity that contrasts Sybil's (French-like) character from her more urbane (English) friend, Blanche, are some examples of Kavanagh's concept of the 'Southern mind'. Like many novels in the nineteenth century, it could be said that Kavanagh's owe much to Madame de Staël's *Corinne* and Corinne's disrespect for the containment of domestic propriety.[47] Kavanagh considered *Corinne* a superior work to *Delphine* primarily because of the novel's depictions of Italy and the nature of its subject matter: '"Corinne [. . .] could only be written by Corinne herself. "Delphine" can be read and forgotten – "Corinne" seems written in light. It has the fine distinctness which is one of the most remarkable attributes of a great book' (II: 299). Kavanagh's main contention is that though the story deals with love, in reality there is but little love in it. It is Corinne who absorbs the reader wholly: 'Like the queen in a classic tragedy, she fills the scene; she even effaces her own love and its sorrows. [. . .] Corinne is not woman's love, passionate and devoted – she is genius, giving to man the adoration that should have been bestowed on art alone' (II: 310–11).

Kavanagh had already dismissed *Corinne* as a true novel when she noted the conflicting interests between the intended love story and the depictions of Italy: 'though a novel ought to be nothing but a novel, and though fiction detracts from reality which is the charm of a book of travels, Madame de Staël's attempt was like Byron's, later, in "Childe Harold," singularly felicitous. It suited her genius – too metaphysical for fiction and too imaginative for mere truth' (II: 299). In her analysis of the novel Kavanagh demonstrates her preference for a more imaginative rendition of reality over what she perceived as a catalogue of metaphysical ideas. In her judgement of *Corinne*, as a love story, there is misunderstanding of the true nature of the union of soul and heart – too much of Madame de Staël's intervention that infiltrates throughout the narrative. For example, while attending a ball in Rome, Lord Neville, a major character in the novel, is asked by a Frenchman what he thinks of Rome, and is met with the indecorous response: '"One cannot speak seriously in a ball-room; and *you know I cannot speak otherwise*"' (II: 313). It is such moments, Kavanagh contends, that expose Madame de Staël's weakness, as here, she is the one who is, in fact, doing the talking. However, what Kavanagh perceived as Madame de Staël's weakness as a novelist, she hailed as the gifts of an extraordinary woman. '"Corinne"', she states, 'was more than a novel' just as Madame de Staël 'was more than a novelist. We have seen her but under one aspect of her literary career, and it had many. The eloquent critic, the acute thinker, the clear though dogmatic politician, would show us another Madame de Staël, far more wonderful than the novelist' (II: 318). Her two novels, *Delphine* and *Corinne*, were, for Kavanagh, the 'gentle aspect of that great and powerful mind which would not depart without having told us what it thought of love and woman' (II: 319). Perhaps this, Kavanagh's concluding comment on Madame de Staël, is an appropriate ending to her study of French women writers as she gives the final word to one who, she was undoubtedly aware, had already proved her influence on writers in the mid nineteenth century.

English *Women of Letters*

Writing in *The Athenaeum* Geraldine Jewsbury said that in *English Women of Letters* Kavanagh writes of women 'who have been the first in their own style'.[48] As with her choice of French women writers, Kavanagh pleads impartiality in her selection, which, she says, is based on 'great celebrity, original or suggestive power, and great attraction'. As before, she has chosen ten authors, all novelists. In her preface to *English Women of Letters* she has added little to her previous comments and merely uses it as an opportunity to remind her reader that she has included only dead authors who have 'already stood the test of all merit – time'. Her selection is compiled of: Aphra Behn (1640–89), Sarah Fielding 1710–68),[49] Madame D'Arblay (Fanny Burney) (1752–1840), Charlotte Smith (1749–1806), Ann Radcliffe (1764–1823), Elizabeth Inchbald (1753–1821), Maria Edgeworth (1768–1849), Jane Austen (1775–1817), Amelia Opie 1769–1853) and Lady Morgan (Sydney Owenson) (1775–1859). Kavanagh is interested in these writers as individual women in their time as well as the literary impact and historical relevance afforded to their novels. Although her biographical information has, occasionally, been proved wrong (as will be discussed later), her sincerity of purpose, a phrase she could also have applied to her subjects, is beyond refute.

Aphra Behn

As was the case in France, prejudice against women's literary emancipation in England during the seventeenth century was rife and it was considered morally reprehensible for a woman to step beyond the given boundaries of behavioural acceptance. Moreover, for an Englishwoman to publish, and to publish for money, was, more or less, tantamount to prostitution. As in France, anonymity of women's writing was the preferred path. In England a woman who published her work openly made herself public and vulnerable to social discrimination.[50] It was in this culture of restraint that in 1688 the conduct-book writer the Marquis of Halifax had remarked in relation to such women as Aphra Behn, 'the unjustifiable Freedom of some of your Sex have involved the rest in the penalty of being reduced'.[51] Since her death in 1689, Aphra Behn had been a particular target of what Maureen Duffy refers to as 'the rising waters of late eighteenth century neo-puritanism'.[52] Kavanagh is of the opinion that the noble examples of Mademoiselle de Scudéry and Madame de La Fayette were lost on Aphra Behn, who, though familiar with the object of their works, 'wrote not one coarse passage the less for either' (11). While she argues that the women of France did their best to ennoble women and 'compel them into delicacy', Aphra Benn, she suggests, is guilty of encouraging women to sink to the level of man's coarseness in that neither she nor her pupils attempted, or cared, to raise men to woman's moral standards. Writing in the mid nineteenth century, Kavanagh's censure is somewhat typical of the time, as Aphra Behn was then still perceived as a writer of depravity and coarseness. Geraldine Jewsbury took exception to Kavanagh's inclusion of Behn in her study. She considered Behn to be a woman who had 'wasted her genius and profaned her gifts' and that Kavanagh 'would have done better to leave both novel [*Oroonoko*] and author where she found them, in the Mausoleum of the British Museum'. Kavanagh was well aware of the reaction of puritan severity, which, she noted, had defiled English literature far and wide, and that Behn had been an open target. However, it seems that for all her objections to what she perceived as Behn's lack of moral consciousness in her writing, Kavanagh was, nevertheless, intrigued by her outright defiance of implied laws of decorum for women: 'She wrote dramas which, though not worse than those of her contemporaries, revolted the public as proceeding from a woman, yet, braving censure and reproof, with an independence worthy [of] a better cause, she persisted in her course' (11). Overall, Kavanagh recognised Behn as a woman with many sides to her nature, or, to use Janet Todd's phrase, as 'an unending combination of masks'.[53] In Kavanagh's view Behn was a woman who fell short of the accepted notion of seventeenth-century femininity in both her conduct and her writing, but in so doing was able to assert an independence that was flamboyantly defiant of imposed social mores.

In the mid nineteenth century, when Kavanagh was undertaking her own research, the few available sources pertaining to Aphra Behn's life offered little in the way of enlightenment. Indeed, it was not until Maureen Duffy's biography in 1987 that many issues and facts concerning her true birth and circumstances were verified. Janet Todd's biography, published in 1996, begins with the comment, 'What is securely known about Aphra Benn outside her works could be summed up in a page'.[54] Conscious of the paucity of biographical information – 'Of her life as a writer and a woman we do not know much' – Kavanagh draws solely on material available in the biographical source attributed to '"one of the fair sex"',[55] a writer who, Kavanagh notes, was 'one who knew her long and well, who loved her truly and defended her warmly, but with more zeal than boldness' (10). From this source Kavanagh deduces that Behn had two great passions, the 'mightiest was pleasure; the second literature' which she combined 'in an unusual degree'. She goes on to discuss the accepted geniality of this voluptuous and sociable woman as portrayed by her biographer. She refers briefly to some of the major events in Behn's life, notably her time in Holland as an English spy, her Dutch lovers and her experience of unrequited love with the man she referred to as Lysander or sometimes Lycidas. However Kavanagh does express some doubts as to the authenticity of some of the information in her source and so offers a brief overview of Behn's progress and contribution as a writer in her time, of which she says:

She wrote for her bread, and wrote much and carelessly. She borrowed from French, Spanish, and English authors. She published three volumes of miscellaneous poems, in which Rochester and Sir George Etherege, among the rest, were her coadjutors. Her poems were bad, though she contributed the paraphrase of 'Oenone's Epistle to Paris,' in the English translation of 'Ovid's Epistles,' and received the following handsome compliment from Dryden in the preface to that work: – 'I was desired to say that the author, who is of the fair sex, understood not Latin. But if she does not, I am afraid she has given us account to be ashamed who do.' Her plays, some of which had great success, were so coarse as to offend even that coarse age. Her novels were open to the same objection and were rarely original. Sometimes, but not often, she openly acknowledged her translations, as in the case of La Rochefoucauld's 'Maxims,' and Fontenelle's 'Plurality of Worlds.' Towards the close of her life, she included mathematics, philosophy, theology even, in her pursuits, but it must be confessed that she excelled in nothing. Like all persons of lively minds, she took interest in many things; she found pleasure in those 'rare flies, of amazing forms and colours,' which she brought from Surinam, and presented 'to his Majesty's antiquary,' and, at a later period, she took amusement in the arid details of chronology, but her versatility was productive of no substantial result. (9–10)

It is, nevertheless, in the descriptions of Surinam, the (purported) country of Behn's early years, which Kavanagh finds the more palatable and acceptable planes of Behn's writing. It is here that, she argues, the bountiful and beautiful surroundings natural to that environment fired Behn's imagination and unleashed her powers of observation: 'Aphra Behn's description of this luxuriant country is remarkable; in this, and in the forcible portraiture of character, lay her strength, and that of the future English school of fiction which she not unworthily opened' (4). It is Kavanagh's awareness of Behn's contribution to fiction, and the fact that she praises Behn at all, that sets her apart from other nineteenth-century commentators. Two decades after Kavanagh's publication John Doran vehemently attacked Behn's plays in particular, claiming that 'Behn dragged the Muses down to her level "where the Nine and their unclean votary wallowed together in the mire"'.[56] Eric Robertson also felt the need to apologise for including Behn in *English Poetesses* (1883) when he declared, 'It is a pity, [that] mention should be made of so unsexed a writer as Mrs. Aphra Behn'.[57] Although Kavanagh voices her admonition of Behn's dramatic works in particular, within this climate of Behn censure, she also speaks out in favour of Behn's strengths as a writer. Ezell has argued that, owing to her lack of '"feminine"'characteristics, Robertson and Kavanagh see Behn as both a failed female and a failed writer and goes on to suggest that in their eyes 'success in the second category depends primarily on success in the first'.[58] As Kavanagh's praise of Behn suggests, she is not wholly of that opinion, and therefore to hook her on to another critic's prejudice negates the positive qualities that Kavanagh affords to Behn as a writer.

After Behn returned to England, she met Charles II who, on being moved to pity by the 'tragic history of Prince Oroonoko', suggested she should publish her novel. This novel, in which Behn draws her material from her experience of early colonialism and slavery, the triumphs of human dignity and the redemptive force of love, appealed directly to Kavanagh's own understanding of what she perceived as the power of fiction to convey truth. If Kavanagh was unable or unwilling to consider Behn's other works worthy of comment, she was deeply touched by the political exposure and expressed humanity in *Oroonoko* (1688). In this context she compares Behn's ability to convey a sense of 'truth' with that of her French contemporaries:

> To that deep feeling of a great wrong inflicted on a noble nature, Mrs. Behn owed the power, the dignity, and the tenderness with which she told the story of Oroonoko; and it is a noble thing and a rare gift to feel the truth with such depth and keenness. Let us compare Oroonoko with the 'Grand Cyrus' with the exquisite 'Princess de Clèves' itself, we shall feel nothing there that comes so much home to our feelings, nothing that is so true of every time, as this story. (22–3)

However, regardless of the merit afforded to Behn's ability as a writer of 'truth', for Kavanagh it was not enough to erase the offensive nature of the majority of Behn's works. Kavanagh's critical rejection of Aphra Behn as a great writer rests on Behn's lack of 'delicacy', the generic quality, which, in Kavanagh's view, takes precedence over all others. It is interesting, therefore, that in her appraisal of *Oroonoko* she acknowledges Behn's superiority over her French contemporaries. She goes on to suggest that the two French authors (Mademoiselle de Scudéry and Madame de La Fayette) in dispensing with the indelicacies would, no doubt, each have produced a weakened and lesser novel but still have created a classic.[59] She considers:

> though Mrs. Behn's indelicacy was useless, and worse than useless, [. . .] she had two gifts which she far excelled either of the French ladies – freshness and truth. 'Oroonoko' is not a good book, but it is a vigorous, dramatic, and true story. True in every sense. The descriptions are bright, luxuriant, and picturesque; the characters are rudely sketched, but with great power; the conversations are full of life and spirit. Its rude and careless strength made it worthy to be one of the first great works of English fiction. In some of the nobler attributes of all fiction it failed, but enough remained to mark the drawing of that great English school of passion and nature, of dramatic and pathetic incident, which, though last arisen and slowly developed, has borrowed least and taught most. (23)

Kavanagh's final comment here suggests that she did, in fact, admire Aphra Behn more than she was able to admit. The very fact that she chose to open her discussion on English women writers with an appraisal of this writer is significant and, although she dismissed Behn's other works, her comments on *Oroonoko*[60] suggest that she felt a sense of gratification that it was a woman who, in producing such a work, had the courage of her convictions. Considering Kavanagh's recognition of Behn in this respect, she offers no concession to Clara Reeve's earlier comments on Behn in *The Progress of Romance*. While Reeve notes the impropriety of Behn's works, she defends her on the grounds that she possessed 'marks of genius':

> Among our early Novel writers we must reckon Mrs. Behn. – There are strong marks of genius in all this lady's works, but unhappily, there are some parts of them, very improper to be read by, or recommended to virtuous minds, and especially to youth. – She wrote in an age, and to a court of licentious manners, and perhaps one ought to ascribe to these causes the loose turn of her stories. – Let us do justice to her merits, and cast the veil of compassion over her faults.[61]

Kavanagh's own critical stance projects both historical censure and an accepted nineteenth-century cultural admonition of Behn's writing. Yet, like Clara Reeve, who was writing in the second half of the eighteenth century, she was also conscious of the significance of Behn as a woman writing in the politically charged yet sexually cloistered world of seventeenth-century England. It is arguable that alongside history's censure of Behn there is another strand in history in which the positive aspects of this writer have met with recognition and critical acceptance. Kavanagh is a part of that strand when she defiantly speaks out for Behn's finer contribution to women's writing, which precedes by almost seventy years Virginia Woolf's well-known assertion in the early twentieth century that it was Aphra Behn 'who earned [women] the right to speak their minds'.[62] It is this voice which suggests that, in spite of the objections she raises to Behn's lack of 'delicacy', Kavanagh, nevertheless, perceived Behn as one who had the ability to portray a sense of 'freshness and truth' at a time when it was itself considered 'indelicate' of women to write fiction at all.

Not such 'silly young creatures'

Kavanagh argues that the impact of women's writing in England during the eighteenth century had brought about a significant change in so far as women had introduced 'delicacy' into a literary culture which, when it was not licentious or profane, was, nevertheless, 'coarse'. Evidence of her own feminist thinking is visible in her objections to the portrayal of women by the earlier male novelists which was that of 'silly young creatures made to delight man, to amuse, tease, and obey him' (96). And for Kavanagh this depiction of woman's worth was coarseness indeed. She argues that 'We had not the perfect and twofold human being until women wrote' (96). Richardson, she claims, who respected women, was the only male writer of his age to do them justice, namely in his creation of Clarissa whom she considers 'a great and noble creature' (96). Smollet and Fielding she dismisses outright and it is with a sense of irony that she speaks of Goldsmith: 'the delicate, tender, and certainly refined Goldsmith – could not go beyond Sophia Primrose. She was his ideal of a heroine: a handsome, sensible, and quiet girl, capable of appreciating a superior man' (96–7). She goes on to suggest that it was the woman novelist who put an end to this 'low ideal of womanhood' and introduced heroines with substance. Fanny Burney's Evelina, for example, is one such : 'Instead of standing in the background, a lovely young creature, ready to be wooed and won, she is a prominent figure, and acts a leading part from first to last' (97). She puts forward a similar case for Burney's Cecilia and Charlotte Smith's Emmeline, a heroine who impressed Madame de Genlis to such an extent that she predicted that women would soon reach a 'supremacy in literature' (98). In Kavanagh's view women did fulfil this prophecy – an accomplishment, she argues, that cannot be overestimated. She contends that 'The ambition of women [in England] seems to have been to establish a standard of their own excellence, essentially different from that which men prized' (98). This 'excellence' however was the result of progressive literary development over the century. Outside of the very small, aristocratic Blue Stocking Circle, led by Lady Elizabeth Montagu, who would meet to discuss matters of social and cultural significance, engagement in intellectual pursuits was considered unwomanly and it was not until the last quarter of the eighteenth century, when there was a significant increase in women's literary production, that this prejudice dissolved. There are numerous reminders of such prejudices in women's writing: in Fanny Burney's *Evelina*, Mr Lovell says, 'I have an insuperable aversion to strength, either of body or mind, in a female'[63] and, as Jane Austen pointedly remarked in *Northanger Abbey* (1818), 'imbecility in females is a great enhancement of their personal charms'.[64] The concealment of learning was tantamount to femininity, as Dr Gregory famously advised women, 'If you happen to have any learning, keep it a profound secret'.[65] For much of the century women who appeared 'learned' put themselves at risk of public ridicule. Kavanagh notes that in her early drama *The Witlings*[66] Fanny Burney herself expressed 'a strong dislike to learning in women' – not that she considered learning in women objectionable in itself, but through fear of public ridicule. Burney's friends compared *The*

Witlings to Molière's *Femmes Savantes*, which ridicules learned women, and the play was never performed. Kavanagh also notes that, although Burney had a knowledge of Latin (her teacher was Dr Johnson), she did not delight in her studies as 'The dread of being thought learned was greater than the pleasure of acquiring a dead language' (46). Burney had noted in her journal, 'I would a thousand times rather forfeit my character as a writer than risk ridicule or censure as a female'; as Judy Simons succinctly puts it, 'the personal dilemma she describes embodied the perplexities of the age.'[67]

Sarah Fielding

Following her discussion on Aphra Behn, Kavanagh offers only a cursory glimpse of Sarah Fielding. She contends that as 'Aphra Behn's ideal of womanhood was coarse and low; Miss Fielding's was uncertain; like her brother, she dealt more with humours of human nature than with its secret springs' (97). She notes that 'Three quarters of a century had elapsed since Aphra Behn had published her "Oroonoko," so fresh and vigorous with all its rudeness, when Miss Fielding produced her "David Simple," in 1744' (27). Considering the amount of biographical information Kavanagh allocates to each of the women in her study, unpredictably Sarah Fielding's background is wrapped up in one short, clipped paragraph:

> Sarah Fielding, born in 1714,[68] died at Bath in 1768. She was the friend of Richardson, and some of her letters are included in his correspondence, not far from the begging epistle of poor, starving Laetitia Pilkington; we also find her alluded to by Johnson. (25)

She is similarly sparing in her commentary on her work. Sarah Fielding, Kavanagh argues, was one who did not quite fit into the age in which she wrote. She contends that Fielding's novel *David Simple* walked a fine line between the declining picaresque and the emerging English school of fiction, and suggests that Sarah Fielding would have made a better essayist than novelist.

Fanny Burney (Madame D'Arblay)

By contrast Kavanagh offers a fuller picture of Fanny Burney (1752–1840), who became Madame D'Arblay, the name she has chosen to head her section on this writer. Kavanagh opens her chapter on Fanny Burney's novel *Evelina* (1778) with a flourishing recognition of Burney's talent:

> More than a hundred and thirty years after the fame of Mademoiselle de Scudéry had reached its acme, the name of Frances Burney redeemed

English literature from the reproach of having produced no woman of genius sufficient to rule, for a time at least, the world of fiction. For some years Miss Burney was certainly the greatest of living English novelists. Her 'Evelina' and 'Cecilia' had, in their day, as much power and importance as the 'Great Cyrus' and her 'Princess of Clèves' in another. They were the books which the appearance created delighted surprise or impatient expectations. Goldsmith was dead, and Walter Scott was not yet in his teens. Miss Burney long stood first. (58)

Kavanagh's account of Fanny Burney's life, taken mainly from Burney's diaries, tells of a demure, grave young creature who, because of her shyness, was known in the household as 'the old lady'. However, she notes that, 'beneath that solemn exterior concealed, not merely an unusual amount of talent, but an exquisite sense of the ridiculous, and a rare and penetrating knowledge of character' (39). She conveys a sense of the congenial home life headed by Fanny Burney's father, Dr Charles Burney, who, Kavanagh distinctly notes, was a descendant of the MacBurneys of Shropshire and who could probably claim descent from the Irish O'Byrnes of Wicklow. Fanny Burney's childhood and formative years were spent in the harmonious company of the intelligent and cultured, including Mrs Thrale (Hester Lynch Piozzi), for whom she was a favourite, and luminaries such as Dr Johnson, who treated her as his pet. Nevertheless, Kavanagh is selective in what she chooses to write about. Although she goes into some detail about Burney's life and her progression as a writer, there are conspicuous gaps. She gives information relating to the period between 1786 and 1790 when Burney reluctantly agreed to undertake the position of the Second Keeper of the Robes for Queen Charlotte; her marriage to the French aristocrat Alexandre D'Arblay, whom she met while he was domiciled in England; and the birth of their son and the times she spent in Paris. However, she makes no reference to Burney's battle with breast cancer and the mastectomy she underwent, without anaesthetic, in Paris on 30 September 1811.[69] Considering the biographical significance of this event, it is puzzling as to why Kavanagh omitted it! It may be that she considered the subject too indelicate for inclusion. She records the events leading up to the publication of *Evelina* in 1778,[70] which was published anonymously and for which Burney received the princely sum of £20. Interestingly an entry in Burney's diary later records that, owing to the unforeseen success of *Evelina*, this agreement had incurred the loss of £1500. Kavanagh notes that, unable to keep the news of publication to herself, Burney felt obliged to acknowledge the existence of the work to her father who appears to have found his daughter's enterprise amusing. In view of the prejudices towards women and print at that time, Kavanagh finds his congenial response disconcerting:

It does not seem to have occurred to this thoughtless father that by this book his daughter might compromise for ever her reputation or her prospects – for he must have known how futile was her dream of incognito – still less that this shy, quiet little brown lady of twenty-six could possibly have written a tale of merit'. (42)

Evelina was a tremendous success and was applauded by Dr Johnson who (being no admirer of Fielding) declared that '"Harry Fielding knew nothing but the shell of life," gallantly leaving Miss Burney the kernel' (43). Kavanagh also records that Edmund Burke and Sir Joshua Reynolds read *Evelina* enthusiastically and Mrs Thrale 'liked it better than Madame Riccoboni's tales', a writer who, Kavanagh notes, 'was in the noon of her fame' (43). There was also much curiosity about the author, which led to speculation that the novel might have been written by Anstey, the author of the *Bath Guide*, or even by Horace Walpole. When her identity was eventually disclosed, Burney found herself the prize of fashionable society.

Circulating libraries, which conveniently facilitated the rising number of women readers, had first appeared in the 1740s.[71] Such a readership would, no doubt, help to explain the appeal of Burney's novel in which the problems of domestic life are viewed from a female perspective. Evelina is a heroine of her age when manners and etiquette were a young woman's currency and Kavanagh sees the novel's strength in its exposure of vulgarity. Although she does not consider Burney a writer of great human depth, she gives much credit for her ability to convey an astute sense of realism in her satirical portrayal of social pretensions:

Miss Burney lived in the very heart of the world of her day. She saw, she heard, and she painted. Her vision was keen, her hand unerring. She was too genuine a woman of her times to appeal to the feelings or to the imagination. No presentiment of a new school – of still undiscovered horizons – of regions fair and fruitful – disturbed her quick sense of the present. Sufficient for her were the men and women whom she saw, and their manners, their oddities, their vulgarity, their coarseness, insolence, or pride [. . .] She revelled especially in pictures of high-born or middle-class vulgarity. Her sense of the humourous *sic* and the ludicrous was keen – too keen for geniality. (58–9)

Of Burney's novel *Cecilia* (1782) Kavanagh suggests that, though it lacks the seduction of *Evelina*, it is 'an acute mirror of the passing follies of the day' (71). Again, she praises the power of Burney's observations on the follies of human weakness in which she advocates that 'Manners and characters, perplexities of incident, were Miss Burney's *forte*' (81), yet she contends that 'the subtle graces of tenderness, of those vague feelings which scarcely know how to leave the heart, she knew not how to deal with' (81). *Camilla*, which came out in 1796, was testament to what Kavanagh judged as Burney's 'falling off' as a novelist, and *The Wanderer* which followed in 1814 she considered a failure (87). She argues that in these novels Burney's attempts to engage with the complexities of woman's lot in the world were not as convincing as, say, those of Madame de Staël, whose heroines Corinne and Delphine, though subject to censure are, nevertheless, more sympathetic as women on the grounds that 'the teaching of the tale is that genius, independence, and generous feelings ought not to be so strictly fettered by social laws' (86). It is Kavanagh's opinion that Burney failed in the plight of woman's rights because she did not allow her heroines to explore beyond the narrow confines of their socially defined world:

> her heroines are amiable, correct, and good; but so inexorable is she to the least dereliction from the right path of prudence – for virtue is never questioned – that she is ready to inflict every sorrow and every humiliation upon them if they take a step beyond its narrow limits. The world is right, and always right – if they suffer, let them thank their own folly for their sorrows. (86)

She compares Burney's heroines unfavourably with those of 'Mrs. Inchbald' and 'Miss Edgeworth' in so far as, unlike these two novelists who knew 'where the springs of life lie hidden', the sorrows of Burney's heroines stem predominantly from the external world and 'never spring from within' (89). For Kavanagh a consideration of the 'inner life' is important if a writer is to convey a truer picture of the heroine's subjectivity. Kavanagh's comparison with Madame de Staël's flawed heroines suggests that she would have preferred Fanny Burney to have taken more risks with her heroines and to have gone beyond the social ideal of the conventional virtuous woman.[72] It is clear that Kavanagh's recognition of Burney's contribution to the English novel is established less in the depiction of her heroines – though she notes that *Evelina* 'is valuable and interesting as a woman's picture of English life and society in the year 1778' (70) – and more for her scrupulous observations of the society in which she lived. These observations, which, Kavanagh notes, did not originate in women's writing, are, nevertheless, born out of domestic life, the domain of the woman writer in which Fanny Burney excelled.

Charlotte Smith

In her discussion of Charlotte Smith, Kavanagh refers to details of this writer's background that had already been made public by Sir Walter Scott in 1829 and Anne Elwood in her 1843 publication *Memoirs of the*

Literary Ladies of England from the Commencement of the Last Century.[73] However, whereas Anne Elwood sees merit in Charlotte Smith's poetry, Kavanagh merely reminds her reader that 'as a poetess she is forgotten' (91). Charlotte Smith, though she was born in London, was formerly Charlotte Turner whose family hailed from Sussex. Orphaned when she was four years of age, she was raised by her aunt and educated in London. As a result of family circumstances, the aunt considered that marriage would offer the best long-term security for her beloved niece who was then aged fourteen. Kavanagh's somewhat dry delivery of this arrangement gives some indication of the sense of resignation and duty that she imagined was Charlotte's experience. She tells us:

> A Mr. Smith, aged twenty-one, was found and prepared to fall in love with her niece, who also received the injunction to welcome his passion; the young people proved docile; and in February, 1765, Miss Turner [now aged fifteen] was married. (92)

Family respectability was guaranteed by the fact that the groom's father was a West India merchant and a Director of the East India Company. All did not turn out as planned, however, and Kavanagh writes that, although the union was unfortunate in that neither was happy, for Charlotte it was the cause of 'a long source of misery' (92). Domestic circumstances also worked against the two young people, as Kavanagh continues: 'The home and family to which a young, romantic, and accomplished girl found herself introduced, were enough to chill any bride's heart'. The couple lived in a grim part of London, in 'A house in one of the narrowest and dirtiest lanes in the city, and in which the sun's beams had never shone' (92). To add to her torment, Charlotte was forced to suffer the debilitating eccentricities of her in-laws. The waywardness of her financially irresponsible and pleasure-seeking husband soon led to him serving seven months' imprisonment in 1783 for debt. As his wife, Charlotte was obliged to accompany her husband in this grim ordeal, after which she then withdrew to her beloved Sussex where, Kavanagh records, Charlotte's temporary elation was soon dashed by poverty and cares. She began writing to help support her eight children[74] (she gave birth to twelve children in all), publishing her *Elegiac Sonnets and Other Essays* in 1784 at her own expense. She also worked as a translator and produced pamphlets as well as novels which were the main source of her livelihood. After ten years of marriage Charlotte, worn down by cares, left her husband in 1785 and subsequently published *Emmeline* in 1788.

Kavanagh sees Charlotte Smith as a brave but sad woman who, in the history of women's writing, helped to 'fill the vacant space between Miss

Burney and Mrs. Radcliffe'. While she considers her inferior to these two writers, having neither 'the vigour of the one, or the picturesque faculty of the other' (91), she is of the opinion that Charlotte Smith was one of the best novelists of the day. This view is interesting in so far as Kavanagh argues that, while Charlotte Smith was addicted to poetry, it was 'bitter necessity that made her a novelist' (94). At the same time Charlotte Smith was conscious of the political influences of her day and her views are expressed in her novel *Desmond* (1792). This aspect of Charlotte Smith's work is fully recognised by Kavanagh when she notes that 'Mrs. Smith was, like Mrs. Inchbald, a partisan of the new doctrines of the day, and like her, she lived in the intimacy of many fiery spirits of those exciting times' (93). She argues that although Charlotte Smith wrote much and with 'unequal success' she wrote in haste, which, coupled with 'the gloom that overshadowed her life, robbed her of a durable literary fame' (91). Nevertheless she considers Charlotte Smith 'worthy of record', seeing her as a 'connecting link between opposite schools [Fanny Burney and Ann Radcliffe], and the most characteristic representative of the modern domestic novel' (95). In fact Kavanagh goes on to suggest that 'She is quite distinct in this respect from the writers of her times, and the combination, though in an inferior degree, of merits so different, is her claim to originality' (95). *Emmeline*, *Ethelinda* (1789) and *The Old Manor House* (1793), she considers the most agreeable and representative of Charlotte Smith's work and refers to these three novels in her discussion. While she accepts that there are tender and pleasing passages in *Emmeline*, she dismisses it because of the improbability of the details. The more successful aspect of both this novel and her successive work, *Ethelinda*, she judges to be Smith's depiction of 'the lady'; a much imitated phenomenon, she argues, that remains 'far beyond anything similar in contemporary literature, French or English' (98).

It is in this section of her discussion that Kavanagh focuses predominantly on sexual politics and the developments of the woman novelist. She raises here the 'vexed question' pertaining to the lack of understanding between the sexes when, she says, 'the more delicate workings of either must ever escape the other's penetration' (99). Women novelists, she argues, offered a greater variety of heroines in their novels, including Charlotte Smith's multi-dimensional idea of the active woman as 'lady'. While Kavanagh contends that in *The Old Manor House* the heroine, Monimia, lacks interest, the more secondary character Mrs Grace Rayland, the rich and haughty inhabitant of the Old Manor House itself, is 'admirably drawn'. Kavanagh applauds the imaginative rendering of this elderly woman, which is 'free from caricature or exaggeration'

and 'seems to have been suggested [. . .] by Queen Elizabeth' (103). She
sees her as a powerful and despotic influence on others:

> The character of this haughty, selfish, jealous woman is excellently sus-
> tained throughout. She lives away from the freedom of modern manners,
> in a solemn world of her own, and everyone who enters that charmed circle
> must adopt her antediluvian notions. She keeps within her ancestral pride
> within an impregnable fortress. Capricious, mistrustful, and supercilious,
> she maintains the Somerives [her relations] in a slow fever of suspense.
> What will become of her vast property when she is gone to her venerable
> ancestors? No one knows, not even the reader. (102–3)

By contrast to this powerful and intriguing despot, Kavanagh perceives
the younger 'heroine', Monimia, the hero Orlando's beloved, as engaging but puerile and ignorant. And although Monimia shares the same
culturally imposed weakness of other heroines, particularly her more
intelligent counterparts, Emmeline and Ethelina, Kavanagh finds her
quite unacceptable:

> Her weakness is one which they shared, and to which the heroines of
> women are still liable: she is too sensitive, too easily frightened, and she
> weeps too much and too often. The number of times she is near fainting
> during her stolen interviews with Orlando is irritating, and the facility with
> which her tears flow is childish (105).

Clearly, Monimia has little appeal for Kavanagh, who contends that,
regardless of the intentions of the story, interest is sustained primarily by
the powerful presence of the old lady, Mrs Grace Rayland. As a writer
Kavanagh considered Charlotte Smith to be 'above mediocrity but below
genius' (114). She praises her 'great charm her gift and her power' but
maintains that her work is tinged with the stamp of sadness that the
author herself endured in her own life.

It is understandable that Kavanagh considered Charlotte Smith's
young heroine insipid. Monimia was representative of an all too characteristic acceptance of female frailty that served to measure her sexual
desirability as a woman. The association of frailty and desirability was
related very much to the type of education women received which, in the
main, was designed to keep women childlike and dependent. This
specific aspect of female conditioning was particularly irksome to
Kavanagh, and the issue of women's education during the seventeenth
and eighteenth centuries infiltrates Kavanagh's perspective of both
French and English women writers. As was the case with her French contemporary, an English woman was not required to spell correctly or, in
her case, to write 'decent English'. Moreover, Kavanagh argues that this

attitude to women was detrimental to their wider understanding of knowledge, as she says that women's knowledge, 'such as it was, rarely went far or deep – opinion, prejudice, and society restricted it within the narrowest bounds, and, as a rule, women lacked that culture from within, without which even genius can achieve no perfect work' (122).

Ann Radcliffe

It was this very lack of education that, in Kavanagh's view, prevented Ann Radcliffe from reaching her full potential as a novelist. Although she considered that Ann Radcliffe wrote passages of 'great beauty, told in beautiful language', she maintained that 'these productions, one and all, betray a mind which had long lain dormant, and that wakened too late to the consciousness of great gifts' (122). Maria Edgeworth, she notes, gained much as the recipient of her loving father's intellectual endeavours as an 'educator'; however, Edgeworth was amongst the exceptional few as most women were socialised against intellectual enquiry. As Kavanagh argues:

> Nature has set a difference, and a great one, between man and woman, but education has set one still greater. It is not the Greek and Latin of boys that gives them a future advantage over their more ignorant sisters. It is that they are trained to act a part in life, and a part worth acting, whilst girls are either taught to look on life, or, worse still, told how to practise its light and unworthy arts. (202–3)

Along with many other women, Ann Radcliffe was a recipient of such an inadequate system.[75] In Kavanagh's view the educational gender imbalance was an effective barrier to women's progress:

> Had Ann Radcliffe been John Radcliffe, and received the vigorous and polished education which makes the man and the gentleman, we might have had a few novels less, but we would assuredly have had some fine pages more in that language where, spite their merit, her works will leave no individual trace. (123)[76]

The cult of female sensibility took precedence in educational matters and Kavanagh argues that Radcliffe's 'want of knowledge' left her ignorant, awkward and impatient, failings that proved to work against her. However, while she contends that Radcliffe failed to portray character, failed in penetration, historical knowledge and cultivated taste, she was never vulgar. Her great strength was in her understanding of Nature and her ability to waken a sense of 'Terror' in her reader. Although nowhere in her commentary does Kavanagh attempt to engage in unravelling the psychodynamics of terror in the stories, particularly those concerning the heroine's development – or lack of it – in each novel, she is conscious of the psychological complexities that terror suggests. In her commentary on Radcliffe's second novel, *A Sicilian Romance* (1790), she suggests that Radcliffe's powers of description, though exaggerated and not developed as fully as in her later novels, 'enabled her to reveal to many minds a taste, a passion, that had lain all but dormant till she came [. . .] For in what novels and romances, till she took up a pen, shall we find places and scenery substituted for the human interest?' (124–5). It was the heady mix of terror and the sublime that Kavanagh considered to be part of the human condition and the mark of genius in Radcliffe's novels.

Ann Radcliffe follows in the Romance tradition associated with Horace Walpole and Clara Reeve but, as Kavanagh argues, like Sir Walter Scott himself, in their portrayal of gothic times and manners, they failed in so far as they could produce only a one-sided picture. She maintains that Walpole's *Castle of Otranto* (1764) and Reeve's *Old English Baron* (originally published as *The Champion of Virtue* in 1777), two signature gothic Romances, took no account of the paralleled joys and cruelties of that distant age. In delivering their tales to suit the convention of the times, she claims that, in an attempt to comply with a sense of eighteenth-century decorum, these writers are guilty of giving a false picture of the past:

> The knight has been clothed in modern gentleness, politeness, and refinement, and in that smoothing down of features offensive to modern taste, the largeness, that great characteristic of the Middle Ages, and perhaps the greatest, the manly and noble frankness, have been irremediably lost. (117)

From this 'evil', she contends, 'Mrs. Radcliffe' kept clear. In fact Kavanagh argues that, unlike her predecessors, Ann Radcliffe was thoroughly original in her work to the extent that she founded a new school that 'spite its faults', after two generations its stores remain abundant.[77] In her judgement Ann Radcliffe was, quite simply, a better writer than her predecessors. Kavanagh was not alone in her opinion; as noted by Bonamy Dobrée in his introduction to Radcliffe's *The Mysteries of Udolpho*, De Quincey had referred to her as 'the great enchantress of that generation' (*Confessions of an English Opium Eater*, Masson, III, p. 282), and Scott had declared her to be 'the first poetic novelist' in English literature.[78] During her lifetime Radcliffe's reputation as a novelist was without question and she was the recipient of much critical acclaim.[79] As Dobrée has noted, favourable attention persisted through Laetitia Barbauld's Introduction to volume XLIII of *The British Novelists* (1810) until the 1830s when a new phase of novel-writing based on social experience took over.[80] In fact, until that period, Radcliffe was designated 'required reading' by those who considered themselves educated or cultured. Jane Austen took it for granted that her readers would be familiar with Radcliffe's *The Mysteries of Udolpho* when in *Northanger Abbey* (written in 1798 but published in 1818) Catherine Morland referred to General Tilney as having 'the air and attitude of a Mononi'. However, Thackaray, writing in 1860, assumed that his readers would not be familiar with the novel:

> Valancourt, and who was he? Cry the young people. Valancourt, my dears, was the hero of one of the most famous romances which ever was published in this country. The beauty and elegance of Valancourt made your grandmammas' gentle hearts to beat with respectful sympathy. He and his glory have passed away. (*Roundabout Paper* in about 1860 (no. xxiv))[81]

Like Thackeray, Kavanagh was also of the opinion that, in accordance with the dictates of changing literary taste, Radcliffe's romances would soon be forgotten, relegated to 'remote provinces and old fashioned libraries' (122). She puts this down to the fact that, unlike the social and domestic novels of 'Miss Burney, Charlotte Smith, Miss Edgeworth and Mrs. Inchbald' (122), in order to fully appreciate Ann Radcliffe a wider historical knowledge and understanding of the world of romance is required. Without this knowledge, she argues, Radcliffe's originality and gifts are lost.

Little is known about Ann Radcliffe's private life, and, although she kept records of her impressions of the external world, she left no diaries that give any notion of her inner life or letters to reveal her friendships. It is known that Christina Rossetti, for want of material, was forced to abandon the idea of writing Radcliffe's biography,[82] while Kavanagh claimed that 'An existence so serene and modest leaves little to biography'. Though conscious of the problems such a life evokes, Kavanagh readily accepts the limitations of her own undertakings as a biographer:

> The care with which she shunned attention has concealed even the few incidents of Mrs. Radcliffe's life. We know what books she wrote, what journeys she took, and there ends our knowledge. How it fared with her in that inner world which it is both the art and the charm of biography to unravel, we may vaguely surmise, but can never know. (118)

Owing to the paucity of biographical sources available, Kavanagh had to rely on the *Annual Biography and Obituary* for 1824 for most of her information. This same account was the source also for Scott in the *Lives of the Novelists*,[83] a text with which Kavanagh was undoubtedly familiar. As Kavanagh has noted, Ann Radcliffe preferred her quiet domestic environment to the glamour of the literary world (ironically, an observation that reflected Kavanagh's desire for privacy in her own life). She records that in 1809 Radcliffe was reported to be dead, a report that

Radcliffe herself ignored. Later on it was thought that she had become the 'the victim of her own wild imaginings' and was the inmate of a lunatic asylum. Kavanagh notes that throughout this juncture Ann Radcliffe remained 'calmly silent', untouched by the speculations of the world outside her own self-contained domestic environment: 'What the world said or thought of her, so long as it affected not her integrity was a matter of little moment to her in her happy retirement' (118). In May 1823, the year of Radcliffe's actual death, a writer in the *Edinburgh Review* made the comment that

> The fair authoress kept herself almost as much incognito as the Author of Waverly; nothing was known of her but her name on the title page. She never appeared in public, nor mingled in private society, but kept herself apart, like the sweet bird that sings its solitary notes, shrowded and unseen.[84]

Radcliffe was born in London in July 1764, to tradespeople with gentle connections.[85] Kavanagh notes that as a young woman her physical appearance was unexceptional and her educational achievements were average:

> She was shy; she showed no extraordinary genius, and the times were not propitious to the development of female intellect. The young girl's person was probably more admired than her mind. She was short, but exquisitely proportioned; had a lovely complexion, fine eyes and eyebrows, and a beautiful mouth. She had a sweet voice, too, and sang with feeling and taste. (119)

At the age of twenty-three Ann married William Radcliffe, a graduate of Oxford. As the proprietor of the *English Chronicle*, William spent much of his time at his workplace. However, as Kavanagh records, conscious of her literary ability and as a means of occupying her time during his absence, this 'clear-sighted' husband encouraged his wife to write. It was during the long solitary evenings spent by her fireside that Ann Radcliffe engaged in her short but successful career as a novelist (she wrote for eight years, from the age of twenty-five until the age of thirty-three). It was, Kavanagh notes, after her last two works, *The Mysteries of Udolpho* and *The Italian*, that she stopped writing and, as a result of the financial rewards they produced[86] and an inheritance received on the death of relatives, she and her husband settled to a retirement of pleasant independence. The couple loved to travel but had visited the Continent only once, to Holland and the Rhine and then, as Kavanagh states, 'they only saw but a small portion of it' (120). The inspiration for Radcliffe's famous descriptive passages on nature and of the sublime comes from her own love of landscape paintings and travel books. Kavanagh writes that during the last twelve years of her life Ann Radcliffe was 'afflicted with spasmodic asthma', a condition that blighted an otherwise rewarding and happy existence until her death, at the age of fifty-nine in February 1823.

Kavanagh bases her brief discussion of Radcliffe's work around the four novels *The Sicilian Romance* (1790), *The Romance of the Forest* (1791), *The Mysteries of Udolpho* (1794) and *The Italian* (1797). While she refers to Radcliffe's first novel, *The Castles of Athlin and Dunbayne* (1789), she does so only to suggest that in this story is to be found 'the germ of what was to be one of Mrs. Radcliffe's excellencies – fine and striking simile' (124). Kavanagh argues that in *The Sicilian Romance* Ann Radcliffe presents passages that 'suggests terror far more than she seems willing to create it' (129), a feature that has raised much comment from modern critics of Radcliffe's work. In *The Romance of the Forest*, which, Kavanagh notes, was inspired by one of Radcliffe's favourite haunts, Windsor Forest, she argues that it is this novel that is 'perhaps the least defective of the five she wrote, and though not the best, it is that which has most unity of purpose, and which strives least after that mixture of the real and the supernatural that was both Mrs. Radcliffe's charm and error' (132). Kavanagh follows this comment with a skeletal sketch of the story in which the forest itself features strongly in the narrative, noting that 'in making the forest the home of her characters she appealed to a feeling as subtle, as mysterious, and as deep as superstition; man's secret though seldom gratified passion for solitude' (136). Much of the appeal of this novel for Kavanagh is Radcliffe's power of delivery in her depiction of Nature as represented by the forest. At the same time she suggests that, while it is a story that steps fleetingly on the threshold of the supernatural, it is all too human in its rendition of romance. However, *The Mysteries of Udolpho*, Radcliffe's subsequent novel, Kavanagh argues, is the one that is most representative of Radcliffe's descriptive powers. Moreover, she claims that, unlike Radcliffe's other novels, once read, *The Mysteries of Udolpho* is never forgotten. Again her commentary focuses on Radcliffe's interaction of storyline with descriptive passages. Although the novel is set in France in the year 1584, Kavanagh argues that the date is immaterial and the story belongs to no specific time, 'Her characters are modern; they speak, think, and act like modern people' (139). She contends that it is a novel with its 'faults, as well as its beauties' both of which are 'wonderful' and 'stamped with a mighty impress' (139). The story is built around a series of journeys, which, Kavanagh suggests, reflect Ann Radcliffe's own love of travel:

> Pleasure journeys were the events and the romance of Mrs. Radcliffe's life. She liked travelling. She liked that vivid succession of images and

pictures; the road left behind, the road spreading on, the strange, dreamy charm of passing motionless through so much earth and sky. She had a wonderful power in describing it: no wonder that she filled her tales with journeys. Her heroes and heroines seem wanderers upon earth. Happy or persecuted, they are ever winging their flight to the charming regions, or to the grand and sublime scenes Mrs. Radcliffe so often described and never saw. (140)

She mentions (142) that Byron's opening of his fourth canto of 'Childe Harold's Pilgrimage' is borrowed directly from Radcliffe's description of Venice. Another reference point for Kavanagh is the phenomenon of the mysterious veiled picture. She describes the terror and fear that the young heroine, Emily, experiences on encountering this picture at the castle of Udolpho but does not reveal its secret, something, she tells us, is apparent only at the end of the novel. It is such episodes that contribute to the success of the story: 'the effect is produced – the circumstance has seized on our imagination, and haunts us with a sort of torment. This was what the author wanted, and truly her object is accomplished' (145). Kavanagh was of the opinion that in Ann Radcliffe's novels no incident is subordinate to the sense of terror surrounding it and it is such techniques that draw on the reader's imagination and make for compelling reading.

While Ann Radcliffe's powers of description and her ability to sustain disbelief in matters of suspense met with Kavanagh's undisputed approval, she was less impressed with other aspects of Radcliffe's writing. Her characters, she claimed, are either too good or too bad, but even here she concedes that they are the stuff of gothic fiction. Two such characters are St Aubert (*The Mysteries of Udolpho*) and Schedoni (*The Italian*) about whom she says:

> St. Aubert is perfectly good, tender, amiable, and true; Schedoni is as entirely bad, perfidious, cruel and relentless; but though neither is true, there is real sweetness in one, and great power in the other. One is like Mrs. Radcliffe's ideal landscapes, and the other like her savage, frowning castles. Both belong to the world of the imagination, and cannot be tried by the laws of real, every day life. (150)

Radcliffe's novel *Gaston de Blondeville*, published posthumously in 1826, was, Kavanagh suggests, 'Mrs Radcliffe's rendition of the struggle between right and wrong and though she feels that, in this respect, it is a far more noble effort than her previous works, it is inferior. In this work, which makes use of the 'only genuine supernatural agency she ever used' (159); she argues that Ann Radcliffe was less inspiring than when she relied on suggestion rather than actual supernatural agencies to create a sense of terror. Though her novels have gone out of fashion, it is in her powers of suggestion, Kavanagh argues, that Radcliffe's influence lives on beyond her own age.

Elizabeth Inchbald

In her day Elizabeth Inchbald was known more for her work in the theatre than as a novelist. Her first play, a farce entitled *The Mogul Tale*, in which she also acted, was performed at London's Haymarket on 6 July 1784. She received 100 guineas for this work and, with it, as Kavanagh notes, 'The foundation of a theatrical fortune was now laid' (167). This success was followed by a succession of plays, including *Such Things Are*, written in 1788, which brought in £900, a sum which, after a period of financial struggle that she and her late husband had been forced to endure, offered a degree of financial security. However, in order to help her relatives whose circumstances were always needy, she chose to live frugally in order to make this amount and her subsequent earnings stretch further. It was only later in life that she published her two novels, *A Simple Story* (1791)[87] and *Art and Nature* (1796).

Born in October 1753 to a Catholic farming family who lived in Suffolk, Elizabeth Simpson was one of eight children and, like her four sisters, was remarkable for her beauty. Her formal education was, Kavanagh writes, one which 'her sex and station in life rendered adequate according to the feeling of the times' (160–1). However, such was her desire to learn, Elizabeth took refuge in her love of reading and her passion for the theatre. When she was eighteen she left Suffolk for London, hoping to find work as an actress but was soon met with the realities of life. In this regard Kavanagh notes that 'Elizabeth does not seem to have been ignorant of the perils she ran. But she had firm confidence in her own virtue, and, spite that reserve of manner which the impediment[88] in her speech had strengthened, a daring, independent heart' (161). Kavanagh writes extensively about Elizabeth Inchbald's life, in which she refers to Inchbald's encounters in London, her marriage to Joseph Inchbald, a 'second-rate actor' seventeen years her senior, their theatrical experiences, their travels and their hardships when work was hard to come by – at one time they were so hungry they were compelled to eat turnips straight from the field – her friendship with the actress Mrs Siddons,[89] her childless marriage and the sudden death of her husband in 1779. A widow at the age of twenty-six, after a marriage of seven years, Mrs Inchbald vowed that she would never marry again.

Throughout her life Elizabeth Inchbald was admired for her beauty and she readily accepted the acknowledgement of such by others, as Kavanagh puts it: 'Conscious of her beauty, and like many beautiful women exacting in the recognition of its rights, she allowed and liked respectful worship' (164). Following Anne Elwood's[90] biography of Elizabeth Inchbald in 1843, Kavanagh identifies, but focuses far more than Elwood on, Inchbald's many admirers, including William Godwin, and her friendship and love for John Kemble, the actor and Jesuit-educated brother of Mrs Siddons. However, Kavanagh notes that, in addition to her beauty and her charm, Inchbald was a woman of quick temper and, like her heroine, Miss Milner, in *A Simple Story*, had in her a streak of 'perversity'. The one man whom, had he proposed, Kavanagh feels sure Elizabeth would readily have accepted, was her dear friend John Kemble. However, after the death of her husband, Kemble shied away:

> he tempered his friendship with prudence. With her heedless frankness, Mrs. Inchbald confessed 'that she would have jumped to have him;' but Mr. Kemble, much as he liked and admired her, had seen her faults too closely to make this dangerous venture. (165)

Though perverse temperament may have denied her the man she loved, paradoxically, it is this very 'perversity' that Kavanagh notes in both author and fictional heroine that is significant – they each offer a refreshing antidote to the usual template virtuous heroine of the time. In 1789 Elizabeth Inchbald gave up the stage, a profession for which Kavanagh considered her ill-suited, and earned her living through her writing. She lived in increasingly frugal conditions and moved from one lodging to another according to the dictates of financial circumstances. However, these circumstances did not deter others from seeking her company. Many, including various members of the aristocracy as well as other women writers such as Madame de Staël, Maria Edgeworth, Ann Radcliffe and Amelia Opie, held her in high esteem.

In her account of this remarkable woman's life it becomes apparent that Kavanagh had a particular fondness for her subject as both a woman and a writer. Elizabeth Inchbald's generosity and charity were given freely at the expense of her own material comforts. As a writer she drew on a sense of social realism that was, no doubt, gained from her own experience and independence. It is with much regret Kavanagh notes, that before her death Elizabeth Inchbald, 'yielding to the advice of her friend', one Dr Poynter, 'and to her own conscientious scruples', took the decision to destroy (burn) her memoirs.[91] Kavanagh writes that in doing so 'she ultimately destroyed a record that was probably more amusing than edifying' (168) and is relieved that no Dr Poynter was around to step in between Mrs Inchbald and her 'beautiful tale' that finally became *A Simple Story*. Kavanagh's portrayal of Elizabeth

Inchbald is one that acknowledges her as an extraordinarily gifted and politically liberal-minded woman who, as she grew older, gradually retreated from society in favour of a more singularly contemplative existence. In a letter to Mrs Opie, dated 19 December 1820, the last letter she wrote before her death, Elizabeth Inchbald expresses her growing concerns with an afterlife, as she writes, '"I have so many reflections concerning a *future* world, as well as concerning the *present*, and there are on that awful subject so many books still unread, that I think every moment lost which impedes my gaining information from holy and learned authors"' (181). Her final residence was Kensington House, a genteel establishment for Catholic ladies, where on 1 August 1821, she died, aged sixty-eight.[92] She is buried in Kensington churchyard, a short distance from where Kavanagh herself once lodged. The touching tribute with which Kavanagh concludes her sketch bears witness to her admiration for Elizabeth Inchbald, as she recalls, 'A few years ago an Irish lady, grieved to see the weeds that overran and defaced the sunken tombstone, had it cleared, and caused flowers to be planted around the grave of the authoress of "A Simple Story"' (182).

Kavanagh is of the opinion that of all women writers Elizabeth Inchbald is the least literary 'in the good and honourable sense of the word'. She writes that in *A Simple Story* Elizabeth Inchbald had a story to tell and the result is 'wonderful' (182–3). Later on she states:

> Mrs. Inchbald's style is faulty, incorrect, but it has a rare gift: that of producing strong and direct impressions; vigour and pathos were the characteristics of her genius. Her stage education also gave her dramatic power and knowledge. To that, too, we think she owed the nice distinctions in her men and women. They have none of the conventional perfection common in novels. The human representatives of heroes and heroines, whom she had seen moving on the stage, had helped to clothe them in flesh and blood, and suggested fallibility with their very looks. (198)

Mr Dorriforth, the thirty-year-old guardian of seventeen-year-old Miss Milner, is a man of 'inexorable will' and, though he has his virtues, his stern and immovable character offers a challenge to the otherwise conventional patterned hero of the day. Kavanagh notes that 'it is said that in Miss Milner Mrs. Inchbald, to a great extent, painted herself' (186–7). Kavanagh maintains that Miss Milner is full of faults, she is 'vain, wilful and provoking', but it is she who engages the reader's sympathy. She argues that while Miss Milner lacks the innocence of Evelina, the dignity of Cecilia and the sweetness and intellectual turn of Emmeline and Ethelinda, she is, nevertheless, 'a new woman, a true one, a faulty one, introduced for the first time to the world [. . .] There had been no

Miss Milner before this one' (199). Kavanagh herself takes great pleasure in comparing this 'perverse' self-willed and defiant young woman
with her companion, the very 'wooden' and unmistakably unreal Miss
Fenton, who, she argues, Inchbald draws with a 'touch of satire':

> Miss Fenton is a pattern young lady. She is exquisitely beautiful, and as
> exquisitely correct. She has not a fault, and everyone [. . .] seems to con-
> sider her providentially meant for faulty Miss Milner's improvement and
> imitation. And, of course, Miss Milner detests her, and is more perverse
> than ever. (187)

Not surprisingly, it is to Kavanagh's delight that Miss Fenton is soon
ejected from the story.

Though conscious of its merits, Kavanagh is critical of *A Simple Story*
in several ways, not the least of which is the seventeen-year gap between
the first and second parts of the novel. She is of the opinion that Inchbald
would have been advised to end her novel with the marriage of Mr
Dorriforth and Miss Milner as this would have offered a more acceptable conclusion to the intended love story. Notwithstanding this consideration, an aspect of Inchbald's writing with which Kavanagh takes
serious issue is her attempt at educational theory, 'the most dangerous
syren a novel-writer ever heeded' (193). As she had previously argued in
relation to French women writers, such practice destroys enchantment.
Moreover, she considers that Elizabeth Inchbald's views on education are
oversimplified and, as such, are detrimental to both her purpose and to
human understanding. These views are demonstrated by the fact that
Miss Milner's faults are considered to be the result of her having had a
'bad education', whereas her daughter, who appears in the second part
of the novel, and who received a 'good education', is meant to be 'proper
and virtuous'. In Kavanagh's view Inchbald sacrificed her heroine to a
somewhat specious theory that only falsifies and demoralises in its reduc-
tionism. *Nature and Art*, a novel which, in Kavanagh's opinion, 'has little
of the charm and none of the truth of *A Simple Story*', she claims is too
engaged with the social theories of the French Revolution which out-
weigh the 'interest of the tale' (199). As with *A Simple Story*, she gives a
brief commentary and outline of the storyline; however, *Nature and Art*,
she concludes, is too didactic in its oppositional representation of good
and bad. Dale Spender has argued that the imposition of Victorian
morality had inhibited Kavanagh's response to this novel,[93] however,
Spender's view does not take in Kavanagh's objections to what she perceived as the novel's overall two-dimensional representation of society.
The oppositional convenience and placement of good and bad characters, namely victim and oppressor, is detrimental, in Kavanagh's view, to

a fuller understanding of social and sexual injustices such as those presented in this novel. Nevertheless, she gives credit for Inchbald's brevity
and delivery of one section in particular. When a young woman, Hannah,
is brought to court for killing her illegitimate child, she is sentenced to
death by the child's father, William, who is now a Judge, and who, having
previously seduced then abandoned Hannah, failed to recognise her in
court. Kavanagh refers directly to the text here and suggests that it is
delivered in 'the manner of true pathos' (201). Elizabeth Inchbald, she
claims, 'though never a fine writer', had the ability to wholly engage the
reader's sympathy, in this case, she argues: 'Hannah's anguish [is] told
with a repressed strength that [is] deeply affecting; it is as if we witnessed
some great, pent up agony, which broke the heart from which it could
not escape' (202). It is this sense of delivery that can be found in both of
the novels she discusses that, Kavanagh maintains, marks Elizabeth
Inchbald as a true writer. In 1987 Dale Spender argued that the absence
of Elizabeth Inchbald from the literary tradition is not only a loss – it is
a disgrace.[94] In writing about Elizabeth Inchbald, Kavanagh was one
woman writer who hoped that this would not happen.

Maria Edgeworth

Kavanagh introduces her next writer as one whose '"manly understanding"' is complemented by 'the most vigorous though the least masculine
of female writers, in that great touchstone of temper and genius – style'
(203). In this context Kavanagh attributes much of Maria Edgeworth's
understanding of the world to the influence of her remarkable Anglo-
Irish father, Richard Lovell Edgeworth (1744–1817).[95] In his own right
Richard Edgeworth was a notable educator and a reformer whose impact
was very much in evidence, especially on Edgeworthstown, his socially
progressive, though somewhat secluded, estate in County Longford.
Although Kavanagh gives an engagingly graphic account of his notably
egregious ancestry, whose history, she says, 'reads like a romance' (203),
it is as the father of Maria Edgeworth that he is best remembered.[96] Her
justification for such a digression stems from the dearth of information
concerning Maria Edgeworth herself, suggesting that 'the mixture of
wisdom, virtue, and romance of the race from which she sprang will give
us a fair clue to her real temper and nature' (208). It is interesting and surprising that few biographical sources were made available in the mid nineteenth century, particularly as during the height of her writing career,
Maria Edgeworth was undoubtedly the most commercially successful and
prestigious female novelist of her day.[97] At the time Kavanagh was
writing, apart from Richard Lovell Edgeworth's *Memoirs*, which had
been completed by Maria after his death, along with a few published

items,[98] there was little else to go on. Maria Edgeworth's own much-guarded *Memoir* was not published until 1867, five years after Kavanagh's study appeared.[99]

Kavanagh writes that Maria Edgeworth was one of twenty-one children,[100] the collective offspring of Edgeworth's four wives. Since her death in 1849 biographical studies have differed in relation to Maria Edgeworth's exact place and date of birth. Kavanagh states that she was born in the village of Hare Hatch, near Reading (the house occupied by her parents at the time) on 1 January 1767 (207) but more recent sources have confirmed that she was born at Black Bourton, the home of her mother's family in Oxfordshire in 1768.[101] Kavanagh merely states that Maria was the daughter of Edgeworth's first wife, an English woman, formally Anna Maria Elers, whose birth had been the cause of her mother's death. In fact she was incorrect about the details of Anna Maria's death. Maria was the third child after Anna Maria had already given birth to two boys. After Maria's birth Anna Maria had two more daughters before she died, probably of puerperal fever, ten days after the birth of her fifth child in 1773 when Maria was five years old.[102] Kavanagh refers to Maria Edgeworth's involvement in the writing of her father's *Memoirs*, but offers nothing more in relation to her mother's death. In 1782, when she was fifteen, Maria left England to live in Edgeworthstown where, apart from the occasional visits to Scotland, England and France,[103] she remained until her death in 1849.

Prior to her writing novels, Maria helped her father run the estate, acted as his amanuensis and, under his guidance, engaged herself in works on education, including in 1798, under their joint authorship, the Rousseau-inspired two-volume work *Practical Education*. It is interesting that, while Kavanagh makes no significant reference to the influence of Charles Burney on his daughter Fanny (Dr Burney's influence is referred to constantly in modern accounts of Burney's life), she pays considerable attention to the father–daughter relationship enjoyed by Richard Lovell Edgworth and Maria. Undoubtedly this was a more prominent partnership than that of the Burneys, but unlike the Burneys these two saw little of each other until Maria's move to Ireland.[104] Kavanagh argues that Richard Lovell Edgeworth's direct influence on his daughter's writing was not always to her advantage, although she suggests that, indirectly, she gained much from his 'vigorous and active mind' (202). Her first novel, *Castle Rackrent* (1800), was written in secret and was the only novel she wrote without consulting her father. Critics' opinion regarding Edgeworth's influence on Maria's writing has differed over time. While Virginia Woolf in *The Common Reader* (1925) writes of him as nothing less than an egotistical despot and a portentous bore,[105] later critics see him in a more positive light, particularly in relation to Maria, and repudiate claims of his negative interference with her fiction.[106] Kavanagh contends that Maria Edgeworth always enjoyed the critical advice of her father, so much so that with his death, at the age of seventy-four, on 31 May 1817,[107] ceased 'his daughter's literary history' (209). Maria Edgeworth stopped writing when she was fifty years old and, as Kavanagh points out, she 'can scarcely have been exhausted.' It is with an echo of disappointment that she writes, '[Maria] had long relied on [her father's] guidance; too long, perhaps, for her own good'. To demonstrate her point she turns directly to Maria Edgeworth's own words:

> 'Whenever I thought of writing anything,' she has said herself, 'I always told him my first rough plans, and always with the instinct of a good critic, he used to fix immediately upon that which would best answer his purpose – *"Sketch that, and show it to me."* These words, from the experience of his sagacity, never failed to inspire me with hopes of success. His decision in criticism was particularly useful to me. It was the happy experience of this, and my consequent reliance on his ability, decision, and perfect truth, that relieved me from the anxiety to which I was so much subject, that I am sure I should not have written or finished anything without his support.' (209)

Kavanagh feels strongly that Maria Edgeworth was wrong to rely so much on her father, regardless of his overall benevolence and critical wisdom: 'She had genius and facility enough to strike out a path of her own' (209). After his death she feels that Maria lost confidence and, although she owed him much in terms of life experience, Kavanagh argues that, had he died earlier, Maria Edgeworth would have been a completely different writer. Moreover, she argues that Maria's lack of imagination in her fiction was a direct consequence of her education, which, admirable as it was, discouraged more 'tender and amiable' qualities from emerging in her writing. Kavanagh blames Richard Lovell Edgeworth for the lack of romance in his daughter's fiction: 'It was the fault of Mr. Edgeworth – a fault which he imparted to his daughter – to keep the romance of the family for real life, and to repress it where it is graceful and becoming in fiction' (210).

Though Kavanagh laments the lack of romance in Maria Edgeworth's novels, it is obvious in her discussion that she is sympathetic with her as a woman whose personality and driving force is characteristically 'Irish':

> Maria, born in England, of an English mother, was, nevertheless, very Irish in temper, far more so than in her writings. She had the hopeful ardour, the sensitiveness of the Irish character, its enthusiasm and its spirit of mirth and enjoyment, all save its imagination. (210)

This perspective is interesting from one who acknowledges Maria Edgeworth as a national writer. At the same time one cannot help but suspect that Kavanagh takes the opportunity here to indulge her own patriotic sensibilities.

By the mid nineteenth century Maria Edgeworth had ceased to attract the praise her work had previously enjoyed but she was still highly complimented as a woman: as Marilyn Butler has pointed out, 'She had a personality that has always had a strong appeal for the kind of biographer, almost invariably a woman, that likes to like her subject'.[108] Kavanagh was no exception; she liked this writer who, regardless of the changing literary fashions, was to her one whose sense of 'moral truth' was unchanging.

Kavanagh writes extensively on Maria Edgeworth's merits as a writer while, at the same time, she is aware of the changing response to her work. She praises her techniques of exposing human folly by ridiculing pretentiousness and notes her perceptive understanding of social mores and her penchant for the romantic idealism of 'prudence, honour, principle; and every virtue under heaven' (217). Her weakness, she maintains, was tied in with her insistence on the delivery of practical truths – facts. It is this insistence on facts, Kavanagh argues, that interfered with her ability to believe in the 'mysterious, involuntary nature' of romantic love. While acknowledging *Castle Rackrent* as Maria Edgeworth's 'great Irish story', resplendent in its wit and humour, she writes that, in her delivery of prominent realism, Edgeworth omits a sense of romance, the result of which, she argues, renders the novel 'Dreary in the extreme'. Maria Edgeworth's preference for reason over emotion was clearly not to Kavanagh's taste. She saw this novel more as a didactic, educational tract with her later novels offering little more: 'in some of her subsequent works, Miss Edgeworth introduced a sort of conventional romance; it was not very real indeed, but it gave the mind a sense of rest from much formal teaching' (220). Maria Edgeworth's acknowledgement of the nature of 'propinquity' and the truth of 'stubborn facts' was, Kavanagh argues, her Achilles' heel. She suggests that, in her appeal to judgement and reason, Maria Edgeworth 'shunned the road that leads to the heart' (226). She discusses several of Edgeworth's works, including *Castle Rackrent*, *Belinda* (1810) and *Tales of Fashionable Life* (1809–12), noting her significant influence on Sir Walter Scott and the respect and admiration she justly earned as a writer in her time.

Throughout her discussion Kavanagh gives little time to politics and religion, choosing to focus on the stylistic properties of Maria Edgeworth's own brand of domestic realism. She considers that Maria Edgeworth's overwhelming desire for usefulness, a trait gleaned from the influence of her father, coupled with her need to educate, interfered with the 'real' writer who, she contends, had she been left to her own devices, would have been at greater liberty to explore the powers of her imagination.

Jane Austen

Notwithstanding her admiration for Maria Edgeworth as a satirist, Kavanagh was clearly more at ease in her commentary on Jane Austen, whom she considered to be a woman of 'amiable temper and gentle heart' (250). She engages wholly with the sensibilities of this writer whose 'little bits of ivory two inches wide' (250) were produced within the 'quiet obscurity of domestic life' (247). She journeys amicably through Austen's six novels, stopping here and there to denote some particularly poignant moment characteristic of Austen's strength and pointing out the delicacy of her pen in her depiction of reality. However, she says little of Jane Austen's own experience of life, offering little more than a paragraph with the barest of biographical details from her birth on 16 December 1775 at Steventon, Hampshire, to her death from consumption in July 1817. It is a telling fact, perhaps, that, in this instance, Kavanagh wished to concentrate less on the biography and more on Jane Austen's novels.

For Kavanagh it is Austen's focus on the details of everyday life and her characterisation that set Austen apart from other writers, including herself:

> That young lady had a talent for describing the involvement of feelings and characters of ordinary life, which is to me the most wonderful thing I ever met with. The big bow wow strain I can myself do, like any now going, but the exquisite touch which renders ordinary commonplace things and characters interesting from the truth of the the description and sentiment is denied to me. What a pity such a gifted creature died so early! (250–1)

She contends that at the heart of Austen's superiority is 'delicacy', that all too evident requirement in women's writing that for Kavanagh, with only a few exceptions,[109] determines the success of a novel. It is interesting that she did not perceive Jane Austen as a creative or inventive writer; her stories, she says, are only 'moderately interesting' and her heroes and heroines 'are not such as to charm away our hearts'. Austen's power, she claims, is in her delivery of the ordinary: 'never has character been displayed in such delicate variety as in her tales; never have commonplace men and women been invested with so much reality' (252). More importantly Kavanagh believed that Jane Austen possessed something much rarer and more significant, she was 'a seer' (252). She argues that, though

Austen's range of vision was limited, she delivered her tales of commonplace with such a keenness and power of perception that little escaped
her. To this gift, she says, 'Miss Austen added another equally rare – she
knew where to stop' (252). Brevity and judgement, she contends, are the
reasons behind Austen's continuing success.

During her lifetime Austen published her works anonymously and it
was only after her death with the publication of *Northanger Abbey*, published posthumously in 1818, and *Persuasion*, also published in that
year, that her name appeared in print. As a means of gleaning some
aspect of what Kavanagh terms Austen's own 'literary idiosyncrasy', she
turns to Catherine Morland, who in *Northanger Abbey* says:

> 'Yes, novels; for I will not adopt that ungenerous and impolitic custom, so
> common with novel-writers, of degrading by their contemptuous censure,
> the very performances to the number of which they are themselves adding;
> joining with their greatest enemies in bestowing the harshest epithets on
> such works, and scarcely ever permitting them to be read by their own
> heroine, who, if she accidentally takes up a novel, is sure to turn over its
> insipid pages with disgust. Alas! if the heroine of one novel be not patron-
> ised by the heroine of another, from whom can she expect protection and
> regard? I cannot approve of it.'

Kavanagh goes on to say:

> 'It is only a novel' found no favour with Miss Austen; she justly and indig-
> nantly exclaimed: 'It is only Cecilia, or Camilla, or Belinda, or, in short,
> only some work in which the greatest powers of the mind are displayed, in
> which the most thorough knowledge of human nature, the happiest delin-
> eation of its varieties, the liveliest effusions of wit and humour are conveyed
> to the world in the best chosen language.' (250)

Kavanagh considered *Northanger Abbey* to be the 'least pleasing' of
Austen's six novels and, although she notes that many consider *Mansfield
Park* (1814) the most perfect, her own preference is for *Persuasion*. She
argues that *Mansfield Park, Sense and Sensibility* (1811) and *Persuasion*
are three tales that reveal 'the phase of [Austen's] literary character which
she chose to keep most in the shade; the tender and the sad' (271).
Persuasion, she argues, was the most powerful in this respect and, one
feels, the one that held most appeal for Kavanagh because it focuses on
what she understood as the inimitable quality of woman's silent endurance
and disappointment in love. She cites the case of Anne Elliot, who, at the
advice of others, breaks her engagement with the only man she could ever
love, Captain Wentworth, and as a result spends her youth regretting her
decision. Kavanagh argues, 'Here we see the first genuine picture of that
silent torture of an unloved woman, condemned to suffer thus because she

is a woman and must not speak' (272). And although the tale ends in happiness with the couple's marriage, for Kavanagh it is the prominence of sadness in Anne Elliot that distinguishes this from Austen's other tales.

In her conclusion Kavanagh suggests that Jane Austen's failing was due to the singularity of tone in her delivery of strong feeling. In *Pride and Prejudice* (1813), for example, the indignation felt by Lady Catherine de Bourgh on hearing of the marriage between Mr Darcy and Elizabeth Bennet, Kavanagh maintains, was partially lost in delivery. However, in spite of her raising such an objection, one feels that Kavanagh was not entirely happy with her own criticism. Although she had already noted Austen's weaker moments in her discussion, her criticism here hangs on to her otherwise positive response like an unwelcome coda to an otherwise delightful melody. It is as if, by including such observation, Kavanagh is performing a tiresome duty, the execution of which, she feels, is necessary to attaining a critically balanced point of view. Far more convincing is her approbation of Austen's method which is clearly visible in her apologetic conclusion:

> By choosing to be all but perfect, she sometimes became monotonous, but rarely. The value of light and shade, as a means of success, she discarded. Strong contrasts, bold flights, she shunned. To be true, to show life in its every-day aspect, was her ambition. To hope to make so much out of so little showed no common confidence in her own powers, and more than common daring. Of the thousands who take up a pen to write a story meant to amuse, how many are there who can, or who dare, be true, like Jane Austen. (274)

It is to Jane Austen that Kavanagh attributes the greatest accolade: delicacy – the quality that defines her work and the reason why, in her conclusion, Kavanagh decrees Austen the only woman writer in her study whose novels will stand the test of time.

Amelia Opie

It is with a gracious sense of *difference* that Kavanagh discusses her next writer:

> Of all the women who have written 'Mrs Opie is the one who succeeded most by qualities distinct from those generally called literary, or, better still, intellectual. She was not much of a thinker, still less of a writer. Her style is careless, and often incorrect; her pictures of life are not such as we can value. Strong character she neither conceived nor painted. Yet she succeeded in an age where men and women, far beyond her in power and attainments, might have made the public fastidious; and that success, a matter of fact, not of assertion, entitles her to consideration. Great though her deficiencies were, it was merited. Mrs. Opie had but one gift – a great

one, a beautiful one, a woman's gift – a gift which won and ruled hearts amenable to no other power; better than any in her generation she knew how to appeal to the heart. (289)

It was Amelia Opie's ability to 'appeal to the heart', Kavanagh argues, that engaged the reader in tales that were little more than 'the exhausted staple of romance'. Her stories, she claims, had no individuality of their own and they lacked originality, yet they yielded an 'affecting sweetness' and this alone, she contends, is her great achievement.

Taking much of her background material on Amelia Opie from Cecilia Lucy Brightwell's biography of 1854,[110] Kavanagh introduces the young Amelia Alderson. Born in Norwich in 1769, only child of the respected physician Dr James Alderson, a strong Unitarian, and her mother who died when Amelia was fifteen, leaving father and daughter bereaved but blessed in their mutual devotion. Dr Alderson, a socially compassionate and progressive man, allowed his daughter much liberty and Kavanagh writes that, at the age of sixteen, Amelia was already a cultivated young woman with extraordinary tastes. She would take herself off, alone, to the law courts, namely the *Nisi Prius* Court and witness the day's proceedings, relishing the pageantry and the excitement that accompanied the various hearings, the scenes and incidents of which later found their way into her works. Amelia's interest in the system of judicial practice, Kavanagh reports, was to last all of her life. She was a frequent visitor to London and by the age of twenty-five she had become acquainted with several celebrated people, including Godwin, Mary Wollstonecraft, Elizabeth Inchbald and Mrs Siddons. It was in London that she met her husband, the portrait painter John Opie, whom Kavanagh describes as 'self taught, low born and high minded'.[111] Nevertheless, their meeting is portrayed with overtones that would not be out of place in a romantic novel of the same period, as Kavanagh writes:

> He saw Miss Alderson at an evening party, for he was then a popular and admired artist, and from the moment that the door opened and admitted her, clad in blue, with bare neck and arms, her bright auburn hair flowing down her shoulders, and gentle ardour in her beaming face, he was smitten with love life-long and deep.[112] We doubt if, from her own showing, Amelia Alderson really returned his passion, but she esteemed and liked him, she felt his strong love, and though she vowed at first that his chances of success were but one to a thousand, she allowed his will to rule hers, and married him in Marylebone Church, on the 8th of May, 1798. (280)

As it turned out, the union was fortuitous in terms of Amelia's writing. Kavanagh notes that Amelia Opie's early preference was for writing poetry, a literary form which was not to her husband's taste and from which he may have helped to divert his wife's interest: 'he had the good sense and the good feeling to wish her to cultivate her talents as an author' as Amelia Opie herself had written: '"Knowing, at the time of our marriage, that my most favourite amusement was writing, he did not check my ambition to become an author; on the contrary, he encouraged it, and our only quarrel was, not that I wrote too much, but that I did not write more and better"' (280). Undoubtedly Kavanagh would have agreed with John Opie on the quality of his wife's prose, the faults of which she attributes to Amelia's love of liberty at the expense of her early education: 'Her careless and incorrect style alone would prove that she did not receive solid or genuine instruction' (281). The marriage lasted for eight years until April 1807, when John Opie met his death prematurely at the age of forty-six. Throughout their marriage the Opies had engaged in a full and satisfying social life and enjoyed the company of many literary celebrities. However, while her husband relished society, Amelia was not always so inclined and from time to time she left her husband in London to indulge her need for quieter reflection with her father in Norwich. Kavanagh notes that one of the highlights of their marriage was a visit in 1802 to Paris where they met many well-known people who are to be found in Amelia Opie's account of that visit written thirty years later. After the death of her husband, Amelia Opie returned, a childless widow, to her father's house in Norwich where she stayed until Dr Alderson's death in 1825. Prior to his decease she became increasingly interested in the Quaker movement, an interest that met with her father's approval, and, on a renewed acquaintance with her early friend Elizabeth Gurney, later Mrs Fry, she was received into the Society of Friends. This development did not prevent Amelia Opie from engaging in her love of travel, however, and she returned to Paris, historically the place of so much carnage and heroism, and continued to meet with interesting and engaging people, including her hero, General La Fayette, as well as Benjamin Constant and the elderly Madame de Genlis. Kavanagh suggests that Amelia Opie's love of travel also accommodated an epicurean tendency redolent of one who can readily engage with the material world. It is this very curiosity in the world around her, Kavanagh argues, that induced in her a weakness of purpose, which proved to be her great infirmity. Kavanagh accepts without question Celia Brightwell's Memoirs of Amelia Opie, and concludes her own biographical section on a note of resignation that for want of more purpose, her subject, who died at the age of eighty-four on 2 December 1853, would have been a better writer.

Although before her marriage Amelia Opie was unknown to the public, Kavanagh argues that some of Opie's best pieces were written in her youth, including *The Dangers of Coquetry*, which was published anonymously in 1790. She considers Amelia Opie's next novel, *Father and Daughter*, published in 1801 under her own name, to be her best. It is, she says, 'a beautiful and pathetic tale, which had rapid and genuine success' (281). It was also a tale that had brought tears to the eyes of the French painter David, and to Sir Walter Scott who had told Amelia Opie '"that he had cried more over her 'Father and Daughter' than he cried over such things"' (284). In Amelia Opie's next novel, *Adeline Mowbray* (1804), Kavanagh accepts that this tale is based on incidents in Mary Wollstonecraft's life: 'Mrs Opie knew Godwin before he married Mary Wolstonecraft *sic*, and if she did not know that generous and noble-minded though erring woman, she was well acquainted with her history' (293). She proffers the argument that, unlike *Father and Daughter*, which is held together by moral sentiment, *Adeline Mowbray* is concerned more with the refutation of theories, and, in spite of the 'tender and beautiful' conception of the heroine, it fails to seduce the reader. She gives a brief overview of both of these novels and refers in passing to a selection of Amelia Opie's other tales, which, in the main, compare unfavourably with other women writing in similar fields. As she believed was the case with several other women in her study, Kavanagh attributes Opie's weaknesses as a writer to a 'defective education' and, in her case, also a 'want of experience'. She sees her as a woman of virtuous mind and moral intentions but one who, when attempting to convey a moral lesson, lacked the power of Maria Edgeworth's wit, or the didactic impact of Hannah More. If Amelia Opie's tales taught anything, Kavanagh contends, it was pathos, and it is this quality, along with her ability to engage her own element of 'sweetness', that explains her appeal and success in her own time.

Sydney Owenson, Lady Morgan

Kavanagh's final discussion centres on Sydney Owenson, Lady Morgan. For Kavanagh, Lady Morgan and her works represent an Ireland that Kavanagh herself can relate to only in her imagination. She introduces her as a writer who 'is not one that can or will be readily forgotten'. Although she claims that her 'genius' is not that over which time has no power, she is of the opinion that her name will live on in both 'the political and literary history of her times' (297), even after she has ceased to be read, and her books have been forgotten. To an extent Kavanagh's prediction has been fulfilled. With the exception of *The Wild Irish Girl* (1805), Lady Morgan's novels have been largely forgotten, but she has been the subject of several biographies, testimony to the interest and fascination in her as a woman as well as a writer. Lady Morgan was at once a charming and formidable woman who both embraced and defended her work with the energy and vigour of a defiant general, and it is this element of her character that Kavanagh found both fascinating and endearing. 'Her celebrity', she says, is like that of Madame de Staël, both 'personal and literary'. Kavanagh herself was writing only three years after Lady Morgan's death in 1859 and, in her very first paragraph, she places Lady Morgan, the writer, into a social perspective:

> She was a brilliant woman of the world – she travelled and saw much – she wrote upwards of seventy volumes – she was original, witty, and fearless – she had vehement and cruel enemies and ardent friends – she braved sarcasm and slander, and kept good her stand against a host. Her very faults – and they were open – extended her celebrity. She talked admirably, and both talked and wrote a good deal about herself. Few of the women who have written have done more than Lady Morgan, by the very bent of her nature, to be remembered long. (297)

At the time of writing Kavanagh judges that, evidence suggests that as well as a celebrated writer, Lady Morgan was also of a generous nature and a woman of 'sterling qualities'. However, Kavanagh's enthusiastic portrayal of Lady Morgan is marred by a number of incorrect statements relating to her early life. Geraldine Jewsbury had drawn attention to these errors when she said, 'In writing the chapter on Lady Morgan, Miss Kavanagh has been unfortunate: amongst the many statements she makes, hardly one is correct'.[113] Kavanagh writes that Sydney Owenson was born to parents who were both actors, when, in truth, her mother hated the stage and kept her distance. Sydney's mother, Jane Hill, was an Englishwoman and a highly religious Wesleyan who was devoted to order and cleanliness. Nevertheless, she seems to have been overwhelmed by her future husband's more congenial character and Gaelic charm. The circumstances surrounding Sydney's birth have been the subject of much conjecture, made up of part myth and part reality. Kavanagh writes that Sydney was born to her English mother and Irish father, Robert MacOwen (who later changed his name to the more anglicised Owenson), between Ireland and England on the Irish Sea in the year 1788.[114] Her parentage, like her birth, Kavanagh writes, 'seemed to decree that she should belong to neither country' (297). The question of Sydney's birthplace is one which has intrigued biographers; in 1988 Mary Campbell wrote that it was a tradition among Owenson's fellow actors that his daughter had been born at sea, but, whether fact or fiction, she is of a similar mind as Kavanagh when she states that, although, temperamentally, Lady Morgan was 'typically Irish', she was caught between the two countries. In her *Memoirs* Lady Morgan claimed Dublin as her true birthplace, as Mary Campbell has noted:

In later years Sydney claimed to be a trueborn native of Dublin, and described in her *Memoirs* with almost total recall, her nativity, when the bells of all the churches of the city, led by the great bell of St. Patrick's rang out for the birth of Jesus, and of Sydney Owenson.[115]

Lady Morgan's early years were spent in Ireland, where her father pursued his theatrical career. The young Sydney, or Siddy, as she was affectionately known, and her younger sister Olivia, who was eight years her junior, lost their mother to an illness diagnosed as 'gout in the stomach' and it was left to her widowed husband to care for his two young daughters. He proved a gentle and tender protector, taking great care of their health and education. Kavanagh writes that Sydney was 'educated at Miss Crowe's, North Earl Street, Dublin. This lady, a milliner and a schoolmistress, a not uncommon conjunction in those unpretending times, was considered a good teacher, and her seminary was even distinguished by the epithet of eminent' (298–9). Again Kavanagh is guilty of misrepresentation, a common failing of Lady Morgan's early biographers and one which had already incurred Lady Morgan's wrath. As Geraldine Jewsbury had pointed out, the young Sydney Owenson and her sister were not educated at Miss Crowe's establishment but spent their first three years of formal education at a prestigious and expensive Huguenot boarding school in Clontarf run by one Madame Terson. The girls were then transferred to a less select establishment, Mrs Anderson's Finishing School in Dublin. However, Kavanagh is right when she notes that, while Sydney inherited much of her father's wit, she was as much self-taught as instructed. Her early penchant was for poetry and it was not until she was aged twenty-three in 1801, when her father found himself in 'straitened circumstances', that Sydney became a 'professional authoress'. Her poems, or, as Kavanagh puts it, her 'juvenile performances', were printed in Ireland and then published in London, drawing the attention of the Countess of Moira whose patronage helped launch the young writer into Dublin society.

Kavanagh writes of Lady Morgan's appearance, her personality and talents and the impact of her literary success as having equal magnitude, as if these separate entities were conjoined historically as one singular item:

> She was short, of the smallest size of woman, not pretty, though she had an expressive face and fine eyes. She was even slightly deformed, but with the mixture of Irish blood which flowed in the veins of the MacOwens, she had inherited exquisite musical taste; she played on the harp with spirit, and sang sweetly. Better still, matchless vivacity and much wit were her own; she possessed in its perfection the untaught art of conversation; she was eloquent and lively, somewhat satirical, a fault that increased with years and success, but, when she chose, irresistibly captivating. Thus began, in the

first years of this century, the long literary career and the social triumphs
of the future Lady Morgan. (299)

It is noticeable here that the reference to Lady Morgan's 'Irish blood', once
again, presented an opportunity for Kavanagh to voice her own patriotism
for the country of her birth. Moreover, Kavanagh's description of Lady
Morgan's appearance is not dissimilar to that attributed to Kavanagh
herself by those who knew her. Later on she relates the experience of one
who had seen Lady Morgan dressed in Celtic attire on two occasions in
Dublin and who declared that she was 'Hardly more than four feet high
[. . .] with a slightly curved spine, uneven shoulders and eyes' (305).[116] In
spite of her physical idiosyncrasies, the young Sydney Owenson had her
suitors, and Kavanagh writes of her marriage to 'Mr. Morgan', an English
surgeon whom Sydney had met at Baron's Court in Tyrone, the seat of the
Marquis of Abercorn. Kavanagh is both intrigued and amused at the story
of how Sydney procured Morgan's knighthood while attending a private
ball given by the Duke of Richmond. When he asked Miss Owenson if he
should congratulate her on her marriage, Kavanagh notes:

> Her reply, if genuine, shows plenty of ambition and worldly prudence: 'The
> rumour respecting Mr. Morgan's *devouement* may or may not be true; but
> this I can at least, with all candour and sincerity, assure your Grace, that I
> shall remain to the last day of my life in single blessedness unless some more
> tempting inducement than the mere change from Miss Owenson to Mistress
> Morgan be offered me.' [Whereupon] the good natured Duke knighted Mr.
> Morgan on the spot, and on the 20th of January, 1812, Sir C.T. Morgan
> was married to Sydney Owenson, at Baron's Court, Tyrone. (301)

The marriage, she adds, 'though long and childless, was blessed with
more then common happiness' (301).

Notwithstanding the undoubted grief Lady Morgan felt at the death
of her father, one month after her marriage, Kavanagh contends that 'her
marriage and the great war with critics are the only two leading events
in Lady Morgan's life' (301). In 1811, one year prior to her marriage,
Sydney Owenson had published *The Missionary*, a novel Kavanagh
deemed 'one of her worst and most imperfect books' (300). Two of her
publications, *France* (1817), a two-volume work on society in that
country, and a novel, *O'Donnel* (1813), were met with extreme animosity in some quarters. Although very successful when it was published, by
the middle of the nineteenth century, Kavanagh maintains, *France* had
lost much of its value. When it did appear it procured its author celebrity,
money and enemies, which resulted in the most vitriolic criticism that
went beyond her authorship and attacked her personal morals and her
appearance. While Kavanagh expresses her own deep sense of outrage at

this response she is also conscious of the fact that Lady Morgan heedlessly 'courted attack' when, as she puts it, 'she called in sarcasm to her aid, and sarcasm invites retaliation' (302). The Irishman John Wilson Croker was a notably vicious commentator, whose animosity Kavanagh considered to be particularly misogynistic.[117] His ceaseless criticism was not without its repercussions, however, and it is with a sense of delight that she reports on Lady Morgan's prompt revenge. In her novel *Florence Macarthy* (1818) Lady Morgan modelled the extremely unsympathetic character Counsellor Con Crawley specifically on Croker who, it is said, 'winced' at the obvious association.

Kavanagh's account of Lady Morgan's life is littered with anecdotal references to her individuality and the impact her extraordinary personality had on society. Throughout her discussion she singularly embraces the writer and the woman in one voice: 'If few women were attacked with more virulence by those who did not know her, few, more than lady Morgan, enjoyed the liking and approbation of those who did' (305). She criticised her writing for want of 'simplicity' but she praised it also for creating romantic landscapes and castles without the associated terror and gloom that was so prevalent in Mrs Radcliffe's novels. She gives credit for the fervour and sincerity invested in her stories, particularly *The Wild Irish Girl* (1805), a tale about which, she says, 'the interest never flags' (308). Kavanagh considers that one of the more innovative and significant aspects of this novel is Lady Morgan's ability to invest 'her characters with far more romance than she gave to external scenery, or, to speak more correctly, she made the romance of nature dependent upon them' (311). She suggests that it is this inversion of formula that gives Lady Morgan's novels a resonance that was absent in the gothic canvas of Mrs Radcliffe's stories. Moreover, it is within this romantic paradigm, she argues, that Lady Morgan was able to introduce a new type of heroine and one that clearly influenced Sir Walter Scott's heroine's of later years. Of the wild Irish girl, Glorvina, Kavanagh says:

> even more than Miss Milner in 'A Simple Story' is the prototype of a favourite heroine of our own days – the bright, gifted, and joyous girl. But she has features which Miss Milner had not, features which she was the first, we believe, to introduce in romantic fiction. Glorvina is spirited and generous. She is patriotic and ardent too. She is no cold epitome of virtue, no mere embodiment of frivolous vanity. She is young, gay, and graceful, but she is also a noble woman. She has not the power of intellect of Corinne, but she is far more natural and fascinating. (314)

However, Kavanagh is less impressed with the heroines scattered throughout Lady Morgan's other novels, whose finer qualities, she argues, are marred by a want of the simplicity that is characteristic of 'all great and noble natures' as exemplified by Glorvina. Though she is generally enthusiastic about Lady Morgan's intentions in her novels, the heroes fare little better than the heroines in this context. Kavanagh suggests that, while Lady Morgan did not select great historical characters for her heroes, she gave them 'all the charm of greatness' (327), characteristics which, she claims, had they been modelled on eminent men, would have been more successful. She argues that the failings of Lady Morgan's characters were small in relation to her objective as a novelist, which was to 'serve and vindicate her country' in all she wrote. Unlike Maria Edgeworth who shunned Irish politics, Kavanagh writes that Lady Morgan was fearless in her endeavours to include politics in her writing and, although Kavanagh argues that this trait cost her dearly, she contends that, as a writer, Lady Morgan was superior in that 'she had far more vigour, and especially originality, than women usually show' (329). Though Kavanagh's admiration for Lady Morgan's political voice seeps through her critical overview of this 'temperamentally Irish' writer, she concludes her discussion of Lady Morgan on a note of disappointment. She argues that notwithstanding the fact that her Irish novels 'are bold, energetic conceptions', she was weak in execution and, with a little more discipline, Lady Morgan would have held one of the very highest places held by a woman in English literature.

In drawing attention to this small sample of women novelists, it was Kavanagh's intention to keep their history alive. Her belief in this venture is matched only by her prevailing sense of optimism that although, at the time of writing, many women had been relegated by the literary canon as merely writers of their time, she refused to see them removed to the peripheral outpost of literary history. She had written that her studies of both French and English women of letters are parts of one whole, made up of those who, though no longer read, are deserving of recognition, a sentiment she makes clear at the end of her study: 'We cannot open a novel of to-day on which these past and faded novelists have not left their trace. And whilst the human mind, its toils, its pleasures, are worth noting, that trace, however fine and often invisible, is worthy of attention and record.'

A Summer and Winter in the Two Sicilies

In *An Anthology of Women's Travel Writing*, Shirley Foster and Sara Mills point out that during the nineteenth century British women travel writers were writing from a perspective that was characterised by the very nature of their own domestic experience. They draw attention to the fact that, during that period, most women writers were aware of the textual constraints imposed by gender appropriateness and that the 'narrator's femininity [. . .] had to be guaranteed in order for her work to be appropriately authenticated in gender terms'.[1] Writing in the mid nineteenth century, Kavanagh, of course, was no exception to the strictures placed on the female travel writer and, like others before her, she would also have been subject to a form of gender censure and restrictiveness.[2] Foster and Mills contend that the activity of travel itself, wherein mobility is defined by variables including 'gender, race and class parameters as well as by topography', was more problematic for women, simply because domestic upheaval was greater for women than for men. Moreover, while they acknowledge that not all women travel or write in the same way, it is the woman writer who is more likely to comment on issues of a domestic nature:

> It is partly because such questions of gender were thus foregrounded for them that travellers focus on similar areas in foreign environment – how women dress, their family and societal roles, the degree of personal freedom available to them, and so on. In reflecting on the domestic habits of the female Other, they were, too, enabled to take a revisionary look at their own position, although this did not necessarily produce a radical subversion of the colonialist, white supremacist stance into which they may have been locked. The accounts themselves show the complexity of the narrative position which is produced: the narrating 'I', both authorised by her 'proper' knowledge of the material she is presenting and self-marginalised by speaking from the locus allotted to her, is able to offer new interpretations of femaleness in a context which involves self-evaluation as well as sympathetic observation.[3]

In *A Summer and Winter in the Two Sicilies*, published in 1858, Kavanagh adopts a similar domestic approach as she comments on the cultural contradictions and gender politics of life in the two Sicilies[4] from a predominantly female social perspective.[5] Such a perspective was not unique to Kavanagh, of course, as Italy had already been written and rewritten by British travel writers many times. However, throughout my discussion I will refer mainly to women travellers, although some of the considerations raised here are not necessarily restricted by gender. From the early nineteenth century British women had perceived Italy as a land of liberty.[6] Moreover, a consideration of gender representation in women's travel writing and particularly the idea that such perspectives appropriated a *feminisation* of Italy has provoked much critical discussion in recent years.[7] As one commentator has noted, Madame de Staël's 1807 novel *Corinne ou l'Italie* had set up what was to become a dominant nineteenth-century view of the way *la bella libertà* became *synonymous* for women and for Italy.[8] This view was not lost on Kavanagh, who took advantage of the increasing public interest in the reports and experiences of women travellers at that time. Writing about Victorian women travellers, Maria H. Frawley has poignantly observed:

> That so much of the travel writing of the period was written by women suggests that publishing houses and editors of the periodicals were willing and eager to capitalize on the ostensibly different perspectives that women were able to bring to literature about the wider world. Women travellers, in turn, were eager to capitalize on the publicity that their activities abroad could bring.[9]

Kavanagh is a prominent voice here in that she draws on the context of cultural 'differences' in English[10] and Italian women, and in this respect her interest and cogent delivery of women's experience is itself a form of political writing.

Despite publishers' interest in women's travel writing, however, Kavanagh's publication met with a poor response in *The Athenaeum*.[11] Henry Fothergill Chorley, a regular and usually enthusiastic reviewer of Kavanagh's works, disliked *The Two Sicilies* on the grounds that, unlike 'Mrs. Wollstonecraft's "Letters from Norway," Madame Dudevant's "Winter in Majorca," [or] Mrs. Butler's "Year of Consolation"', all of whom, he contends, 'look through a clear glass', Kavanagh 'does not appear to have seen clearly' and that her 'telescope – besides exaggerating and diminishing familiar objects with a caprice the theorem of which we have not found – has cloud on its *lenses*'.[12] While Fothergill Chorley's argument throws into focus travel writing as seen from experientially different perspectives, Kavanagh makes it very clear that she was interested in the domestic life of the people and she records their cultural practices and their stories alongside her own experiences of travel in the two Sicilies. In this context her observations were recognised as a strength by the reviewer in the *Dublin Review*, who was of the opinion that:

> The extracts will show the justice and good feeling of Miss Kavanagh's strictures upon the character of the people with whom she spent some time, and inclines us to adopt her views, as far as they go, of Italian society. And this we do the more decidedly because she does not attempt too much. She does not generalize or amplify beyond what a traveller's limited means of observation would justify, and we find ourselves attaching a certain value to impressions, which though slight, are so evidently genuine. [13]

What is significant about Kavanagh's account is that she is as interested in relating the fortunes, customs and prejudices of the people she engages with as she is in documenting her experiences as a traveller. Moreover, it is this element in her writing in which the social and sexual politics are apparent as she relates to the manners and practices which help to divide communities as well as hold them together. Writing from within the discourse of her own social and historical position, she makes no direct reference to Italian politics but notes the accepting attitude of a people whose horizons are contained within the boundaries of their daily existence:

> But this much I can safely say – political opinions the people here have none. Of a united Italy, republican or monarchical, they do not dream. Northern Italy is to them a remote, unknown land – they neither like nor dislike it – they know nothing about it. Their patriotism scarcely goes beyond the limits of their birthplace, and rarely passes the frontiers of the state. [. . .]
>   Political rights are to them words devoid of meaning. Panem et Circenses, give them bread and festas; let food be cheap, and holydays frequent, they ask for no more.
>   This is a low state of feeling, yet why censure this people? What does the cry for political rights mean all the world over? It implies the existence of great wrongs, and here the people, as a class, are anything but oppressed. There is no cry against landlords and masters, for land is divided by inheritance, and commerce is not strong enough to crush the weak. The rich and the strong of the land do not sit assembled in Senate to make laws for a class who, whether right or wrong, matters not [. . .] Social freedom compensates for the absence of political liberty. (I: 134–6)

In spite of her observations here, Kavanagh is aware of the material differences imposed by social class and privilege but is intrigued by the general respect and lack of disdain shown to those who are at the very bottom of society. Beggars are everywhere, she tells us, and, when alms cannot be given, they are turned away with a genuine plea to 'have patience', *Figlia mia* (I: 121). Everywhere there is a sense of acceptance without repulsion of the very poor:

> The beggar sits in the sun, unmolested by the polizia; he kneels in the church by the side of the daintiest lady, unawed by pews, beadles, and respectability. When he wants food he goes to the gates of the convent, and receives it without the fear of being captured and locked up in the monk's cell. His wife will persecute you for a grano, his children will handle your garments and pull your cloak, like beings of one race with ourself. You may want occasionally; but starvation, as I have already said, is unknown.
>
> 'Our people would not bear hunger,' said an Italian liberal to me; 'the least rise in provisions brings on a riot.'
>
> The fertility of the country, the mildness of the climate, softens the hardships of poverty. The poor need not much care about the misery of their homes, when they live in the open air, and when the street and the sun are as free to them as to the rich. They are wretched and degraded, it is true, for poverty is wretched and degrading all the world over, but it should never be forgotten that they are not in this land of despotism what they would be in lands of liberty and civilization – the lepers of society, nay, if one may judge by the laws made against them – its born enemies. (I: 136–7)

Here Kavanagh neither romanticises nor sentimentalises a poverty that is accommodated by both climate and social attitude. Her observations relate more to the paradox of democracy and poverty in other 'lands of liberty', presumably Britain, where, she contends, the poor are perceived by the rest of society as a diseased species. It is interesting that a review in the *Dublin University Magazine* accepted her comments only on the understanding that 'if it were the fair inference from what the writer herself had seen and observed, it were less just to take her to task for it'.[14] Nowhere does Kavanagh see herself as anything other than a privileged and accepted guest in the region and as such she is intrigued by the pattern of everyday life as well as the customs of the people she encounters. She takes a particular delight in the energy and industry invested in the celebrations and festivals held throughout the year. Her description of a Neapolitan *festa* is one example, regardless of status, of communal rejoicing:

> The first time we entered Naples was on a July night. We came from Rome, but by land. Accordingly, we drove along the quays. It was a festa, and I never had seen such a sight. Everywhere churches were illuminated, and looked more like Chinese pagodas than like churches; festoons of lamps crossed the streets; petards were firing off, with a deafening noise, at every corner. A little pig, tied in a doorway – too young to be accustomed to Neapolitan ways – was sorely frightened, and screamed with all his might. He was the first of his species whom I had seen in a city, and therefore struck me.

A crowd of men, women and especially children, that seemed endless, swarmed in the streets, on the quays, and around the stalls. These stalls were an epitome of Italian manners. The[re] were so many kitchens. Fires were burning, and pans were whizzing everywhere around us. The night which was dark, heightened the effect. The whole scene looked like the feeding of a nation. Hunger seemed out of the question here; and seen by daylight, the dirty bye-streets of Naples, even without the rejoicing of a festa, convey the same feeling. The abundance and cheapness of meat, vegetables and fruit put starvation out of the question. Every street is a market, and every market is a picture of plenty. The town is dirty, the shipping in the port is unworthy of the magnificence of the bay; but a people can live here, and that is a very redeeming fact. (II: 134–5)

Nevertheless, her fascination for Neapolitan street life did not cloud her awareness of the less appealing aspects of unaccompanied travel, which she relates without hesitation:

The men of the lower classes are certainly tiresome and impudent in their pertinacity. It is next to impossible to get rid of them, if they once fasten on you. The very good-humour with which they bear repulse and reproach is most irritating.

The vice, the cruelty, of which they are accused, we have not seen. We have even gained no practical knowledge of the dishonesty for which they are so famous. It is true, we were so warned against the thieves of Naples, that we have been unusually careful. (2: 157)

It seems that although Kavanagh had some knowledge of Italian, understandably she had some problems with language in the South. At one point, she tells of an episode with a guide who 'did not know Italian and I was not more learned in Sicilian' (II: 23). However, as she travelled within the southern regions for at least a year, evidence suggests that during that time she did manage to overcome some of her difficulties with the different dialects.[15]

In the mid nineteenth century travel writing enabled the woman writer to break into a predominately masculine genre and record the experience of travel from a woman's perspective. It was also a means of broadening horizons. Maria H. Frawley argues:

To a significant extent, women writers achieved a degree of public recognition for their travel writing because it was considered to be a nondomestic genre and hence by implication an unusual and risky choice for the woman writer. Whereas many of the women who wrote fiction were thought of as popular novelists – entertainers – women who wrote nonfiction demanded a different, perhaps more serious, kind of recognition.[16]

The list of women travellers during the nineteenth century is extensive, and, as Shirley Foster has commented, 'By the end of the century there were few parts of the globe that remained unvisited by women determined to extend their horizons, and many took pride in boasting that they were the first female visitors in particular areas'.[17] However, Kavanagh was not a pioneer: she did not travel far afield and into unknown territories.[18] Far from it, she remained in Europe and, it appears, always travelled with her mother. Throughout her account she simply states 'we' but refers to her 'mother' directly on two occasions (II: 122 and II: 188). The desire for better health could be one explanation why Italy was a chosen venture – it was a warm, hospitable and naturally beautiful country that, for the British visitor, afforded cheap travel.[19] In the preface to her book, however, Kavanagh gives another consideration:

> Opening a volume of letters written by the accomplished Mr. Pope and his friends, I fell on the following passage:–
>
> The Rev. Dean Berkeley, afterwards Bishop of Cloyne, writing from Naples, October 21st, 1717, observes:– 'I have long had it in my thoughts to trouble you with a letter, but was discouraged for want of something that I could think worth sending fifteen hundred miles. Italy is such an exhausted subject that I dare say you would easily forgive my saying nothing of it; and the imagination of a poet is a thing so nice and delicate, &c.'
>
> Surely, I thought, if Italy was exhausted a hundred and thirty-one years ago, and if, nevertheless, the public have been able to find amusement and instruction in the vast number of accounts that have since then been given of this beautiful country, the subject is an inexhaustible one.
>
> Satisfied with this logical inference, and comforted by a vision of piles of yet unwritten books of Italian travels, destined to a public yet unborn, I resolved that these two volumes should take their fate.

Like Lady Morgan and Mary Shelley,[20] who also wrote extensively about their travels in Italy, Kavanagh records her experience of the domestic as well as the aesthetic. Although many aspects of life were observed, there are sections when all three women focus ostensibly on the social and political status of women within the economic subcultures throughout Italy. Fothergill Chorley in *The Athenaeum* took exception to Kavanagh's comments on marriage, however, referring to them as 'sweeping illustrations'. In fact, as Kavanagh perceived the traditions surrounding marriage – as the local people related these to her – her comments are founded on an understanding of sexual difference in which the woman, in each case, had little choice but to follow custom. For example, when referring to the social and economic customs of the materially prosperous Sorrento business class, Kavanagh notes that there is little choice for women between marriage and becoming a nun:

> When they are ladies their life is retired, domestic and dull. They marry, they enter a convent, or they become house-nuns; that is to say, they take

the vows, but live at home like the virgins of the early church. But married women or nuns it seems that they must be. Of course in this populous country, where the families are large, every girl cannot marry, and it will often happen that she who cannot get a husband or who will not take the one she can get, enters a convent and becomes a nun for the sake of having a position. Unconquerable, indeed, is the horror of Italian girls at remaining single in the world, where nothing awaits them save a life of restrictions that converts a house into a prison, and makes a convent a place of comparative freedom. I know one young girl, rich but plain, who, hating the idea of being married to a man who would take her for her money, and no less hating the prospect of remaining in the house that was to become her brother's one day, threatened to throw herself out of the window unless she were allowed to enter a monastery.

It is rather a pitiable case that single women should be considered and should consider themselves as only fit to be locked up for life; but setting aside the immorality of doing from worldly reasons what should never be done save from the highest and purest motives, it should not be forgotten by those who condemn this system that these Italian nuns are at least provided for. The poor girls who hunt for husbands for the sake of a position until great writers proclaim to the world in bitter and eloquent pages their misery and their degradation; the wide and unhappy class of gently matured and educated women, who are flattered in the bloom of their youth, sneered at in its decline, made the butt of jests, more or less good natured, in their old age, who are handed about all their lives, the bore and burden of a family, who will teach your children for the sake of a home, who daily fill the columns of newspapers with their sad advertisements, and who are a living reproach to the society that gives them liberty and denies them its privileges, are here, either of them, unknown as a class. (I: 94–6)

In his study of marriage and the family in early nineteenth-century Italy, Marzio Barbagli discusses the statistical changes in household structures over time. His findings are based on the Census data for Florence in 1810 but he notes that 'The Florentine situation was mirrored in other Italian cities as well, and despite their great diversity in most other respects they were extraordinarily similar in terms of household structure'.[21] Barbagli's study is interesting in so far as outside of the larger cities cultural change was slower, which helps to put into perspective Kavanagh's disdain, forty years or so later, of women and society. Barbagli writes:

[The unmarried] remained in the households where they had grown up, either with both their parents or only one. When the parents died the offspring had to find some other solution, and they either lived on their own (forming a single-person household), or formed a non-conjugal household (with an unmarried brother or cousin) or else joined the household of a married brother (creating an extended household). For those over forty-five, the most common solution was to live alone, although there were important differences between men and women. Bachelors were more often to be found living alone, whereas spinsters were more likely to join either extended family households or non-conjugal households.[22]

Kavanagh was one amongst other travellers in Italy (including European, American and Australian women) who wrote about the customary lack of social liberty endured by Italian women. Earlier travellers had addressed this subject of course, including in the mid seventeenth century Lady Anna Miller in her *Letters from Italy*. Anna Miller was appalled at the custom of arranged marriages, which she perceived as women 'being led to the altar as victims, for sacrifice to any disagreeable wretch their parents think proper to bestow them upon'.[23] One hundred years later in 1867 and a few years after Kavanagh's publication, the suffragist Jane Strachey also expressed her concern. In a letter to her husband, she wrote, 'It is heart-breaking to think of the sufferings in intellect and affection which hundreds of women endure from their socially enslaved position.'[24] However, regardless of Kavanagh's sense of outrage at the subservience of women in Italy, she is not without a sense of comic irony concerning what she terms the 'dangerous nature' of womankind. While remaining critical of the practice, she tells us that in Sorrento marriages undergo a form of parental arrangement. She is told by a young peasant woman, Carmela, that

The parents settle the match between themselves, and then refer to the young people; I need not say that in England the young people settle it first then refer to the old. However, compulsion is, I believe, quite out of the question. The marriage being agreed upon by all parties, it is solemnized either in the open day, a proceeding held shameless, barefaced, or at twilight, when the bride steals out to church, escorted by a few friends. She is dressed in her best, has plenty of chains and rings, and wears a gold spadella and flowers in her hair. We once met one of these decorous twilight brides, and very pretty and modest she looked, leaning on the arm of her father, who gravely scattered sugar-plums to the boys in the street. She was going to the cathedral and the bridegroom was invisible. In Rome they make sure of being never seen, by marrying at four in the morning which must make the wedding-day feel rather tedious. The Sorrento sposa does not leave her new home for a week during which she is all but invisible; after this she appears once more, and acts her usual part. I am sorry to say that Italian wives are not very happy. Their husbands rarely trust or honour them; they treat them like children, and are as jealous as Turks. An Italian wife rarely knows the price of anything, not even of meat or vegetables, for it is the man who buys, even in the middle-class. A Roman wife told me that when she married, she could not have five baiocchi without her husband's knowledge. He was kind and fond of her, but mistrustful and jealous. In Sorrento, and in all the south, it is still a rule that peasant women, though taught how to read, must not

know how to write; *the reason is obvious*; if these frail and dangerous creatures knew how to write they would invite love-letters at once. (I: 103–4)

Marriage and courtship between young Sorrentini held much fascination
for Kavanagh, and Carmela's tales of love, jealousy and possession are a
source of endless enlightenment, particularly from the perspective
offered by this 'unmarried' young woman. She includes an interlude on
the discussion of marriage:

> I was once questioning Carmela concerning her aversion to marriage,
> which seemed remarkably strong. She replied with some warmth:–
> 'Signora, when you marry a man, he is fond of you, but after two or three
> years, he either begins to look at and talk to other women, or to beat you
> for jealousy.' I thought she was exaggerating, but she gave me instances that
> startled me, and which other testimony confirmed, at least, so far as the
> jealousy went, for I need not say that the flirting which offended her so
> much is not peculiar to Sorrento. A young woman once went with her
> husband to a festa; she happened to look at another man; at once her
> husband took her home, and beat her till he was tired. The offended wife
> made a vow which she religiously kept: that never again would she go out
> with her husband. Repentance and entreaties availed him not; they never
> again appeared together out of their home. (I: 104–5)

Carmela also relates the tale of one woman who had the misfortune
to marry a man whose possessiveness was the cause of her voluntary
imprisonment:

> A widower married a middle-aged woman; from her marriage day that
> woman never left her husband's house. There was a church opposite their
> door, and she never crossed the street to enter that church and hear mass;
> her husband went, and she stayed at home; and this had lasted something
> like twenty years. When Carmela mentioned the facts, witnesses, who
> could not be mistaken confirmed the story. The man was also harsh to his
> only son by a first wife, and was liked by no one; he was only an enriched
> peasant, but he had the spirit and the domestic tyranny of any feudal old
> Cenci. His wife must have stood in mortal fear of him for he neither locked
> her up, nor stayed within to watch her. His will was stronger than bolts or
> bars, and imprisoned her like gates of adamant. (I: 105–6)

Taken at face value these tales of women and marriage do appear to be
sweeping, especially to suggest that Italian wives are not very happy, but
this is exactly how Kavanagh understood these stories. She is also aware
that the tales she is told are 'extreme cases'. Her informant, Carmela, is
the unmarried daughter of a neighbour and is twenty-three years old,
molto vecchia (very old). She is part of 'a large comfortable and industrious farming family' and her opinion of the 'male sex', Kavanagh sus-

pects, is 'more poetic than charitable'. She tells us that after relating this incredible story, Carmela 'took an apple from the table, and said, impressively: "A man is like this apple; he is fair and smooth without, but there is a worm within"' (I: 106).

Throughout her book Kavanagh talks extensively about women and marriage and the change this has on women's lives. She is intrigued by Carmela's instructive accounts of peasant traditions here, but she is equally aware that this is only part of a larger picture:

> Yet, for all Carmela may think, the women of the people seem happier to me than the ladies, who are prisoners at large, and bound hand and foot by decorum; and infinitely happier in many respects are both the men and the women of the people than the more educated men and women above them. (I: 106–7)

I note here that Kavanagh makes a distinction between 'women' and 'ladies', the implication being a difference between the natural and the contrived. (As has been demonstrated in this study and elsewhere, such divisions evoke further consideration of the notion of gendered subjectivity.) Interestingly, Kavanagh's comment also denotes the paradox of her own position as a visitor from a country where, for a woman, 'femininity' is also synonymous with class and social acceptance.

It is interesting that in her travel book *Italy*, published in 1821, Lady Morgan also comments on the attitude to marriage, this time by the aristocracy in Sardinia:

> The bond of marriage was one of mere accommodation. The necessity (originating in fashion) which every man was under, of neglecting his own wife, and entering into the services of his neighbours, while it undermined morality, deprived taste of its preference, and passion of its excitements: and general gallantry was so blunted by authorised libertinism, that lovers became as stupidly loyal, as husbands were confessedly faithless.[25]

Similarly, when Mary Shelley documented her experience of Italy in her two-volume account, *Rambles in Germany and Italy, 1840, 1842 and 1843*, she noted that 'The unmarried [women] in Italy are usually of good conduct, while marriage is the prelude to a fearful liberty'.[26] The travel writer Thomas Watkins had already noted this 'fearful liberty' to which Shelley is referring when in 1792 he wrote:

> Before marriage their women are nuns, and after it libertines. At twelve years they are immured in a convent, from which there is no return, but upon the hard conditions of receiving from their parents a husband whom they have never seen. If dissatisfied with him (as it generally happens) they are at liberty (from universal custom) to chuse their *Cavalieri Serventi, or Cecisbei*, who attend them to all public places, for the husbands dare not,

assist at their toilette, and, in a word, do every thing they are ordered; for which the ladies sacrifice their own virtue, and their husband's honour.[27]

Together Morgan's, Shelley's and Kavanagh's accounts of marriage customs serve to compound a consciousness of cultural difference as perceived by these women visitors. It is clear, too, that all three women were interested in sexual politics and the customs and boundaries to which women, regardless of class or social standing, were subject.[28] Kavanagh offers her readers a glimpse of tradition, but she is also sufficiently intrigued by the stories that proliferate around marriage concerning the empowerment of women once they have entered into this institution.

Kavanagh also comments on the lack of educational provision for the poor, especially girls. Her time in Italy preceded the liberation of Naples from Bourbon rule in 1859–60, too soon for her to witness the attempts at reform that followed.[29] At the time she would also have been unaware of the philanthropic efforts of a wealthy Englishwoman, Julie Salis Schwabe, who, like Kavanagh, was a defender of Garibaldi and the Italian national cause.[30] In response to Garibaldi's request that more be done for children orphaned by the wars, Salis Schwabe and her Italian colleagues founded a number of schools for the peasantry in and around the region of Naples. Nevertheless, Kavanagh does note the educational provision for girls in Sorrento:

> There are six convents in Sorrento, the monastery of San Paolo, where only ladies of noble birth are received; this is one of the few feudal relics of the place; another monastery, the convent Delle Grazie, which is open to every class, and the conservatorio, or asylum, for poor girls, which has been founded by the charitable Canon, called the Santo. They are his children, and he gives them all he has. They are lodged free of expense, but must work for their support. They never go out, unless in case of illness. (I: 87–9)

She observes that 'The religious education of the people is here, as it is everywhere, in the hands of the priests, and it is very carefully attended to; but beyond reading and writing for boys, and reading and knitting for girls, there is little education. [. . .] Such education as there is, is general and open to all – cheap, but not always gratuitous' (I: 88–9). The only other direct reference is, interestingly, contained within a discussion on marriage. While in Naples, Kavanagh engages with a man whom she describes as a 'learned Neapolitan' who declares that he will never marry on the grounds that it is not conducive to happiness as the couple are ill prepared beforehand for such a commitment. Kavanagh suggests to the man that the 'low state of female education makes wives dull company at home'. His reply to this is a revealing comment on patriarchal attitudes to women: 'There it is, there it is! [. . .] but men will not look at the root of the evil. And yet I assure you Signore, our women are not naturally inferior. They are good-natured, amiable, and lively; but that liveliness goes away with youth or with the cares of marriage, and then they get heavy and dull. And that is why I stay at home with my books, and will not change my state' (II:1 68).

If the 'root of evil' produces the uneducated woman who makes life dull for her husband, then this is not necessarily the situation in all cases. In 1821 Lady Morgan noted that the advances made in women's education were impressive:

> Of all the benefits which the Revolution has conferred upon Italy, the greatness, and most permanent is the new and liberal system of female education, raised upon the ruins of that demoralizing bigotry, which calculated to make women concubines and devotees, but which could not produce good wives and good mothers. In most of the great capitals, Bonaparte, or the Italian governments that acted under his influence, have formed establishments for the education of girls of all ranks, and endowed them with sufficient revenues; being fully aware how powerfully women contribute in determining the character of society; and how much a generation of well-educated females must contribute to raise it from that gulf of immorality into which the vices and feebleness of the old Governments had plunged this part of Europe.[31]

Less overtly political than Lady Morgan in her comments on women's education, Kavanagh is, nevertheless, as actively interested in women's place as she is in the art, landscape and all the aesthetic bounties that country had to offer. Her writing is most alive when she is either involved directly with domestic life or overwhelmed by the beauty and diversity of the people. With reference to the latter, she did slip into the discourse of Victorian imperialism in so far as she conjectured that the most beautiful of the Italians were descended from the Greeks, whereas the coarseness of others she considered 'Moorish'. Above all Kavanagh was intrigued by the beauty of Italian women and, as did some other women travellers before her, she often objectified these women in terms of art, or equated them with mythological figures. However, there is a sense of genuine appreciation of aesthetic difference in Kavanagh's response to one woman whom she encountered outside Sorrento. Here she expresses an unashamed sensuous delight in her acceptance of the woman's beauty:

> She came down the mountain path with the step and mien of a mountain nymph. Her dark hair was drawn back from her white brow; her brown eyes had the clear light of stars; her features were open and radiant with smiles and beauty; her complexion of pure red and white had never felt the burning sun; all her life she had lived in cool orange-gardens. She was richly

dressed, too, in a violet silk jacket and shirt, with long gold earrings and numberless rows of chains passed around her white neck and falling down to her waist. But I thought more of her beauty. I looked at her, mute and breathless. Did she guess that I found her handsome? I cannot say; but her rosy lips parted in a smile that showed two rows of pearl, and, bending her head, she sweetly said, '*Buon giorno*,' and passed on.

Oh! to be a painter, I thought, and fix that delightful face on canvas for ever. (I: 165)

Kavanagh's description is no less seductive for its iconic associations with art, a convention, which, no doubt, offered an acceptable form of expression to a Victorian readership. Throughout she is constantly alert to the sights and customs of different regions in which the women are adorned in vivid costumes and which, as Shirley Foster has noted, 'Victorian woman had been taught to distrust'.[32] The ambiguous nature of Kavanagh's response is associated with a fear of the unfamiliar, which, when placed within the safety net of an artist's perspective, provided a convenient frame for the onlooker's gaze. This type of displacement activity was not entirely confined to the Victorians, however; earlier women travellers have been shown to react in a similar way by displacing the erotic element of their response to other women within the discourse of art. Moreover, Kavanagh's description here holds the same fascination for the exotic – woman as 'Other' – as those women famously beheld by Lady Mary Wortley Montagu on her visit to a Turkish baths. Writing from Adrianople, on 1 April 1717, to an unknown female correspondent, Lady Montagu stresses the beauty of the women she witnesses:

They Walked and mov'd with the same majestic Grace which Milton describes of our General Mother.[33] There were many amongst them as exactly proportion'd as ever any Goddess was drawn by the pencil of Guido or Titian, and most of their skins shineingly white, only adorn'd by their beautifull Hair divided into many tresses hanging on their shoulders, braided either with pearl or riband, perfectly representing the figures of the Graces. I was here convinc'd of the Truth of a Refflexion that I had often, that if twas the fashion to go naked, the face would be hardly observ'd. I perceiv'd that the Ladys with the finest skins and most delicate shapes had the greatest share of my admiration, thô their faces were sometimes less beautiful than those of their companions. To tell you the truth, I had wickedness enough to wish secretly that Mr. Gervase[34] could have been there invisible. I fancy it would have very much improv'd his art to see so many fine Women naked in different postures, some in conversation, some working, others drinking Coffee or sherbet, and many negligently lying on their Cushions while their slaves (generally pritty Girls of 17 or 18) were employ'd in braiding their hair in several pritty manners.[35]

Kavanagh was familiar with Lady Montagu's letters and it is interesting that, again, she expresses a similar response to female beauty when, on her return boat journey, she encountered 'a beautiful Armenian girl of fifteen' about whom she states:

> She was the first specimen of Eastern beauty I had seen, and she reminded me of the raptures Lady Mary Wortley Montagu has bestowed on Turkish ladies. Her features were almost perfect; her complexion was of lilies and roses; her long, dark, almond eyes were like no other eyes; her laugh, her look, her smile, were bewitching and irresistible. (II: 271–2).

It may be that, by associating her own response to this young woman's beauty with that of Lady Montagu's depiction of Turkish women, Kavanagh had found a convenient point of reference in which to record her own aesthetic appreciation. In this way she was able to acknowledge the sensuous as well as the aesthetic nature of her own feelings without overstepping the boundaries of Victorian propriety.

While recording the merits or otherwise of the women she encounters, Kavanagh's account of the two Sicilies is one that both respects the livelihood and the liveliness of the Italian people, who, she says, 'have the easy manners and the freedom from all vulgarity which seem the privilege of the Italian race' (I: 127).[36] Her appreciation mirrors that of other women travellers to this bountiful country who have been equally fascinated by the culture and sense of difference which has inadvertently given rise to a greater awareness of their own cultural 'Otherness' and identity as visitors. In 1789 Hester Piozzi, one of the first women to have published travel writing under her own name in Britain in the eighteenth century,[37] was also intrigued by what she saw as the God-given benefits of the Italian people:

> God has kindly given to Italians a bright sky, a penetrating intellect, a genius for polite and liberal arts, and a soil which produces literally, as well as figuratively, almost spontaneous fruits. [. . .] The mind of an Italian is commonly like his country, extensive, warm, and beautiful from the irregular diversification of its ideas; an ardent character, a glowing landscape.[38]

Much as she was enamoured of the Italian people and their attractions, however, as a woman travelling (with her mother) without the 'protection' of a male companion, Kavanagh was all too aware of the obstacles and constraints that 'unaccompanied travel' entailed.[39] But, as Martha Vicinus has argued, 'Women are never passive participants in the larger culture but actively transform and redefine their external constraints'.[40]

Kavanagh is realistic and revealing of the dangers for 'unescorted' women travellers (including those discomforts that affect all travellers regardless of gender) such as the possibility of being robbed, the need to constantly haggle the price of transport, loss of luggage and other inconveniences. Nonetheless, in spite of these disadvantages, she refused to be daunted in her determination to experience and appreciate Italy. She travelled economically and without unnecessary privilege, paying no more than was necessary whether on land or sea. Her accommodation was comfortable but never luxurious, staying when possible as a paying guest in various Italian houses or respectable hotels. The contribution that Kavanagh has made to travel writing has helped us to understand and redefine her as a writer in so far as the account of her journey throughout the two Sicilies significantly voices her own experience of some of the cultural contradictions faced by women in that region. Kavanagh's interests engage with the complexities of women's experience, which, as she herself had to make her own way in the world, Vicinus's comment is appropriately poignant.

As the opening sentence of her Preface suggests, Kavanagh saw herself as a predictable but privileged guest in the two Sicilies: 'This book was written in the scenes it describes, for the class of readers to whom it will not, it is hoped, seem an intrusive or an impertinent visitor, but, on the contrary, a welcome, even though not very novel, guest.' While she was fully conscious of the everyday realities of the lives of the people she encountered on her journey, like the heroine in her novel *Grace Lee* she readily engaged in the joys and aesthetic pleasures of her experience. At the end of her two-volume account, the novelist's imagination comes to the fore when, as the boat on which she is travelling sails into the port of Marseilles, she states, 'The day was fine, the sun was shining; coming from London or Paris we should have thought the sky a splendid sky; but coming from Naples it looked grey and dull, and told us plainly that a year of light and splendour was over.'

Postscript

In this study of Julia Kavanagh the emphasis has been on the politics of writing which, I believe, serves to demonstrate Kavanagh's own approach to writing. However, this book is only the beginning and much work is yet to be undertaken on this diverse and gifted writer. The full range of her novels, her short stories, fairy tales, poetry, shorter pieces of non-fiction and her biographical work *Women of Christianity*, by necessity of selection, has not been covered here. In focusing on the sexual politics in Kavanagh's writing, I wished to draw attention to her consciousness of women's place in society and how her awareness of social and sexual difference is impacted in her works. From the middle of the 1840s until the end of the nineteenth century Kavanagh's novels helped to fuel the imagination of her readers, and in so doing played their part in drawing attention to the cultural anomalies that affected the quality of women's lives. Her biographical studies of French women during the eighteenth century and her critical studies of both French and English women writers acknowledge the significance of women in history. She is no less enthusiastic about women and culture in her travel writing, as her observations of women and their social roles in the region of the two Sicilies testify. While she was an almost forgotten writer during the twentieth century, in the last few years facsimiles of her works have reappeared in paperback. Now, over one hundred and thirty years since her death in 1877, Julia Kavanagh is attracting the attention of literary scholars who are taking a fresh look at her contribution to women's writing during the mid nineteenth century.

Notes

Chapter 1

1 Central Library, Birmingham: MS 135.

2 In her novel *Dora* (1868) Kavanagh describes Rouen as if she were familiar with that city. It may be the case that her description of Rouen came from a secondary source. Normandy is also the setting for several of Kavanagh's novels, including *Nathalie* (1850). A few encyclopaedia entries suggest that the family lived in Normandy after leaving London but none of them gives specific evidence.

3 Correspondence from Morgan Kavanagh to the Literary Fund Society is the most reliable source for the family's movements between London and Paris: see Royal Literary Fund, [RLF] File 548 on Morgan Kavanagh, held in the British Library. There are no other primary sources available to shed light on the dates of movement between countries. Information is also taken from the earliest bibliographical records of Julia Kavanagh: H. G. Adams, ed. (1857), *A Cyclopaedia of Female Biography*, London, Groombridge, p. 433; Thompson Cooper (1875), *Men of the Time: A Dictionary of Contemporaries, containing Biographical Notices of Eminent Characters of Both Sexes*, Ninth Edition, London, Routledge, p. 599; Sidney Lee, ed. (1892), *Dictionary of National Biography*, vol. XXX, pp. 246–7; *The Catholic Encyclopedia* (1913), vol. 8, London, Caxton Publishing Co., p. 613.

4 Charles W. Wood, 'Mrs. Henry Wood, In Memoriam', Part Three, *Argosy*, 43, June (1887).

5 Madeline House, Graham Storey and Kathleen Tillotson, eds (1995), *The Letters of Charles Dickens*, vol. 8, 1856–1858, Oxford, Clarendon Press. Letter from Charles Dickens to Alfred Hachette, 9 June 1856, p. 133. The editors also note that this is the first evidence that Dickens was acquainted with Lady Georgiana Fullerton and Julia Kavanagh personally. See note 7.

6 R. C. Terry (1983), *Victorian Popular Fiction, 1860–80*, London, Macmillan, pp. 5–6.

7 Terry's list also includes: Katherine Macquoid, Hesba Stretton, Florence Marryat, Annie Thomas, Ellen (Mrs Henry) Wood, Amelia Edward, Dinah Mulock (Mrs Craik), Holme Lee (Harriet Parr), Anne Manning, Emma Marshall, Anna Marsh (later Marsh-Caldwell), Elizabeth Lynn Linton,

Mrs J. H Riddell (Charlotte Elizabeth Lawson Cowan), Matilda Betham Edwards, Sarah Tytler, Helen Mathers, Emma Worboise, Charlotte Yonge and Mrs Oliphant.

8 John Sutherland (1988), 'Victorian Novelists: A Survey', *Critical Quarterly*, 30: 1, 57. Sutherland's fascinating study reveals that bibliographic profiles for the 'total number of novels published can be retrieved for about 1,200 of the (estimated) 7,000 Victorian novelists' (p. 51).

9 Ibid., p. 57.

10 For a full discussion of Mudie's Library see Guinevere L. Griest (1970), *Mudie's Circulating Library and the Victorian Novel*, Bloomington, Indiana University Press. See also Gaye Tuchman with Nina E. Fortin (1989), *Edging Women Out: Victorian Novelists, Publishers, and Social Change*, New Haven and London, Yale University Press.

11 Elizabeth K. Helsinger, Robin Lauterback Sheets and William Veeder (1983), *The Woman Question: Society and Literature in Britain and America, 1837–1882*, vol. III, New York, Garland Publishing, pp. 48–9.

12 Rita Felski (1995), *The Gender of Modernity*, Cambridge, MA, Harvard University Press, p. 1.

13 For further discussion on Romance see Janice Radway (1984), *Reading the Romance: Women, Patriarchy and Popular Literature*, Chapel Hill and London, North Carolina University Press. In this study Radway argues that in reading romance women can escape from the everyday limitations of their restricted lives.

14 Notably Virago's successful launch of reprints of women writers in the 1970s.

15 Amy Cruse (1935), *The Victorians and Their Books*, London, George, Allen and Unwin.

16 Kate Flint [1993] (1999), *The Woman Reader*, Oxford, Clarendon Press.

17 Alison Booth (2004), *How to Make it as a Woman: Collective Biographical History from Victoria to the Present*, Chicago and London, The University of Chicago Press. See particularly pp. 347–87 for Bibliography of Collective Biographies of Women, 1830–1940.

18 See Margaret Kelleher (2001), 'Writing Irish Women's Literary History', *Irish Studies Review*, 9: 1, 5–14. This is not to say that Kelleher is sympathetic to the 'linear model of history implicit in the concept of "foremothers" [that was] employed by many late twentieth-century feminist critics', which she rejects outright. Kelleher questions the feasibility of such arguments put forward by Margaret Ezell in her 1993 work, *Writing Women's Literary History*, when she asserts that Ezell's argument: 'contains a persuasive critique of such "linear historiography", whereby one looks for "'origins' and significant turning points in an evolutionary pattern that leads up to and explains the contemporary situation"; a view of literary history in which "ancestors" serve to document "the legitimacy of current women's literary activities" [17]. This latter tendency, asserting legitimacy for the present the presences or absences of the past, is very common in the

Irish context; many of the recent retrievals of lesser known Irish women writers are presented in these terms' (pp. 8–9).

19 The Bibliothèque Nationale de France holds several titles translated into French, and the British Library has most of Kavanagh's works in English. Her non-fiction works were also reproduced in English and her novels in English and German by the German publisher, Tauchnitz and in Swedish by Wasmuth Leffler. The Vatican Library also has an Italian version of her story 'By the Well' (*Al pozzo*, Palermo, D. Lao e S. de Luca, 1891). This story was originally published in *Temple Bar*, 841, April (1868), 23: 76, and later in *Forget-Me-Nots* (1878), and Mrs McQuoid (1897), *Women Novelists of Queen Victoria's Reign, A Book of Appreciations*. To date I have found three of Kavanagh's short stories from the collection *Seven Years and Other Tales* (1859) reproduced in German for a series of English/German translations entitled *Sprachen-Pflege*. The series covers translations of work by several other nineteenth-century authors including George Eliot, Maria Edgeworth, Charles Dickens and Anthony Trollope. No publication date is given but judging from the cover design it could be late nineteenth or early twentieth century.

20 Letter in private ownership.

21 Kavanagh was very popular in America, particularly on the East Coast where her work was published in New York, Boston and Philadelphia. *Littel's Living Age* is the only journal I have been able to trace but there may well be others.

22 To put Kavanagh's productive outlet into context, John Sutherland's survey of Victorian novelists reveals that 'The per-author lifetime total breaks down to 17.6 novels per writer. Sexually, women novelists averaged 21 titles against men's 15.7.' Moreover, he also states that 'Almost half of all Victorian novels seem to have been produced by authors clocking up 40–50 titles' (p. 59).

23 This enterprise was known as the Victoria Press and opened on 25 March 1860. The Press also printed *The English Woman's Journal* (1858–64) and *Transactions* (an octavo volume of 900 pages) of the Association for the Promotion of Social Science. See Adelaide Procter, ed. (1861), Preface to the *Victoria Regia*, Victoria Press, p. vii. To date no evidence has emerged to suggest that Kavanagh was associated with the Langland Place Circle; a group of middle-class women, headed by Barbara Leigh Smith Bodichon, who had drawn up the married women's property petition of 1856 and published *The English Woman's Journal*.

24 In her study of English Women Novelists of the 1850s Monica Correa Fryckstedt notes that 'Three hundred copies were available of Miss Manning's *The Old Chelsea Bun House* (December 23, 1854, p. 1542), 400 of Julia Kavanagh's *Grace Lee* (February 24, 1855, p. 218), and 500 of Elizabeth Sewell's *Cleve Hall* (June 30, 1855, p. 770)'. See Monica Correa Fryckstedt (1987), 'Defining the Domestic Genre: English Women Novelists of the 1850's', *Tulsa Studies in Women's Literature*, 6: 1 (Spring, 9–25 (11–13).

25 H. G. Adams, ed. (1857), *A Cyclopaedia of Female Biography*, Part 7, London, Groombridge, p. 433.

26 *Academy*, 10, November (1977), 449.

27 Julia Kavanagh, Obiturary, written by Charles W. Wood, *The Athenaeum*, 2612, 17 November (1877), and *The Times*, 19 November (1877).

28 Mrs C. Martin, 'The Late Julia Kavanagh', *Irish Monthly Magazine*, 6 (1878), 96.

29 Sidney Lee, ed. (1892), *Dictionary of National Biography*, vol. 30, pp. 246–7.

30 *Catholic Encyclopaedia*, p. 613.

31 Percy Fitzgerald (1913), *Memories of Charles Dickens*, Bristol, J. W. Arrowsmith, p. 276.

32 Ernest A. Baker (1937), *The History of the English Novel from the Brontës to Meridith*, no. 8, *Romanticism in the English Novel*, London, H. F. and G. Witherby, p. 109.

33 John Sutherland (1988), *The Longman Companion to Victorian Fiction*, London, Longman, p. 343.

34 In this context I have come across one male commentator, Joseph Kestner, who has considered Kavanagh's radical perspective in her novel *Rachel Gray* (1856). See Joseph Kestner (1985), *Protest and Reform: The British Social Narrative by Women 1827–1867*, London, Methuen.

35 B. G. MacCarthy (1946), *The Female Pen: Women Writers and Novelists*, vol. 1, 1621–1744, and *The Later Women Novelists*, vol. 2, 1744–1818, Cork, Cork University Press.

36 Virginia Blain, Patricia Clements and Isobel Grundy, eds (1990), *The Feminist Companion to English Literature*, London, Batsford, p. 598.

37 Lorna Sage, ed. (1999), *The Cambridge Guide to Women's Writing in English*, Cambridge, Cambridge University Press, p. 361.

38 Eileen Fauset (1996), 'The Politics of Writing', *Irish Journal of Feminist Studies*, 1: 02 (Winter), 58–68.

39 Elibron Classics Series, MA, USA. See also J. D. Smith, III, ed. (2006), *Women of Christianity: The Pioneer 1852 Narrative of Women's Lives in the Christian Tradition*, Eugene, OR, Wipf & Stock.

40 Ann Stewart, ed. (1984), *National Gallery of Ireland: Fifty Irish Portraits*, Dublin, National Gallery of Ireland Publication. 'The work is by a French Academic Artist and was probably painted while she lived in Paris. It was exhibited at the Paris Salon and the Royal Academy in London in 1883' (p. 40). Personnel at the Gallery suggest that the portrait is taken from a photograph and so it could have been painted after Julia's death in 1877.

41 Throughout his life Morgan Kavanagh applied five times to the Literary Fund Society for financial assistance towards living costs, three of those times whilst still living with Bridget and Julia. Records show that he placed applications in 1825, 1839, 1844, 1847 and 1850. See RLF: 548.

42 Letter dated 3 September 1839 from Morgan Kavanagh to Octavian Blewitt, Secretary to the Literary Fund Society, London, item 7. See also

item 11, letter from W. Hislop to Blewitt recommending Kavanagh for financial assistance. '[Kavanagh's] situation is peculiarly painful from the circumstance of an only child being afflicted with a disease in the spine which under the care of a physician here was rapidly being conquered – the costs attending which embarrassed him heavily [and] some months ago he was compelled to remove his daughter at the risk of the malady returning in full [r]igour. I earnestly hope that the Literary Fund Society will assist him to the extent of their ability.' See also item 12, letter from Henry Glenton to Octavian Blewitt, 20 October 1839. In this letter Glenton refers to Julia's stay at Dr Harrisson's Spinal Institution, Fitzroy Square, 'could have remained until her cure had been effected, but want of funds would not allow her to remain any longer and was obliged to return to Paris where her case was never perfectly healed or understood.' See also item 10, letter from Le Comte d'Ormesson to Octavian Blewitt, 20 October 1839 (original in French), The contents of this letter also refer to Julia's condition: 'The little girl who has suffered for several years has backache which has confined her to her bed and who will probably find herself in this situation for a long time to come'. RLF: 548,

43 Letter 565 (445) in Wise and Symington, eds (1932) *The Brontës: The Lives, Friendships and Correspondence in Four Volumes*, vol. 3, 1849–1852, Oxford, Shakespeare Head Press, Basil Blackwell, pp. 117–18.

44 Phyllis Bentley (1969), *The Brontes and their world*, London, Book Club Associates, p. 45.

45 Letter to Ellen Nussey, 24 December 1847, in Margaret Smith, ed. (1995), *The Letters of Charlotte Brontë with a Selection of Letters by Family and Friends*, vol. 1, 1829–1847, Oxford, Clarendon Press, p. 584. See also note 7. 'Mary Taylor's sister Martha had died in Brussels in 1842.' See also Winifred Gérin (1969), *Charlotte Brontë*, Oxford Lives Series, Oxford, Oxford University Press. In her discussion of Brontë's friendship with Martha Taylor, Gerin cites Ellen Nussey, who, speaking of Martha, states: 'so piquant and fascinating were her ways. She was not in the least pretty but something much better, full of change and variety, rudely outspoken, lively and original, producing laughter with her own good humour and affection' (p. 64).

46 Charles W. Wood, 'Mrs. Henry Wood, In Memoriam', *Argosy*, 43, April (1877), 251–70.

47 Ibid.

48 In his preface to the poem Martin MacDermot states: 'Whether from that vanity which makes every author an admirer of his own productions, or from a total ignorance of the publishing system, he [Morgan Kavanagh] imagined, or rather was firmly convinced, that he could have no difficulty in disposing of his Poem. Accordingly, he set out from a remote part of Ireland for this city, but soon found his mistake; for instead of meeting with a publisher to purchase his production, he could not even find one who would take the trouble, or incur the expence of having it examined. [. . .]

He remained accordingly in London, unnoticed and unknown, until he was nearly reduced to his last shilling, when a mere accident introduced him to me, or rather to the gentleman by whom he was introduced. I perused his Poem, and recommended its author to a private gentleman, to whom the first and present edition of 'The Wanderings of Lucan' owes its existence, having had it printed at his own expence, for the sole benefit of the author, who is also indebted to him for many subsequent acts of favour.' In Robert Kavanagh (2001), *The Mysterious Irishman: Morgan Peter Kavanagh* (44 pages), p. 8 (document held at the National Library of Ireland: 5682). Robert Kavanagh's study is an attempt to document the life of his great-grandfather, Morgan Kavanagh.

49 In a letter to Octavian Blewitt of the Literary Fund Society, dated 3 September 1839, addressed from Paris, Morgan refers to his poem *The Wanderings of Lucan and Dinah* as being without merit: 'it was a very long poem composed while I was yet very young in the short space of two months but with the exception of a few passages which cost me a little trouble it was very bad indeed'. RLF: 548: 7.

50 Letter from Morgan Kavanagh to William Jerdan, 27 October 1825: 'Sir, Being necessitated from various pressing circumstances, to introduce myself as soon as possible to the Literary Fund Society, and understanding that on such occasions a literary advocate is necessary, I am imboldened, in consequence of what I have already expressed of your kindness, to beg that you would be so good as to lay my case before the committee at the next sitting. Having a wife and child to support besides myself, I have been for at least this half year past in a situation sufficiently wretched to authorize me to put in my claim of relief much sooner: but as I am a stranger here and without friends, it is my intention, should the Literary Fund allow me the means to remove with my family to my native country, where from being known it is likely that I should soonest obtain a livelihood.' RLF: 548: 1.

51 Letter from Morgan Kavanagh to Octavian Blewitt, Literary Fund Society, 3 September 1839, addressed from Paris. In this letter, Morgan states: 'for the last fourteen years I have with the exception of one year resided in Paris as professor of the English language, supporting by this means myself and family as well as I could. A more lucrative situation, the representative of a French company in England being offered me near the close of the year 1837 I willingly gave up all I possessed here to accept it. Having, through no fault of mine, had the misfortune to lose this place at the end of a year I saw myself under the necessity of removing back to Paris with my family, hoping to recover at least a part of my former connexions. But my arrival has been too late in the season for that, for though I have been here since the month of March I have not been able to obtain employment of any kind; nor do I now expect to earn a shilling before the commencement of the winter season.' RLF: 548: 7.

52 Ibid.

53 It is not known exactly when the family separated but letters written by Morgan to the Literary Fund Society suggest that they were together until around 1847. See RLF: 548.

54 See above, letter to Edward Walford from Julia Kavanagh, Champs Elysées, Paris, 1861.

55 It is possible that at some time between early 1852 and 1853 Julia and Bridget were travelling in southern Italy. See *A Summer and Winter in the Two Sicilies* (1858). They may also have travelled to northern Italy either during this period or at a later time. See Julia Kavanagh, 'A Glimpse of Northern Italy', *The Month*, I July (1864), 112–22.

56 The Franco-Prussian War lasted from July 1870 to May 1871.

57 *The Catholic Encyclopedia* (1913), p. 613.

58 Both Julia and Bridget were buried at this cemetery. A family vault was not acquired until 28 March 1879 in the *Allée du Bruloir, Cimetiere du Château*. Their bones were exhumed after 14 March 1968 (the date on which the vault was officially considered as being 'abandoned') and placed in a communal ossuary: *Archives Municipales de Nice, Registres D'Etat Civil Décés, Fiche de Depouillement*. Information is courtesy of The Princess Grace Irish Library, Monaco.

59 Bridget Kavanagh was born in 1802 and died aged 86 on 20 December 1888 in Nice: The Princess Grace Irish Library, Monaco.

60 According to the 1876 Census form for Nice, Julia's and Bridget's neighbours were English, Italian and French professional lower middle-class which suggests that the address was respectable and accommodating. Flat 93, 24 rue Gioffredo, Nice, is the address on Julia's death certificate: The Princess Grace Irish Library, Monaco.

61 Information is courtesy of The Princess Grace Irish Library, Monaco. Attempts to trace information concerning the beneficiaries of Bridget's Testament (Miss Kate Ray and Miss Lucy Otteo, London) have proved fruitless.

62 In an application to the Literary Fund Society, dated 13 November 1844, Morgan gives his approximate date of birth as 1799, which would have made him twenty-two or twenty-three years of age in 1822. RLF: 548: 15.

63 Letter from W Sherwood to Jerdan, 27 October 1825: 'The inclosed is a letter to you from Mr. Kavanagh, who is the author of The Wanderings of Lucan & Dinah of which I am the publisher, I have no doubt that he and his family are at present in a distressed state, and as regards his Moral Character, I know of nothing objectionable in it.' Letter from Jerdan to Joseph Snow, 30 October 1825: 'The enclosed application for relief to the Literary Fund, will explain itself; and all that I have to add is that the work referred to is a respectable poem (a long octavo volume) displaying considerable talent – the author an unfortunate aspirant from humble life and his production much commended by several critical writers. I consider him a very proper object for relief and his necessities point to the First Meeting.' RLF: 548: 2 and 3.

64 Letter from Morgan Kavanagh to Octavian Blewitt, Secretary of the Literary Fund Society, 18 June 1844: Morgan's address at this time was 27 Alfred Street, Bedford Square, London: RLF: 548: 16.

65 Robert Kavanagh (2001), p. 21. Morgan Kavanagh Manuscript of 670 pp. (1855), held at the National Library of Ireland: 6354.

66 Letter is held at the Harry Ransom Humanities Research Center, University of Texas at Austin.

67 Julia's and Bridget's address here is probably 7 Allason Terrace, Kensington.

68 Letter 565 (445) dated 12 June 1850, in Wise and Symington, 3, pp. 117–18. See also letters from Kavanagh to Leitch Ritchie: William and Robert Chambers, National Library of Scotland, Edinburgh. Ref. Dep. 341.

69 Ibid.

70 Ibid.

71 Ibid.

72 For a demographic study of Irish settlement in Britain see David Fitzpatrick (1989), '"A Peculiar Tramping": The Irish in Britain, 1801–70' in W. E. Vaughan, ed., *A New History of Ireland: Ireland under the Union*, vol. 5, Oxford, Clarendon Press, Chapter 29, pp. 623–60; See also Lynn Hollen Lees (1979), *Exiles of Erin, Irish Migrants in Victorian London*, Manchester, Manchester University Press; see also Roger Swift and Sheriden Gilley, eds (1989), *The Irish in Britain 1815–1939*, London, Pinter Publishers.

73 On 19 November 1847 Morgan wrote to Octavian Blewitt concerning his application for an amount of money to cover his passage from London to Paris. In the concluding paragraph he states that he has 'an old friend residing in Lambeth'. It is possible that this person is known to Bridget and Julia: RLF: 548: 27.

74 On 24 November 1847 Morgan made a fourth application to the Literary Fund Society for funds to return to Paris. His address on correspondence is 15 Leicester Place, Leicester Square, London: RLF: 548: 21.

75 Letter from Julia Kavanagh to Mrs Williams: Trinity College Dublin, MS6235/1–177. This letter is without an address but it is likely to have been Allason Terrace, Kensington.

76 *Household Words*, 27 July 1850. According to the magazine's records, this story was co-written or revised by W. S. Wills. See Michael Forsyth, unpublished Ph.D. Thesis, 'Julia Kavanagh in Her Times', The Open University, Milton Keynes, 1998.

77 Hollen Lees, p. 70.

78 *Household Words*, 3 September (1853), 8: 8,16.

79 Gavan Duffy (1898), *My Life in Two Hemispheres*, vol. 2, London, T. Fisher Unwin, pp. 11–12.

80 Ibid., pp. 120–1.

81 MS. 17 745: National Library of Ireland, Dublin.

82 MS. S757: National Library of Ireland, Dublin.

83 There are no records to show how long Morgan lived at this address but correspondence suggests that it was about three years.

84 Yvonne Kapp (1972), *Eleanor Marx*, vol. I, London, Lawrence and Wishart, p. 23.

85 See above: correspondence referring to *The Hobbies*.

86 Other residents living at 28 Dean Street included a male cook and his wife, a male confectioner and two female servants: people whose professions suggest they would require cheap lodgings.

87 I am grateful to Mary Campbell who kindly allowed me to see the manuscript of an article 'Mr. Kavanagh's Lodgers – a Soho Episode' published in *The Irish Times* in the 1960s. Unfortunately attempts to trace the article have been unsuccessful.

88 Public Health Act 1848.

89 Kapp (1972), p. 23.

90 Ibid. p. 23 (notes).

91 Letter to Octavian Blewitt in support of his fifth application for financial assistance; addressed from 6 Rupert St/Coventry St, London, dated 1 May 1850: RLF: 548: 30.

92 RLF: 548: 33.

93 See Jacques-Philippe Saint-Gerand, *Morgan Kavanagh: Condylure Oublié en Histoire des Sciences du Langage?*: internet source: http://www. chass.utoronto. ca/epc/langueXIX/kavanagh/. According to Saint-Gerard, Morgan made seven unsuccessful attempts at this prize in 1847, 1850, 1857, 1869, 1870, 1871 and 1873.

94 B. Nicolaievsky and O. Maenchen-Helfen (1976), *Karl Marx: Man and Fighter,* in Isaiah Berlin (1978), *Karl Marx: His Life and Environment*, Oxford, Oxford University Press, pp. 142–3.

95 Maximilien Rubel, trans. (1965), Mary Bottomore, *Marx Life and Works*, London, Macmillan Chronology Series, Reference, p. 28.

96 Letter from Julia Kavanagh to Mrs Williams. MS6235/1–177: Trinity College, Dublin.

97 Coroner's Inquest on Morgan Kavanagh, Islington, 14 February 1874 (London Metropolitan Archives) reports that while waiting for a tram car, he 'stepped back to avoid a passing carriage and fell, fracturing his skull'. In Robert Kavanagh, (2001) p. 21.

98 Application for financial assistance to the Literary Fund Society dated 4 November 1844, RLF: 548: 15.

99 Robert Kavanagh (2001), p. 16.

100 Ibid. Martin MacDermot, 'On the Genius of Spenser, and the Spenserian School of Poetry', *The European Magazine*, October (1822), 331–41, and continued in November (1822), 431–40 (ref. 39), p. 24.

101 Robet Kavanagh (2001), p. 8.

102 *Nouvelle Biographie Générale*, pp. 490–1.

103 Application for the sum of £25 dated 4 November 1844. RLF: 548: 15.

104 Robert Kavanagh, (2001), p. 4.

105 *The Athenaeum*, 1546, 13 June (1857), 761.

106 *The Athenaeum*, 1547, 20 June (1857), 792–3.

107 *The Athenaeum*, 1548, 27 June (1857), 822.

108 *The Athenaeum*,1549, 4 July (1857).

109 *The Spectator*, 11 July (1857), 735.

110 Kavanagh gives Paris as her address in her Preface to *French Women of Letters* (1862).

111 The absence of a marriage certificate does not necessarily mean that Morgan and Marie-Rose did not undergo a marriage ceremony. Such a marriage would have made Morgan a bigamist. Robert Kavanagh is of the opinion that no marriage in the lawful sense took place. Robert Kavanagh (2001), p. 4.

112 Ibid.

113 Ibid.

114 Letter from Julia Kavanagh to L. Wiederman, dated 10 January 1868.

115 Robert Kavanagh (2001), p. 6.

116 Morgan Kavanagh (1871), *Origin of Language and Myths*, vol. 1, p. x in Robert Kavanagh (2001), p. 4.

117 Elizabeth Kowaleski-Wallace (1991), *Their Fathers' Daughters: Hannah More, Maria Edgeworth, and Patriarchal Complicity*, Oxford, Oxford University Press, p. 12.

118 Ibid., p. 11.

119 Ibid., p. 11.

120 Letter to Williams, dated 13 January 1848 signed C. Bell, in Margaret Smith, ed. (2000), *The Letters of Charlotte Brontë: with a Selection of Letters by Family and Friends* vol. 2, 1848–1851, Oxford, Clarendon Press, p. 12. See also *Brontë Society Transactions*, 91:1:18 (1981), 118–19.

121 For further discussion see Phyllis Bentley (1969), p. 24.

122 Letter to Ritchie, 6 October 1847: National Library of Scotland, Ref. Dept. 341.

123 Letter 342 (265) in Wise and Symington, eds (1932), *The Brontës: Their Lives, Friendships and Correspondence in Four Volumes*, vol. 2, 1844–1849, Oxford, Shakespeare Head Press, Basil Blackwell, pp. 181–2.

124 Ibid., letter 359 (279), pp. 200–1.

125 Margot Peters (1981), 'An Unpublished Bronte Letter: The Second Edition of "Jane Eyre"', *Brontë Society Transactions*, 91: 1: 18, 116.

126 Letter 400 (312) in Wise and Symington, vol. 2, pp. 268–70.

127 Ibid., letter 403 (314), pp. 286–8.

128 Ibid., letter 421 (329), pp. 306–7. See also Margaret Smith (2000), p. 361. Charlotte Brontë's desk contained a list of books, dated 18 March 1850, sent to Charlotte Brontë from Smith and Elder containing a copy of *Woman in France*, vols I and II.

129 See Tuchman, p. 118.

130 Letter 597 (467) in Wise and Symington, vol. 3, pp. 155–6. See also

Margaret Smith (2000), pp. 462–3 and note 1. See also in Smith, letter from Charlotte Brontë to Mrs Gaskell, 6 August 1851, in which Brontë comments on Catholics and Elizabeth of Hungary, pp. 676–7.

131 Letter 761 (567) in Wise and Symington, vol. 3, p. 326.

132 Ibid., letter 600, pp. 158–60.

133 Margaret Smith (2000), pp. 224–5 (BPM 451 (356)).

134 Letter 603 (470) in Wise and Symington, vol. 3, pp. 161–2.

135 Ibid., letter 639, p. 203.

136 J. A. V. Chapple and Arthur Pollard, eds (1997), *The Letters of Mrs Gaskell*, Manchester, Manchester University Press. The editors have placed a question mark against the recipient's name ?Edward Coward. This could, in fact, be Edward Walford whom Kavanagh addresses above. See letter 321, p. 423.

137 Julia Kavanagh to George Smith: Harry Ransom Research Center, University of Texas at Austin.

138 British Museum. Additional MS. 46,615, Agreement between Richard Bentley and Julia Kavanagh dated 3 July 1848.

139 British Museum Additional MS. 46,615, Agreement dated 22 June 1848 and 46,616, Agreement dated 18 October 1852.

140 To put Kavanagh's earnings into perspective, in 1848, Charlotte Brontë received a payment of £100 for *Jane Eyre*. Margaret Smith notes that 'The payment of £100 was probably the firm's acknowledgment that sales of *JE* had been so good as to warrant a 2nd edn. Smith, Elder paid £500 each for the copyrights of *JE*, *Shirley*, and *Villette* in their three-volume format, though for *Villette* CB recorded the actual receipt of £480. In addition she was paid £100 for the cheap one-volume edn. of *JE* (1850) and £82. 10s. for the foreign copyright of *Villette*.' See Margaret Smith (2000), note 2, p. 29. While Kavanagh was required to make a living from her writing, it seems that she was relatively fortunate in the amounts she earned. As Tuchman has noted, 'Most authors earned little by writing. Since they had few occupational alternatives, women were more likely to be among those struggling to get by' (p. 150). Tuchman also notes that, 'Judging from the Macmillan Archives [compiled from 1866], a typical, mediocre novelist might receive from £50 to £100, equivalent to $225 to $450, for the sale of a novel's copyright. If an author published a book a year, this sum was sufficient to maintain a family in the middle class – not prosperous, but wealthy enough to keep more than one servant. Thus, in an age when writing for money was no longer socially condemned, increasing numbers of people would not have written novels had they not expected some modest profit' (pp. 40–1).

141 Elaine Showalter (1978), *A Literature of Their Own: British Women Novelists from Brontë to Lessing*, London, Virago, pp. 19–20.

142 *The Athenaeum*, 2: 1622, 27 November (1858), 681.

143 Mary Lyndon Shanley (1989), *Feminism, Marriage, and the Law in Victorian England*, Princeton, Princeton University Press, p. 4.

144 Anthony Wohl, ed. (1978), *The Victorian Family*, New York, St Martin's Press, pp. 9–10, in Shanley (1989), p. 5.
145 Shanley (1989), p. 3.
146 Robert A. Colby (1968), *Fiction with a Purpose: Major and Minor Nineteenth Century Novels*, Bloomington, Indiana University Press, pp. 196–7. See also Shirley Foster (1988), '"A Suggestive Book" A Source for *Villette*', *Etudes Anglaises*, 35: 2, 177–84.
147 Mrs C. Martin (1878), p. 97.
148 Shirley Foster (1985), *Victorian Women's Fiction, Marriage Freedom and the Individual*, London, Croom Helm, p. 19.

Chapter 2

1 Terry Eagleton [1975] (1988), *Myths of Power: A Marxist Study of the Brontës*, London, Macmillan, p. xix.
2 The concept of separate spheres is not new of course; feminist criticism of the 1970s and 1980s particularly explored many aspects of women's literary history from this perspective.
3 Lorna Sage, 'The Case of the Active Victim', *Times Literary Supplement*, 26 July (1974), 803–4, in Elaine Showalter (1978), p. 86.
4 Coventry Patmore's *The Angel in the House* (1855–56) and John Ruskin's 'Of Queens' Gardens' in *Sesame and Lilies* (1865) were extremely influential in spreading the ideal of womanhood.
5 In her study of Victorian women's fiction Shirley Foster draws attention to the fact that as early as 1842 some writers were conscious of maintaining a sexual distinctiveness. She points out that 'Miss Stodart, in her *Female Writers: Thoughts on their proper Sphere and on their Powers* (1842) was one of the first to suggest that womanly qualities of delicacy, sensitivity, quick sympathy, and powers of observation commit women novelists to a particular literary mode – the depiction of home and family; [. . .] Anne Mozley posits that the most admirable female writers are those who turn their gifts to social and domestic account, who refrain from making themselves "exceptions from the ordinary domestic type of women", and who write "on subjects especially open to feminine treatment" with their natural "delicate fingering . . . soft touch, and quick perception."' Foster (1985), pp. 2–3.
6 'The Lady Novelists of Great Britain', *Gentleman's Magazine*, 18–25 July (1853), 18. See also J. M. Ludlow, review of *Ruth*, in *North British Review*, 19: May (1853), 169. Here Ludlow argues against the idea of unmarried women writing novels because they lack the emotional 'wifely and motherly experience' of their married counterparts.
7 Ibid., p. 20.
8 G. H. Lewes, 'The Lady Novelists', *Westminster Review*, 58 (1852), 129–33.
9 Ibid.
10 Elizabeth Strutt (1857), *The Feminine Soul: Its Nature and attributes with thoughts upon marriage, and friendly hints upon feminine duties*, London.

Elizabeth Strutt said, '"familiar and sentimental fiction" was like "lyric and elegiac poetry" – a field where women might excel with "felicity of tact," "acuteness of perception and apprehension," and "depth and warmth of feeling."' In Elizabeth K Helsinger, et al. (1983), p. 48.

11 Lewes (1852), 134–5.

12 G. H. Lewes, 'Currer Bell's "Shirley"', *Edinburgh Review*, 91, January (1850), p. 155, in Foster (1985), p. 3.

13 Ibid., p. 3.

14 George Eliot, 'Silly Novels by Lady Novelists', *Westminster Review*, 66 (1856), 460.

15 Ibid.

16 Margaret Fuller Ossoli, *Woman in the Nineteenth Century* (1845), in New and Complete Edition, Arthur B. Fuller, ed., introduction by Horace Greeley, (1968) New York, Greenwood Press.

17 George Eliot, 'Margaret Fuller and Mary Wollstonecraft', *The Leader*, 13 October (1855). See Ashley Tauchert, ed. (1995), *Mary Wollstonecraft: A Vindication of the Rights of Woman* [1792], London, Everyman Series, Dent, p. 322.

18 W. R. Gregg, 'False Morality of Lady Novelists', *National Review*, 8 (1859), 145–7.

19 Florence Nightingale, *Cassandra* (1928), [1852, rev. 1859]; reprinted in R. Strachey (1978), *The Cause*; in J. M. Golby (1986), *Culture & Society in Britain 1850–1890*, Oxford, Oxford University Press, pp. 244–56.

20 Cynthia Eagle Russett (1989), *Sexual Science: The Victorian Construction of Womanhood*, Cambridge, MA, Harvard University Press, pp. 1–2. See also in Eagle Russett: ref. to John Stuart Mill and Harriet Taylor Mill, *Essays on Sex Equality*, with an Introductory Essay by Alice S. Rossi (1970), Chicago, University of Chicago Press, pp. 125, 148, 149. On *The Subjection of Women.* see also Josephine Kamm (1977), *John Stuart Mill in Love*, London, Gordon and Cremonesi. See also Eugene August (1975), *John Stuart Mill: A Mind at Large*, New York, Charles Scribner & Sons.

21 For a full discussion of the 'feminine' writers see also Elaine Showalter (1978).

22 Along with Currer Bell and George Eliot they include 'Holme Lee, Ennis Graham, F.G. Trafford, Allen Raine, Lucas Malet, John Strange Winter, Lanoe Falconer, George Egerton, Lawrence Hope, Vernon Lee, Claude Lake, Ross Neil, John Oliver Hobbes, Martin Ross, and Michael Fairless. [. . .] In public terms, the pen name reflects the novelists' desire to protect themselves from personal attack and to win the serious respect of reviewers. In private terms, the masculine name suggests the fantasy of acquiring a more exciting identity and the guilt of choosing a vocation in direct conflict with woman's status.' In Helsinger et al. (1983), p. 65.

23 Letter 313 (239) to W. S. Williams, 28 October 1847, in Wise and Symington, vol. 2, pp. 150–1.

24 Henry Fothergill Chorley. Kavanagh's works were reviewed regularly in the periodicals, most notably in *The Athenaeum* by Fothergill Chorley and Geraldine Jewsbury.

25 *The Athenaeum*, 1203, 16 November (1850), 1184–5.

26 Some reforms were met but the Acts of Parliament were few and far between and the process of change was long drawn out. The 1857 and 1878 Matrimonial Causes Acts and the 1870 Married Women's Property Act were followed in 1874 by the Married Women's Property Amendment Act, and later, the 1882 Maried Woman's Property Act.

27 Also known as the 1857 Divorce Act. See Shanley (1989), p. 26.

28 Joan Perkin (1989), *Women and Marriage in Nineteenth-Century England*, London, Routledge, pp. 30–1.

29 Valerie Saunders (1999), 'Marriage and the Antifeminist Woman Novelist' in Nicola Diane Thompson, ed., *Victorian Woman Writers and the Woman Question*, Cambridge, Cambridge Studies in Nineteenth Century Literature and Culture 21, Cambridge University Press, p. 25.

30 Lady Caroline Norton was also instrumental in effecting some change in the laws pertaining to child custody. Her pamphlet *A Plain Letter* influenced the passing of the Infant Custody Act in 1839 and her pamphlets *English Laws for Women*, 1854, and *A Letter to the Queen*, 1855, supported the Matrimonial Causes Act (1857) and the Married Women's Property Act (1870).

31 Common law rules based on the doctrine of coverture stipulated that a married woman was incapable of signing any contract without being joined by her husband as co-signer. See Shanley (1989), p. 26.

32 Shanley (1989) outlines the unsatisfactory outcome of the Act, which failed to achieve equality for women: 'What Parliament accomplished in the Divorce Act must in the final analysis be judged in the light of what it failed to do. Usually hailed in histories of English jurisprudence as a watershed statute that created both the action for civil divorce and the new Court of Divorce, the Divorce Act also sanctioned and perpetuated a patriarchal understanding of the marriage bond. Parliament was so deeply wedded to notions of marital hierarchy that the contractarian arguments of Caroline Norton, Barbara Leigh Smith, and others for equal grounds for divorce made very little impression, even when they were advanced in Parliament by such eminent figures as Lords Lyndhurst and Brougham. When presented with proposals to allow married women to control their own property and to equalize the grounds for divorce for men and women, Parliament rejected both almost out of hand. Only in providing that a deserted or separated wife could be treated as a femme sole did Parliament grant nominally married women any legal autonomy' (p. 47).

33 Ibid., pp. 26–7.

34 Ibid., pp. 21–3.

35 Dolores Dooley (1996), *Equality in Community*, Cork, Cork University Press, p. 19. The text cited is from the *Appeal on Behalf of Women* (1825).

36 Jenni Calder (1976), *Women and Marriage in Victorian Fiction*, London, Thames and Hudson, p. 33.

37 Patsy Stoneman (1996), *Brontë Transformations*, Hemel Hempstead, Harvester Wheatsheaf, p. 22.

38 Foster (1985), p. 19.

39 Bird imagery also appears in Kavanagh's other novels, particularly in *Daisy Burns*, vol. 1, pp. 346–7.

40 Eagle Russett (1989), pp. 42–3.

41 Letter 639, Charlotte Brontë to Julia Kavanagh, 21 January 1851, in Wise and Symington, vol. 3, p. 203.

42 Mrs. Charles Martin, 'The Late Julia Kavanagh', *Irish Monthly Magazine*, 4 (1878), 98.

43 Michel Foucault [1976] (1984), *The History of Sexuality*, vol. 1, London, Penguin.

44 Foster (1985), p. 18.

45 Jane Moore (1992), 'An Other Space: A Future for Feminism' in Isobel Armstrong, ed., *New Feminist Discourses*, London, Routledge, pp. 65–79.

46 Nancy Armstrong (1987), *Desire and Domestic Fiction: A Political History of the Novel*, Oxford, Oxford University Press, p. 21.

47 Sally Shuttleworth (1999), *Charlotte Brontë and Victorian Psychology*, Cambridge, Cambridge University Press, p. 18.

48 See Tuchman, Chapter 8, 'The Critical Double Standard', pp. 175–202.

49 Letter 832 (627) to W. S. Wiliams, 9 March 1853, in Wise and Symington, eds (1932) *The Brontës: Their Lives, Friendships and Correspondence in Four Volumes*, vol. 4, pp. 50–1.

50 *The Athenaeum*, 1321, 19 February (1853), 220–1.

51 'The Progress of Fiction as an Art', *Westminster Review*, 60 (1853), 372.

52 'There is at least one other writer of considerable gifts, whose books are all so many reflections of *Jane Eyre*. We mean no disparagement to Miss Kavanagh; but from *Nathalie* to *Grace Lee*, she has done little else than repeat the attractive story of this conflict and combat of love or war – for either name will do [. . .].' Mrs Margaret Oliphant, 'Modern Novelists – Great and Small', *Blackwood's Edinburgh Magazine*, 1: 37, May (1855), 559. There are numerous similarities between names; for example, Daisy's own name, Burns, is reminiscent of Jane's friend Helen Burns; Daisy's grandfather is a Thornton, who lives at Thornton House, echoing Thornfield; a cousin is Edward Thornton, a young aristocrat who is protective towards Daisy and whose name is an amalgamation of Edward Rochester and Thornfield Hall. Edward also has a sister, Bertha, who, unlike Bertha Mason, is sane and also extremely beautiful, a reminder, perhaps, of a once beautiful and desirable Bertha Mason. Moreover, like Jane, Daisy is also an orphan.

53 To avoid confusion I shall refer to her as Daisy from the beginning.

54 Shuttleworth (1999), p. 9.

55 Ibid., p. 9.

56 Ibid., p. 72.

57 William Michael Rossetti, ed. [1904] (1935), *The Poetical Works of Christina Georgina Rossetti,* London, Macmillan, p.330. Christina was often a model for her brother's paintings and although in this poem she is referring to Elizabeth Siddel, Dante Gabriel Rossetti's model/muse and wife, she is conscious of her own situation.

58 *Jane Eyre*, Chapter 14.

59 Westminster Review, 60 (1853), 370.

60 Rape seed oil was used mainly in the manufacture of lubricants for the fast growing railways throughout Europe.

61 Henry Fothergill Chorley in *The Athenaeum*, 2051, 16 February (1867).

62 R. L. Stevenson's *The Strange Case of Dr. Jekyll and Mr. Hyde* (1886) is probably the most well known of this type of doubling in nineteenth-century literature, but it is interesting to note that Kavanagh's text predates Stevenson by nineteen years.

63 The usual spelling of the English translation is Sibyl.

64 Marina Warner (2002), *Fantastic Metamorphoses, Other Worlds: Ways of Telling the Self*, Oxford, Oxford University Press, p. 164.

65 Robert Rogers (1970), *A Psychoanalytic Study of the Double in Literature*, Detroit, MI, Wayne State University Press. Rogers offers an enlightening discussion of the latent and manifest double in literature from a Freudian perspective.

66 *Jane Eyre*, Chapter 17.

67 *Jane Eyre,* Chapter 25.

68 Helen Michie has noted that 'Elizabeth Gaskell, the Brontës, and even George Eliot use plumpness in their female characters as a sign of fallen nature. In *Villette*, Ginevre Fanshaw grows visibly fatter as she draws closer to her elopement; in fact, she often eats the "lion's share" of Lucy's bread, cream, and wine, while Lucy, silent, sanctimonious, and puritanical, refuses food throughout the novel. Hetty Sorrel is also characterized by her plumpness and by her associations with cream and other dairy products, while Dinah grows thin sharing her bread with the poor.' In Helen Michie (1987), *The Flesh Made Word: Female Figures and Women's Bodies*, Oxford, Oxford University Press., p. 22.

69 Shuttleworth (1999) has argued that 'Male erotic arousal is given acceptable social form by linking it entirely with the social duty of procreation' (p. 83). For further discussion on medical science, evolution and women's reproductive role see also Eagle Russett, chapters 3 and 4.

70 It is interesting that Hunt exhibited this painting at the Royal Academy in 1854 alongside his *The Awakening Conscience*, the first Victorian picture to embrace the notion of the kept woman, a picture which shocked the establishment in its reference to the underside of domestic life.

71 While *Grace Lee* was deemed 'exciting and meritorious' by *Putnam's Monthly Magazine of American Literature, Science and Art, The United States Democratic Review* was of the opinion that the early sales of six

thousand copies were sufficient proof of its literary merit and popular appeal, declaring that it is 'a work of singular fidelity and power; the writer has realized to advantage that nature is more wonderful than art; and that, to interest human passions, [Kavanagh] must describe both human scenes and human character. Most carefully and vividly does she illustrate this axiom; and while "Grace Lee" has many scenes of the most exciting and absorbing interest, there is not one which puts a strain upon credulity. Any attempt at an analysis of plot so intricate and convolute, so versatile in progress and elaborate in its evolvement, we feel would be out of place and impossible in the limits to which we find ourselves confined. We can but recommend the book to all who prefer the truth of character and feeling to the meretricious romance of verbiage, sentiment, and situation.' See *Putnam's Monthly Magazine of American Literature, Science and Art*, 5: 30, June (1855), 663, and *The United States Democratic Review*, 35: 5, May (1855), 413. See also *The North American Review*, 81: 168, July (1855), 263.

72   'The story is not only improbable, but the absolute impossibility of it stares the reader in the face and asserts itself in every page. [. . .] Grace Lee, the heroine, is intended to be an elaborate ideal of a woman "equal to either fortune," sufficient to herself and queen over her own will. This may be a grand abstract idea; but the contradictions of human nature are a tribe of wild Arabs, and have never yet been brought "within the belt of rule" by any abstract idea or theory that has ever been put forth, – and to attempt it in a book professing to be a record of life and character is resented by the reader as an attempt to take him into custody. Grace Lee does not fill out Miss Kavanagh's intentions. She is simply a fantastic, self-willed, eccentric young woman, who loves her own self better than anything else in the world, – and egoism, no matter how disguised or decorated, makes a poor figure when it comes to be dissected, as every one who knows his own heart can testify.' *The Athenaeum*, 1429, 17 March (1855), 313–14.

73   For a full report on Mudie's titles (1987), see Fryckstedt, p. 11. A first printing of 1000–1500 copies, most of which were sold to the circulating libraries, was usual for novels. The average cost of a three-volume novel was 1 guinea or 31 /6.d which meant that purchase was beyond the reach of most people. Julia Kavanagh's earlier novel *Daisy Burns* (1853) had an initial printing of 1000 copies published by Bentley. See Bentley papers, MS.46, 616 in the British Library.

74   *Jane Eyre*, Chapter 37.

75   It is likely that Kavanagh was familiar with the Catholic scholar Lamartine, whose works she may have encountered as a young Catholic girl educated in France. Alphonse de Lamartine, *Souvenirs, impressions, pensées et paysages, pendant un voyage en orient (1832–1833)*, Brussels, Wahlen, 1836. 'Visite à Lady Esther Stanhope', pp. 184–209.

76   On a visual level, in this passage Kavanagh also alludes to imagery in Milton's *Paradise Lost*, e.g. 'God and light of heaven' (III, 73); 'The golden sun in splendour likest heaven' (III, 572); 'Like those Hesperian gardens

famed of old' (III, 568); 'If stone, carbuncle most or chrysolite / Ruby or topaz, to the twelve that shone / In Aaron's breastplate, and a stone besides' (III, 596–8).

77 Lamartine (1836), p. 202.
78 See the *New Larousse Encyclopedia of Mythology* [1959] (1972), London, Hamlyn, 'Hesperides are three or four in number [. . .] Their abode was beyond the river-ocean, at the extreme western limits of the world, where they personified the clouds gilded by the setting sun. They lived in a wondrous garden and guarded the golden apples which grew there. Since, however, the Greeks had two identical words for "apple" and for "flock of sheep", it has been wondered if the Hesperide were not rather guardians of the celestial flocks which in Indo-European mythology symbolised clouds' (p.144).
79 Lamartine (1836), p. 203.
80 In this respect Mrs Chesterfield is a parody of one of Milton's fallen angels.
81 *Jane Eyre*, Chapter 35.
82 Catherine Belsey (1994), *Desire: Love Stories in Western Culture*, Oxford, Blackwell, p. 34.
83 Coventry Patmore, *The Angel in the House*, published in four parts, *The Betrothal*, (1854), *The Espousals* (1856), *Faithful for Ever* (1860), *The Victories of Love* (1863). It is likely that Kavanagh would have known the first two parts, which were available when *Grace Lee* was published.
84 *The Athenaeum*, 1472, 12 January (1856), 40–1.
85 Robert Kavanagh (2001), p. 21.
86 *The Leader*, 7, 5 January (1856), 19.
87 Ibid.
88 Kavanagh is not mentioned in the 1851 Census. See Chapter 1.
89 For a comprehensive discussion on conditions in the needlework industry see Helen Rogers (1997), '"The Good Are Not Always Powerful, Nor The Powerful Always Good": The Politics of Women's Needlework in mid-Victorian London', *Victorian Studies*, 40:4, Summer, 589–623.
90 Kestner (1985), p. 187.
91 Helen Rogers notes that 'The 1841 Census recorded 20,780 dressmakers and milliners in London (24 Oct. 1850, Mayhew 518); by 1864 this figure had risen to 54,870 (Lord 69). Many workers were employed as sweated outworkers in the "slop" or "dishonourable trades" rather than in the "honourable" private dressmaking establishments. In 1850, Mayhew estimated that at least 10,000 dressmakers worked in the "dishonourable" sector (31 Oct. 1850), 527). The 1841 Census noted a further 12,849 females working in other needle trades, including seaming, shirt and corset-making (23 Nov. 1849, Mayhew 194–6). The terms "dressmaker," "sempstress," and "needlewoman" therefore incorporated a range of occupations employing women from different social classes' pp. 591–2.
92 The needlework industry was the topic of several influential novels during the mid nineteenth century. Charlotte Tonna's *The Wrongs of Women*

(1844) and Charles Kingsley's *Alton Locke* (1850) are well known, as is Thomas Hood's poem 'Song of the Shirt', which became an anthem for reformers.

93 Public attention was alerted to the plight of the needlewomen by the Report for the Children's Employment Commission, conducted by Richard Dugard Grainger in 1843. In the Victorian imagination the underside of the 'genteel' needlewoman was one of prostitute. In her article Helen Rogers cites Grainger on the vulnerability of the needlewoman in an overstocked labour market, noting his anxieties concerning the ' "proverbial" immorality among the dressmakers (F33). Grainger's use of the word "proverbial" suggests that his apparently factual findings were interlaced with powerful cultural narratives about the nature of the single woman worker' Helen Rogers (1997), p. 591.

94 Sonnet XVI, in John Carey, ed. (1971), *Milton: Complete Shorter Poems*, London, Longman, pp. 327–8.

95 J. M. Ludlow, 'Ruth', *North British Review*, 19 (1853) 151–74. See also Kestner (1985), p. 190.

Chapter 3

1 Kavanagh's information is taken from a variety of different sources and although she states these – ninety are listed – she seldom identifies a specific source in her discussion.

2 Kavanagh lists Saint-Beuve as one of her sources and it is likely that she was referring to his *Portraits de Femmes*, published in 1840. Edmond and Jules de Goncourt published their *La Femme au dix-huitième siècle*, 2 vols (Paris) in 1862, twelve years after Kavanagh's publication in 1850. See also Booth (2004), pp. 347–87.

3 *The Athenaeum*, 2 March (1850), 226.

4 Quarterly Review, 88, 2, 176, March (1851), 352.

5 *The Nation*, 16 March (1850), 458.

6 P. M. Hall, 'Duclos's *Histoire de Madame de Luz*: Woman and History', in Eva Jacobs et al., eds (1979), *Woman and Society in Eighteenth-Century France*, London, Athlone Press, p. 143. Hall notes that this comment is 'a generalization which fails to take account of certain exceptions, such as for instance the figure of the warrior-female or the politically active queen. In these cases, the female activity is overtly intruding on activities specifically masculine and offers a rather different problem'. See note. 13, p. 263.

7 Susan R. Kinsey, 'The Memorialists' in Samia I. Spencer, ed. (1984), *French Women and the Age of Enlightenment*, Bloomington, Indiana University Press, p. 219.

8 Maïté Albistur and Daniel Armogathe, *Histoire du féminisme français du moyen âge à nos jours* (Paris: Editions des femmes, 1977), p. 175: in Kinsey, in Spencer (1984), p. 219.

9 Madame Tallien and Madame de Staël.

10 A period of civil war in France 1648–53 followed by war with Spain 1653–59.

11 Saint-Simon records that, after thirty-five years of influence and power, Madame de Maintenon's death at Saint-Cyr on 15 April 1719 passed unnoticed in Versailles and was scarcely mentioned in Paris. However, Lucy Norton in her notes states that Saint-Simon 'greatly exaggerates Mme de Maintenon's influence in the government of France'. Lucy Norton, ed. and trans. (1972), *Historical Memoirs of the Duc de Saint-Simon* (shortened version), vol. 3: 1715–1723, London, Hamish Hamilton, p. 240.

12 Elizabeth Suddaby and P. J. Yarrow, eds (1971), *Lady Morgan in France*, Newcastle, Oriel Press, p. 102.

13 George Eliot, 'Woman in France: Madame de Sablé', *Westminster Review*, 62, October (1854), 448–73, reprinted in Thomas Pinney, ed. (1963), *Essays of George Eliot*, London, Routledge and Kegan Paul, p. 56.

14 Ibid. George Eliot argues in favour of the superiority of French women writers over English writers in the seventeenth century, stating that 'Patriotic gallantry may perhaps contend that English women could, if they had liked, have written as well as their neighbours; but we will leave the consideration of that question to the reviewers of the literature that might have been' (p. 54).

15 Presumably Kavanagh is referring to Molière's *Précieuses Ridicules* (1660) and *Les Femmes Savantes* (1673).

16 Kinsey, in Spencer (1984), p. 215.

17 Philippe, Duc d'Orléans, and nephew of Louis XIV, became Regent against the wishes of Madame de Maintenon, who had favoured Louis XIV's illegitimate son to Madame de Montespan, the Duc du Maine, later legitimised by Louis.

18 Of the numerous accounts of the Duc d'Orléans's character, G. P. Gooch, taking Saint-Simon as his source, expands on Kavanagh's sketch: 'The best feature in his complex character was his steady affection for Liselotte [Philippe's mistress], who made allowance for the fact that he had not been permitted to choose his wife, and in that dissolute age no one expected him to be a faithful husband. "He is quite crazy about women," she reported. "Provided they are good-tempered, indelicate, great eaters and drinkers, he troubles little about their looks." When she complained of his choice of ugly women he blandly rejoined: "*Bah! Maman, dans la nuit tous les chats sont gris.*" The orgies of the Palais Royal became the talk of Europe, but, like his uncle, he allowed his mistresses no political influence. A second failing was drunkenness, though in fairness we must remember that two or three glasses were enough to upset him. A third was his licentious talk, so gross that his long-suffering wife dared not invite decent folk to their table. A fourth was his open scorn of religion, and he was said to read a volume of Rabelais during Mass. No wonder Louis XIV called him *un fanfaron de crimes* and dreaded his rise to power. On the credit side, however, there were some excellent qualities. He was gracious, human, generous, tolerant,

open-minded, deeply interested in science and art, and fully aware of France's desperate plight. No Bourbon prince came so close to the pattern of a Renaissance ruler, combining military prowess and intellectual tastes with unbridled lusts of the flesh. "He has the best intentions," reported his mother, "and he loves his country more than his life. He works all day and wears himself out. He would like to see everyone happy. For tradition he cares nothing. He is very nice to me, shows me real friendship, and would grieve to lose me. His daily visits are a joy. Histories always make me laugh. I should be an unnatural mother if I did not love him with all my heart." The fairies, she added, had been invited to his birth, and each had given him a talent; but one of them had been forgotten and, arriving later, remarked that he would possess all the talents except the capacity to use them. He pities his wife, who bore him eight children, even more than himself, for he possessed compensations which she was denied.' C. P. Gooch (1956), *Louis XV: The Monarchy in Decline*, London, Longmans, pp. 31–2.

19 Saint-Simon records that 'neither his mistresses, nor Mme la Duchesse de Berry, nor his *roués,* not even when he was quite drunk, ever extracted anything at all from him concerning the government or the business of the State. He lived openly with Mme de Parabère, and with many other women too. He revelled in their jealousies and complaints, but continued on equally good terms with all of them. Thus the scandal of his public harem, and the lewdness and impiety of his nightly suppers soon became generally known throughout the whole of France.' In Norton (1972), p. 64.

20 Norton records that Madame 'had particularly loathed Mme de Maintenon, whom she called *die alte Zote* (the old whore), which may have coloured Saint-Simon's exaggerated language when he referred to her as *la vieille ordure* (the filthy old creature). Note 2, p. 209.

21 Norton notes that Charlotte Aglae d'Orléans, Demoiselle de Valois (1700–61), was the Regent's third daughter and, in 1737, married the Duke of Modena (p. 157).

22 Kavanagh states that the Duchesse de Berri was married at a very young age. See also Gooch (1956), p. 38.

23 Norton notes: 'There had been a terrible scene in 1711, after Saint-Simon had warned her father about scandalous rumours of incest. Orléans had repeated his words and the Duchesse de Berry had attacked poor Madame de Saint-Simon.' See also note 1, p.63. Madame was deeply distressed by the rumours about her son and the Duchesse de Berry, but did not, of course, believe a word of them (there was never any proof). She hated to hear that notices were stuck on the Palais Royal: 'Here be Lotteries and most subtle poisonings.' 'By lotteries,' she wrote, 'they imply that my son lives with his daughter after the manner of Lot.' Gooch notes 'the Regent's passion for his eldest daughter the Duchesse de Berry, which led contemporaries to talk openly of incest and twentieth-century scholars to leave the question open' (note 1, p. 28).

24 Saint-Simon records Armand Auguste, Comte de Rions (1692–1741). Kavanagh's spelling 'Riom' is incorrect.

25 Demoiselle de Valois (1700–61) married the Duke of Modena in 1737. See Norton (1972), notes, p. 157.

26 Norton (1972), p. 440.

27 In 1703 Madame du Maine created 'The Order of the Honey Bee', an organisation devoted to the protection of the honey bee. The order was to have thirty-nine members only, each to dress in dark red satin dresses embroidered with bees. There was also a golden medal with the motto 'baroness of Sceaux, perpetual dictator of the order of the bee'.

28 Kavanagh gives no date for this correspondence but it is likely that it occurred after the Cellamare episode as she goes on to mention a visit at this time by the Duchess of Modena, formerly Madame de Valois, who, it has been suggested, agreed to this marriage in order to save Richelieu from punishment for his part in that Conspiracy.

29 Kavanagh states: 'The liberal policy, affected by the Duke of Orleans at the opening of the regency, was soon relinquished by him; with it vanished his brief popularity. The privileges granted to the parliamentary party had rendered them desirous of emulating the freedom and power of the English Commons. In order to check this spirit, the Duke of Orleans broke their edicts, and finally deprived them of the right of remonstrance. This arbitrary conduct created deep discontent in Paris. The provinces were equally inimical to the regent. The despotic centralisation of monarchy under Richelieu and Louis XIV, which led to future greatness and freedom, was still considered oppressive and tyrannical. The sense of local independence was so strong in Brittany, that the states refused to pay the taxes laid upon them by the regent, and carried on secret intrigues with Alberoni; offering to recognise his master, Philip V., regent, provided their province should become once more an independent duchy' (I: 49).

30 Guillaume Dubois, first minister to the Duc d'Orléans.

31 Kavanagh may have also read an article by G. H. Lewes, entitled 'A Charming Frenchwoman' in *Frazer's Magazine*, 2451, May (1848), 509–18. In this article Lewes discusses the content of Madame de Staal's *Memoirs*, including her early experiences, which he suggests reads like a novel and is superior to ordinary romance.

32 Judith Curtis, 'The Epistolières', in Spencer (1984). Curtis's essay refers to Mlle Delaunay before she became Madame de Staal (p. 227). See also note 3, p. 239.

33 Marguerite Jeanne Cordier (1683–1750), known in society as Rose de Launay or Delaunay. Brought up in a Rouen convent whose family name she adopted, she was left destitute after the death of her godmother, the abbess of the convent. See Curtis, in Spencer (1984), p. 226.

34 Madame de Staal-Delaunay, née 'Marguerite Jeanne Cordier, *Mémoires*, ed. G. Doscot (Paris: Mercure de France, 1970), p. 29. See Kinsey, in Spencer (1984), p. 215.

35 See G. Doscot (1970), p. 29: 'Mon âme, n'ayant pas pris d'abord le pli que lui devait donner la mauvaise fortune, a toujours résisté à l'baissement et à la sujétion où je me suis trouvée: c'est là l'origine du malheur de ma vie.' (My soul, not having acquired in the beginning the bent that an ill fortune was to impose on it, has always resisted the humble and subordinate position in which I have found myself: therein lies the source of all my unhappiness). See Curtis in Spencer (1984), p. 239.

36 *Mémoires*, p. 230.

37 Kavanagh notes that M. de Ferriol's slave probably died young, for there is no other record of her fate save that she came to France with her master (I: 75).

38 In order to uphold the secrecy of the pregnancy, a plan was derived to prevent a scandal. Kavanagh notes that 'With the connivance of Madame de Villette [Bolingbroke's companion], who feigned to take her to England, whilst she left her in a retired quarter of Paris, she gave birth to a daughter, unsuspected. Her child was afterwards placed in a provincial convent, where she passed under the name of Miss Black, niece of Lord Bolingbroke' (I: 79).

39 Kavanagh records that Aïssé's scruples were probably strengthened by the destiny of the Comte de Nogent, who, having imprudently married the beautiful slave, brought, like her, from Constantinople by M. de Ferriol, had, in consequence, been subjected to the most bitter insults (I: 80).

40 Curtis notes that Eugène Ritter cast doubt on the standard arrangement of the letters, suggesting that sections have been shifted from their proper place in the sequence and reminding us of the possibility of other sorts of tampering as well (Eugène Ritter, 'Notes sur les *Lettres de Mlle Aïssé*,' in *Mélanges offerts . . . à Gustave Lanson* (Paris, Hachette, 1922), pp. 313–18, note 98). She also argues that some letters suggest 'a side of the writer that makes a pointed contrast with the idealized figure first presented in the 1787 biography'. Prior to those letters pertaining to her incompatible yearnings, Curtis notes that evidence suggests that Aïssé was also 'gossipy, practical, outspoken, smug about her own moral delicacy, and much less ingenuous than the commentators would lead us to believe. [. . .] Moreover, in her letters, [Aïssé] seeks to impose on her reader an ingratiating self-image, the meek, noble, pitiable image of the legend.' In Spencer (1984), p. 229.

41 For further information on the French romantic novel see Pierre Fauchery (1972), *La Destinée féminine dans le roman européen du dix-huitième siècle*, Paris, A. Colin.

42 See Curtis in Spencer (1984), pp. 228–9.

43 See Warren Hunting Smith (1938), *Letters to and from Madame du Deffand and Julie de Lespinasse*, New Haven, Yale University Press. In his introduction Hunting Smith has noted that 'Julie was born when her mother was still the wife of the Comte d'Albon, and she was therefore technically legitimate' (p. viii). See also note 43. Kavanagh names both Ségur and Ségur, De, in her list of authors consulted.

44 Ibid., pp. vi–vii. See also Benedda Craveri (1994), *Madame du Deffand and Her World*, London, Peter Halban. Taking Ségur as the main source, Craveri notes that 'Madame d'Albon who was separated from her husband at the time had already given birth to an illegitimate child [a boy] the year before Julie's birth. Unlike her brother who was brought up secretly in a convent in Lyons and of whose fate we know nothing, Julie was given a family surname, welcomed into her mother's house and openly recognised as her daughter. Her unknown father did not completely disappear but turned up seven years later in a remarkable new guise; he came not as Madame d'Albon's lover, but as her son-in-law, not as Julie's father but as her legitimate half-sister's husband' (p. 111).

45 Hunting Smith (1938) has suggested that 'The Vichys had reasons for keeping Julie under their wing. [. . .] they couldn't run the risk of her laying claim to the d'Albon rank and fortune. [. . .] Her mother's husband and son were still alive, and would resent any claim on their property [. . .] Vichy did not want his scandalous connection with his mother-in-law to be made public. Furthermore, he hoped that he or his son would inherit Madame du Deffand's comfortable fortune – Julie, in Paris, would be a rival heir' (pp. viii–ix).

46 Ibid., pp. viii–ix.

47 Ibid., p. xiii.

48 See particularly Craveri (1994).

49 See Fernand Nozière, 'Le Salon de Madame Geoffrin' in *Les Grands Salons Littéraires (XVIIe et XVIIIe siècles): Conférences du musée Carnavalet* (Paris: Payot, 1928), p.135, in Sara Ellen Procious Malueg, 'Women and the Encyclopédie' in Spencer (1984), p. 260 and note 5, p. 270.

50 Hunting Smith (1938) notes that on her removal to Paris in 1754 Madame du Deffand gave Julie an annuity of 692 livres and made a new will bequeathing her 15,000 livres (p. xiii).

51 Ibid., p. 164.

52 Ibid., p. 166.

53 Hunting Smith (1938) notes that 'A few months after Julie came to Paris, two Irishmen named Taaffe were presented at Court by the English ambassador. Though their identity is not absolutely certain, it seems highly probable that they were Theobald and John Taaffe, who, according to *Notes and Queries*, were sons of Stephen Taaffe of Dublin. The family must have had property also in Dowanstown, County Meath, since John Taaffe's will is indexed under his name with the caption "formerly of Dowanstown."' He suggests that John Taaffe was not the sort of man whose attentions to a young girl are to be encouraged. He was a gambler and not of good character. However, he also notes that 'According to the Duc de Luynes, John Taaffe was inclined to be a 'philosophe,' and Madame du Deffand herself said afterwards that he was 'a man of good sense and good society' (pp. xiii–xv).

54 Ibid., p. 168.

55 Craveri (1994) argues that 'Although Madame du Deffand's behaviour was unexceptional from the point of view of form, her intervention seemed offensive to Julie. Mademoiselle de Lespinasse was naturally driven by her heart, not her head. She wanted to love and be loved and she found the brutal return to reality unbearable. To sacrifice a love affair that occupied her heart and mind to a code of behaviour which turned against her at every opportunity without ever protecting her must have been the ultimate injustice. Her reaction was one of violent hysteria. Besides Madame du Deffand's letter to Taaffe, we have La Harpe's description of Julie's condition at the time. Although La Harpe does not relate to Julie's crisis specifically to the episode with Taaffe, of which, in any case, he appears to be ignorant, his description is very effective' (p. 169).

56 Ibid., pp. 168–9.

57 Hunting Smith (1938) discusses the reasons why John Taaffe is in Paris and gives the background to his relationship with Julie: 'With Julie he flirted so violently that she quite lost her head (as she usually did when her emotions were aroused).' Referring to correspondence between Madame du Deffand and Taaffe, he notes: 'While he was writing this letter, one was already on its way from Madame du Deffand, ordering him to make honourable proposals to Julie (if his passion had really overpowered him) or else to give her up. Julie in the meantime had received such a scolding for her imprudence that she was having concussions and fainting-spells, apparently caused by an overdose of opium. She was well enough, however to read Madame du Deffand's letter before it was sent; in fact it was originally intended that she should transcribe the letter in her own handwriting. Madame du Deffand had perhaps hesitated to use Wiart as the amanuensis for this delicate and personal negotiation; the rough draft of the letter is in an unknown hand' (p. xvi).

58 J. F. La Harpe, *Correspondance Littéraire*, p. 385, in Craveri (1994), p. 169 and notes p. 459.

59 Craveri writes that P. M. Ségur had recorded that an acquaintance, Madame de la Ferté-Imbault, observed that '"In her fury, the young lady took such a dose of opium that it affected her for the rest of her life." Ségur was of the opinion, however, that the overdose was "a violent *crise de nerfs* which she sought to calm by repeated doses of opium in keeping with the fatal habit which she developed then and in which she persisted for the rest of her life"' (p. 169) and notes p. 459. Kavanagh presents these facts in a more sympathetic light; she states that later, 'while struggling with the torments of her soul', Mademoiselle de Lespinasse, 'sinking under the pressure of woe and disease', found opium a source of enervation, 'to which her want of rest compelled her to resort' (I: 187).

60 Linda Gardiner's 'Women in Science' gives a comprehensive list of Madame du Châtelet's publications, including a book on the metaphysics of natural science (the *Institutions de physique*), an essay on the nature of fire and heat (the *Dissertation sur la nature et propagation du feu*) and two short

pieces on the problem of measuring physical force. Other works include a translation of Mandeville's Fable of the Bees. She co-authored, anonymously, Voltaire's popularisation of Newtonian physics, *Eléments de la philosophie de Newton*, as well as a translation of Newton's *Principia mathematica*, with a commentary, which was published posthumously. In Spencer (1984), p. 184.

61 Jean François, Marquis de Saint-Lambert.

62 Voltaire was at Cirey from 1734 to 1749. Kavanagh makes no reference to the fact that he was given refuge at Cirey by the Marquise owing to the fact that he was obliged to leave Paris because of his criticism of French institutions.

63 See references to Mademoiselle Delaunay's and Madame du Deffand's letters in M. F. A. de Lescure, ed. (1865), *Correspondance complète*, vol. 1, Paris, Plon, 1865, in Curtis, in Spencer (1984), pp. 230 and notes 4 and 10, p. 239.

64 Whilst Kavanagh expresses a respect for Madame du Châtelet's love of science, her sympathies for this woman's involvement with Voltaire are indirectly exposed in her reference to Madame Denis, Voltaire's favourite niece with whom he developed a close relationship, whom she described as 'an ugly, agreeable woman, who wrote tragedies she could never get acted' (I: 152).

65 See Roseann Runte, 'Women as Muse', in Spencer (1984), p. 451ff. See also D. J. Adams, *La Femme dans les contes et romans de Voltaire*, Paris: Nizet, 1974, pp. 21–2., p. 154, in Runte, note 35.

66 Roland Bonnel and Catherine Rubinger (1994), *Femmes Savants et Femmes d'Esprit*, New York, Peter Lang, p. 27.

67 Madame d'Epinay's published work on education include *Lettres à mon fils* (1759) and *Les Conversations d'Emilie* (1774). See Rosena Davison, 'Madame d'Epinay's Contribution to Girls' Education' in Bonnel and Rubinger (1994), pp. 219–41. See also Samia I. Spencer, 'Women and Education' in Spencer (1984), pp. 83–96.

68 Madame Geoffrin contributed two hundred thousand livres to the Encyclopédists' project. See Louis R. Gottschalk (1929), *The Era of the French Revolution, 1715–1815*, Boston, Houghton Mifflin Company, p. 82. See also Runte, in Spencer (1984), pp. 149. Runte notes that in the eighteenth century it was common practice to give women names such as '"mama," "little mother," or "little sister." [and] tenderness, rather than passion is evoked by the attribution of such terms. These roles evoke names in the family, not in society at large. It appears that authors sought the intimacy of the family but were obliged to seek in the family circle names for the roles of women played outside.' See Philippe Ariès, *Essais sur l'histoire de la mort en Occident du moyen âge à nos jours*, Paris: Le Seul, 1975, p. 154, also in Runte, note 30.

69 Stanislaus 1 of Poland (1677–1766). Stanislaus was King during the years 1704–9 when he abdicated. He became king a second time for the three years

1733–36 before circumstances forced him to abdicate for a second time, after which he settled at Lunéville in Lorraine and founded the Academia Stanislaus. He is also the father of Marie Lecsinska, wife of Louis XV.

70 Kavanagh extends her argument later on, noting: 'the gossiping Englishman' (I: 173). Walpole's response to the decline of the *bureaux d'e-sprit*s: 'Like all those who resorted to Paris for amusement, Walpole noticed this alteration with evident displeasure. "They may be growing wiser," he pettishly observes, "but the intermediate change is dullness." The era for bureaux d'esprit was, however, gone beyond recall. Philosophy, indeed, no longer sought the aid of their fostering care; it did not even need them as those central points whence it formerly disseminated its doctrines far and wide. The whole spirit of the nation had become philosophic; every drawing room was now a fit arena. It thus happened that when the three great bureaux d'esprit had ceased to exist, no effort was made to replace them. That such assemblies would be as needless now as they had formerly been useful, seemed to be felt almost by intuition. New wants, new feelings had arisen. Like many prouder institutions, as soon as their appointed task of good or evil was fulfilled, the bureaux d'esprit were forgotten; and their sentimental successors now spoke of them as slightingly as they had probably spoken of the soirées of the Hôtel Rambouillet and the *ruelles** of the seventeenth century. *The *précieuses* of the seventeenth century generally received their morning visitors before they had risen. Their guests were thus invited to take seats in the *ruelle*, or space extending between the bed-side and the wall, and which was sufficiently wide to accommodate several persons. From this circumstance a morning conversazione became known under the name of *ruelle*' (II: 18).

71 George Eliot, 'Woman in France: Madame de Sablé' in Pinney (1936), pp. 60–1.

72 Madame de Genlis published over eighty books, the most important including: *Théâtre à l'usage des jeunes personnes*; *Adèle et Théodore, ou lettres sur l'éducation* (1782); *Les Veillées du Château* (1784); *Leçons d'une gouvernante à ses élèves* (1791); *Précis de la conduite de Mme de Genlis depuis la Révolution* (1796); *Mademoiselle de Clermont* (1802); *La Duchesse de la Vallière* (1804); *Mémoires*, 10 vols (1825).

73 'Mme de Genlis elaborated with great detail on the distinction in knowledge, treatment, social status, and salary between a *gouverneur* (governor) and a *gouvernante* (governess). While the former was considered a friend of the family who shared their meals, the latter was counted among the servants and ate at their table.' *Discours sur la suppression des couvents*, Paris: Onfrois, 1790, p. 14. In Spencer (1984), p. 96.

74 The Duc de Chartes (Duc d'Orléans) later changed his name to Philippe Egalité, As the Duc d'Orléans, he subsidised radical pamphleteers in 1789 and voted for the death of his cousin, the former Louis XVI. See Sarah Maza (1993), *Private Lives and Public Affairs: The Causes Célèbres of Prerevolutionary France*, Berkeley, University of California Press, p. 83.

75 Madame de Genlis escaped the guillotine during the Reign of Terror and, after travelling throughout Europe during the 1790s, returned to France to receive a pension from Napoleon.

76 Kavanagh (1852), *Women of Christianity*, Chapter 22.

77 Madame de Nesle (Madame de Vintimile) died in childbirth in 1741.

78 Kavanagh is consistent in addressing the women in her study Mademoiselle or Madame; Madame de Châteauroux was previously the Marquise Louis de La Tournelle before she inveigled the King to make her Duchesse de Châteauroux.

79 Jeanne-Antoinette Poisson was born in Paris on 29 December 1721. A fortune-teller prophesied her future at the palace and she received an education and acquired those accomplishments suitable for a King's mistress. See Christine Pevitt Algrant (2003), *Madame de Pompadour: Mistress of France* London, Harper Collins.

80 Ibid., p. 150.

81 On the morning of 6 October 1789 several men and women attempted, unsuccessfully, to enter the Queen's chamber at Versailles to assassinate her.

82 Kavanagh gives no direct source for Marie Antoinette's response and, as the young dauphine was unaware of Madame du Barry's status at the time, Kavanagh's comment that she 'deeply resented the indignity of supping with a courtesan' is questionable.

83 Kavanagh's wording here is significant in that she attempts to detract from any suggestion of overt prurience inferred from the young dauphine's response. Antonia Fraser offers a more poignantly suggestive translation and also states that it is the Comtesse de Noailles who responds to Marie Antoinette's question: 'Marie Antoinette fell into the trap of asking the Comtesse de Noailles the identity of this lady; [. . .] When the Comtesse tactfully replied that the lady was there to give pleasure to the King, the Dauphine cheerfully said: "Oh, then I shall be her rival, because I too wish to give pleasure to the King." Fraser (2002), *Marie Antoinette: The Journey*, London, Phoenix Paperback, p. 79. Fraser's source is taken from Andre Castelot (1957), *Queen of France: A Biography of Marie Antoinette*, New York, p. 29.

84 Ibid., p. 143.

85 Antonia Fraser (2002) draws attention to the ways in which pornography was used as a means of casting doubt on the Queen's innocence: 'Even the theme of the diamonds was a help to pornographers since the word for jewels (*bijoux*) was a code for the female genitalia. (*Les Bijoux Indiscrets* a tale by Diderot, had the eponymous "jewels" relating their adventures.) [. . .] the web of fantasy spun around the innocent Queen and the foolishly naïve Cardinal was much easier to accept than the actual truth: that the whole thing was a criminal conspiracy' (p. 282).

86 Antonia Fraser notes that 'It was well put by a modern historian. Sarah Maza in "The Diamond Necklace Affair Revisited" (1991), that although the total innocence of Marie Antoinette was obvious, standard accounts of

the affair viewed her as guilty, "because large numbers of people wanted to believe in her guilt"'. In Fraser (2002, p. 281). See also in Fraser, p. 565 n11, 'Maza, 'Diamond Necklace', p. 64, p. 85 note 7'.

87 Ibid., p. 316.

88 Gita May (1970), *Madame Roland and the Age of Revolution*, New York, Columbia University Press, p. 251.

89 Kavanagh relates that after the September massacres of 1792, 'The soul of Madame Roland was filled with horror at what she saw and heard. If anything increased her despair, it was the consciousness that her husband, though minister of the Interior, could not prevent, could not do anything. "We are under the knife of Robespierre and Marat," she despairingly wrote to a friend, on the 5th of September; and on the 9th she added, "You know my enthusiasm for the revolution; well, I am ashamed of it now: it has been sullied by monsters; it is hideous." The proclamation of the republic which at another time would have filled her with joy, now seemed to her prophetic soul but the forerunner of the fall of the men by whom that republic had been founded' (II: 135).

90 May (1970), p. 246.

Chapter 4

1 In *Shirley* (1849) Charlotte Brontë satirises the stigma associated with the French novel. In a heated interchange with his niece, Shirley, Mr Sympson blames Shirley's lack of principle on her choice of reading: 'You read French. Your mind is poisoned with French novels'. (Chapter 31). See also Flint (1999), who outlines the attitudes and prejudices of the English establishment towards the French novel, particularly pp. 138, 164, 265, 288 and 303. In contrast Kavanagh deliberately goes against the grain when, in her novel *Dora* (1868), she recalls the romantic associations of Mademoiselle de Scudéry's novel *Clélie* (I: 307 in Tauchnitz edition).

2 Ezell notes that 'Between 1675 and 1875, there were at least twenty-five biographical encyclopedias and anthologies specifically devoted to chronicling the lives and labours of literary Englishwomen. From the early accounts of "Women among the Moderns Eminent for Poetry" in Edward Phillips's *Theatrum Poetarum* (1675) to Jane Williams's *Literary Women of England* (1861) and Eric Robertson's *English Poetesses* (1883), curious readers could peruse the lives of female writers. Starting with *The Nine Muses* (1700) and Colman and Thornton's *Poems by Eminent Ladies* (1755 and 1780) up through Frederic Rowton's *Cyclopedia of Female Poets* (1848–74), they could ponder exactly what style, subject, or domestic circumstance were revealed as "feminine" in the selections of women's writing presented in these anthologies.' In Margaret J. M. Ezell (1996), *Writing Women's Literary History*, Baltimore and London, The Johns Hopkins University Press, pp. 68–9. In addition to this selection I would include *Memoirs of Eminent Englishwomen* (1844) by Louisa Stuart

Costello (1799–1870). Unlike Kavanagh, both Costello and Jane Williams concentrate on women poets. See also section on 'Bibliography of Collective Biographies of Women 1830–1940' in Booth (2004), pp. 347–87.

3 Ezell (1996), pp. 68–9.

4 Janet Todd, ed. (1987), *A Dictionary of British and American Women Writers 1660–1800*, London, Methuen, p. 2. See also Ezell (1996), p. 93.

5 Full title: *The Progress of Romance, Through Times, Countries, and Manners; With Remarks on the Good and Bad Effects of it, on them Respectively; In a Course of Evening Conversations.* For further discussion and reprint of this text see Gary Kelly, ed. (1999), *Bluestocking Feminism: Writings of the Bluestocking Circle, 1738–1785*, vol. 6, Sarah Scott and Clara Reeve, London, Pickering & Chatto.

6 English Showalter (1972), *The Evolution of the French Novel: 1641–1782*, Princeton, Princeton University Press, p. 4.

7 Ibid., p. 29.

8 English Showalter (1972) outlines the core of the debate when he suggests that the novel 'lacked ancestors': as a genre without rules it 'was always in danger of excess, and the absence of fixed standards seemed to paralyse critics, when it did not provoke scorn, as from Boileau: "Dans un Roman frivole, aisément tout s'excuse [Nicolas Boileau-Despréaux, *L'Art Poétique*, Chant 3, line 119] ". The prefaces of the Scudérys responded to this general attitude, by attempting to place the *roman* within the epic tradition. Critics and theorists of fictional genres failed to comprehend the changes that the authors were making. Huet, for example, [. . .] drew his own conception of the *roman* from the Scudérys; and his *Lettre sur l'origine des romans* (1670) was regarded as authoritative well into the eighteenth century' (pp. 29–30).

9 George Eliot opens her essay 'Woman in France: Madame de Sablé' with the following: 'In 1847, a certain Count Leopold Ferri died at Padua, leaving a library entirely composed of works written by women, in various languages, and this library amounted to nearly 32,000 volumes. We will not hazard any conjecture as to the proportion of these volumes which a severe judge, like the priest in Don Quixote, would deliver to the flames, but for our own part, most of those we should care to rescue would be the works of French women. [. . .] in France alone woman has had a vital influence on the development of literature; in France alone the mind of woman has passed like an electric current through the language, making crisp and definite what is elsewhere heavy and blurred; in France alone, if the writings of women were swept away, a serious gap would be made in the national history.' In Pinney (1936), pp. 52–3.

10 I have kept to Kavanagh's spelling of Madame de la Fayette in her text but have used the more conventional Madame de La Fayette in my own discussion.

11 Faith E. Beasley, 'Altering the Fabric of History: Women's Participation in

the Classical Age' in Sonya Stephens, ed. (2000), *A History of Women's Writing in France*, Cambridge, Cambridge University Press, p. 64. See also Joan DeJean (1991), *Tender Geographies: Women and the Origins of the Novel in France*, New York, Columbia University Press (see particularly Appendix: Bibliography of Women Writers: 1640–1715, pp. 201–21.).

12 The desire for anonymity covers many areas. It was generally known who was the author of a specific work. For most writers, background and class dictated propriety and it was considered improper for both male and female authors to make money by publishing their work. There were exceptions, of course, and Marie Catherine Desjardins and Madame de Villedieu did sign their work. Mademoiselle de Scudéry and Madame de La Fayette often placed a man's name on the cover. See also Beasley, in Stephens (2000), p. 70. See also DeJean (1991) who argues: 'The first practitioners of literary exclusionism had little use for critical indirection. Following the lead of Nicolas Boileau, the individual who, with royal backing, imposed his authority as supreme arbiter of French literary taste, commentators displaced all the fictional content of women's writing onto reality. They refused to grant these novels any subtlety, denied them any role in the creation of construction of gender. According to the argument thus promoted, these novels had to be suppressed because they propagated a socially and politically subversive vision: women's writing constituted a threat to the foundation of the nation state, the family, and manly virile virtue' (p. 14).

13 See DeJean (1991), p. 126. Bonnel and Rubinger (1994) refer to the problems associated with writing and sexual difference during the period of the Enlightenment: 'The various entries of the *Encyclopédie* dealing with women are often ambiguous. There is no "doctrine," no single voice. There is, however, a certain discernible consensus about the relationship between sexes. Men and women have been designed by Nature with different attributes for different roles. [. . .] Even in the apparently innocuous genre of the novel, women writers immediately encountered hostility. At the height of the "nouvelle querelle des femmes" which centred on the novel in the middle of the century, only a small minority, notably Laclos and Lenglet Dufresnoy, spoke out for the literary equality of the sexes as Fénelon had done at the end of the seventeenth century' (p. 13).

14 DeJean (1991) notes that in his *Dictionnaire historique et critique* (1695–1697) Pierre Bayle raised objections to the so called 'new novelists' whose success in simulating history 'have thrown a shadow over real history'; readers cannot 'separate fiction from true fact' (p. 136). See also Beasley, who argues the case for the more historically accurate *nouvelle historique* which gained popularity around 1660, after the demise of the more outdated ponderous heroic genre made popular by Mademoiselle de Scudéry: 'Readers also preferred more believable stories. To this end, novelists grounded the *nouvelle* in often meticulously researched, primarily sixteenth-century French history. The resulting fictions so closely resembled

history that it was difficult to distinguish fact from fiction. Novelists played upon the ambiguity of the French term *'histoire'*, which can mean both history and story. They filled in the lines of history primarily by adding plausible motives for well-known events, often with love and women as the principal forces. As official history became more and more co-opted by Louis XIV as a vehicle of propaganda, women writers used the *nouvelle historique* to rewrite the historical record to include women, thus using the pen to revolt against such a monarch who would relegate them to power-lessness and silence' (in Stephens (2000), pp. 72–3).

15 Kavanagh does not engage in the politics of the Fronde and only occasion-ally mentions the women involved. Three of the principle *frondeuses* who opposed the regency were the Duchesse de Montpensier, the Duchesse de Longueville and the Princess de Condé. See also Antonia Fraser [2006] (2007), *Love and Louis XIV: The Women in the Life of the Sun King*, London, Phoenix Paperback.

16 When Louis XIV took over the government in 1661 he also took control of all intellectual and creative output in which Louis and Versailles took centre stage. Women were discouraged from writing and the period until the end of the century became known as 'le grand renfermement de la femme' ('the great confinement of women'). See also Beasley, in Stephens (2000), pp. 66 and 83.

17 In this connection Kavanagh notes an interlude when Mademoiselle de Gournay called in several of her 'renowned *purists*' contemporaries to con-sider the significance and inclusion of the word *raffinage* into the French language (I: 27).

18 *Précieuses* is the name attributed to those women who gathered in the salons for conversation.

19 The term 'salon' is a nineteenth-century substitute for the earlier term *ruelle*. While Kavanagh acknowledges this term she uses the term 'salon' in her discussion.

20 Although Kavanagh notes the opening of the Hôtel Rambouillet as 1600, modern scholars give the date as 1620. See Beasley, in Stephens (2000), p. 67. See also Nicole Aronson (1978), *Mademoiselle de Scudéry*, Boston, Twayne Publishers. Aronson points out that 'Gustave Charlier's remark-able article "La Fin de l'Hôtel de Rambouillet" has clearly established that the activities of the Hôtel Rambouillet continued well after the *Fronde*' (p. 37). See Gustave Charlier (1939), 'La Fin de l'Hôtel de Rambouillet,' *Revue Belge de Philosophie et d'Histoire*, 18, 409–26.

21 Aronson (1978) also notes that Mademoiselle de Scudéry 'detested pedantry and loved the joys of witty conversation. In her letters she con-fessed to her taste for puns, witticisms and jokes, and this must have allowed her to feel quite at ease with the group surrounding Mme de Rambouillet' (p. 27).

22 Ricovrati Prize for women in the Arts.

23 Kavanagh notes that Mademoiselle de Scudéry was, in fact, 'ugly', going

on to say that 'she knew it, and said it frankly. When the celebrated Nanteuil improved her face, in the crayon portrait he drew of her, she sent him the pretty verse:– *"Nanteuil; en faisant, mon image. / A de son art divin signalé le pouvoir, / Je hais mes yeux dans mon miroir, / Je les aime dans son ouvrage."'* (I: 50). See also Aronson who notes that 'Although the Nanteuil portrait of Mlle de Scudéry has unfortunately been lost, there is one by Elisabeth Chéron that verifies the fact that she was, indeed, not physically attractive' (p. 27).

24 Kavanagh tells us: 'Madeleine's education was not merely intellectual, though she studied Italian and Spanish, which she knew thoroughly, and read the best authors of every language, [. . .] dancing, drawing, painting, music, and needlework were included in her education. What she was not taught she learned of her own accord, and thus became acquainted with agriculture, gardening, cookery, house-keeping, and medicine – she even acquired no mean proficiency in the lady-like art of concocting potions, perfumes, and distilled waters, and was evidently resolved that no feminine accomplishment should escape her' (I: 41). Aronson (1978) notes that the details of Mademoiselle de Scudéry's early life are to be found in the *Mémoires* of Valentin Conrart, the founder of the Académie Française, in whom Mademoiselle confided: Aronson's reading (p. 21) from Conrart is very similar to that of Kavanagh who, presumably, used the same source.

25 In her biography of Mademoiselle de Scudéry, Aronson has noted that during her lifetime none of this writer's works, with the exception of *Célinte, Mathilde d'Aguilar* and later editions of *Conversations* printed in Amsterdam, was published in her own name. While he was alive, George de Scudéry appeared as the author. When he died she published anonymously (p. 18).

26 Beasley, in Stephens (2000), p. 70.

27 Modern critics would disagree with Kavanagh's reductive view. In her chapter 'What Do Women Want?' Joan DeJean (1991) argues to the contrary, suggesting that Scudéry's heroines reflected the loss of personal freedom that marriage incurred. As marriages were made to protect family property, Scudéry's suggestion of *marriage d'inclination*, marrying for love, threatened the status quo and the politics of inheritance. See pp. 114–15.

28 Aronson (1978), p. 44.

29 Victor Cousin, 1792–1867. Kavanagh gives no textual source. It is likely that she is referring to *La Société française au XVII siècle d'après le Grand Cyrus de Mlle de Scudéry* (1858). See also 'Company Manners' in *Household Words*, IX, 20 May (1854), pp. 323–31 with reference to Cousin's comments on Mademoiselle de Scudéry.

30 DeJean (1991) argues that 'In ancien régime France, a woman became an author when she made the novel the site of speculation on questions as essential to the organization of society as the right of individuals to choose their marriage partners rather than have their lives directed by the interests

of the family and State. In this tradition, female authorship was a political act: these novels are never solely about love, but always stress the political and social implication of affective choices' (p. 11).

31 Kavanagh notes that it was to the Duc de la Rochefoucauld that Madame de La Fayette devoted the best part of her life. Almost twenty years her senior, Rochefoucauld was fifty when Madame de La Fayette was thirty-two and he provided the company and friendship that was lacking in her marriage.

32 Jean Renaud Ségrais (1624–1701). Poet and novelist, elected to the Académie Française in 1662.

33 See DeJean (1991), p. 106.

34 The company included Edward Gibbon, Denis Diderot and Jean d'Alembert.

35 The young Germaine had no playmates of her own age until she was eleven when her mother invited Mademoiselle Huber to visit. Mademoiselle Huber describes their first meeting: 'Mlle Necker grasped my hand, [. . .] embraced me, told me she had been waiting for me for an eternity, she was sure she would love me till she died, I would be her only true friend, this moment would determine an everlasting affection.' Catherine Rilliet Huber, 'Notes sur l'enfance de Madame de Staël', *Occident et Cahiers Staëliens*, 5–6 (30 June 1933: March 1934), 5:42, in Gretchen Rous Besser (1994), *Germaine de Staël Revisited*, New York, Twayne Publishers, pp. 2 and 149n.

36 Kavanagh refers to a letter written by Madame de Genlis after Madame de Staël's death in which she writes: '"Often, in thinking of her, I have regretted that she was not my daughter or my pupil. I would have given her good literary principles, just ideas, and simplicity; and with such an education, and her fine mind and generous soul, she would have been an accomplished woman, and the most justly celebrated authoress of our times"' (II: 197).

37 Kavanagh writes: 'M. de Guibert – is said to have been bewitched by Germaine Necker. Under the name of Zulmé he thus painted her in the fervour of her youth. Setting aside the inflated taste of the age [. . .] this portrait gives us singular and powerful impression of what Germaine Necker was in her youth:– "Zulmé is only twenty, and she is the most celebrated priestess of Apollo. She is the favourite of the god [. . .] From amidst the sacred maidens one steps forth. My heart will ever remember it. Her large black eyes beamed with genius; her hair, the colour of ebony, fell on her shoulders in waving locks; her features were more characteristic than delicate; they told of something beyond the destiny of her sex. Thus might we paint the muse of poesy, or Clio, or Melpomene. 'Here she is! Here she is!' all cried when she appeared, and breath seemed gone"' (II: 203).

38 The marriage lasted approximately ten years from 1786 to 1797 when they were formally separated. Kavanagh gives little background to the marriage, only that wealthy, middle-class M. and Mme Necker considered it advantageous for their daughter to marry into the aristocracy. Modern

biographical sources suggest that Germaine Necker considered this man unworthy of her. She was an extremely wealthy and eligible heiress and all he could offer was a title. See Angelica Goodden (2000), *Madame de Staël: Delphine and Corinne*, London, Grant and Cutler Ltd.

39 One year after her marriage to her first husband, Baron de Staël, Madame de Staël gave birth in 1878 to their daughter, Gustavine, who lived for twenty months. Her two sons to Narbonne, Auguste and Mathias-Albert, were born in 1790 and 1792 respectively and Constantine's daughter, Albertine, was born in 1797. She later gives birth secretly to Rocca's son, Louis-Alphonse, in 1812. See Rous Besser (1994).

40 Madame de Staël fled from Paris in 1792 to escape the September massacres, crossing the Channel to England. She then went on to Switzerland before returning to France, only to be exiled again by Napoleon whose rage she encountered as a result of her political ideas and also the free-thinking aspects of her novel *Delphine* (1802). During this time she travelled extensively throughout Europe before returning to Paris on the abdication of Napoleon in 1814, but later resumed her travels in 1815. See Goodden (2000).

41 *De l'Allemagne* (1810) provided Madame de Staël's French audience with their first manifesto of romanticism. This work, which had taken six years to complete, was eventually published in England in 1813.

42 Goodden (2000), pp. 14–15.

43 Ibid., p. 11.

44 Ibid., p. 11.

45 From a review by W. R. Gregg of *The Life and Times of Madame de Staël* by Maria Norris, London, 1853, in *The North British Review*, November (1853) 39, 20, 18.

46 Goodden (2000), pp. 22–3.

47 In Diana Craik's novel *Olive* (1850) Corinne is cited as a free spirit and a woman who has broken free from rules of duty and social acceptance: 'A Michelangelo can stand alone with his genius and so go sternly down unto a desolate old age. But there scarce ever lived a woman who would not rather sit meekly by her own hearth, with her husband at her side, and her children at her knee, than be the crowned Corinne of the Capitol' (Chapter 2).

48 Geraldine Jewsbury, Review of *English Women of Letters: Biographical Sketches* by Julia Kavanagh, 2 vols (Hurst & Blackett), in *The Athenaeum*, 1826, 25 October (1862), 527.

49 Kavanagh gives Sarah Fielding's year of birth as 1714 but all modern sources give 1710.

50 For a fuller discussion on the subject of women and publishing see Elizabeth Eger, ed. (1999), *Bluestocking Feminism: Writings of the Bluestocking Circle, 1738–1785*, vol. 1, London, Pickering & Chatto, Introduction, pp. xvi–xix.

51 Janet Todd (1996), *The Secret Life of Aphra Behn*, London, André Deutsch, p. 3. See also Eger (1999), subheading, 'Woman in the Conduct

Book Tradition: From the Glorious Revolution to Cultural Revolution' for discussion of the impact of the Marquis of Halifax's *The Lady's New-Year's Gift; or, Advice to a Daughter* (1688) (pp. xxxv–xxxviii).

52 Maureen Duffy, ed. (1987), *Love Letters Between a Nobleman and His Sister*, by *Aphra Behn*, London, Virago, p. vii.

53 See Todd (1996), p. 12.

54 Ibid., p. 1.

55 Maureen Duffy notes that this text, published in 1698, was an extended version of *The History of the Life and Memoirs of Mrs Behn*, which appeared prefixed to a collection of her *Histories & Novels* first published in 1696 and anonymously attributed to 'One of the Fair Sex', though the first version is admitted to be by Charles Gildon, the editor, who indeed repeats the main biographical facts in his rewrite of Langbaine's *An Account of the Dramatic Poets*. See Maureen Duffy (1977), *Aphra Behn 1640–89: The Passionate Shepherdess*, London, Jonathan Cape, p. 17. See also Todd (1996), who casts further doubt on the legitimacy of this source as biography (p. 12). Todd states that: 'a colleague of Gildon's called Samuel Briscoe was eager to exploit and sensationalise the dead author. He wanted to publish a volume of the collected stories of which *Oroonoko* was the crown and he too needed a biography. So he commissioned "The Life and Memoirs of Mrs. Behn. Written by One of the Fair Sex". In the third edition this was expanded into a patchwork by the inclusion of some love letters, thought of originally as a short story, and some comic letters purportedly written when Aphra Behn was in Flanders. Any one of Behn's female friends might have written the "Memoirs" or the impecunious Sam Briscoe himself might have supplied it, or Gildon in less austere mood may have performed again' (p. 12).

56 John Doran, *Their Majesties' Servants. Annals of the English Stage* London, 1888, vol. 1. p. 239. Doran is referring to a volume of poetry by women, sometimes referred to as 'the Daughters of Behn', *The Nine Muses*, published in 1700 and edited by Delarivier Manley. See Todd (1996), p. 4. and p. 436n.

57 Ezell (1996), p. 93. See also Eric S. Robertson (1883), *English Poetesses: A Series of Critical Biographies, with Illustrative Extracts* London, p. 9.

58 Ezell (1996), p. 93.

59 B. G. MacCarthy (1994) notes: 'It is noteworthy and very characteristic of Aphra Behn that, having chosen him [Oroonoko], she did not by the fraction of a shade abate his negritude, as Mrs. Kavenagh believed Mme de la Fayette or Mlle de Scudéry would have done' (p. 160). It is arguable that Kavanagh saw Oroonoko as a romantic hero. Jane Smiley has recently suggested that '*Oroonoko* owes quite a bit to the romance' and that Oroonoko himself is a romantic hero. See Jane Smiley (2006), 'Picaresque Polemic', *Saturday Guardian*, 15 April, 22.

60 I would argue that Kavanagh perceived Oroonoko's 'noble nature' as a universal and that her understanding was not confined to associations of race or colour.

61　Clara Reeve (1785), *The Progress of Romance*, Colchester, W. Keymer.
　　p. 117.

62　Virginia Woolf (1929), *A Room of One's Own*, London, Hogarth Press,
　　p. 65. For insight into the associations of writing and modesty and the cul-
　　turally systematic silencing of women during the seventeenth centuries see
　　also Angela Goreau, 'Reconstructing Aphra Behn' in Mary Ann O'Donnel,
　　Bernard Dhuicq and Guyonne Leduc, eds (2000), *Aphra Behn (1640–
　　1689) Identity, Alterity, Ambiguity*, Paris, L'Harmattan. See also the intro-
　　duction in Angela Goreau (1985), *The Whole Duty of a Woman: Female
　　Writers in Seventeenth-Century England*, New York, Dial.

63　Edward A. Bloom, ed. (1982), Fanny Burney, *Evelina*, Oxford, Oxford
　　University Press, pp. 361–2.

64　Jane Austen (1818), *Northanger Abbey*, Chapter 14.

65　Hester Chapone, *Letters on the Improvement of the Mind* (1773) in Judy
　　Simons (1987), *Fanny Burney*, Writers and Their Work Series, London,
　　Macmillan, p. 2.

66　'The Witlings' satirised the pretensions of the Blue Stocking Circle headed
　　by Lady Elizabeth Montagu.

67　Simons (1987), p. 23.

68　Modern biographical sources give Sarah Fielding's birth date as 1710.

69　See Kate Chisholm (1998), *Fanny Burney: Her Life*, London, Chatto &
　　Windus, pp. 191–217.

70　*Evelina* was subsequently published in four editions. See Simons (1987), p. 47.

71　Dale Spender notes that during the mid eighteenth century it was 'out of
　　the question for respectable women to venture into bookshops which were
　　very much the preserve of men. Even as late as the end of the eighteenth
　　century it was still impossible for decent women to walk into a bookshop
　　as Mary Somerville found when she wanted a copy of Euclid's *Elements of
　　Geometry*: there was simply no way she could get it.' Dale Spender (1986),
　　Mothers of the Novel, London, Pandora, p. 92.

72　In the light of her censure of Aphra Behn, whose disregard for the rules of
　　feminine decorum shocked generations that followed, Kavanagh's opinion
　　here may seem confusing and contradictory. However, whereas Kavanagh
　　objected to Behn's 'coarseness', in the context of women novelists and their
　　progression throughout the eighteenth century, her argument relates
　　directly to Burney and her contemporaries.

73　See Sir Walter Scott [1861] *Miscellaneous Works*, and Anne Katharine
　　Elwood (1843), *Memoirs of the Literary Ladies of England from the
　　Commencement of the Last Century*, London, Colburn. Kavanagh may
　　also have had access to Anna Laetitia Barbauld (1810), *British Novelists*,
　　London, F. C. & J. Rivington.

74　Kavanagh notes that during the couple's imprisonment the children had
　　stayed in Sussex (presumably with relatives).

75　One early twentieth-century biographer notes that 'So far as her
　　[Radcliffe's] formal education is concerned, we are able to learn little. The

general impression given by her biographers is that it was the ordinary education of the young girl of that day, and that, according to modern ideas, it would seem, if not superficial, decidedly incomplete.' Clara Frances McIntyre (1920), *Ann Radcliffe in Relation to Her Times*, New Haven, Yale University Press, pp. 9–10.

76 McIntyre (1920) gives Ann Radcliffe more intellectual credit than Kavanagh seems to suggest in this comment: 'From Mrs. Radcliffe's own work we might, perhaps be inclined to give her credit for rather more knowledge than [Kavanagh's] comment implies. Her references to authors, both in her journals and in her novels, show not only thorough familiarity but genuine appreciation, and the quotations which she uses as headings to her chapters suggest a considerable range of reading.' McIntyre gives evidence of other areas of interest and intellectual enquiry as recorded by 'Mrs. Elwood' in her *Memoirs of Literary Ladies*, and the writer of the sketch in the *Annual Biography and Obituary* who 'speaks of her "gratification in listening to any good verbal sounds"; and says that she "would desire to hear passages repeated from the Latin and Greek classics; requiring, at intervals, the most literal translations that could be given, with all that was possible of their idiom, how muchsoever the version might be embarrassed by that aim at exactness." This would make it appear that she had no understanding of the originals' (p. 10). See also David S. Miall's article 'The Preceptor as Fiend: Radcliffe's Psychology of the Gothic', first published in Laura Dabundo, ed. (2000), *Jane Austen and Mary Shelley and Their Sisters*, Lanham, MD: University Press of America, pp. 31–43. Miall gives some interesting insights into Radcliffe's (Ann Ward's) education and experience and suggests that in her novels she reacts against the cult of sensibility which formed a young woman's education at that time.

77 In relation to Kavanagh's comments, Spender (1986) puts forward the case that Ann Radcliffe 'was one of the founders – if not the founder of the romantic movement'. She draws attention to the fact that the historical sexual bias associated with the terms 'romantic' and 'romance' was to the detriment of women writers. '[Ann Radcliffe] was followed by many men who were influenced by her work and who acknowledged their great debt to her. But while the men who drew on her work for inspiration have been granted the prestigious status of writers of the *romantic* school, the woman who started it all is consigned to the derisory status of the writer of *romance*.' Spender (1986), p. 238.

78 Bonamy Dobrée (1996), Introduction to Ann Radcliffe's *The Mysteries of Udolpho*, London, Oxford University Press, p. x.

79 For a full list of reviews in journals and magazines see McIntyre (1920).

80 Dobrée (1996), p. xv.

81 Ibid.

82 Frances Thomas (1994), *Christina Rosetti: A Biography*, London, Virago, p. 236.

83 McIntyre, (1920) p. 7.

84 Ibid., p. 6.

85 Kavanagh's spelling of Radcliffe's first name 'Anne' contradicts other references; for example, McIntyre (1920), who used the same biographical source (*Annual Biography and Obituary*, 1823) notes the spelling 'Ann'. See McIntyre, p. 27.

86 Kavanagh reports that *The Mysteries of Udolpho* brought in £500 and *The Italian* £800.

87 *A Simple Story* was written initially in 1779 and was turned down by the London publisher. The story was revised and published in 1791 when it went into a second edition within three months.

88 Anne Elwood, writing in 1843, refers to this impediment as 'an imperfection in her organs of utterance, which for some time rendered her speech indistinct, induced her, in early youth, to fly from company, and hide her defect in solitude; seeking in books for that recreation which she denied herself in the world'. Elwood also makes reference to Inchbald's approach to education: 'The nature of her education, or, rather absence of it, may be gathered from an observation of her own. "It is astonishing how much all girls are inclined to literature, to what boys are. My brother went to school seven years, and could never spell; I, and two of my sisters, though we were never taught, could spell from infancy."' See Anne Elwood (1843), pp. 310–11.

89 Kavanagh is quick to pick up on the resourcefulness of Mrs Siddons, who was obliged to organise her time to accommodate both home life and career. She relates that Elizabeth became acquainted with Mrs Siddons when she and her husband were performing in Liverpool, noting that 'Mrs. Siddons, who was not yet the great tragic actress of later years, but a sorely-tried, hard-tasked woman, who acted at night in the stately parts for which her genius and her person fitted her so well, but who washed and ironed her children's clothes in the morning' (164).

90 See also James Boaden, ed. (1833), *Memoirs of Mrs. Inchbald: Including her Familiar Correspondence*, 2 vols, London, Richard Bentley.

91 Kavanagh notes that one publisher offered Inchbald the sum of 'one thousand pounds' for the manuscript without even seeing it (169).

92 As Kavanagh points out, Elizabeth Inchbald was an astute business woman and, in spite of her frugal mode of living, she had invested enough funds to ensure an annual income sufficient to cover her needs. One modern source states that Elizabeth Inchbald died a rich woman, leaving £5000. See Lorna Sage, ed. (1999), *The Cambridge Guide to Women's Writing in English*, Cambridge, Cambridge University Press, p. 341.

93 Spender (1986), p. 214.

94 Ibid., p. 215.

95 It is interesting that, over one hundred years after Kavanagh's comment, George Watson in his Introduction to *Castle Rackrent*, suggests that 'It is Maria's tutelage to her father, which persisted devotedly until his death in 1817, that makes her the *least* [my italics] feminine of female novelists'.

George Watson, ed. (1964), Introduction, *Castle Rackrent*, Oxford, Oxford University Press, p. x. In her biography of Maria Edgeworth, Marilyn Butler suggests that most of the studies on Edgeworth written by women in the latter part of the nineteenth and the earlier twentieth centuries 'all seemed bent on making Maria Edgeworth attractively feminine'. Marilyn Butler (1972), *Maria Edgeworth: A Literary Biography*, Oxford, Oxford University Press, p. 6.

96 As a prelude to her discussion on Maria Edgeworth, Kavanagh gives a brief but qualified account of Richard Lovell Edgeworth's colourful aristocratic ancestry, which dates back to the reign of Elizabeth I.

97 For her novel *Patronage* (1814) Edgeworth earned £2100, three times the amount (£700) that Scott earned for *Waverley* published in the same year. Altogether she earned £11,062 8s 10d from her writing. See Todd (1987), p. 111.

98   See J. Boaden, ed. (1833); includes letters from Maria Edgeworth and Robert Lovell Edgworth to Mrs Inchbald.

99 See *A Memoir of Maria Edgeworth*, with a selection from her letters by the late Mrs [Frances] Edgeworth, 3 vols, 1867 (privately printed) in Butler (1972), pp. 4 and 506.

100 Butler (1972) writes that there were twenty-two children (p. 7).

101 Ibid., p. 36.

102 Ibid., p. 45.

103 Todd (1987) includes Switzerland in this list (p. 110).

104 Butler (1972) gives a full account of Richard Lovell Edgeworth's interests, which took him away from his family for many months at a time when Maria was a child.

105 Virginia Woolf [1925] (1948), *The Common Reader*, London, The Hogarth Press, pp. 151–2.

106 Todd (1987), p. 112.

107 Butler (1972) gives the date of death as 13 June 1817 (p. 401).

108 Ibid., p. 2.

109 Kavanagh suggests that Aphra Behn 'had no delicacy of intellect or of heart, but she had sympathy. Perhaps only a woman could have written "Oroonoko"' (p. 251).

110 Cecilia Lucy Brightwell (1854), *Memorials of the Life of Amelia Opie*, Norwich, Fletcher and Alexander, and London, Longman, Brown & Co.

111 It is interesting to compare Kavanagh's sharp description of John Opie with that offered by a writer in 1883 who, also taking Brightwell as her source, refers to him as 'a simple, high-minded Cornishman, whose natural directness and honesty were unspoiled by favour, unembittered by failure'. Miss Thackerary (Mrs Richmond Ritchie) (1883), *A Book of Sibyls*, London, Smith, Elder & Co. (p. 164).

112 See Brightwell (1854), who describes the scene as thus: 'The first time Mr. Opie saw his future wife, was at an evening party, at the house of one of her early friends; among the guests assembled, were Mr. Opie, and a family,

personally known to the writer of these Memoirs. Some of those present were rather eagerly expecting the arrival of Miss Alderson; but the evening was wearing away, and still she did not appear; at length the door was flung open, and she entered, bright and smiling, dressed in a robe of blue, her neck and arms bare; and on her head a small bonnet, placed in somewhat coquettish style, sideways, and surmounted by a plume of three white feathers. Her beautiful hair hung in rich waving tresses over her shoulders; her face was kindling with pleasure at sight of her old friends; and her whole appearance was animated and glowing' (p. 63).

113 While Geraldine Jewsbury points out that Kavanagh is incorrect in relation to several issues concerning Lady Morgan's early life, she is generally enthusiastic about *English Women of Letters* as a whole. Her concluding paragraph reads: 'On the whole, this work of Miss Kavanagh's will be a pleasant contribution to the literature of the times; and in raising a shrine to the merits of some of the leading English women of literature, Miss Kavanagh has also associated her own name with theirs.' *The Athenaeum*, 1826, 25 October (1862), 528.

114 There has been some discrepancy over the exact year of Sydney Owenson's birth and bibliographical information speculates any time between 1776 and 1783. Mona Wilson (1924), *These Were Muses*, London, Sidgwick & Jackson, suggests 1783 (in Spender (1986), p. 303). One earlier twentieth-century biographer decided that she had been born in 1776, on grounds that this date 'is based on a process of elimination which left this as the only date conforming with all the facts'. See Lionel Stevenson (1936), *The Wild Irish Girl: The Life of Sydney Owenson, Lady Morgan (1776–1859)* London, Chapman Hall. Dale Spender opts for Kavanagh's 1778 on the grounds that Kavanagh's date is more substantiated. Spender (1986), p. 303. More recent biographical information suggests 1776.

115 Mary Campbell (1988), *Lady Morgan: The Life and Times of Sydney Owenson*, London, Pandora Press, p. 17.

116 Campbell (1988) notes that '[Lady Morgan's] eyes always attracted comment, and so did the slightly crooked shoulder; in later life Lady Morgan attributed this to her habit of leaning on one side while writing or playing the harp' (p. 111).

117 John Wilson Croker was born in Galway in 1780. According to Mary Campbell, he was one of those Irishmen who, in his attempts to succeed, became more English than the English. Turning his back on his own country, he was a high Tory and his slashing attacks on Lady [Sydney Owenson] Morgan's novels were dictated by his Tory politics. See Campbell (1988), pp. 153–9.

Chapter 5

1 At the same time Foster and Mills draw attention to the fact that a considered 'female representation' could well have been strategic and could relate

more to the fact that writers wanted to get published. Shirley Foster and Sara Mills, eds (2002), *An Anthology of Women's Travel Writing*, Manchester, Manchester University Press, p. 10.

2 Foster and Mills (2002) give several examples of travel writers who stress the significance of domestic considerations, including Harriet Martineau, who, they note, 'stressed that the kinds of experience accessible only to women are needed to complete knowledge of the foreign: "I am sure, I have seen much more domestic life than could possibly have been exhibited to any gentleman travelling through the country [North America]. The nursery, the boudoir, the kitchen, are all excellent schools in which to learn the morals and manners of a people."' Elizabeth Rigby also 'claims that the domesticity which is the supreme characteristic of English womanhood not only makes women good travellers (punctual practical, brave and independent) but also equips them for sharp observatin and attention to subjects that might otherwise pass disregarded' in Foster and Mills (2002), p.10. See also Harriet Martineau (1837) *Society in America*, 2 vols London, Saunders and Otley, vol. I, 8, xiv, and E. Rigby, 'Lady Travellers', *Quarterly Review*, LXXVI, No. CLI (1845).

3 Foster and Mills (2002), pp. 9–10.

4 After the Napoleonic era in 1816, the Bourbon king, Ferdinand IV of Naples, bestowed the name of the Kingdom of the Two Sicilies on his domain of southern Italy and Sicily, after which he became known as Ferdinand 1 of the Two Sicilies. The Kingdom survived revolutions until 1860 when it became part of Italy.

5 By 'female perspective' I am referring to the discourse of social and historical positioning, which is not to be confused with any notion of biological essentialism.

6 Glenda Sluga, 'Gender and the Nation: Madame de Staël or Italy', in Barbara Caine, ed. 'La bella Libertà: Women and the Flight to Italy', *Women's Writing*, 10: 2 (2003), 241–51 (p. 241). See also Chloe Chard (1999), *Pleasure and Guilt on the Grand Tour: Travel Writing and Imaginative Geography 1600–1830*, Manchester, Manchester University Press, particularly pp. 34–9.

7 See above, Barbara Caine (2002). The essays in this special edition of this journal are dedicated to issues surrounding gender, liberty and nation in Italy.

8 Ibid.

9 Maria H Frawley (1994), *A Wider Range; Travel Writing by Women in Victorian England*, Cranberry, NJ, Fairleigh Dickinson University Press, Association of University Presses, Inc., p. 28.

10 As no evidence has come to light to suggest that Kavanagh had returned to Ireland after the family removed to London in 1824, one can deduce that, other than France, it was England and English customs that had shaped her experience and I use the term 'English' in the cultural sense only.

11 *The Athenaeum*, 1622, November (1858).

12 Perhaps one way of interpreting Kavanagh's 'clouded lens' today is to consider her approach to language. John Banville has noted a culturally idiomatic aspect of Irish English in so far as it is different from English English or American English. In a recent discussion about writing he commented on the fact that: 'an English writer will try to be clear. Orwell said that good prose should be like a pane of glass. The Irish writer would say: "No no, it's a lens, it distorts everything." You see, the odd thing is that the Irish language died in the 1840's but we still have that deep grammar inside us and it still dictates. The Irish language is an incredibly oblique language. It doesn't say things straightforwardly. Everything is expressed in a very oblique way.' *The Observer Review*, 17 September (2000), 15. Although Kavanagh spent most of her formative years in France, she would have spoken both French and English with her parents who, of course, were of Irish origin.

13 *Dublin Review*, 45, December (1858), 502–10.

14 'Lady Tourists in the Two Sicilies', *Dublin University Magazine*, 53, February (1859), 189.

15 Of the Neapolitans, Kavanagh notes, 'Their ready wit is proverbial. [. . .] Several of their witticisms have been repeated to me, but, to be understood, they require a profound knowledge of the Neapolitan dialect, which is essentially concise'. (II: 150).

16 Frawley (1994), p. 30.

17 Shirley Foster (1990), *Across New Worlds: Nineteenth-Century Women Travellers and Their Writings*, Hemel Hempstead, Harvester Wheatsheaf, p. 4.

18 For example see Sara Mills (1991), *Discourses of Difference: An Analysis of Women's Travel Writing and Colonialism*, London, Routledge. See also Mary Louise Pratt (1992), *Imperial Eyes: Travel Writing and Transculturation*, London, Routledge. See also Shirley Foster and Sara Mills, eds (2002).

19 Amongst its other attractions, Italy in the mid nineteenth century attracted visitors for health reasons. Famously, Elizabeth Barrett Browning set up home in Rome, and the Australian poet and painter Adelaide Ironside spent eleven years there, accompanied by her mother, before dying of consumption in 1867. See Ros Pesman, 'In Search of Professional Identity: Adelaide Ironside in Italy' in Caine (2003), p. 308.

20 Lady Sydney Morgan (1821), *Italy*, 3 vols, London; Mary Shelley (1844), *Rambles in Germany and Italy in 1840, 1842 and 1843*, 2 vols, London.

21 Marzio Barbagli (1991), 'Marraige and the Family in Italy in the Early Nineteenth Century' in John A. Davies and Paul Ginsborg, eds *Society and Politics in the Age of the Risorgimento*, Cambridge, Cambridge University Press, p. 99.

22 Ibid., p. 98.

23 Lady Anna Miller (1776), *Letters from Italy, Describing the Manners, Customs, Antiquities, Paintings, &c of that Country, in the Years 1780 and*

1781, to a Friend Residing in France, by an English Woman, London, 3 vols, London, vol. II., p. 61, in Chard (1999), p. 92.

24 Jane Strachey to Richard Strachey, 2 May 1867, Strachey Papers, India Office Records, British Library, Mss Eur F127/126. in Caine (2003), p237 and 240n.

25 Lady Morgan (1821), *Italy,* vol. 1, p. 91.

26 Mary Shelley (1844), *Rambles,* p.77. Shelley was no doubt aware of the practice of the *cavalieri serventi,* or *cicisbei,* men who were the constant companions (and lovers) of married women. See Mirella Agorni (2002), *Translating Italy for the Eighteenth Century,* Manchester, St Jerome Publishing, p. 126.

27 Thomas Watkins (1794), [1792] *Travels through Switzerland, Italy, Sicily, the Greek Islands to Constantinople; through Part of Greece, Ragusa, and the Dalmatian Isles,* Second Edition, 2 vols, London, vol. II, pp. 371–2, in Chard (1999), p. 92.

28 Marriage in Italy had been the focus of earlier visitors to that country. As Agorni has noted, one of the earliest travel accounts to be published under the name of a woman in Britain in the eighteenth century was Hester Piozzi's *Observations and Reflections Made in the Course of a Journey Through France, Italy and Germany,* published in 1789. Agorni (2002), pp. 111–41.

29 Maura O'Connor, '"Civilizing southern Italy": British and Italian Women and the Cultural Politics of European Nation Building' in Caine (2003), pp. 253–68.

30 Ibid., See Chapter 1, letter from Kavanagh to Mrs W. S. Williams requesting funds for Garibaldi refugees.

31 Lady Morgan (1821), *Italy,* vol. 1. pp. 196–7. See Foster (1990) for further discussion on Victorian women travellers' views on education and women in Italy, pp. 65–8. See also Agorni (2002), for discussion on Lady Morgan and the existence of an Italian tradition of female learning in Italy, pp. 125–30.

32   Foster (1990), p. 62.

33 *Paradise Lost,* IV.304–18.

34 Charles Jervas (1675–1739), portrait painter. In 1710 he had painted Lady Montagu dressed as a shepherdess.

35 Robert Halsband, ed. (1965), *The Complete Letters of Lady Mary Wortley Montagu,* vol. 1, 1708–1720, Oxford, Clarendon Press, pp. 313–14.

36 It could be argued that Kavanagh's perspective of the Italian race as being free from 'vulgarity' is a disguised criticism of the artificial manners and affectations of those nations who consider themselves 'cultivated'. In her chapter on 'Hester Piozzi's Appropriation of the Image of Italy: Gender and the Nation', Agorni argues that 'A representation of Italy in sentimental terms appears particularly suited to a country whose inhabitants had been conventionally depicted by English writers and playwrights as carried away by their strong emotions. [. . .] They are in fact characterised [by Piozzi] as

less "affected" than the English, in a word, less "civilised". It is extremely significant in this respect that one of the most important cultural practices considered to reflect the degree of civilization in a country is travel, which is best exemplified by the tradition of the Grand Tour. Piozzi counters the myth of the cultivated Englishman with that of the sincere Italian, who appears less culturally sophisticated but, accordingly, more in touch with nature' (2002, p. 132).

37 Agorni (2002), p. 119.
38 Hester Lynch Piozzi (1789), *Observations and Reflections . . .*, in Chard (1999), pp. 41–2. The passage here is taken from a longer passage, which Chard cites in relation to Piozzi's attempts to invest England with, amongst other considerations, the benefits of an Italian climate.
39 For a full discussion on women travelling alone see John Premble (1987), *Mediterranean Passion*, Oxford, Clarendon Press: 'all females abroad without male escorts, whether travelling singly, in pairs, or in groups, were classified as "unprotected", and the term carried strong connotations of eccentricity. The unprotected female was an aberration, who found her place in fiction as either a comic or a tragic deviation from the norm' (pp. 77–8).
40 Martha Vicinus (1985), *Independent Women: Work and Community for Single Women, 1850–1920,* Chicago, Chicago University Press, p. 8, in Frawley (1994), p. 29.

Julia Kavanagh: publications

Editions used

Novels

Nathalie, 3 vols. London, Hurst and Blackett, 1850.
Daisy Burns, 2 vols. Leipzig, Bernhard Tauchnitz, 1853.
Grace Lee, New York, Appleton & Co., [1855] 1872.
Rachel Gray, Leipzig, Bernhard Tauchnitz, 1856.
Adèle, 3 vols. London, Hurst and Blackett, 1858.
Sybil's Second Love, 2 vols. Leipzig, Bernhard Tauchnitz [1867], reprinted in Elibron Classics Series, Adamant Media Corporation, Brighton, MA, 2000.

Biography and criticism

Woman in France during the Eighteenth Century, New York and London, P. Putnam & Sons, [1850] 1893.
French Women of Letters, 2 vols. London, Hurst and Blackett, 1862.
English Women of Letters, Leipzig, Bernhard Tauchnitz, 1862.

Travel

A Summer and Winter in the Two Sicilies, 2 vols in one Leipzig, Bernhard Tauchnitz, 1858.

Novels

1848: *The Three Paths: A Story for Young People,* London, Chapman and Hall.
1848: *Madeleine*, London, Bentley.
1850: *Nathalie*, 3 vols. London, Hurst and Blackett).
1853: *Daisy Burns*, 3 vols. London, Bentley.
1855: *Grace Lee*, 3 vols. London, Smith and Elder.
1856: *Rachel Gray*, 3 vols. London, Smith and Elder.
1858: *Adèle*, 3 vols. London, Hurst and Blackett.
1863: *Queen Mab*, 3 vols. London, Hurst and Blackett.
1865: *Beatrice*, 3 vols. London, Hurst and Blackett.
1867: *Sybil's Second Love*, 3 vols. London, Hurst and Blackett.
1868: *Dora*, 3 vols. London, Hurst and Blackett.

1870: *Sylvia*, 3 vols. London, Hurst and Blackett.
1872: *Bessie*, 3 vols. London, Hurst and Blackett.
1875: *John Dorrien*, 3 vols. London, Hurst and Blackett.
1877: *Two Lilies*, 3 vols. London, Hurst and Blackett.

Collections of short stories

1859: *Seven Years and Other Tales*, 3 vols. London, Hurst and Blackett.
1861: 'John's Five Pounds' in Adelaide A. Proctor, ed. (1861), *The Victoria Regia – A Volume of Original Contributions in Poetry and Prose*, London, Emily Faithful & Co. Victoria Press. 259–76.
1877: *The Pearl Fountain and Other Fairy Tales*, London, Chatto and Windus [co-written with Bridget Kavanagh].
1878: *Forget-Me-Nots*, 2 vols. London, Bentley [with an introduction by Charles Wood].

Biography and criticism

1850: *Woman in France during the Eighteenth Century*, 2 vols. London, Smith and Elder.
1852: *Women of Christianity*, London, Smith and Elder.
1862: *French Women of Letters: Biographical Sketches*, 2 vols. London, Hurst and Blackett.
1862: *English Women of Letters: Biographical Sketches*, 2 vols. Hurst and Blackett.

Travel writing

1858: *A Summer and Winter in the Two Sicilies,* 2 vols. London, Hurst and Blackett.
1864: 'Recollections of an old city' [Geneva] in *The Month*, I: 25.
1864: 'A Glimpse of Northern Italy' in *The Month*, I: 112–22.
1865: 'Glimpses of Rome' in *The Month*, 2: 199.

Journals: contributions of non-fiction

1846: 'The Montyon Prizes' in *Chambers Miscellany* [also published by Chambers as a separate pamphlet, London, Chambers, BL shelfmark 8285.a.71 (3.)].
1846: 'The French Working Classes' in *People's Journal*, 2 September: 159.
1846: 'Prizes of Virtue in France' in *People's Journal*, 2 November: 285.
1847: 'Literature of the Working Classes of France' in *People's Journal*, 3 June: 47.

Journals: contributions of short stories

Chambers Edinburgh Journal
1847: 'Gaiety and Gloom', 27 March: 193–7.
    'Young France', 19 June: 387–92.
    'Soirée in a Porter's Lodge', 7 August: 86–92.
    'The Cheap Excursion', 1 April: 212–15.
    'The Mysterious Lodger', 15 April: 243–7.
    'A Comedy in a Courtyard', 15 May: 306–10.
(All reprinted in *Seven Years and Other Tales*)

Household Words
1850: 'An Excellent Opportunity', 27 July: 1:18: 421–6.
(Also reprinted in a revised form in *Seven Years and Other Tales*)

Temple Bar
1868: 'Mimi's Sin', March, 831: 22: 470.
    'By the Well', April, 841: 23: 76.
1869: 'My Brother Leonard', September, 983: 27: 187.
(All reprinted in *Forget-Me-Nots*)
'By the Well' was also published in Mrs McQuoid (1897), *Women Novelists of Queen Victoria's Reign, A Book of Appreciations,* London; and in Italian, 'Al pozzo' [Prima traduzione italiana di E. M. Palermo, D. Lao e S. de Luca, 1891. Vatican Library].

All the Year Round
1868: 'Sister Anne', 9 May: 542; 16 May: 548; 23 May: 572.
(Reprinted in *Forget-Me-Nots*)

Argosy
1872: 'Miller of Manneville', 14: 463.
1873: 'Nina, the Witch', 14: 463.
1877: 'Clement's Love', December: 440–59.
1878: 'Story of a Letter', 26: 30.
1878: 'Perpétue: A sketch', 26: 431.
(All reprinted in *Forget-Me-Nots* and *Littell's Living Age*)
('Clement's Love' reprinted in *Forget-Me-Nots* only.)

Littell's Living Age: Boston, MA.
1870: 'Annette's Love Story', 108: 291
(Also reprinted in *Forget-Me-Nots*)
1876: 'Story of Monique', 128: 293.

Poetry

The only poems traced are those published in *Argosy* after Kavanagh's death.

1891: 'Wouldst thou be happy', January, 51: 47.
    'Yes, I have heard it oft, February', 51: 112.
    'Our Life is one long poem', June, 51: 483.
1894: 'Clough na Molla: a poem', 57: 82.
    'I do not love: a poem', 57: 154.
    'Westward: a poem', 57: 414.

Reviews for *The Athenaeum*

Alphonse de Lamartine (1847), *The History of the Girondins*.
Vol. I, 1014, 3 April (1847) 384–6.
Vol. II, 1015, 10 April (1847) 384–6.
Vol. III, 1018, 1 May (1847) 457–9.
Vol. IV, 1023, 5 June (1847) 592–3.
Vol. V, 1024, 12 June (1847) 619–20.
Vol. VI, 1032, 7 August (1847) 835–3.
Vols. VII and VIII, 1036, 4 September (1847) 935–6.

Selected reprints

Kavanagh's books have also been reprinted in English by Ward Lock & Co., London; Bernhard Tauchnitz, Leipzig; D. Appleton & Co., New York; Henry Holt & Co., New York; G.P. Putnam's & Son, London and New York; J. & D. Sadlier & Co., New York; Lea & Blanchard, Philadelphia; H.L. Kilner & Co., Philadelphia; Whittmore, Niles & Hall, Boston.

Smith, J. D. III, ed. (2006), *Women of Christianity: The Pioneer 1852 Narrative of Women's Lives in the Christian Tradition*, Eugene, OR, Wipf & Stock.

In recent years paperback facsimiles of the Tauchnitz editions of Kavanagh's works have been published in the Elibron Classics Series, by Adamant Media Corporation, USA.

Selected publications in other European languages

French

Madeleine (1850), republished (1860), *Tuteur et pupille*, roman anglais traduit par Mme H. Loreau, Paris, L. Hachette.

Madeleine (1859), second edition (1870), Paris, Putois-Cretté.

Les Trois Sentiers (1867), ouvrage traduit de l'anglais par Marie de Jorel, Paris, P. M. Laroche.

Rachel Gray (1900), par Mrs. L. (*sic*) Kavanagh. Traduit de l'anglais par Mme V. Parise, Toulouse, Société des livres religieux.

Swedish
Daisy Burns (1854), Upsala, C. Wasmuth, C.A. Leffler.

German
Madeleine (1852), Hamburg, Agentur des Rauhen Hauses.
Three of Kavanagh's short stories were published in English and German in
a series of books suitable for learning English, Sprachen-Pflege. These
are 'A Soirée in a Porter's Lodge' (*Eine Abendgesellschaft in einer
Björtnerwohnung*); 'A Cheap Excusion' (*Der Billige Ausflug*); 'The Little
Dancing Master' (*Der kleine Tanzlehrer*).
The dates of publications are unknown, but judging from the one book traced,
Der kleine Tanzlehrer, they are likely to be late nineteenth and/or early twen-
tieth century.

Select bibliography

Biographical directories

Adams, H. G., ed. (1857), *A Cyclopaedia of Female Biography*, London, Groombridge.

Cooper, T. (1857), *Men of the Time: A Dictionary of Contemporaries, containing Biographical Notices of Eminent Characters of Both Sexes*, Ninth Edition, London, Routledge.

Kunitz, S. J. and Haycraft, H., eds (1936), *British Authors of the Nineteenth Century*, New York, The H. W. Wilson Company.

Lee, S., ed. (1892), *Dictionary of National Biography*, vol. 30, London, Smith and Elder.

Read, C. A., ed. (1891), *The Cabinet of Irish Literature*, vol. 3, London, The Gresham Publishing Company.

Watson, G., ed. (1969), *The New Cambridge Bibliography of English Literaure*, vol. 3. 1800–1900, Cambridge, Cambridge University Press.

The Catholic Encyclopedia (1913), vol. 8, London, Caxton Publishing Co.

Nouvelle Biographie Générale, vol. 27, Paris, Firmin Didot Frères, 490–1.

Nineteenth century periodicals

Chorley, H. F. 'Sybil's Second Love', *The Athenaeum*, 2051, 16 February (1867) 218.

────── 'French Women of Letters: Biographical Sketches', *The Athenaeum*, 1779, 30 November (1861) 717–18.

────── 'A Summer and Winter in the Two Sicilies', *The Athenaeum*, 1622, November (1858) 681.

────── 'Daisy Burns', *The Athenaeum*, 1321, 19 February (1853) 220–1.

────── 'Nathalie', *The Athenaeum*, 1203, 16 November (1850) 1184–5.

────── 'Woman in France during the Eighteenth Century', *The Athenaeum*, 1166, 2 March (1850) 226.

Duffy, G. 'Woman in France during the Eighteenth Century', *The Nation*, 16 March (1850) 458.

Eliot, G. 'Silly Novels by Lady Novelists', *Westminster Review*, 66, October (1856) 442–61.

—— 'Margaret Fuller and Mary Wollstonecraft', *The Leader*, 13 October (1855) 988–9.

—— 'Woman in France: Madame de Sablé', *Westminster Review*, 62, October (1854) 448–73.

Gregg, W. R. 'False Morality of Lady Novelists', *National Review*, 8 (1859) 144–67.

Jewesbury, G. 'English Women of Letters: Biographical Sketches', 1862, 25 October (1862) 527–8.

—— 'Adele', *The Athenaeum*, 1429, 17 March (1855) 176–7.

—— 'Grace Lee', *The Athenaeum*, 1429, 17 March (1855) 313–14.

Lewes, G. H. 'The Lady Novelists', *Westminster Review*, 58 (1852) 129–33.

—— 'Shirley [by Charlotte Brontë]', *Edinburgh Review*, [XCI], January (1850) 155.

—— 'A Charming Frenchwoman', *Frazer's Magazine*, 2451, May (1848) 509–18.

Ludlow, J. M. 'Ruth [by Elizabeth Gaskell]', *North British Review*, [XIX], May (1853) 169.

Norris, M. 'The Life and Times of Madame de Staël', *The North British Review*, November (1853) 39.

Oliphant, Margaret, 'Modern Novelists – Great and Small', *Blackwood's Edinburgh Magazine*, May (1855) 559.

Rigby, E. 'Lady Travellers', *Quarterly Review*, LXXVI, No. CLI.

Taylor, Emily, 'Lady Novelists of Great Britain', *Gentleman's Magazine*, July (1853) 18–25.

Wood, C. W. 'Mrs. Henry Wood, In Memoriam', *Argosy*, 43, April (1877) 251–70.

—— 'Mrs. Henry Wood, In Memoriam', Part Three, *Argosy*, 43, June (1877).

Anonymous articles and reviews

'Lady Tourists in the Two Sicilies', *Dublin University Magazine*, 53, February (1859) 1892–5.

'A Summer and Winter in the Two Sicilies', *Dublin Review*, 45, December (1858) 502–10.

'Grace Lee', *The North American Review*, 81: 168, July (1855) 263–7.

'Grace Lee', *Putnam's Monthly Magazine of American Literature, Science and Art*, 5: 30, June (1855) 663.

'Grace Lee', *The United Democratic Review*, 35:5, May (1855) 413.

'Grace Lee', *The Spectator*, 3 March (1855) 245–6.

'Company Manners', *Household Words*, 9, 20 May (1854) 323–31.

'The Lady Novelists of Great Britain', *Gentleman's Magazine,* July (1853) 18–25.

'The Progress of Fiction as Art' [ref. *Daisy Burns*], *Westminster Review*, 60 (1853) 370–2.

'Woman in France during the Eighteenth Century', *Quarterly Review*, 88, 2, 176 (1851) 352.

Obituary

Academy, 10 November (1877) 449.

Martin, Mrs C. 'The Late Julia Kavanagh', *Irish Monthly Magazine*, 4 (1878) 96–100.

Wood, C. W. *The Athenaeum*, 2612, 17 November (1877) 630.

—— *The Times*, 19 November (1877) 6.

Morgan Kavanagh and The Hobbies

The Athenaeum, 1546, 13 June (1857) 761.

—— 1547, 20 June (1857) 792–3.

—— 1548, 27 June (1857) 822.

—— 1549, 4 July (1857)

The Spectator, 11 July (1857) 735.

Reviews in The Athenaeum of Kavanagh's works not discussed in this book

'The Three Paths', 1054, 9 January (1848) 37.

'Madeleine', 1097, 4 November (1848) 1101.

'Women of Christianity', 1265, 24 January (1852) 104–5.

'Seven Years and Other Tales', 1683, 28 January (1860) 133.

'Queen Mab', 1882, 21 November (1863) 675–6.

'Beatrice', 1946, 11 February (1865) 553–4.

'Sylvia', 2223, 4 June (1870) 220–1.

General

Agorni, M. (2002), *Translating Italy for the Eighteenth Century*, Manchester, St Jerome Publishing.

Algrant, C. P. (2003), *Madame de Pompadour: Mistress of France*, London, Harper Collins.

Ariès, P. (1975), *Essais sur l'histoire de la mort en Occident du moyen âge à nos jours*, Paris, Le Seuil.

Armstrong, I., ed. (1992), *New Feminist Discourses*, London, Routledge.

Armstrong, N. (1987), *Desire and Domestic Fiction: A Political History of the Novel*, Oxford, Oxford University Press.

Aronson, N. (1978), *Mademoiselle de Scudéry*, Boston, Twayne Publishers.

August, E. (1975), *John Stuart Mill: A Mind at Large*, New York, Charles Scribner & Sons.

Baker, E. J. (1937), *The History of the English Novel from the Brontës to Meredith vol. 8, Romanticism in the English Novel*, London, H. F. and G. Witherby.

Banville, J. (2000), *The Observer Review*, 17 September, 15.

Barbagli, M. (1991), 'Marriage and the Family in Italy in the Early Nineteenth Century', in J. Davis and P. Ginsborg, eds, Society and Politics in the Age of the Risorgimento, Cambridge, Cambridge University Press, 92–127.

Barbauld, A. L. (1810), British Novelists, London, F. C. & J. Rivington.

Barker, J. (1995), *The Brontës*, London, Phoenix Giants.

Beasley, F. E. (2000), 'Altering the Fabric of History: Women's Participation in the Classical age', in S. Stephens, ed., A History of Women's Writing in France, Cambridge, Cambridge University Press, 64–83.

Belsey, C. (1994), *Desire: Love Stories in Western Culture*, Oxford, Blackwell.

Bentley, P. (1969), *The Brontës and Their World*, London, Book Club Associates.

Berlin, I. (1978), *Karl Marx: His Life and Environment*, Oxford, Oxford University Press.

Besterman, T., ed. (1958), *Lettres de la marquise du Châtelet*, Geneva, Voltaire Foundation.

Blain, V., Clements, P. and Grundy, I., eds (1990), *The Feminist Companion to English Literature*, London, Batsford.

Bloom, E., ed. (1982), Fanny Burney, *Evelina*, Oxford, Oxford University Press.

Boaden, J., ed. (1833), *Memoirs of Mrs. Inchbald: Including Her Familiar Correspondence*, 2 vols, London, Richard Bentley.

Bonnel, R. and Rubinger, C. (1994), *Femmes Savants et Femmes d'Esprit*, New York, Peter Lang.

Booth, A. (2004), *How to Make It as a Woman: Collective Biographical History from Victoria to the Present*, Chicago and London, The University of Chicago Press.

Brightwell, C. L. (1854), *Memorials of the Life of Amelia Opie*, Norwich, Fletcher and Alexander; London, Longman, Brown & Co.

Brontë, C. [1848] (1994), *Shirley*, London, Penguin Classics.

Butler, M. (1972), *Maria Edgeworth: A Literary Biography*, Oxford, Oxford University Press.

Caine, B., ed. (2003), 'La bella Libertà: Women and the Flight to Italy', *Women's Writing*, 10: 2.

Calder, J. (1976), *Women and Marriage in Victorian Fiction*, London, Thames and Hudson.

Campbell, M. (1988), *Lady Morgan: The Life and Times of Sydney Owenson*, London, Pandora Press.

Carey, J., ed. (1971), *Milton: Complete Shorter Poems*, London, Longman.

Chapple, J. A. V. and Pollard, A., eds (1997), *The Letters of Mrs Gaskell*, Manchester, Manchester University Press.

Chard, C. (1999), *Pleasure and Guilt on the Grand Tour: Travel Writing and the Imaginative Geography 1600–1830*, Manchester, Manchester University Press.

Charlier, G. (1939) 'La Fin de l'Hôtel de Rambouillet', *Revue Belge de Philosophie et d'Histoire*, 18, 409–26.

Chisholm, K. (1998), *Fanny Burney: Her Life*, London, Chatto & Windus.

Colby, R. A. (1968). *Fiction with a Purpose: Major and Minor Nineteenth Century Novels*, Bloomington, Indiana University Press.

Craik, D. [1850] (1999), *Olive*, Oxford, Oxford World's Classics.

Craveri, B. (1994), *Madame du Deffand and Her World*, London, Peter Halban.

Cruse, A. (1935), *The Victorians and Their Books*, London, George Allen and Unwin.

Curtis, J. S. I. (1984), 'Epistolières' in Spencer, ed., French Women and the Age of Enlightenment, Bloomington, Indiana University Press, 226–41.

Dabundo, L., ed. (2000), *Jane Austen and Mary Shelley and Their Sisters*, Lanham, MD, University Press of America.

Davis, J. and Ginsborg, P., eds (1991), *Society and Politics in the Age of the Risorgimento*, Cambridge, Cambridge University Press.

Davison, R. (1994), 'Madame d'Epinay's Contribution to Girls' Education', in R. Bonnel and C. Rubinger, eds, Femmes Savants et Femmes d'Esprit, New York, Peter Lang, 219–41.

DeJean, J. (1991), *Tender Geographies: Women and the Origins of the Novel in France*, New York, Columbia University Press.

Dobrée, B., ed. (1996), Ann Radcliffe, *The Mysteries of Udolpho*, Oxford, Oxford University Press.

Dooley, D. (1996), *Equality in Community: Sexual Equality in the Writings of William Thompson and Anna Doyle Wheeler*, Cork, Cork University Press.

Doscot, G., ed. (1970), *Mme de Staal-Delaunay, née Marguerite Jeanne Corder, Mémoires*, Paris, Mercure de France.

Duffy, G. (1898), *My Life in Two Hemispheres*, vol. 2, London, T. Fisher Unwin.

Duffy, M., ed. (1987), *Love Letters Between a Nobleman and His Sister, by Aphra Behn*, London, Virago.

—— (1977), *Aphra Behn 1640–89 The Passionate Shepherdess*, London, Jonathan Cape.

Eagle, Russet, C. (1989), *Sexual Science: The Victorian Construction of Womanhood*, Cambridge, MA, Harvard University Press.

Eagleton, T. [1975] (1988), *Myths of Power: A Marxist Study of the Brontës*, London, Macmillan.

Eger, E., ed. (1999), *Bluestocking Feminism: Writings of the Bluestocking Circle, 1738–1785*, vol. 1, London, Pickering & Chatto.

Elwood, A. K. (1843), *Memoirs of the Literary Ladies of England from the Commencement of the Last Century*, London, Colburn.

Ezell, M. J. M. (1996), *Writing Women's Literary History*, Baltimore and London, The Johns Hopkins University Press.

Fauchery, P. (1972), *La Destinée féminine dans le roman européen du dix-huitième siècle*, Paris, A. Colin.

Fauset, E. (1996), 'The Politics of Writing', *Irish Journal of Feminist Studies*, 1:2, 58–68.

Felski, R. (1995), *The Gender of Modernity*, Cambridge, MA, Harvard University Press.

Fitzgerald, P. (1913), *Memories of Charles Dickens*, Bristol, J. W. Arrowsmith.

Fitzpatrick, D. (1989), '"A Peculiar Tramping": The Irish in Britain, 1801–70' in W. E. Vaughan, ed. A New History of Ireland: Ireland under the Union, 1801–17, vol. 5, Oxford, Clarendon press, 623–60.

Flint, K. [1993] (1999), *The Woman Reader*, Oxford, Clarendon Press.

Foster, S. (1985), *Victorian Women's Fiction: Marriage, Freedom and the Individual*, London, Croom Helm.

—— (1988), '"A Suggestive Book" A Source for *Villette*', *Etudes Anglaises*, 35: 2, 177–84.

—— (1990), *Across New Worlds: Nineteenth-Century Women Travellers and their Writings*, Hemel Hempstead, Harvester Wheatsheaf.

Foster, S. and Mills, S., eds (2002), *An Anthology of Women's Travel Writing*, Manchester, Manchester University Press.

Foucault, M. [1976] (1984), *The History of Sexuality*, vol. 1, London, Penguin.

Fowler, A., ed. (1976), *Milton: Paradise Lost*, London, Longman.

Fraser, A. (2002), *Marie Antoinette: The Journey*, London, Phoenix Paperback.

—— [2006] (2007), *Love and Louis XIV: The Women in the Life of the Sun King*, London, Phoenix Paperback.

Frawley, M. (1994), *A Wider Range: Travel Writing by Women in Victorian England*, Cranberry, NJ, Fairleigh, Dickinson University Press, Association of University Presses, Inc.

Fryckstedt, M. C. (1987), 'Defining the Domestic Genre: English Women novelists of the 1850's', *Tulsa Studies in Women's Literature*, 6:1, Spring, 9–25.

Fuller, A., ed. (1968), Margaret Fuller Ossoli, [1845] *Woman in the Nineteenth Century*, New York, Greenwood Press.

Gardiner, L. (1984), 'Women in Science', in S. I. Spencer, ed., French Women and the Age of Enlightenment, Bloomington, Indiana University Press, 181–96.

Gérin, W. (1969), *Charlotte Brontë*, Oxford, Oxford Lives Series, Oxford University Press.

Golby, J. M., ed. (1986), *Culture and Society in Britain 1850–1890*, Oxford, Oxford University Press in association with The Open University.

Goncourt, E. and Goncourt, J. (1862), *La Femme au dix-huitième siècle*, 2 vols, Paris.

Gooch, C. P. (1956), *Louis XV: Monarchy in Decline*, London, Longmans.

Goodden, A. (2000), *Madame de Staël: Delphine and Corinne*, London, Grant and Cutler Ltd.

Goreau, A. (1985), *The Whole Duty of a Woman: Female Writers in Seventeenth Century England*, New York, Dial.

—— 'Reconstructing Aphra Behn', in A. O'Donnel, B. Dhuicq and G. Leduc, eds, Aphra Behn (1640–1689) Identity, Alterity, Ambiguity, Paris, L'Harmattan, 43–8.

Gottschalk, R. (1929), *The Era of the French Revolution, 1715–1815*, Boston, Houghton Mifflin Company.

Graves, R. [1959] (1968), *New Larousse Encyclopedia of Mythology*, London, Hamlyn.

Griest, L. G. (1970), *Mudie's Circulating Library and the Victorian Novel*, Bloomington, Indiana University Press.

Hall, P. M. (1979) 'Duclos's *Histoire de Madame de Luz: Woman and History*', in Eva Jacobs, et. al., eds, *Woman and Society in Eighteenth-Century France*, London, Athlone Press, 139–51.

Halsband, R., ed. (1965), *The Complete Letters of Lady Mary Wortley Montagu*, vol. 1, 1708–1720, Oxford, Clarendon Press.

Helsinger, K., Lauterback Sheets, R.and Veeder, W. (1983), *The Woman Question: Society and Literature in Britain and America, 1837–1882*, vol. 3, New York, Garland Publishing.

Hollen Lees, L. (1979), *Exiles of Erin, Irish Migrants in Victorian London*, Manchester, Manchester University Press.

House, M., Storey, G. and Tillotson, K., eds (1995), *The Letters of Charles Dickens*, vol. 8, 1856–1858, Oxford, Clarendon Press.

Hunt, L. ed. (1991), *Eroticism and the Body Politic*, Baltimore, John Hopkins University Press.

Hunting Smith, W. (1938), *Letters to and from Madame du Deffand and Julie de Lespinasse*, New Haven, Yale University Press.

Jacobs, E. et. al. (1989), *Woman and Society in Eighteenth Century France*, London, Athlone Press.

Kamm, J. (1977), *John Stuart Mill in Love*, London, Gordon and Cremonesi.

Kapp, Y. (1972), *Eleanor Marx*, vol.1, London, Lawrence and Wishart.

Kelleher, M. (2001), 'Writing Irish Women's Literary History', *Irish Studies Review*, 9: 1, 5–14.

Kelly, G., ed. (1999), *Bluestocking Feminism: Writings of the Bluestocking Circle, 1738–1785*, vol. 6, London, Pickering & Chatto.

Kestner, J. (1985), *Protest and Reform: The British Social Narrative by Women 1827–1867*, London, Methuen.

Kinsey, S. R. (1984), 'The Memorialists', in S. I. Spencer, eds., French Women and the Age of Enlightenment, Bloomington, Indiana University Press, 212–25.

Kowaleski-Wallace, E. (1991), *Their Fathers' Daughters: Hannah More, Maria Edgeworth, and Patriarchal Complicity*, Oxford, Oxford University Press.

Lamartine, Alphonse de (1836), *Souvenirs, impressions, pensées et paysages, pendant un voyage en orient (1832-1833)*, Brussels, Wahlen.

Lescure, M. de. ed. (1865), *Correspondance complète* [The Letters of Madame du Deffand], Paris, Plon.

MacCarthy, B. G. [1946] (1994), *The Female Pen: Women Writers and Novelists*, vol. 1, 1621–1744, and *The Later Women Novelists*, vol. 2, 1744–1818 [in one vol.], Cork, Cork University Press.

MacDermot, M. 'On the Genius of Spenser, and the Spenserian School of Poetry', *The European Magazine*, October (1822) 331–41.

———. 'On the Genius of Spenser, and the Spenserian School of Poetry', *The European Magazine*, November (1822) 431–40.

McIntyre, C. F. (1920), *Ann Radcliffe in Relation to Her Times*, New Haven, Yale University Press.

Martineau, H. (1837), *Society in America*, 2 vols London, Saunders and Otley.

May, G. (1970), *Madame Roland and the Age of Revolution*, New York, Columbia University Press.

Maza, S. (1993), *Private Lives and Public Affairs : The Causes Célèbres of Pre-revolutionary France*, Berkeley, University of California Press.

Maza, S. 'The Diamond Necklace Affair Revisited (1785–1786): The Case of the Missing Queen' in L. Hunt, ed. (1991), *Eroticism and the Body Politic*, Baltimore, John Hopkins University Press, 63–89.

Miall, D. S. (2000), 'The Preceptor as Fiend: Radcliffe', Psychology in the Gothic' in L. Dabundo, ed., Jane Austen and Mary Shelley Their Sisters, Lanham, MD, University Press of America, 31–43.

Michie, H. (1987), *The Flesh Made Word: Female Figures and Women's Bodies*, Oxford, Oxford University Press.

Miller, Lady Anna (1776), *Letters from Italy, Describing the Manners, Customs, Antiquities, Paintings, &c of that Country, in the Years 1780 and 1781, to a Friend Residing in France, by an English Woman*, 3 vols. London.

Mills, S. (1991), *Discourses of Difference: An analysis of Women's Travel Writing and Colonialism*, London and New York, Routledge.

Moore, J. (1992), 'An Other Space: A Future for Feminism', in I. Armstrong, ed., New Feminist Discoursed, London, Routledge, 65–79.

Morgan, Lady Sydney (1821), *Italy*, 3 vols, London, Henry Colburn & Co.

Nicolaievsy, B. and Maenchen-Helfen, O. (1976), *Karl Marx: Man and Fighter*, London, Penguin.

Norton, L., ed, (1972), *Historical Memoirs of the Duc de Saint-Simon* [shortened version], vol. 3, 1715–1723, London, Hamish Hamilton.

O'Connor, M. (2003), "Civilizing Southern Italy": British and Italian Women and the Cultural Politics of European Nation Building' in B. Caine, ed., 'La bella Libertà: women and the flight to Italy', Women's Writing, 10:2, 253–68

O'Donnel, A., Dhuicq, B. and Leduc, G., eds (2000), *Aphra Behn (1640–1689) Identity, Alterity, Ambiguity*, Paris, L'Harmattan.

Perkin, J. (1989), *Women and Marriage in Nineteenth-Century England*, London, Routledge.

Pesman, R. (2003), 'In Search of Professional Identity: Adelaide Ironside in Italy,' in B. Caine, ed., 'La bella Libertà: women and the flight to Italy,' Women's Writing, 10:2, 307–28.

Peters, M. (1981), 'An unpublished Brontë Letter: The Second Edition of "Jane Eyre"', *Brontë Society Transactions*, 91: 1, 18: 116.

Pinney, T., ed. (1936), *Essays of George Eliot*, London, Routledge and Kegan Paul.

Piozzi, Hester Lynch (1789), Observations and Reflections made in the Course of a Journey Through France, Italy and Germany, London, in M. Agorni, ed. (2002), Translating Italy for the Eighteenth Century, Manchester, Manchester University Press, 111–41.

Pratt, M. L. (1992), *Imperial Eyes: Travel Writing and Transculturation*, London, Routledge.

Premble, J. (1987), *Mediterranean Passion*, Oxford, Clarendon Press.

Procious Malueg, S. E. (1984), 'Women and the Encyclopédie', in S. I. Spencer, ed., French Women and the Age of Enlightenment, Bloomington, Indiana University Press, 259–71.

Proctor, A., ed. (1861), *The Victoria Regia*, London, Victoria Press.

Radway, J. (1984), *Reading the Romance: Women, Patriarchy and Popular Literature*, Chapel Hill and London, North Carolina University Press.

Reeve, C. (1785), *The Progress of Romance*, Colchester, W. Keymer.

Rilliet Huber, C. (1933–34) 'Notes sur l'enfance de Madame de Staël', *Occident et Cahiers Staëliens*, 5–6, 5: 42.

Robertson, E. S. (1883), English Poetesses: *A Series of Critical Biographies, with Illustrative Extracts*, London, Cassell.

Rogers, H. (1977), '"The Good Are Not Always Powerful, Nor The Powerful Always Good": The Politics of Women's Needlework in Mid-Victorian London', *Victorian Studies*, 40: 4, Summer, 589–623.

Rogers, R. (1970), *A Psychoanalytic Study of the Double in Literature*, Detroit, MI, Wayne State University Press.

Rossetti, W. M., ed. [1904] (1935), *The Poetical Works of Christina Georgina Rossetti*, London, Macmillan.

Rossi, A. S., ed. (1970),: *Essays on sex equality: John Stuart Mill and Harriet Taylor Mill*, Chicago, Chicago University Press.

Rous Besser, G. (1994), *Germaine de Staël Revisited*, New York, Twayne Publishers.

Rubel, M. (1965) [trans. Mary Bottomore], *Marx Life and Works*, London, Macmillan Chronology Series, Macmillan Reference.

Runte, R. (1984), 'Women as Muse' in S. I. Spencer, ed., French Women and the Age of Enlightenment, Bloomington, Indiana University Press, 143–54.

Sage, L., ed. (1999), *The Cambridge Guide to Women's Writing in English*, Cambridge, Cambridge University Press.

—— 'The Case of the Active Victim', *Times Literary Supplement*, 26 July (1974) 803-4.

Saint-Gerand, J. P. *Morgan Kavanagh: Condylure Oubli En Histoire Des Science Du Langue:* internet source: http://www.chass.utoronto.ca/epc/langueXIX/kavanagh/.

Saunders, V. (1999), 'Marriage and the Antifeminist Woman Novelist', in N. D. Thompson, ed., Victorian Women Writers and the Woman Question, Cambridge, Cambridge Studies in Nineteenth Century Literature and Culture 21, Cambridge University Press, 24–41.

Scott, Sir, W. [1829] (1861), *The Miscellaneous Works of Sir Walter Scott*, vol. 6, Chivalry, Romance and Drama, Edinburgh, Adam and Charles Black.

Shanley, M. L. (1989), *Feminism, Marriage and the Law in Victorian England*, Princeton, Princeton University Press.

Shelley, Mary (1844), *Rambles in Germany and Italy in 1840, 1842 and 1843*, 2 vols, London, Henry Colburn & Co.

Showalter, Elaine (1978), *A Literature of Their Own: British Women Novelists from Brontë to Lessing*, London, Virago.

Showalter, English (1972), *The Evolution of the French Novel: 1641–1782*, Princeton, Princeton University Press.

Shuttleworth, S. (1999), *Charlotte Brontë and Victorian Psychology*, Cambridge, Cambridge University Press.

Simons, J. (1987), *Fanny Burney*, Writers and Their Work Series, London, Macmillan.

Sluga, G. (2003), 'Gender and the Nation: Madame de Staël or Italy' in B. Caine, ed., 'La bella Libertà: women and the flight to Italy,' Women's Writing, 10: 2, 241–51.

Smith, M., ed. (1995), *The Letters of Charlotte Brontë with a Selection of Letters by Family and Friends*, vol. 1, 1829–1847, Oxford, Clarendon Press.

—— ed. (2000), *The Letters of Charlotte Brontë with a Selection of Letters by Family and Friends*, vol. 2, 1848–1851, Oxford, Clarendon Press.

Smiley, J. (2006) 'Picaresque Polemic', *Saturday Guardian*, 15 April, 22.

Spencer, S. I. (1984), *French Women and the Age of Enlightenment*, Bloomington, Indiana University Press.

Spender, D. (1986), *Mothers of the Novel*, London, Pandora Press.

Stephens, S., ed. (2000), *A History of Women's Writing in France*, Cambridge, Cambridge University Press.

Stevenson, L. (1936), *The Wild Irish Girl: The Life of Sydney Owenson, Lady Morgan (1776–1859)*, London, Chapman Hall.

Stewart, A., ed. (1984), *National Gallery of Ireland: Fifty Irish Portraits*, Dublin, National Gallery of Ireland Publication.

Stoneman, P. (1996), *Brontë Transformations*, Hemel Hempstead, Harvester Wheatsheaf.

Strachey, R. [1928] (1978), *The Cause: a short history of the women's movement in Great Britain*, London, Virago.

Suddaby, E. and Yarrow, P. J., eds (1971), *Lady Morgan in France* [France 1816], Newcastle, Oriel Press.

Sutherland, J. (1988), 'Victorian Novelists: A Survey', *Critical Quarterly*, 30:1, Spring 50–61.

—— (1988), *The Longman Companion to Victorian Fiction*, London, Longman.

Swift, R. and Gilley, S., eds (1989), *The Irish in Britain 1815–1939*, London, Pinter Publishers.

Tauchert, A., ed. (1995), *Mary Wollstonecraft: A Vindication of the Rights of Woman* [1792], London, Everyman Series, Dent.

Terry, R. C. (1983), *Victorian Popular Fiction: 1860–80*, London, Macmillan.

Thackeray, Miss (Mrs Richmond Ritchie) (1883), *A Book of Sibyls*, London, Smith, Elder & Co.

Thomas, F. (1994), *Christina Rossetti: A Biography*, London, Virago.

Thompson, N. D., ed. (1999), *Victorian Women Writers and the Woman Question*, Cambridge, Cambridge Studies in Nineteenth Century Literature and Culture 21, Cambridge University Press.

Todd, J. (1987), *A Dictionary of British and American Women Writers 1660–1800*, London, Methuen.

—— (1996), *The Secret Life of Aphra Behn*, London, André Deutsch.

Tuchman G, with Fortin, N.E. (1989), *Edging Women Out: Victorian Novelists, Publishers, and Social Change*, New Haven and London, Yale University Press.

Vaughan, W. E. ed. (1989), *A New History of Ireland : Ireland under the Union, 1801–17*, Vol. 5, Oxford, Clarendon Press.

Vicinus, M. (1985), *Independent Women: Work and Community for Single Women, 1850–1920*, Chicago, Chicago University Press.

Warner, M. (2002), *Fantastic Metamorphoses, Other Worlds: Ways of Telling the Self*, Oxford, Oxford University Press.

Watkins, T. [1792] (1794), *Travels through Switzerland, Italy, Sicily, the Greek Islands to Constantinople; through part of Greece, Ragusa, and the Dalmatian Isles*, Second Edition, 2 vols, London.

Watson, G., ed. (1964), Maria Edgeworth, [1800] *Castle Rackrent*, Oxford, Oxford University Press.

Wilson, M. (1924), *These Were Muses*, London, Sidgwick & Jackson.

Wise, T. J. and Symington, J. A., eds (1932), *The Brontës: Their Lives, Friendships and Correspondence in Four Volumes*, vol. 2, 1844–1849, Oxford, Shakespeare Head Press, Basil Blackwell.

——— eds (1932), *The Brontës: Their Lives, Friendships and Correspondence in Four Volumes*, vol. 3, 1849–1852, Oxford, Shakespeare Head Press, Basil Blackwell.

——— eds (1932), *The Brontës: Their Lives, Friendships and Correspondence in Four Volumes*, vol. 4, 1852–1928, Oxford, Shakespeare Head Press, Basil Blackwell.

Wohl, A., ed. (1978), *The Victorian Family*, New York, St Martin's Press.

Wood, C. (1981), *The Pre-Raphaelites*, London, Book Club Associates, Weidenfeld & Nicolson.

Woolf, V. (1925), *The Common Reader*, London, Hogarth Press.

——— (1929), *A Room of One's Own*, London, Hogarth Press.

Records and miscellaneous documents

Archives Municipales de Nice, Registres D'Etat Civil Décés, Fiche de Pepouillement. [Courtesy of the Princess Grace Irish Library, Monaco.]

Campbell, M. Manuscript, 'Mr. Kavanagh's Lodgers', in private ownership.

Forsyth, M. (1998), Ph.D. Thesis, 'Julia Kavanagh in her Times', The Open University, Milton Keynes.

Kavanagh, M. (1855), 'The Errors of Religion', unpublished manuscript, 670 pp. held at the National Library of Ireland: 6354.

Kavanagh, R. J. (2001), *'The Mysterious Irishman – Morgan Peter Kavanagh'* Ottawa, Canada, held at the National Library of Ireland: 5682.

——— (2003), 'Morgan Kavanagh: Enigmatic Poet, Novelist and Philologist', Ottawa, Canada, held at the National Library of Ireland: MS 39,914

Royal Literary Fund, British Library, File: 548.

Index

EU authorised representative for GPSR:
Easy Access System Europe, Mustamäe tee 50,
10621 Tallinn, Estonia
gpsr.requests@easproject.com

www.ingramcontent.com/pod-product-compliance
Lightning Source LLC
Chambersburg PA
CBHW051143030726
47504CB00004B/1007